خود آموز انگلیسی

This book designed for Farsi speaking students

این کتاب به علاقمندانی که عازم کشورهای: آمریکا- کانادا- انگلستان واسترالیا هستند توصیه میشود

A-Self-Teaching Guide

Improve and Expand
Your English Vocabulary
By
Learning Words in Context!

انگلیسی خود را تقویت کنید
با فرا گیری لغات و کاربرد درست آن
در جمله به
همراه تلفظِ متداولِ روز

نویسنده و گرد آورنده :

مهندس سید رحمت اله موسوی
ارشیتکت- فارغ التحصیل دانشگاه پلی تکنیک کالیفرنیا

A-Self-Teaching Guide

Improve and Expand Your English Vocabulary By Learning Words in Context!

By:

Rahmat Moosavi
Architect

Holding Degree from
California Poly Technic State University

This book is recommended to those people interested to travel to:
USA, England, Canada, or Australia

Order this book online at www.trafford.com
or email orders@trafford.com

Most Trafford titles are also available at major online book retailers.

Printed in the United States of America.

ISBN: 978-1-4269-5539-6 (sc)

Library of Congress Control Number: 2011900865

Trafford rev. 05/03/2011

www.trafford.com

North America & international
toll-free: 1 888 232 4444 (USA & Canada)
phone: 250 383 6864 • fax: 812 355 4082

This book dedicated to my beloved Twin Sons:

Steve Soheyl *Moosavi*
&
Paul Pouyan *Moosavi*

تقدیم به :

تقدیم به دو فرزند دو قلوی عزیزم پویان و شهیل
که در نوشتن این کتاب مرا یاری دادند بویژه
راهنمائیهای پویان عزیزم
از لحاظ مشکلات کامپیوتری

نا گفته نماند ...

ازبزرگوارنی که مشوق من در این رهگذر بوده اند سپاسگزارشان میباشم:

دکتر فهیمهٔ موسوی استاد دانشگاه تهران- روان شاد برادرم امان اله موسوی- آقای رسول رحیمی مهندس امین صلح جو- مهندس نصراله موسوی- دکتر رضوان حبیبیان- بیتا موسوی دبیر زبان و دکتر کامران افشار استاد دانشگاه کالیفرنیا و مهندس داریوش رهبر.

مندرجات

TABLE OF CONTENTS

فصل اول :　　　　　　　　　　　　　　　　　　　　　　　　　　　صفحه

PREFACE: سرآغاز

This book is designed to be a handy reference tool bar for Farsi speaking language aspires to learn word in context.

Before beginning to use this Self- Teaching Guide extensively, get acquainted with the entire book by scanning it from beginning to end.

بنام خداوند جان و خِرد

پیش گفتار:

چند کلمه ائی با خوانندگان و علاقمندان این کتاب

در زمینه بوجود آوردن این اثرکه قریب پنج سال بطول انجامیده هدف این بوده است که مجموعه ای بصورت ***خود آموز کتاب انگلیسی*** در اختیار دانشجویان و دانش آموزان که علاقمند به فراگیری انگلیسی هستند قرار دهم و همواره بر گونه ای باشد که درصورت نیازبتوان بمطالب پیشین مراجعه نمود.

یاد دارم که در ابتدای ورودم به آمریکا جهت ادامه تحصیل-- جوانی پرانرژی و تشنۀ فراگیری بودم. قبل از عزیمت به خارج لغات زیاد و پراکنده حتی با حفظ اسپل آنها بیاد داشتم-- ولی مشکلی که چگونه این لغات با معانی مختلف رادر قالب جملات مربوطه بکاربرم و یا صحیح تلفظ نمایم با خود میگفتم اگردر این زمینه کتابی یا جزوه اتی بیابم بهر قیمت آنرا تهیه و مطالعه خواهم کرد.

هدف از تألیف این خود آموزبرای پیش برد وتقویت زبان به گونه ای است که دانشجو کمتر وقتش را صرف پیدا کردن معانی و تلفظ لغات کند و همه اینها در یک مجموعه در اختیارش قرارگیرد بدون اینکه نیازی به نوار-- DVD -- CD یا چیزهائی نظیرآن باشد .

تألیف دو زبانۀ یک کتاب دارای اشکالات ویژه ائی است که نویسنده باید خیلی بآن توجه کند که کدام معنی لغت را در جای خودش بهمراه درج تلفظ دقیق آن بکار گیرد. این مهم بتدریج طی مدت بیش از سی سال اقامت در آمریکا و حضور در کلاسهای درسی دانشگاه ومحاوره با اساتید فن و با مراجعه به منابع وکتب ویژه زبان ومطالعه و بررسی آنها صورت گرفته است .

برخی از مندرجات شامل بهترین و سهل ترین شیوه ایست که دانش آموزان و دانش جویان فارسی زبان سایر کشورهای فارسی زبان هم بتوانند از آن بهره بگیرند . این کتاب بتدریج شما را آماده میسازد تا از ترس و خجالت فاصله بگیرید وبتدریج برای صحبت کردن و آشنا شدن با تلفظِ اصلی آماده شوید و از طرفی دیگر---اکثرجملات و پاراگرافهای این کتاب ربطی بهم ندارند و مستقل از یکدیگر بوده که میتوان از هرفصل یا صفحه ای از آن از ابتدا مراجعه و لغات وجملۀ جدیدی را تجربه کرد .

جملات ونوشته های این کتاب ازتفسیراخبار، روزنامه و مجله های داخلی و خارجی الهام گرفته ویا اقتباس شده است بطوریکه از حالت فرا گیری درس اجباری دراید و در بعضی موارد احتیاطأ از ذکر اسامی و بعضی موضوعات خاص اجتناب شده است تا حامل هیچگونه پیام خبری و سیاسی نبوده و نسبت به صحت ویا سقم آن بیطرف باشد.

در این کتاب نه تنها شما با تلفظ کردن صحیح لغات ومعانی فارسی آنها آشنامیشوید بلکه همزمان میتوانید نحوهٔ استفاده کردن لغات را در جملات گوناگون مشاهده نمائید . برای هر لغت مورد نظر علاوه بردرج تلفظِ آن در مجاورش چندین معنای دیگر در مجاورت آن آمده است که یکی دوتا از آنها مناسب ترین است وعلت درج معانی دیگر بمنظورِ ارتقاء دانشِ علاقمندان است.

مسلماً این اثر دارای نقاط ضعف میباشد واز هم اکنون در صدد رفع آنها در چاپ های بعدی هستیم--- بنا بر این تذکرات و راهنما ئیهای صاحب نظران برای نویسنده بسیار ارزنده خواهد بود و نویسنده را در رفع نواقص یاری خواهد کرد . نویسنده قصد دارد پس از انتشار این کتاب ---چهارمین اثری که در دست است منتشر نماید. در خاتمه آرزو مینماید به رغم همهٔ نارسائیها توانسته باشد گامی مثبت در این راه بردارد.

برای شما آرزوی موفقیت وپیشرفت مینماید .
مهندس سید رحمت اله موسوی – کالیفرنیا --- ژانویهٔ 2011

فصل اول

راهنما و علامات نقطه گذاری

PUNCTUATION MARKS:

نقطه گذاری شیوه ایست که خواندن و نوشتن راسهل میکند بطوریکه با تغیرات تُنِ صدا مثل بالا وپائین بردن-مکث کردن- نحوهٔ طرز بیان و حرکات صورت معنی کلمه را روشن میکند . معنی اصلی یک نقطه در آخر جمله بمنزلهٔ آنستکه جمله سئوالی یا ندائی نیست .

- Also the period is used to terminate most abbreviations such as:

Mr. , Mrs. , Dr. , US., etc. ← و هم چنین نقطه را مقابل حروف مختصر شده بکار میبرند مثل

a. *It is a sign that he is under serious pressure.* → (statement)

b. *I asked if he would see me.* → (indirect question)

c. *Please order to play symphony.* → (request or command)

- 1. ***period*** (.)

1. the point or character (.) used to mark the end of a declarative sentence, indicate an abbreviation, etc.; full stop.

2. *a full pause, as is made at the end of a complete sentence; full stop.*

- 2. ***question mark*** (?) ***–noun***

The question mark is used to terminate a direct question of any sort e.g.
Why not?, why? Who are you?, Whose car was stolen?

1. Also called ***interrogation point****, interrogation mark. a mark indicating a question: usually, as in English, the mark (?) placed after a question.*
2. something unanswered or unknown: His identity is still a question mark to most of us.

3. **exclamation mark** (!) علامت تعجب :x کِل می شِن

Exclamation point/mark (!) to terminate a strong expression of feeling. *e.g.*

get out of this office at once! , *An exclamation mark is used at the end of a strange statement , it shows shock or surprise. Hey, watch your step!*

Exclamation mark ***–noun***
1. the sign (!) used in writing after an exclamation.
2. this mark sometimes used in writing two or more times in succession to indicate intensity of emotion, loudness, etc.: *Long live the Queen!!*
3. this mark sometimes used without accompanying words in writing direct discourse to indicate a speaker's dumbfounded astonishment:
"His wife just gave birth to quintuplets." (*!*)
Also called exclamation mark .

- 4. **comma** (,)

a. Comma is used between items in a series, *Ex. Words, phrases, clauses or numbers. Frank, John, Fred, Harry and David.*

b. use the comma to set off interjections which are included in sentences.

Ex. Hello, I am glad to see you. Hey, watch your step! Oh, I thought so. Yes, I'll be glad to. However, she caught the train. He, tried moreover, to attain his goal.

- 5. **Semicolon** ***–noun*** (;) سِه مِی- کُو لِن

The punctuation mark (;) used to indicate a major division in a sentence where a more distinct separation is felt between clauses or items on a list than is indicated by a comma, as between the two clauses of a compound sentence. Ex. **a**. *John broke his ankle skiing; than he bought a snowmobile.*
b. *Nations no longer declare war or wage war; they declare or wage mutual suicide.*
c. *A bird does not fly because it has wings; it has wings because it flies.*

- 6. Colons (:)

a. The colon is used in more formal writing to call attention to words that follow it. Use the colon at the end of a sentence to introduce a list, an explanation (or intensification) of the sentence, or an example.

Ex. *The university offers five different majors in engineering: mechanical, electrical, civil, industrial, and chemical engineering.*

b. Colons to Separate Independent Clauses

Use the colon as a substitute for a semicolon to separate two independent clauses when the second amplifies or restates the first clause. *Do not use the colon after a verb or after a phrase like such as or consisted of.* Remember, the colon can only be used after an independent clause.

- 7. **Quotation mark** ***-noun*** (“ ”) علامت نقل قول

one of the marks used to indicate the beginning and end of a quotation, in English usually shown as “ at the beginning and ” at the end, or, for a quotation within a quotation, of single marks of this kind, *as “He said, ‘I will go.” Frequently, esp. in Great Britain, single marks are used instead of double, the latter being then used for a quotation within a quotation.* *e.g. “don’t you know enough to stop?” he asked*

Direct: *He said, “I am going home.”*

Indirect: *He said that he was going home.*

Direct: *She said, “I have a headache. I am going to bed”.*

Indirect: *She said that her head hurt and that she was going to bed.*

- 8. **Apostrophe** ***-noun*** (,) or (’) *e.g. man’s coat, Everybody’s friend, Tomorrow’s assignment, The Joneses’ gardens, three dollars’ worth farmers.*

a. Apart from indication possession, the apostrophe is principally used to indicate letters in a contraction. *e.g. who’s there? , I can’t come*

b. The apostrophe is also used to form plurals of letters, figures, or signs for which there is no acceptable plural.

*e.g. There are three 9’s, twenty-five n’s, and two *’s on the page.*

c. The sign ('), as used: to indicate the omission of one or more letters in a word, whether unpronounced, as in *o'er* for *over,* or pronounced, as in *gov't* for *government;* to indicate the possessive case, as in *man's;* or to indicate plurals of abbreviations and symbols, as in *several* M.D.'s, 3's.

- **9. Hyphen** ***–noun*** (-) *e.g. twenty-one*

a short line (-) used to connect the parts of a compound word or the parts of a word divided for any purpose.

- **10. Dash** (_)

The mark or sign (—) used to note an abrupt break or pause in a sentence or hesitation in an utterance, to begin and end a parenthetic word, phrase, or clause, to indicate the omission of letters or words, to divide a line, to substitute for certain uses of the colon, and to separate any of various elements of a sentence or series of sentences, as a question from its answer

- **11. Parentheses** ( ) پرن تاسس

1. either or both of a pair of signs ( ) used in writing to mark off an interjected explanatory or qualifying remark, to indicate separate groupings of symbols in mathematics and symbolic logic, etc.
2. Usually, parentheses the material contained within these marks.

- **12. Brackets** [ ]

1. a shelf or shelves so supported.
2. Also called *square bracket***.** one of two marks [or] used in writing or printing to enclose parenthetical matter, interpolations, etc.
3. *Mathematics* . brackets, parentheses of various forms indicating that the enclosed quantity is to be treated as a unit.

- **We have 4 types of sentence:**

1.*Declarative*: *stating a fact* اعلانی- اظهاری

2.*Interrogative*: *asked question direct or indirect* پرسشی

3.*Imperative*: *end with* (.) or (!) *ex, what a beautiful sunset!* امری

4.*Exclamatory*: *the house is on fire!* تعجبی- شگفت اور- ندا

ADDITIONAL POINTS ABOUT PUNCTUATION

- Here are a few more points to consider before our discussion of punctuation comes to an end:

- **Punctuation of Business Letters**

Q. I'm writing a business letter. Can I put a comma after the opening salutation, or is it a colon or a semicolon?

A. *The opening salutation of a formal letter is followed by a colon, never a comma or a semicolon. However, use a comma after the salutation in an informal letters. Commas are also appropriate in business letters written to friends.*

- **Slashes**

Q. What are the proper grammatical uses of the slash mark?

A. *The slash mark, also known as the virgule, is used to mark the divisions between words, lines, and numbers. The word* ***virgule*** *comes from the Latin* ***virgule****, meaning " little rod." We often see the slash mark in the expression* ***and /or*** *and in the informal writing of a date between the day and the month and between the month and the year:* ***1/10/2011****. The expression* ***in care of*** *is frequently abbreviated* ***c/o****.*

- Asterisks

  Q. Where did asterisks come from?

  A. *This star like sing (*) is used in print to refer the reader to footnotes, references, omissions, and the like. The word comes from the Greek word **asterisks**, meaning "little star."*

- Bullets

  Q. How do I use bullets?

  A. *as the representative's remarks suggest, bullets mark items in a list. If a sentence follows the bullet, place a period at its end.*

قوانین اسپل کردن
SPELLING RULES:

- Words or roots ending in, ie usually change the ie to y when adding ing. **Ex**: die – dying or lie – lying

- Words end with e, **Ex**: face – facing or rise – rising
- Words end with ce or ge , e will stay when adding suffix.

  Ex: trace – traceable, courage – courageous (کوریج ز)= brave (a courageous soldier).

- One syllable words ending in a single consonant a single vowel ***double the consonant*** when adding the suffixes ed, ing, or er.

  Ex: tap – tapping, sip – sipping

ie and ei

- i before e, except after c or when shouded like a as in neighbor and weigh. وی:کشیدن، سنجیدن، وزن کردن-وزن داشتن

  e.g. 1 : receive, neighbor, weigh

  e.g. 2: neither, leisurely, foreign, sheik, seized, their weird height.

- able versus ---ible, The ending is usually ---ible if the root is not a complete word.

  Examples: credible, impossible, and plausible.

  able versus ible: Also use---ible, if the root end in ns, ss soft c, or soft g.

  Examples: defe**ns**ible, admi**ss**ible, le**g**ible.

- Four words end in efy: liquefy, putrefy, rarefy, stupefy.

  Other are spelled with ify. **e.g.** : magnify, beautify, identify.

- Three words end in –ceed: Exceed, Preceed, Succeed

  One word ends in---sede: <u>Supersede</u>. Others are spelled with cede

- The prefix **in** usually means **not** **e.g.** Visible, invisible or when added to a word starting with L becomes il. & legal, illegal

  لغاتی که بام شروع میشود و پیشوند آن im میباشند مثل Moral, Mature ولی آنکه با p شروع میشود استثنائی است مثل Possible

  Example: Moral→ immoral,

  Mature→ immature

  Possible → impossible

- In grammar, a gerund جِرَند is a noun formed from a verb and expressing an action or state.
  In English, gerunds end in -ing

موارد استعمال ← at, in and on

1. قبل از ایام هفته و....و........ از حروف اضا فهٔ on استفاده میشود مثل :

On Saturday,
On New Year's Day,
On my Birthday,
On the radio and On TV

2. ولی از حروف اضافهٔ In برای اسامی ماهها و چهار فصلِ سا ل و همچنین اوقات روز مثل : صبح- ظهر و عصر

In April, In May
In Spring, In Winter etc. **Or**
In the Morning,
In the afternoon, etc.

3. ساعات روز با حروف اضافهٔ at

at down,
at dinner time,
at noon,
at night,
at the present time or day

4. همچنین at برای بیان محلی که شخصی یا چیزی در آنجاست یا جائی که عملی در آنجا اتفاق میافتد:

The post office is at the corner of the street.
Mr. Brown is at the office or I will meet you at the railroad station.
He is always at it, he never gives himself any rest. He is at it again!

استعمال وبکار گیری حروف بزرگ

When and where we should use Capital Letters?

Capitalize words that name one particular thing, most often a person or place rather than a general type or group of things.

Names that are capitalized can be thought of as legal titles that identify a specific thing. For example, you take a course in Architecture or English (a word not capitalized because it is a general field of study), but the course is offered by a particular department with a specific name, such as Architectural or English Depart ment.

The name of the specific department is capitalized. However, if you take a course in Farsi, the word Farsi is capitalized because it is the name of specific language.

Listed here are categories of words that should be capitalized. If you are not sure whether a particular word fits in these categories, check you dictionary.

- *Persons:* .... ***Robert Gates, Bill Clinton***
- *Places, including geographical regions:* ***Iran, Caspian See, Persian Gulf***
- *Peoples and their languages:* ....***Iranian, Spanish, Dutch***
- *Religions and their followers:* .... ***Muslim, Christianity, Judaism***
- *Members of national, political, racial, social, civic, and athletic groups:* ***Democrat, Iranian-American Los Angeles Lakers***

- *Institutions and organization: ....* **Supreme Court, Legal Aid Society**
- *Historical documents: ....* **The Declaration of Independence**
- *Periods of events: ....* **Middle Ages, Boston Tea Party World War II,**
- *But not century numbers: ....* **eighteenth century**
- *Days, months, and holidays: ....* **Monday, June, Thanksgiving**
- *But not seasons: ....* **spring, winter, summer**
- *Trademark names: ....* **Kodak, Mercedes, Coca-Cola**
- *Holly books and words denoting the Supreme Being: ....* **Quran, Bible, Allah, Lord**
- *Words and abbreviations from specific names: ....* **NATO, CBS, Stalinism**
- *Place words, such as street, park, city, that are part of specific names: ....* **California, New York City Wall Street, Madison Ave, Yosemite National Park**
- *Title that precede people's names:.........* **Governor Jerry Brown Uncle Sam**

Also capitalize the following:

- Capitalize the first word of every sentence (including quoted sentences).
  Ex. **M**y brother said, "**T**ests are not fun and games."

- The first word in salutation and in the complimentary close of Letter:
  Ex. **M**y dear **C**arol, **Y**our sincerely

- All references to the President and Vice President of the United States.

- The first word of each line a poem in traditional verse.

فصل دوم

HOMONYM WORDS:

کلمات همصدا یا مشابه

Homonyms are words that sound alike but are spelled differently. Their meanings are also very different. (متشابه یعنی (درلفظ یکی و در معنی مختلف

Ex: *hear* & *here*, and *pair* & *pare*[1]

1. تراشیدن سم حیوان (در لفظ یکی در معنی و نوشتن متفاوت)

توضیح :

یک سری لغات هستند با معانی مختلف که از دو کلمه تشکیل شده اند متصل بیک دیگر یا جدا ولی موقع تلفظ یکنواخت هستند با اسپل متفاوت مثل:

- allot (v) اِلات — The judge will allot us twenty minutes for our presentation.
- a lot (article +n) — There is a lot material to scrutinize.

- all ways (adj + n) — In all ways, life is a splendid adventure.
- always (adv) — My best friend is always king to me.

- anyone (pro) — Is anyone here dissatisfied?
- any one (adj + num), Pick any one number and bet on it.

- anyway (adv) — Anyway, we wouldn't have had fun if we had gone.
- any way (adj + n) — I will help in any way possible.

- everyday (adj) — We all have certain everyday tasks to perform.
- every day (adj + n) — We perform these tasks every day.

- everyone (pro) — Everyone we loved was present.
- every one (adj + pro), Every one of the watches is fine.

- nobody (pro) — Nobody knows the trouble I've seen.
- no dody (adj + n) — Despite the solid clues, no body was ever found.

(n) → noun **(v)** → verb **(adj)** → adjective (**prep**) →preposition

CONFUSING SPELLINGS:

The following pairs of words defy categorization. دیفای کَتِ گرایزیشن

- boy (n) بُوی Her young boy is quite preconcious.
- buoy (n) بوE Many had trouble spotting the buoy in the channel.

- breadth (n) برِدج They measured the length and breadth of the field.
- breath (n) برِث In polluted air, a breath is sometimes agony.

- decent (adj) Dسِنت Most people are good and decent.
- descent (n) دِ سِنت After the climb, they began their descent.

- latter (n) لَ تِر The latter is closer than the former.
- ladder (n) لَ دِر The technician climbed the ladder onto our roof.

HOMOPHONES *are words that are pronounced alike and that have different meanings but that may not be spelled the same.*
Some homophones are also ***homonyms***. *These are words that have the sam pronunciation and spelling but different meanings.*

- ad (n) اَد The ad for new shoes interested me.
- add (v) I can add up the numbers that you require.

- aid (n) اِید The Red Cross gives aid to people in need.
- aide (n) An aide is always there to give assistance.

- ail (v) اِیل What ails you?
- ale (n) Don't drink too much ale.

- air (n) اِیر The air was stifling.
- heir (n) اِر He was heir to a fortune.

(n) → noun **(v)** → verb **(adj)** → adjective **(prep)** →preposition

• aisle (n)	آی یل	He proudly escorted the bride down the aisle.
• I'll		I'll go to the movies with you.
• isle (n)		Oh, what adventures they had on Gilligan's Isle.
• altar (n)	آل تِر	The altar of the church is magnificent.
• alter (v)		No one can alter the past.
• arc (n)	آرک	The thin arc of the moon illuminated the night.
• ark (n)		The ark almost foundered in the water.
• ate (v)	ایت	We ate our dinner by candlelight.
• eight (n)		The number eight has some strange connotations.
• aught (n)	آت	Many mathematicians say "aught" instead of "zero."
• ought (v)		You ought to learn the homonyms.
• bail (n)	بیل	The bail was set at $1,000,000.
• bail (v)		The survivors must bail the water from their boat.
• bale (n)		We counted three bales of hay.
• band (n)	بَند	The marching band played wonderfully.
• band (n)		Don't snap me with that rubber band!
• band (v)		We will lose the fight unless we band together.
• banned (v)		The authorities banned the film from the festival.
• bare (v)	بِر	Dare you bare your head to the blazing sun?
• bear (v)		I cannot bear that awful noise.
• bear (n)		The grizzly bear was extremely menacing.
• bases (n)	بی سِز	With two men out, the bases are loaded.
• basis (n)		He has no basis for his argument.
• beat (v)	b ت	Can you beat his score?
• beat (n)		The cop walks his beat at night.
• beet (n)		The beet is a nutritious red root.

- beau (n) بُ — She came to the dance with her new beau.
- bow (n) — A red bow adorned the little girl's hair.
- bow (n) — Mehdi of Iran was master of the bow and arrow.
- bow (v) — You must bow before the king.

- been (v) بین — The tourists have been to the plaza in Athens.
- bin (n) — Throw the remnants into the trash bin.
- berry (n) بِری — A freshly picked berry is fine summer treat.
- bury (n) — Bury the evidence quickly!
- berth (n) بِرث — Give that crazy man a wide berth.
- birth (n) — The birth of their first child was a joyous occasion.
- bid (n) بِد — Sara Taf. place the winning bid at the auction.
- bid (v) — The gentleman bid the lovely lady adieu. آدیو

- blew (v) بلو — The winds blew ferociously.
- blue (n) — The color blue is my favorite.

- board (n) بُرد — The rotting, wooden board split in two.
- board (v) — All passengers may now board the airliner.
- bored (adj) — The bored child turned the television off and went outside.

- bolder (adj) بُلدِر — The child grew bolder with each success.
- boulder (n) — A large, granite boulder blocked the trail.

- born (v) بُرن — Roubi M. was born on a glorious day.
- borne (v) — You have borne your troubles majestically.

- brake (n) بریک — My car needs new brakes.
- break (v) — Don't break anything in the china shop.

- bread (n) برد — There are few foods so satisfying as freshly baked bread.
- bred (v) — My uncle bred horses for a living.

(n) → noun **(v)** → verb **(adj)** → adjective **(prep)** →preposition

- bridal (adj) بِ رای دِل We attended the bridal shower.
- bridle (n) The room adjusted the horse's bridle.

- borough (n) بُرو The Bronx is a borough of New York City.
- burrow (v) The mole burrowed under the house.
- burrow (n) The rabbits retreated into their burrow.

- buy (v) بای How much can you buy with so little money?
- by (prep) The tired runner fell by the roadside.
- bye (int) Bye! Have a nice day!

- cache (n) کَش The burglar's cache held all the loot from the robbery.
- cash (n) I don't have enough cash to pay for dinner.

- canvas (n) کَن وِس As an artist, my dad always had a large stock of canvas.
- canvass (v) Senator Bigs canvassed the neighborhood for support.

- capital (adj) کَ پی تول The murderer was given capital punishment.
- capital (n) The capital of Iran is Tehran.
- capitol (n) The United States Congress meets in the Capitol.

- carat (n) کَرِت That diamond is one carat.
- caret (n) Proofreaders use a caret to indicate where missing or additional information should be place within text.

- carrot (n) کَروت Everyone knows about beta carotene in carrots.
- karat (n) The purity of gold is measured in karats.

- cede (n) سی د Hong Kong island was ceded to the British by the Treaty of Nanking in 1842.
- seed (n) Every mighty oak grew from a tiny seed.

- ceiling (n) سیلینگ The ceiling must be painted as well.
- sealing (v) She is sealing the envelope with wax.

(n) → noun **(v)** → verb **(adj)** → adjective **(prep)** →preposition

- cell (n) سِل — Let the villain rot in his cell..(ویلِن ادم پست، تبه کار شریر villain)
- sell (v) — He will sell his car through the classifieds.

- cellar (n) سِ لِر — Siavash kept his fine wine in the cellar.
- seller (n) — The watch seller got a fair price for his wares.

- census (n) سِن سِس — The bureau conducted a population census last year.
- senses (n) — Taste is one of the five senses.

- cent (n) سِنت — One cent used to buy a stick of gum.
- scent (n) — The dog's keen nose picked up the scent.
- sent (v) — The teacher sent the upstart to the principal.

- cereal (n) C ریال — Cold cereal with bananas sounds like a fine breakfast.
- serial (adj) — These murders appear to be the work of a serial killer.

- cession (n) سِ شِن — England's cession of Hong Kong created controversy.
- session (n) — I missed my session with the therapist.

- chased (v) چیست — The police chased the suspect.
- chaste (adj) — He is virtuous and chaste.

- chews (v) چوُز — The cow chews contentedly on her cud.
- choose (v) — You must choose between two sweaters.

- choir (n) کْو آیر — I appreciate the sweet sounds of a fine choir.
- quire (n) — One needs many quires of paper to write a book.

- chord (n) کُرد — The strange musical chord made me shiver*.لرزه*
- cord (n) — They tied the cord around the box.

- chute (n) چوت — Dispose of the papers in the garbage chute.
- shoot (v) — "Stop or I 'will shoot! "

- cite سایت — Always cite your sources when writing essays.
- sight (n) — Is the Statue of Liberty in sight?
- site (n) — The Architect chose this site for the new building.

- climb (v) کِلایم The courageous defy death and climb mountains.
- clime (n) The bird flow south toward gentler climes.

- colonel (n) کِر نِل She attained the rank of army colonels .
- kernel (n) کِر نِل How many kernels are there on an ear of corn?

- complement (v), کام پِل مِنت The debutante's hat complemented her outfit.
- compliment (n), کام پِل مِنت She gave me a flattering compliment.

- conduct (n) کان داکت Benny's conduct in class has been less than admirable.
- conduct (v) Reginald will conduct the tour of the museum.

- core (n) کُر Some people enjoy eating the core of the apple.
- corps (n) کُر The Marine Corps is a force to be reckoned with.

- council (n) کان سِل The city council met in special session.
- counsel (n) His counsel gave him good advice.

- coarse (adj) کُرس The coarse fabric was uncomfortable to wear.
- course (n) The runners followed the course through the forest.
- course (n) She enrolled in a Persian culture course.
- coward (n) کَ اِرد He was labeled a coward after he ran from challenge.
- cowered (v) During the storm, the kitten cowered under the bed.

- creak (v) کِریک The stairs creak at night.
- creek (n) The water of the creek babbled outside my window.

- cue (n) کیو The cue to begin the race was the sound of a gunshot.
- cue (n) She struck the ball with the pool cue.
- queue (n) Standing in a queue requires patience.

(n) → noun **(v)** → verb **(adj)** → adjective **(prep)** →preposition

- currant (n) كُرنت — The black currant is a delicious berry.
- current (n) — The current of the river was swift.
- Current (adj) — It is good to be knowledgeable about current events.

- cymbal (n) سيم بَل — The sound of clashing cymbals is thrilling.
- symbol (n) — The American flag is a symbol of freedom.

- dear (adj) D إر — Dear reader, you should learn these homonyms.
- deer (n) — New Zealanders raise deer as American raise cows.

- desert (v) بِزِرت — The frightened soldier deserted his platoon*. (گروه، جوخهٔ افراد) *
- desert (n) Dزِرت — Only the hardiest of plants survives in the desert.
- dessert (n) Dزِرت — Creme brulee is a special dessert.

- dew (n) دُ — The pearly dew glistened on the lawn.
- do (v) — Please do the work immediately.
- due (adv) — The assignment is due next week.

- die (v) دآی — Water the plant or it will die.
- dye (n) — The dye made the white shirt green.

- discreet (adj) دیس کریت — The diplomat handle the affair in a discreet fashion.
- discrete (adj) — Ours was a discrete department, separate from the rest.

- doe (n) دو — A female deer is a doe.
- dough (n) — The baker kneaded the dough.

- done (v) دآن — The job is done.
- dun (n) — The smog turns the color of the sky to dun.
- dun (v) — Don't dun me for what I owe.

- dual (adj) دُآل — The coupe had dual exhausts.
- duel (n) — The adversaries fought a fearsome duel.

(n) → noun **(v)** → verb **(adj)** → adjective **(prep)** →preposition

- earn (v) اِرن The more you earn, the more you spend.
- urn (n) We keep Grandpa's ashes in an urn.

- elicit (v) اِلِ سیت I elicit thoughtful responses from my pupils.
- illicit (adj) The politician's illicit affair caused quite a scandal.

- ewe (n) یُو Ewes roam the pastures in Scotland.
- you (pro) You are very special.

- exercise (n) اِگزِر سایز My lack of exercise contributes to this unsightly bulge.
- exorcise (v) The priest will exorcise the demon.

- faint (adj) فِینت Faint sounds caught our attention.
- feint (n) With a quick feint, the fencer won the match.

- fair (n) فِر We journeyed to the county fair.
- fair (adj) Children are taught to be fair with each other.
- fare (n) Rapid transit fares seem to go up and up.

- fated (adj) فِی تِد To be fated is to be destined by fate.
- feted (v) For his accomplishment, we feted him.

- faze (v) فِیز Such behavior does not faze me.
- phase (n) She is going through a difficult phase in her life.

- feat (n) فیت The stuntman began another absurd feat of daring.
- feet (n) After a long day, the feet are tired.
- feet (n) There are three feet in a yard.

- find (v) فآیند What did you find in the shipwreck?
- fined (v) The scoundrel was fined $1,000.

- fir (n) فِر The Douglas fir is magnificent tree.
- fur (n) It's all right to wear imitation fur.

- fisher (n) فی شِر The fishers caught their limit at the lake.
- fissure (n) The quake opened several fissures in the ground.

- flair (n) فِلِ یِر My sister has a flair for baking.
- flare (v) Why do you flare up in anger?

- flea (v) فی لی That flea is driving my dog crazy.
- flee (v) The town's inhabitants must flee the volcano's wrath.

- flew (v) فُلو The young birds flew from their nest.
- flu (n) Each winter I catch a nasty case of the flu.
- flue We found it necessary to clean the flue of the chimney.

- flour (n) فِلا اِر I always use unbleached flour in my bread.
- flower (n) Place the flower in the vase.
- flower (v) When she turned thirteen, her musical abilities flowered.

- fore (adj) فُر The fore three seats are empty.
- four (n) The number four is perfect square.

- forbear (v) فُر بِر Forbear from speaking when I am perturbed.
- forebear (n) My forebear gave me some good genes.

- foreword (n) فُر وُرد Many readers ignore the foreword of a book.
- forward (adv) We marched straight forward.

- fort (n) فورت The children gleefully played in their tree fort.
- forte (n) Mathematics has never been my forte.

- forth (adv) فُرس It is time to go forth and seek your fortune.
- fourth (adj) April is the fourth month of the year.

- foul (n) فاَل Wilt didn't like the foul called against him.
- fowl (n) I enjoy eating fowl, especially chicken.

- freeze (v) فی ریز The butcher will freeze the meat.
- frieze (n) The artist did a fine job with the frieze.

- gamble (v) گم بِل Many people gamble away their money for pleasure.
- gambol (v) The children gambol about the playground with joy.

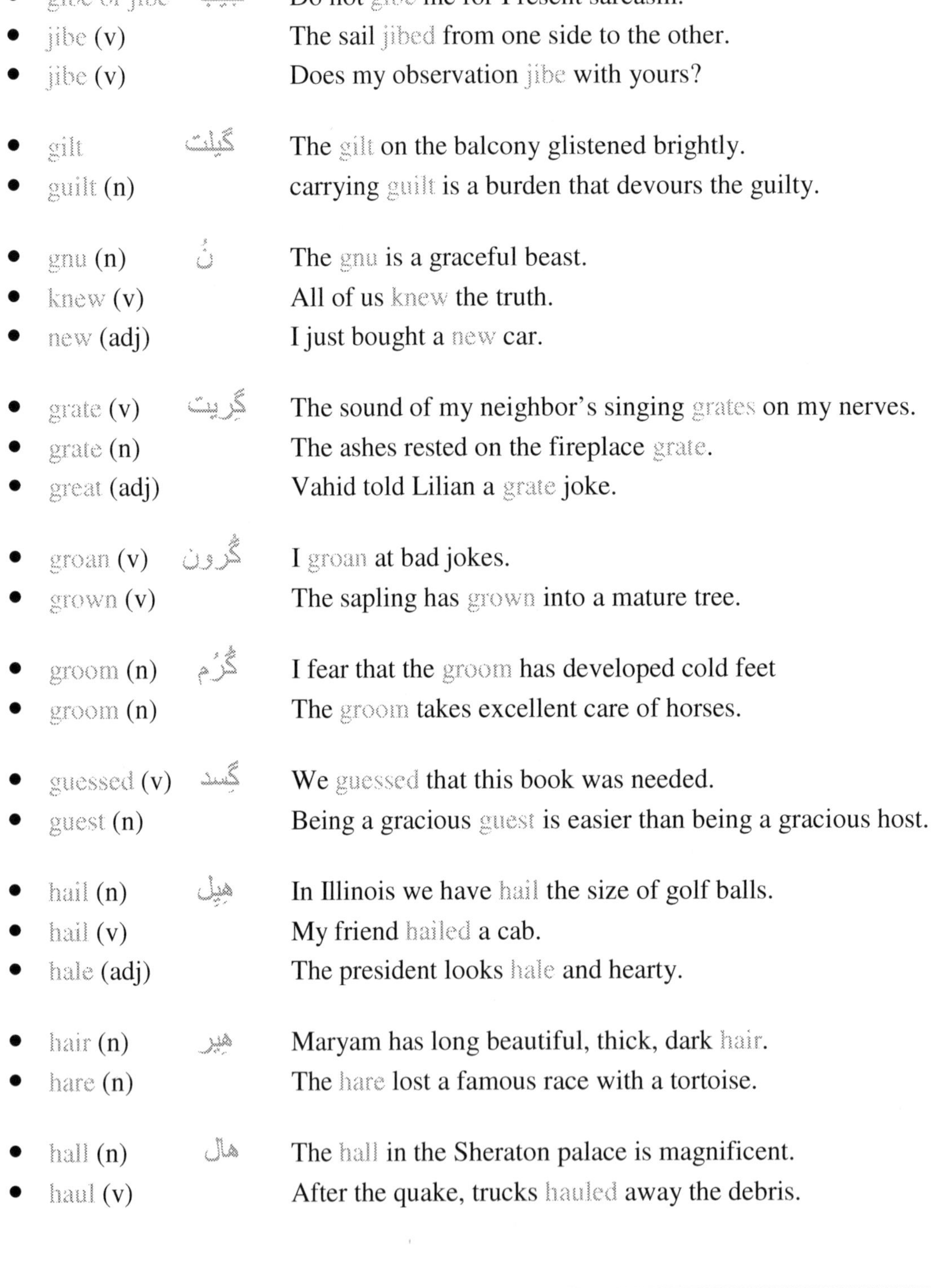

• gibe or jibe	جَیب	Do not gibe me for I resent sarcasm.
• jibe (v)		The sail jibed from one side to the other.
• jibe (v)		Does my observation jibe with yours?
• gilt	گیلت	The gilt on the balcony glistened brightly.
• guilt (n)		carrying guilt is a burden that devours the guilty.
• gnu (n)	نُ	The gnu is a graceful beast.
• knew (v)		All of us knew the truth.
• new (adj)		I just bought a new car.
• grate (v)	گِریت	The sound of my neighbor's singing grates on my nerves.
• grate (n)		The ashes rested on the fireplace grate.
• great (adj)		Vahid told Lilian a grate joke.
• groan (v)	گُرون	I groan at bad jokes.
• grown (v)		The sapling has grown into a mature tree.
• groom (n)	گُرُم	I fear that the groom has developed cold feet
• groom (n)		The groom takes excellent care of horses.
• guessed (v)	گِسد	We guessed that this book was needed.
• guest (n)		Being a gracious guest is easier than being a gracious host.
• hail (n)	هِیل	In Illinois we have hail the size of golf balls.
• hail (v)		My friend hailed a cab.
• hale (adj)		The president looks hale and hearty.
• hair (n)	هیر	Maryam has long beautiful, thick, dark hair.
• hare (n)		The hare lost a famous race with a tortoise.
• hall (n)	هال	The hall in the Sheraton palace is magnificent.
• haul (v)		After the quake, trucks hauled away the debris.

(n) → noun **(v)** → verb **(adj)** → adjective **(prep)** →preposition

- hangar (n) هَن گِر The plane is kept in the hangar.
- hanger (n) My hangers always seem to be on the closet floor.

- hart (n) هارت The hart, a mighty stag, leapt over the rock.
- heart (n) I beg you not to break my heart.

- heal (v) هی یِل Times heals all wounds.
- heel (n) Achilles' heel proved to be his downfall.
- heel (v) In the strong wind, the boat heeled leeward.

- hear (v) هی یِر Can you hear the whispering of the forest nymphs?
- here (adv) We came here on our honeymoon.

- heard (v) هِرد They obviously haven't heard the news.
- herd (n) A herd of bison raced just ahead of our train.

- higher (adv) هایِر The plane flew higher than ever before.
- hire (v) They will hire you if you are literate.

- him (pro) هی م His teacher gave him an A.
- hymn (n) The choir sang a lovely hymn.

- hoard (n) هُرد We discovered a hoard of fine books. اندوخته، ذخیره
- horde (n) A horde of students awaited me.

- hoarse (adj) هُرس One's voice becomes hoarse after a day of lecturing.
- horse (n) My one experience riding a horse was not pleasant.

- hole (n) هُل Alice fell down a very deep hole.
- whole (adj) Our research required a whole set of encyclopedias.

- holey (adj) هُلی The moth-eaten sweater was quite holey.
- holy (adj) In Judaism, Saturday is a holy day.
- wholly (adv) Having cavities filled is a wholly unpleasant experience.

(n) → noun **(v)** → verb **(adj)** → adjective **(prep)** →preposition

- homer (n) هُمِر Timmy hit a homer at the top of the fifth inning.
- homer (n) The ancient Hebrews measure volume in homers.

- hour (n) آوِر My watch shows one minute before the hour.
- our (pro) This is our greatest triumph.

- idle (adj) آی دُل I like to read in my idle time.
- idol (n) My boyhood idol was Joe DiMaggio.
- idyll (n) An idyll is a short poem describing a pleasant, rural scene.
-
- in (prep) این Did you go in the room?
- inn (n) I frequent a certain inn in Greenwich.

- indict (v) این دآیت The drug lord was indicted by a grand jury.
- indite (v) Shelly indited many wonderful poems.

- its (pro) ایتز The dragon returned to its cave.
- it's (contraction), It's going to be fine, sunny day.

- jam (n) جَم It's difficult to find fresh gooseberry jam.
- jamb (n) The door was stuck because the jam was warped.

- key (n) کی Education is the key to unlocked the closed door.
- quay (n) The four-masted schooners unloaded at the quay.

- knight (n) نایت Sir Lancelot was a brave knight.
- night (n) Only marauders and spirits walk a night.

- know (v) نو I now know what his motives were.
- no (adv) No, I haven't seen Elvis in the mall lately.

- lead (n) لید The walls of this building are lined with lead.
- lead (v) Our guide will lead us out of the jungle.
- led (v) لِد Why is he led about so easily?

(n) → noun **(v)** → verb **(adj)** → adjective **(prep)** →preposition

- lean (v) لین Lean on me for support.
- lien (n) The bank has a lien on her property.

- lessen (v) لِ سِن Antibiotics will lessen the infection.
- lesson (n) The first lesson is to pay close attention.

- lie (v) لای Why don't you lie down and take a nap?
- lie (v) Do not lie. A falsehood is always discovered.
- lye (n) Lye is poison used in making soap and lutefisk.

- load (n) لُود We all carry a heavy load in life.
- lode (n) The mother lode was rich in gold.

- made (v) میِد Her success made her happy.
- maid (n) She works as a maid at the Tehran Hotel.

- main (adj) میِن What is your main goal in life?
- mane (n) The horse's mane was long and burnished.

- manner (n) مَ نِر She has a pleasant manner.
- manor (n) A tree-lined road leads to the Vanak's country manor.

- marshal (n) مار شا ل A marshal carries out court orders.
- marshal (v) The colonists marshaled their defenses against the British.
- martial (adj) She studies the martial arts.

- meat (n) میت Being a vegetarian, he didn't eat meat.
- meet (v) Please meet us at noon.
- mete (v) My teacher metes out A's as if they were made of gold.

- mean (adj) مین That was mean, wicked act.
- mien (n) He has a noble mien.

- might (v) مایت Things might have been different between us.
- might (n) Her might was expressed in her mind and her muscles.
- mite (n) The mite is a minuscule creature.
- mite (n) This farting, only a mite, is hardly worth anything.

- miner (n) مای نِر Miners often develop black lung disease.
- minor (adj) The petty theft was only a minor infraction.

- missed (v) میسد We missed you at dinner tonight.
- mist (n) The mist hovered over the tranquil lake.

- morn (n) مُرن On Christmas Day, the children awoke in early morn.
- mourn (v) At funerals, we mourn the death of a loved one.

- morning (n) مُرنینگ The morning of the twelfth, I took the train to London.
- mourning (v) Some never stop mourning the loss f a loved one.

- naval (adj) نِی وِل The naval battle was fought at Trafalgar.
- navel (n) Your navel is your belly button.

- one (n) وآن One comes just before two.
- one (pro) One can do anything one sets one's mind to.
- won (v) These knights have won many battles.

- overdo (v) اُور دُو Do not overdo it.
- overdue (adj) This is your seventh overdue library book.

- paced (v) پیسد He paced about the room nervously.
- paste (n) Only paste held the costume together.

- packed (v) پَکت She packed her bags and left.
- pact (n) The countries signed a pact to codify the peace agreement.

- pail (n) پیل The pail was filled with fresh, warm milk.
- pale (adj) His pale color after surgery was quite shocking.

- pain (n) پین My tolerance for pain is high.
- pane (n) The stone broke the pane of glass.

(n) → noun **(v)** → verb **(adj)** → adjective **(prep)** →preposition

- pair (n) پِر What a lovely pair of vases.
- pare (v) Please pare the fruit.
- pear (n) There is no fruit better than a ripe, juicy pear.

- passed (v) پَست The time passed so quickly.
- past (prep) She ran past the lake.

- peace (n) پیس The enemies ceased fighting and declared peace.
- piece (n) That piece of strudel is fattening.

- peak (n) پیک The adventures climbed to the mountain's peak.
- peek (v) Peek behind the curtain and see if he's there.
- pique (v) The discovery piqued my curiosity.

- peal (n) پیل The peal of the bells rang through the town.
- peel (n) The peel on the avocado is thick.

- peer (n) پِر Don't give in to pressure from your peers.
- pier (n) Fishermen cast their lines from the end of the pier.

- plain (n) پ لِین A great, barren plain stretched before us in every direction.
- plain (adj) I prefer plain colors to busy patterns.
- plane (n) The plane began a sharp descent through the clouds.

- pleas (n) پی لیز We can still hear their pleas for help.
- please (v) A firm back rub will always please me.

- polish (v) پآلیش We must polish the silver before the company arrives.
- polish (adj) I love the favor of a polish sausage with mustard and kraut.

- pole (n) پُل The barber's pole is an ancient symbol.
- poll (n) The latest election poll bodes ill for the incumbent.

- poor (adj) پُور The poor farmers do not need another summer of floods.
- pore (n) Sweat passes through the pores in your skin.
- pour (v) Pour the milk, please.

- populace (n) پاپ یو لِس The populace rallied to overthrow the monarchy.
- populous (adj) A populous city has a large population.

- port (n) پورت The ship returned to its port of call.
- port (n) Father has a number of fine bottles of port in his wine cellar.

- praise (n) پریز The book has received nothing but high praise.
- prays (v) He prays for humankind's well-being.
- preys (v) The tiger preys on smaller, weaker animals.

- present (n) پرزنت I bought her a birthday present.
- present (n) Many of us think of the future, while ignoring the present.
- present (v) I will present my findings to the committee.

- principal (adj) پی رین سِپال The principal ideas are the main ones.
- principal (n) The principal of the school was my pal.
- principle (n) The Golden Rule is my guiding principle.

- profit (n) پرآفیت He failed to make any profit on the risky investment.
- prophet (n) The prophet foretold a time f peace and prosperity.

- quack (n) کُو آک I heard the quack of a duck close by our shelter.
- quack (n) Do not put your faith in the medical miracles of that quack.
- quail (n) کُو ایل The quail warbled merrily in its nest.
- quail (v) The explorers quailed at the sound of the raging rapids.

- rack (n) رَک I have no need for a gun rack.
- wrack (n) The storm brought wrack and ruin to the town.

- rain (n) رین We seldom see rain in Southern California.
- reign (n) The reign of the last czar proved to be tragic.
- rein (n) It is sometimes difficult to hold on to the reins of the horse.

- raise (v) ریز Please raise your hand if you have a question.
- raze (v) This demolition team can raze a city block in one afternoon.
- rays (n) The rays of the sun can be harmful.

- rap (n) رَپ A loud rap at the door woke us.
- rap (n) The patsy took the rap for a crime he didn't commit.
- rap (v) You can rap with your friends when the lecture is over.
- wrap (v) The salesman will wrap the package in festive paper.

- read (v) رید Please read me a story.
- reed (n) Oboes and clarinets are both fitted with reeds.

- real (adj) ری یِل Real life is often stranger than fiction.
- reel (n) The fisherman used a fine reel to land the marlin.

- rest (n) رِست A long rest after this hike will do us good.
- wrest (v) The thief could not wrest the briefcase from my hands.

- rhyme (n) رآیم The poem has a pleasing, melodic rhyme.
- rime (n) The freezing temperatures coated the windows with rime.

- right (adj) رآیت The contestant failed to provide the right answer.
- right (n) The right to privacy should be guaranteed to everyone.
- rite (n) They must pass an initiation rite when they turn thirteen.
- Wright (n) A Wright is a worker.
- write (v) Please write a letter to her soon.

- ring (n) رینگ The ring on her finger glittered with diamonds.
- ring (n) Please ring the bell before entering.
- wring (v) I wring my hands as a nervous habit.
- road (n) رُد Few cars travel this desolate, desert road.
- rode (v) They rode in the car.

- role (n) رُل The politician vehemently denied his role in the scandal.
- roll (v) Roll out the red carpet.

- root (n) رُوت The police discovered the root of the problem.
- route (n) A paper route is a good way to make some money.

(n) → noun **(v)** → verb **(adj)** → adjective **(prep)** →preposition

- rows (n) رُاَز There are rows and rows of seats at The Hollywood Bowl.
- rows (v) He rows the boat.

- rote (n) رُت My brother learned the names of the presidents by rote.
- wrote (v) I wrote to my friend today.

- sail (n) سیل The wind ripped the sail from the mast.
- sale (n) They're having a sale on velvet paintings.

- scene (n) سین The next scene in the movie is dreadful.
- seen (v) None of us had ever seen a sunset so beautiful.

- seam (n) سیم The seam in my pants came undone.
- seem (v) It may seem silly at first, but his plan has merit.

- serf (n) سِرف A serf is a little more than a slave.
- surf (n) The sand and surf give me a peaceful feeling.

- serge (n) سِرج Serge is a heavy material suitable for winter wear.
- surge (v) When the show starts, the crowd will surge forward.

- sew (v) سُ I will sew the button onto your shirt.
- so (adv) Those basketball players are so tall.

- shear (v) شی یِر Some farmers shear their sheep.
- sheer (adj) The face of the cliff was sheer granite.

- shone (v) شُن The midnight moon shone on the lake.
- shown (v) Our daughter's teacher has shown us her fine grades.

- slay (v) اِس لِی The prince will slay any who dare to challenge his power.
- sleigh (n) We rode in a one-house, open sleigh.

- sleight (n) اِس لآیت The magician's sleight of hand is unbelievable.
- slight (adv) The rescue team has only a slight chance of success.

(n) → noun **(v)** → verb **(adj)** → adjective **(prep)** →preposition

- sloe (n) اِس لُو The blackthorn fruit sloe is often used to flavor gin.
- slow (adj) The journey was a slow one.

- soar (v) سُر Airplanes soar above the clouds
- sore (n) The physician examined the sore.

- soared (v) سُرد The toy rocket soared into the sky.
- sword (n) Excalibur was the name of Arthur's sword.

- sole (n) سُل My favorite dish , Dover sole, was listed on the menu.
- sole (n) I have a corn on the sole of my left foot.
- soul (n) Blues music speaks to my soul.

- some (pro) سام Some of them are actually angry.
- sum (n) She embezzled a substantial sum of money.

- son (n) سان His son has made him very proud.
- sun (n) The sun is bright today.

- sow (v) سُا In the spring, I will sow the seeds into the fertile earth
- sow (n) A sow is an adult, female hog.

- spade (n) اِس پید He dug in the earth with his spade.
- spayed (v) My dog Gertie was spayed after her first litter was born.

- stair (n) اِس تِر The third stair from the top always creaks.
- stare (v) Don't stare at others.

- stake(n) اِس تیک To destroy a vampire, pound a stake through its heart.
- steak (n) Barbecued steak is my favorite summer meal.

- stationary (adj), اِس تِی شِنِری She rides a stationary bike at the gym after work.
- stationery (n), Our new stationery is printed on recycled paper.

- steal (v) اِس تی یل Many workers steal office supplies.
- steel (n) Steel now fortifies the infrastructures of most buildings.
- steel (v) Steel yourself against the temptation of chocolate.

- staid (adj) اِس تِید His staid character prevents him from overreacting.
- stayed (v) They stayed on in London until their fortune was spent.

- steer (n) اِس تِر We raised a steer for slaughter, but it became a household pet.
- steer (v) Steer the car to the right.

- straight (adj), اِس تِریت The arrow flew in a straight line
- strait (n) It was a rocky journey through the strait to Morocco.

- suite (n) سُو نیت Most travelers rent a single room rather than suite.
- sweet (adj) Every day can be as sweet as candy or as bitter as vitriol.

- tail (n) تِ یل The puppy's tail wagged happily.
- tale (n) I love to spin a tale of adventure.

- tare (n) تِر A tare is a seed of a herbaceous plant.
- tier (n) I have a tear in my shirt.

- taught (v) تَات My teachers taught me well.
- taut (adj) His taut nerves have been stretched to their breaking point.

- team (n) تیم The basketball team is out of town.
- teem (v) In summer, the air will teem with flying insects.

- their (pro) دِر Their gifts sat under the Christmas tree.
- there (adv) There she goes again.
- they're (contraction), They're my friends.

- threw (v) ثُور She threw the bouquet to her bridesmaids.
- through (prop), We ran through the woods.

- throes (n) ثُرز He was in the throes of a special passion.
- throws (v) Buddy throws a mean curve ball.
- thrown (v) Someone had thrown a snowball at the car.

(n) → noun **(v)** → verb **(adj)** → adjective **(prep)** →preposition

• tide (n)	تآید	The motion of the tide is as certain as death and taxes.
• tied (v)		We tied the burglar to a chair.
• to (prep)	تُو	The hikers walked to the falls.
• too (adv)		You study too much.
• two (n)		One plus one is two.
• troop (n)	تْرُوپ	He led a Boy Scout troop.
• troupe (n)		Many adventures would love to join a circus troupe.
• undo (v)	آن دُ	Sometimes you cannot undo what has already been done.
• undue (adj)		Your actions caused undue commotion.
• vain (adj)	وِین	He is vain and egotistical.
• vane (n)		The weather vane swung slowly in the breeze.
• vein (n)		The miners stumbled upon a rich vein of gold.
• wade (v)	وِید	Let's wade into the cool, shallow water.
• weighed (v)		They weighed the apples on the grocery scale.
• waist (n)	وِیست	This old belt no longer fits around my waist.
• waste (n)		His death is a terrible waste.
• wait (v)	وِیت	Please wait here.
• weight (n)		The weight of a car is related to its performance.
• waive (v)	وِیو	Don't waive your voting rights.
• wave (v)		She waved to me.
• want (v)	وآنت	If you want it, you must work for it.
• wont (adj)		You are wont to eat too much; it is a bad habit.
• ware (n)	وِر	He tried to sell us his cheap wares.
• wear (v)		Wear your jacket.
• where (adv)		Where in the world have you been?

(n) → noun **(v)** → verb **(adj)** → adjective **(prep)** →preposition

- way (n) وی Do you know the way to Shiraz?
- weigh (v) I weigh myself on a digital scale.
-
- weak (adj) ویک She makes my knees feel weak.
- week (n) The week flew by.

- weather (n) ویذر The weather is cloudy and cool.
- whether (conj), Whether or not you may go has yet to be decided.

- which (pro) ویچ Which purse will go best with your outfit?
- witch (n) Glinda, the good witch, charms me still.

- whine (v) وآین No one enjoys a child who whines.
- wine (n) A merlot is a fine wine for any occasion.

- whose (pro) هُوز Whose book is this?
- who's (contraction), Who's coming to your party?

- wood (n) وُد These floors are of polished wood.
- would (v) We all wish that peace would prevail.

(n) → noun (v) → verb **(adj)** → adjective (**prep**) →preposition

انواع جملات انگلیسی جهت فرا گیری لغات با تلفظ و معانی آنها به فا رسی

An inflection is a change in the sound of your voice when you speak. also spelt inflexion. This enables you to listen to the fine inflections in someone's voice.... She spoke in a low voice, always without inflection.

<An inflection is also a change in the form of a word that shows its grammatical function or number.> <...French and Spanish names with inflections.>
(این فلِک شِن : انحناء صرف فعل ، کج کردن- منحرف کردن)

Homonym words: متشابه، کلمه هائیکه تلفظ ان با کلمه دیگر یکسان ولي معني ان دگرگون باشد
Ex. whose, who's, lead, led, read, reed, to, too, two

Synonym words تلفظ هم معنی- مترادف tyrant & oppressor→ (ستمگر- ظالم)
Antonym words متضاد : good & bad , beautiful & ugly, cold & hot

---

- *HIV/AIDS* ***Symptoms and Signs***. Many people with HIV do not know they are infected. Many people do not develop symptoms after they first get infected with HIV. **...**

Human Immunodeficiency Virus (HIV) *is a lent virus (a member of the retrovirus family) that causes acquired immunodeficiency syndrome. (AIDS), a condition in ...*

Acquired[1] **I**mmune[2] **D**eficiency[3] **S**yndrome[4] (AIDS)

1.(اَ کوُاِر : اکتسابی)
2.(اِمی میون : مصون ، آزاد)
3.(دِ فی شِنَ سی : نقص)
4.(سین دِ رُم : مجموعه از نشانه ها که از علت واحدی ناشی شده باشند یا طوری با هم و بطور مشترک پدید آیند که ماهیت کلینیکی مشخصی را تشکیل دهند.)

<u>مَعانی یا بکار گیری لغات فوق در جملات دیگر:</u>

acquire ***–verb (used with object),*****-quired, -quir·ing.**
1. to come into possession or ownership of; get as one's own: *to acquire property.*

2. to gain for oneself through one's actions or efforts: *to acquire learning.*
3. *Linguistics*. to achieve native or native like command of a language or a linguistic rule or element.

immune ***–adjective***
1. protected from a disease or the like, as by inoculation.→ تلقیح، مایه کوبي
2. of or pertaining to the production of antibodies or lymphocytes that can react with a specific antigen: *immune reaction.*
3. exempt or protected: *immune from punishment.*
4. not responsive or susceptible: *immune to new ideas.*
–noun
5. a person who is immune.

deficiency ***–noun, plural*-cies.**
1. the state of being deficient; *lack; incompleteness; insufficiency.*
2. the amount lacked; a deficit.

syndrome ***–noun***
1. ***Pathology, Psychiatry***. a group of symptoms that together are characteristic of a specific disorder, disease, or the like.
2. a group of related or coincident things, *events, actions, etc.*
3. the pattern of symptoms that characterize or indicate a particular social condition.
4. a predictable, characteristic pattern of behavior, action, etc., that tends to occur under certain circumstances: *the retirement syndrome of endless golf and bridge games; the feast-or-famine syndrome of big business.*

WHAT IS THE ORIGIN OF THE WORD (F.*.C.K.) ?

- *In ancient England, people could not have sex without consent[1] from the King... When people wanted to have a child, they had to solicit[2] permission to the monarchy[3]; in turn they would supply a plaque to hang on their door when they had sexual relations.*
  The plaque read ... "Fornication[4] Under Consent of the King".
  This is the origin of the word.
  Fornication Under Consent of the King (*F.U.C.K.*)

1.(کانسِنت : رضايت، موافقت، راضي شدن، رضايت دادن)

2.(سا لی سی ت : درخواست کردن- خواستن، تقاضا کردن خواستاربودن)
3.(ما نار کی : رژیم سلطنتی)
4.(فورن کی شِن : جنده بازی- زنا)

Word History: The word fornication had a lowly beginning suitable to what has long been the low moral status of the act to which it refers.
Our word is first recorded in Middle English about year 1303. voluntary sex between an unmarried man and an unmarried woman;" extended in the Bible to adultery.

- Gordon Brown, Former English prime minister appears serious and statesmanlike[1]. *Statesman, states/manly* 1.سیاستمدارانه – سیاستمدار

مَعانی یا بکار گیری لغات فوق در جملات دیگر:

statesmanlike ***–noun, plural*-men.**
1. a person who is experienced in the art of government or versed in the administration of government affairs.
2. a person who exhibits great wisdom and ability in directing the affairs of a government or in dealing with important public issues.

- Afghan political leaders invoked[1] Afghan and Islamic traitors[2] in an attempt to shame the Taliban into releasing 18 females.

1. (درخواست کردن، استمداد کردن، فراخواندن،استناد کردن)

2.(تری تُر : خائن، خیانتکار - خائن به کشور)

<u>مَعانی یا بکار گیری لغات فوق در جملات دیگر:</u>

invoke ***–verb (used with object),*-voked, -vok·ing.**
1. to call for with earnest desire; make supplication or pray for: *to invoke God's mercy.*
2. to declare to be binding or in effect: *to invoke the law; to invoke a veto.*
3. to appeal to, as for confirmation.
4. to petition or call on for help or aid.

*traitor–**noun***
1. a person who betrays another, a cause, or any trust.
2. a person who commits treason by betraying his or her country

Prays and preys (*spoil*) پِ رِی : شکار

predatory: one that preys, destroy or devours شکارگر-غارتگر

pray → دعا کردن، نماز خواندن بدرگاه خدا استغاثه کردن خواستارشدن، درخواست کردن

***prey* –noun** پِ رِی

1. an animal hunted or seized for food, esp. by a carnivorous animal. حیوان گوشتخوار
2. a person or thing that is the victim of an enemy, *a swindler, a disease, etc.; gull.*
3. the action or habit of preying: *a beast of prey.*

- 110 bodies exhumed[2] in Bosnia grave.

2.از قبر بیرون آوردن- از بایگانی اطلاعات بیرون آوردن
3.(اِکس زو مِی شِن) نبش قبر Exhumation[3]

- Advice (اَدوآیس : پند، نصیحت) is a noun.
  Ex: *she always offers too much advice.*
  Advise (اَدوآیز : آگاهی دادن- مشورت کردن- نصیحت کردن) is a verb.
  Ex: *would you advise me about choosing the right course?*
  Or (*we advise you that, be advised by me*) → سخنم را بپذ یرید
- Her name and location being withheld because she fears retribution.
  رِت را بیوشِن : کیفر، تلافی، مکافات
- Palestinian president outlaws[2] Hamas militias as blockade[3] of Gaza intensifies[4]
  2.(از قانون بی بهره /از شهر بیرون کردن)

  . **3**. راه بند کردن- محاصره کردن **4**. شدید شدن- سختیها

- A purported[1] Taliban spokesman said the hard-line militia had extended (تمد ید کردن) by 24 hours the deadline.

1.(پِرپورت : مفهوم بخشیدن- به نظر آمدن)

***purport* –verb (used with object)**

1. to present, esp. deliberately, the appearance of being; profess or claim, often falsely: *a document purporting to be official.*
2. to convey to the mind as the meaning or thing intended; express or imply.
–noun

3. the meaning, import, or sense: *the main purport of your letter.*
4. purpose; intention; object**:** *the main purport of their visit to France.*
5. *The document purports that ….*

انچه از این سند مفهوم میشود این است که...

- Fan see a tainted hero ← قهرمان آلوده
  ورزشکار و قهرمان مورد علاقه مردم داروی غیرقانونی مثل استرویدز steroids مصرف میکرد
  از این رو مردم او را قهرمان فاسد شناختند.

Taint شائبه، لکه، آلودگی
taintless بی شائبه و بی لکه

- Afghan president criticized the Taliban kidnapping of "*foreign guests*" especially women as contrary[1] to the tenets[2] of Islam and national traditions.

1.(کان ترری :مخالف، معکوس، مغایر) 2. (تِ نِت : عقیده و اصو ل، مرام ، متعقدات مذهبی)

contrary ***–adjective***
1. opposite in nature or character; diametrically or mutually opposed:
contrary to fact; contrary propositions.
2. opposite in direction or position: *departures in contrary directions.*
3. being the opposite one of two: *I will make the contrary choice.*
–noun
6. something that is contrary or opposite: *to prove the contrary of a statement.*
7. either of two contrary things.

tenet ***–noun***
any opinion, principle, doctrine, dogma, etc., esp. one held as true by members of a profession, group, or movement. ***—Synonyms*** ; *belief, position.*

- First battalion[1] 24 marines in Iraq when a concussion[2] become a mortar[3] broke his left leg.

1.(بَ تَ لی یَن : یک گردان نظامی) **2**. (کَن کا شِن : تکان، تصادم ، صدمه، ضربت، ضربه مغزی)
3 . (هاون، اما در اینجا یعنی خمپاره انداز کوچک)

مَعانی یا بکار گیری لغات فوق در جملات دیگر:

*battalion****–noun***
1. *Military.* a ground force unit composed of a headquarters and two or more companies or similar units.
2. an army in battle array.
3. Often, **battalions.** a large number of persons or things; force:

battalions of bureaucrats.

concussion ***–noun***
1. *Pathology*. injury to the brain or spinal cord due to jarring from a blow, fall, or the like.
2. shock caused by the impact of a collision, blow, etc.
3. the act of violently shaking or jarring.

- Bridge crumples[1] into Mississippi River during such hours, flinging[2] cars into the water.

.1(کرامپل : مچاله، مچاله کردن)
.2(فی لینگ : پرت کردن *fling, flung, flung*)

<u>مَعانی یا بکار گیری لغات فوق در جملات دیگر:</u>

crumpled --- **Verb**
If someone or something crumples, they collapse suddenly in an untidy and helpless way.
He crumpled into a heap.

fling ***–verb (used with object)***
1. to throw, cast, or hurl with force or violence: *to fling a stone.*
2. to move (oneself) violently with impatience, contempt, or the like: *She flung herself*
3. to put suddenly or violently: *to fling a suspect into jail.*
4. to project or speak sharply, curtly, or forcefully: *He flung his answer at the questioner.*

- A burning truck and a school bus clung (کِلان : چسبیدن) to one slanted slab. (کِـلِـنْ) → Cling, clung, clung سه قسمت لغت

*cling****–verb (used without object)***
1. to adhere closely; stick to: *The wet paper clings to the glass.*
2. to hold tight, as by grasping or embracing; cleave: *The children clung to each other in the dark.*
3. to be or remain close: *The child clung to her mother's side.*
4. to remain attached, as to an idea, hope, memory, etc.: *Despite the predictions, the candidate clung to the belief that he would be elected.*
5. to cohere.

- As drivers plumed (پِلومد) the waters, other rescuers searched frantically[1] for victims arrived broken bridge.

.1 دیوانه وار- با شدت خشم- سراسیمه

plume ---a vertically or longitudinally moving, rising, or expanding fluid body, as of smoke or water.

frantic----adj.
Highly excited with strong emotion or frustration; frenzied: *frantic with worry.*
Characterized by rapid and disordered or nervous activity:
made a frantic last-minute search for the lost key.

- Team officials decided to play the game after conferring[1] with public safety officials, since sending up to 25,000 people back into traffic could hinder[2] secure efforts, said team president.

1. مشورت یا مذاکره کردن .. 2. هین دِر: به عقب انداختن- ممانعت

hinder ***–verb (used with object)***
1. to cause delay, interruption, or difficulty in; hamper; impede: *The storm hindered our progress.*
2. to prevent from doing, acting, or happening; stop:
to hinder a man from committing a crime.

- City aims to lure its share of valley visitors (Napa valley in Calif.).

لور: به دام انداختن، تطمیع کردن

- Iraqi parliament adjourns[1] without touching key bills. Legislation on hold as Iraqi lawmaker's adjourns[1] for month. Iraq's parliament shrugged[2] off us criticism on Monday and adjourned
for a month.

1.(اَجِرن : خاتمه دادن، به وقت دیگر موکول کردن) **2**.(شرَاگ : شانه بالا انداختن)

<u>مَعاني يا بكار گيرى لغات فوق در جملات ديگر:</u>

adjourn ***–verb (used with object)***
1. to suspend the meeting of (a club, legislature, committee, etc.) to a future time, another place, or indefinitely: *to adjourn the court.*
2. to defer or postpone to a later time: *They adjourned the meeting until the following Monday.*
3. to defer or postpone (a matter) to a future meeting of the same body.
4. to defer or postpone (a matter) to some future time, either specified or not specified.

–verb (used without object)

5. to postpone, suspend, or transfer proceedings.
6. to go to another place: *to adjourn to the parlor.*

shrug–***verb (used with object)***
1. to raise and contract (the shoulders), expressing indifference*, disdain, etc.

*خونسردي، بي علاقگي،

–verb (used without object)
2. to raise and contract the shoulders.
–noun
3. the movement of raising and contracting the shoulders.
4. a short sweater or jacket that ends above or at the waistline.

- For less snooty[1] looking down the nose or showing disdain[2]

1. (اِس نو تی : دارای قیافه تکبر امیز- پرافاده)
2. (دیس د ین: اهانت، ناز، قابل ندانستن تکبر)

<Snooty people who won't speak to their neighbor>
characterized by snobbery. {s ناث snot فین –ان دماغ}
Snotty با یک اُ به معنی فین بینی، کثیف- که تلفظ آن اِسناتی است

- He disdains دیس دین to talk with me. از اینکه با من صحبت کند عا ر دارد.

disdain–***verb (used with object)***
1. to look upon or treat with contempt; despise; scorn.
2. to think unworthy of notice, response, etc.; consider beneath oneself: *to disdain replying to an insult.*
–noun
3. a feeling of contempt for anything regarded as unworthy; haughty contempt; scorn.

- Afghan President Hamid Karzai denounced the kidnapping of women and foreign guests as un-Islamic.

خبر دادن، اشاره کردن

- For Hajji Ali, a tribal elder from the east of the country, it is abhorrent this is not the culture of Afghanistan to take women hostage.

تنفر، زشت، مغایر

abhorrent ***–adjective***
1. causing repugnance; detestable; loathsome: *an abhorrent deed.*
2. utterly opposed, or contrary, or in conflict (usually fol. by *to*): *abhorrent to reason.*
3. feeling extreme repugnance or aversion (usually fol. by *of*): *abhorrent of waste.*
4. remote in character (usually fol. by *from*): *abhorrent from the principles of law.*

- Neighbors tried to pry[1] them off with broomsticks. (Pried, prying)
  1. جدا کردن (پ رای) - این مطلب در رابطه بادعوای سگهاگفته شده است

- "NATO has said there has been no spring offensive" says Pakistani author Ahmad. This is the offensive. تهاجم
  Police investigators continue to implore the public to help forward with information on the vehicle that struck a bicycle on June 12 and was driven from the scene. درخواست کردن، التماس کردن

<u>مَعانی یا بکار گیری لغات فوق در جملات دیگر:</u>

offensive ***–adjective***
1. causing resentful displeasure; highly irritating, angering, or annoying: *Offensive television commercials.*
2. unpleasant or disagreeable to the sense: *an offensive odor.*
3. repugnant to the moral sense, good taste, or the like; insulting: *an offensive remark; an offensive joke.*
4. pertaining to offense or attack: *the offensive movements of their troops.*
5. characterized by attack; aggressive: *offensive warfare.*
–noun
6. the position or attitude of aggression or attack: *to take the offensive.*
7. an aggressive movement or attack: *a carefully planned naval offensive.*

implore ***–verb (used with object)***
1. to beg urgently or piteously, as for aid or mercy; beseech; entreat: *They implored him to go.*
2. to beg urgently or piteously for (aid, mercy, pardon, etc.): *implore forgiveness.*
–verb (used without object)
3. to make urgent or piteous supplication

- *Barbarian at the airport gate*: این عنوان اصلی روزنامه بوده
  The arbitrary (آر بی تر ری) power wielded (و – یلد : گرداندن ، اداره کردن)
  by airport security personnel is an affront. (آشکارا توهین کردن)

<u>مَعانی یا بکار گیری لغات فوق در جملات دیگر:</u>

arbitrary ***–adjective***
1. subject to individual will or judgment without restriction; contingent solely upon one's discretion: *an arbitrary decision.*
2. decided by a judge or arbiter rather than by a law or statute.

3. having unlimited power; uncontrolled or unrestricted by law; despotic; tyrannical: *an arbitrary government.*
4. capricious; unreasonable; unsupported: *an arbitrary demand for payment.*

***wield*–verb (used with object)**
1. to exercise (power, authority, influence, etc.), as in ruling or dominating.

***affront* –noun**
1. a personally offensive act or word; deliberate act or display of disrespect; intentional slight; insult: *an affront to the king.*
2. an offense to one's dignity or self-respect.
–verb (used with object)
3. to offend by an open manifestation of disrespect or insolence:
His speech affronted all of us.
4. to make ashamed or confused; embarrass.

- Citing[1] tenets[2] of Islam chivalry[3] (شِ وِلری) fails to win release of 18 female captives.

1. اصل لغت cite است به معنی ذکر کردن. Citation یعنی ذکر کردن و نقل قول، که در حقوق به معنی احضار است.
2. عقیده- اصول
3. سلحشوری- جوانمردی

مَعانی یا بکار گیری لغات فوق در جملات دیگر:

***tenet*–noun**
any opinion, principle, doctrine, dogma, etc., esp. one held as true by members of a profession, group, or movement.

***chivalry* –noun, *plural*-ries**
1. the sum of the ideal qualifications of a knight, including courtesy, generosity, valor, (وَلِر) and dexterity in arms.
2. the rules and customs of medieval knighthood.
3. the medieval system or institution of knighthood.
4. a group of knights.
5. gallant warriors or gentlemen: *fair ladies and noble chivalry.*

- Afghan top political leaders invoked[1] Afghan and Islamic tradition of chivalry[2] and hospitality Sunday in attempts to shame the Taliban into releasing 18 female South Korea captives.

1.این وُک : متوسل شدن 2.(شِ ور لی : سلحشوری-جوانمردی)
(طلب یاری-استمداد-توسل =invocation)

invoke ***–verb (used with object),*** **-voked, -vok·ing.**
1. to call for with earnest desire; make supplication or pray for: *to invoke God's mercy.*
2. to call on (a deity, Muse, etc.), as in prayer or supplication.
3. to petition or call on for help or aid.

- Reputed: *having a good repute,* *reputation*شهرت- اعتبار.

- A purported [1] Taliban spokesman said the hard-line militia had extended by 24 hours the deadline. Also a purported Taliban spokesman shrugged[2] off the demands and instead set a new deadline. *Purported=reputable*

1 . (پریورتد: معتبر، مشهور) 2.(شِ راگ : شانه بالا انداختن)

purport ***–verb (used with object)***
1. to present, esp. deliberately, the appearance of being; profess or claim, often falsely: *a document purporting to be official.*
2. to convey to the mind as the meaning or thing intended; express or imply.
–noun
3. the meaning, import, or sense: *the main purport of your letter.*
4. purpose; intention; object: *the main purport of their visit to France.*

*shrug****–verb (used with object)***
1. to raise and contract (the shoulders), expressing indifference, disdain, etc.
–verb (used without object)
2. to raise and contract the shoulders.
–noun
3. the movement of raising and contracting the shoulders.
4. a short sweater or jacket that ends above or at the waistline.
<Free shrug pattern و Shrug jacket و Shrug sweater>

- In the volatile (والاتُل: بی ثبات، متغیر) northwest tribal region of Pakistan Islamic militants detonated (دِ تَ- نیت : با صدا منفجر کردن یا شدن).

<u>مَعانی یا بکار گیری لغات فوق در جملات دیگر:</u>

volatile ***–adjective***

1. evaporating rapidly; passing off readily in the form of vapor: *Acetone is a volatile solvent.*
2. tending or threatening to break out into open violence; explosive: *a volatile political situation.*
–noun a volatile substance, as a gas or solvent.

detonate–***verb (used without object)***
1. to explode with suddenness and violence.
–verb (used with object)
2. to cause (something explosive) to explode.

- Neutering[1] or spaying[2] cat or dog to control their population.
  1.(نوت رینگ، خنثی کردن) 2 . (اس پ اینگ :اخته کردن)

- Some dissenters (مخالف عقیده عموم) blame the crackdown (*an act or instance of cracking down*) on regime's fear of a US effort to undermine (نقب زدن- زیر جایی را خالی کردن- به تدریج ضعیف کردن) it as tenacious (تِ نِی شِس :سرسخت، محکم، استوار) over Iran's nuclear program intensify. → شدید کردن- افزودن

مَعانی یا بکار گیری لغات فوق در جملات دیگر:

dissenter–***noun***
1. a person who dissents, as from an established church, political party, or majority opinion.
2. (*sometimes initial capital letter*) an English Protestant who dissents from the Church of England.

undermine ***–verb (used with object),*-mined, -min·ing.**
1. to injure or destroy by insidious activity or imperceptible stages, sometimes tending toward a sudden dramatic effect.
2. to attack by indirect, secret, or underhand means; attempt to subvert by stealth.
3. to make an excavation under; dig or tunnel beneath, as a military stronghold.
4. to weaken or cause to collapse by removing underlying support, as by digging away or eroding the foundation.

tenacious ***–adjective***
1. holding fast; characterized by keeping a firm hold (often fol. by *of*): *a tenacious grip on my arm; tenacious of old habits.*
2. highly retentive: *a tenacious memory.*
3. pertinacious, persistent, stubborn, or obstinate.

- *Eido* is at least the 7th Lebanese anti-Syrian luminary[1] assassinated[2] since Feb. 2005.

(لُومِنِری: شخصیت برجسته- یا یک شخص روشن و فهمیده- جسم نورانی - چهره تابناک).1

(أَسَّ سِی نِیت : کشتن، بقتل رساندن، ترورکردن).2

luminary ***–noun***
1. a celestial body, as the sun or moon.
2. a body, object, etc., that gives light.
3. a person who has attained eminence in his or her field or is an inspiration to others:
one of the luminaries in the field of Medical science.
–adjective
4. of, pertaining to, or characterized by light.

assassinate ***–verb (used with object),*** **-nat·ed, -nat·ing.**
1. to kill suddenly or secretively, esp. a politically prominent person; murder premeditatedly and treacherously.
2. to destroy or harm treacherously and viciously: *to assassinate a person's character.*

- Syria, Iran and their pawns (سرباز پیاده در شطرنج) have ensured political gridlock (گرفتگی و درگیری سیاسی) in Beirut since last November.

Gridlock definition: *A government, business or institution's inability to function at a normal level due either to complex or conflicting procedures within the administrative framework or to impending change in the business.*

gridlock –noun

1. the stoppage of free vehicular movement in an urban area because key intersections are blocked by traffic.
2. the blocking of an intersection by vehicular traffic entering the intersection but unable to pass through it.
3. any situation in which nothing can move or proceed in any direction:
a financial gridlock due to high interest rates.

- Former Lebanon premier Fouad Siniora's government with protests attempting to topple[1] it.

overthrow <*topple a dictator*> (واژگون کردن) .1

topple ***–verb (used without object)***

1. to fall forward, as from having too heavy a top; pitch; tumble down.
2. to lean over or jut, as if threatening to fall.
–verb (used with object)
3. to cause to topple.
4. to overthrow, as from a position of authority: *to topple the king.*

- We will not be blackmailed (باج سبیل، رشوه).

Extortion of money or something else of value from a person by the...

blackmail–noun
1. any payment extorted by intimidation, as by threats of injurious revelations or accusations.
2. the extortion of such payment: *He confessed rather than suffer the dishonor of blackmail.*
–verb (used with object)
4. to extort money from (a person) by the use of threats.
5. to force or coerce into a particular action, statement, etc.: *The strikers claimed they were blackmailed into signing the new contract.*

- India vows to eliminate the widespread practice of aborting (سقط) female fetuses (فی تِس : جنین).

An unborn or unhatched vertebrate (وِرتِ برِت: جانور مهره دار)

abort –verb (used without object)
1. to bring forth a fetus from the uterus before the fetus is viable; miscarry.

–verb (used with object)
6. to cause to bring forth (a fetus) from the uterus before the fetus is viable.
7. to cause (a pregnant female) to be delivered of a nonviable fetus.
8. to cause to cease or end at an early or premature stage: *We aborted our vacation when the car broke down.*
9. to terminate (a missile flight, mission, etc.) before completion.
10. to put down or quell in the early stages: *Troops aborted the uprising.*
–noun
11. a missile, rocket, etc., that has aborted.

- K-9 dog sniffed out armed suspects and hidden narcotics that evaded officers. (ائی وِید : طفره رفتن - فرار کردن)

evade –verb (used with object)

1. to escape from by trickery or cleverness: *to evade one's pursuers.*
2. to get around by trickery: *to evade rules.*
3. to avoid doing or fulfilling: *to evade an obligation.*
4. to avoid answering directly: *to evade a question.*
5. to elude; escape: *The solution evaded him.*
–verb (used without object)
6. to practice evasion.
7. to elude or get away from someone or something by craft or slyness; escape.

- Avoid mumbling or slurring (اِس لِر: لـه کـردن چیـزی در تلفـظ یـا نوشـتن) your words.

slur–***verb (used with object)***
1. to pass over lightly or without due mention or consideration (often fol. by *over*): *The report slurred over her contribution to the enterprise.*
2. to pronounce (a syllable, word, etc.) indistinctly by combining, reducing, or omitting sounds, as in hurried or careless utterance.
3. to cast aspersions on; calumniate; disparage; depreciate:
The candidate was viciously slurred by his opponent.

–verb (used without object)
4. to read, speak, or sing hurriedly and carelessly.
–noun
5. a slurred utterance or sound.

- Gazing (گِی زینگ: چشم دوختن خیره شدن) out the window or reading a look at your seat ... (*Gaze*= گیز)

gaze ***–verb (used without object)***
1. to look steadily and intently, as with great curiosity, interest, pleasure, or wonder.
–noun
2. a steady or intent look.

- Tuesday when 100 heads of cattle symbolizing the boving گـاوی theme (تیم: موضـوع- مطلـب- مقالـه) of this year's OC. Fair were steered onto the sand near the Huntington beach pier.

theme اسم است ed نمی گیرد- معنی دیگر آن گوساله نر- گاو اخته شده .

Steer (اِس تِر: راندن-بردن)

Boving: Free checklist of **Boving** resources, including online databases, obituaries, surname histories, census and military records, and **Boving** message boards

theme ***–noun***
1. a subject of discourse, discussion, meditation, or composition; topic:
The need for world peace was the theme of the meeting.
2. a unifying or dominant idea, motif, etc., as in a work of art.
3. a short, informal essay, esp. a school composition.
4. *Music.*
a. a principal melodic subject in a musical composition.
b. a short melodic subject from which variations are developed.

- General faces demotion (دِمُوشِن: تنزل درجه و مقام) in his partner's death.

demote–***verb (used with object),*****-mot·ed, -mot·ing.**
to reduce to a lower grade, rank, class, or position (opposed to promote):
They demoted the careless waiter to busboy.

- He was an FBI informant (مخبر-خبررسان).

informant ***–noun***
1. a person who informs or gives information; informer.
2. a person who supplies social or cultural data in answer to the questions of an investigator.
3. *Linguistics.* a native speaker of a language who supplies utterances and forms for one analyzing or learning the language

---

- ex offenders (آفِن دِر: متخلف- مجرم) who took student ....
An offender is a person who has committed a crime; a formal use. *In 1965, 42% of convicted offenders ended up in prison.... ...thieves, vandals, sex offenders and muggers.... ...the harsh treatment of young offenders.*

- Obese (چاقی بیش از حد- اُبیس) kids face pervasive[1] bias, the stigmatization directed at obese children by their peers (هم ردیف), parents, educators and others in pervasive (نفوذ/سرایت کننده).1
Stigmatize= لکه دار کردن - بی آبرو کردن- (استیگ م تایز)

pervasive ---adj.
Having the quality or tendency to pervade or permeate: *the pervasive odor of garlic.*

stigmatize **–verb (used with object),-tized, -tiz·ing.**

1. to set some mark of disgrace or infamy upon: *The crime of the father stigmatized the whole family.*

2. to mark with a stigma or brand.
3. to produce stigmata, marks, spots, or the like, on.
Also, *especially British*, **stig·ma·tise**.

peer*–noun*
1. a person of the same legal status: *a jury of one's peers.*
2. a person who is equal to another in abilities, qualifications, age, background, and social status.
3. something of equal worth or quality: *a sky-scraper without peer.*
4. a nobleman.

- 4500 Mexican have died trying to cross borders controls in late 1994 to stem (اِس تِم : جلوگیری کردن- سد کردن) illegal immigration.

stem **–noun**
1. the ascending axis of a plant, whether above or below ground, which ordinarily grows in an opposite direction to the root or descending axis.
2. a cut flower: *We bought roses at the flower market for 50¢ a stem.*
3. the handle of a spoon.
4. stems, *Slang*. the legs of a human being.
–verb (used without object)
5 to arise or originate: This project stems from last week's lecture.

- Mother of one girl respected (رجوع کردن) to police and then it was corroborated (کُراب ریت : تایید کردن- ثابت کردن) by each of other girls.
corroborate = *to support with evidence or authority= confirm*

respect= رجوع، مراجعه احترام ، ملاحظه، احترام گذاشتن به، محترم داشتن بزرگداشت، بزرگداشتن
*respect***–noun**
1. a particular, detail, or point (usually prec. by *in*): *to differ in some respect.*
2. relation or reference: *inquiries with respect to a route.*
3. esteem for or a sense of the worth or excellence of a person, a personal quality or ability, or something considered as a manifestation of a personal quality or ability: *I have great respect for her judgment.*
4. deference to a right, privilege, privileged position, or someone or something considered to have certain rights or privileges; proper acceptance or courtesy; acknowledgment: *respect for a suspect's right to counsel; to show respect for the flag; respect for the elderly.*
5. the condition of being esteemed or honored: *to be held in respect.*
6. respects, a formal expression or gesture of greeting, esteem, or friendship: *Give my respects to your parents.*

–verb (used with object)
7. to hold in esteem or honor: *I cannot respect a cheat.*
8. to show regard or consideration for: *to respect someone's rights.*
9. to refrain from intruding upon or interfering with:
to respect a person's privacy.
10. to relate or have reference to.
—Idioms
11. in respect of, in reference to; in regard to; concerning.
12. pay one's respects,
a. to visit in order to welcome, greet, etc.: *We paid our respects to the new neighbors.*
13. b. to express one's sympathy, esp. to survivors following a death: *We paid our respects to the family.*
15. with respect to, referring to; concerning: *with respect to your latest request.*

- Officers shoot man who officers say was brandishing (تاب دادن) a knife outside his brother's apartment.

*brandish***–*verb (used with object)***
1. to shake or wave, as a weapon; flourish: *Brandishing his sword, he rode into battle.*
–noun **2.** a flourish or waving, as of a weapon.

- Civil strife (اِس تِ رایف: جنگ-نزاع) in Palestine.

strife ***–noun***
1. vigorous or bitter conflict, discord, or antagonism: *to be at strife.*
2. a quarrel, struggle, or clash: *armed strife.*
3. competition or rivalry: *the strife of the marketplace.*
4. *Archaic.* strenuous effort. (*Archaic* : آرکِ یک کهنه، قديمي، غير مصطلح)
an archaic manner; an archaic notion

- As a result of the virulent (وی ریالِنت : -کینه آمی زهراگین، سم دار، تلخ، تند کینه جو، بدخیم) Nazi persecution (پِر سی کیوشِن: آزار-در اینجا تعقیب برای آزار دادن)..........

virulent ***–adjective***
1. actively poisonous; intensely noxious: *a virulent insect bite.*
2. *Medicine/Medical.* highly infective; malignant or deadly.
3. *Bacteriology.* causing clinical symptoms.
4. violently or spitefully hostile.
5. intensely bitter, spiteful, or malicious: *a virulent attack.*

*persecution***–*noun***
1. the act of persecuting.

2. the state of being persecuted.
3. a program or campaign to exterminate, drive away, or subjugate a people because of their religion, race, or beliefs: *the persecutions of Christians by the Romans.*

- Palestine remained in abeyance[1] during world war two.

1.(اَبِ یَ نس : بی تکلیفی- وقفه)

abeyance ***–noun***
1. temporary inactivity, cessation, or suspension:
Let's hold that problem in abeyance for a while.
2. *Law*. a state or condition of real property in which title is not as yet vested in a known titleholder: *an estate in abeyance.*

- The victims of extremists .... (افراطی)

extremist***–noun***
1. a person who goes to extremes, esp. in political matters.
2. a supporter or advocate of extreme doctrines or practices.
–adjective
3. belonging or pertaining to extremists.

- The Jews were allotted (اِلات : تخصیص دادن) Eastern Galilee.

allot–***verb (used with object),*-lot·ted, -lot·ting.**
1. to divide or distribute by share or portion; distribute or parcel out; apportion:
to allot the available farmland among the settlers.
2. to appropriate for a special purpose: *to allot money for a park.*
3. to assign as a portion; set apart; dedicate.
<*allot ten minutes for the speech*> , < *allot seats to the press*>.

- Israel people as envisaged (اِن وِ زِجد: روبرو یا مواجه شدن) in the Belfour declaration (اعلامیه).

envisage–***verb (used with object),*-aged, -ag·ing.**
1. to contemplate; visualize: *He envisages an era of great scientific discoveries.*
2. *Archaic*. to look in the face of; face.
(*Archaic* : آرکِ یِک کهنه، قدیمي، غیر مصطلح)
an archaic manner; an archaic notion

- Several month's fierce (فی یِرس: سخت، بیرحمانه) fighting interspersed by periods of truce (تو روس: مهلت- متارکه جنگ).

Interspersed (این تِر س پِرسد: پراکنده/پخش کردن-گُله گُله پاشیدن)

fierce ***–adjective,*** **fierc·er, fierc·est.**
1. menacingly wild, savage, or hostile: *fierce animals; a fierce look.*
2. violent in force, intensity, etc.: *fierce winds.*
3. furiously eager or intense: *fierce competition.*
4. *Informal.* extremely bad or severe: *a fierce cold.*
truce ***–noun***
1. a suspension of hostilities for a specified period of time by mutual agreement of the warring parties; cease-fire; armistice.
2. an agreement or treaty establishing this.
3. a temporary respite, as from trouble or pain.

- After the armistice[1] of 1949. (armistice means truce)
 To separate the belligerents[2] and safeguard shipping. Withdraw behind the 1949 armistice lines.

1.(آرمیس تیس : دولت محارب)

2.(بِ لِ جِرنت : متخاصم- *(علوم نظامي)* نيروي شورشي، ماجراجو اشوبگر)

armistice ***–noun***
a temporary suspension of hostilities by agreement of the warring parties; truce: *World War I ended with the armistice of 1918.*

belligerent ***–adjective***
1. warlike; given to waging war.
2. of warlike character; aggressively hostile; bellicose: *a belligerent tone.*
3. waging war; engaged in war: *a peace treaty between belligerent powers.*
4. pertaining to war or to those engaged in war: *belligerent rights.*
–noun
5. a state or nation at war.
6. a member of the military forces of such a state.

- After 2003 conviction for a lewd[1] and lascivious[2] a 14-year-old girl.

1. (لود-هرزه،شهوت پرست)
2. (لِ سِه وی یَس: شهوت پرست)

مَعانی یا بکار گیری لغات فوق در جملات دیگر:

lewd ***–adjective*****-er, -est.**
1. inclined to, characterized by, or inciting to lust or lechery; lascivious.
2. obscene or indecent, as language or songs; salacious.

3. *Obsolete.*
a. low, ignorant, or vulgar.
b. base, vile, or wicked, esp. of a person.
c. bad, worthless, or poor, esp. of a thing.

***lascivious* –adjective**
1. inclined to lustfulness; wanton; lewd: *a lascivious, girl-chasing old man.*
2. arousing sexual desire: *lascivious photographs.*
3. indicating sexual interest or expressive of lust or lewdness: *a lascivious gesture.*

- Dingy patterned sheets. (دین جی: تیره رنگ، چرک)

Dingy means: dirty, unclear, shabby, squalid

- Infrastructure: *the underlying foundation or basic framework as of a system or as organization.*

Lying= (لا اینگ: کاذب، دروغگویی) , underlying=زیربنایی

Why is infrastructure important?
The importance of infrastructure is directly related to the services that you get from it. Infrastructure encourages new investment, as well as helps the flow of ideas and goods.

- 300 Spartans (from ancient Sparta :اسپارتن) against a marauding Persian army at the battle of Thermopile.

(مرادینگ: برای غارت حمله کردن-غارتگر)

Re Spartan and more info visit site : → www.300**spartan**warriors.com

***marauding* –adjective**
1. engaged in raiding for plunder, esp. roaming about and ravaging an area: *marauding bands of outlaws.*
2. undertaken for plunder: *a marauding raid.*

- Iraq's government was walking unsatisfactory progress in effort to purge (پرج : پاک سازی کردن) the police of shite militia one of the elusive (ائی لوُ سیو : طفره آمیز- اغفال کننده) benchmarks* set for stabilization.

*(نشان ، نشانهاي در اندیس که مهم است و قابل مقایسه با سایر نشانه هاست، معیار، محک)

***purge* –verb (used with object)**
1. to rid of whatever is impure or undesirable; cleanse; purify.

2. to rid, clear, or free (usually fol. by *of* or *from*): *to purge a political party of disloyal members.*
3. to clear of imputed guilt or ritual uncleanliness.
4. to clear away or wipe out legally (an offense, accusation, etc.) by atonement or other suitable action.
5. to remove by cleansing or purifying (often fol. by *away, off,* or *out*).
6. to cause evacuation of the bowels of (a person).

elusive:
1. eluding clear perception or complete mental grasp; hard to express or define: ***an elusive concept.***
2. cleverly or skillfully evasive: ***a fish too elusive to catch.***
thing that purges, as a purgative medicine or dose.

- Transportation officials plan to begin tackling[1] fine notorious[2] (انگشت نما- شرور- بد) traffic check points within the next four years.

1.(از عهده برامدن داراي اسباب و لوازم كردن بعهده گرفتن، افسار كردن، تكل كردن)
2.(نُو توری یوس : انگشت نما- شرور- بد)

***tackling* –noun** Archaic. (*Archaic*→ آر کِه یِک :کهنه، قديمي، غير مصطلح)
equipment; tackle.

***notorious* –adjective**
1. widely and unfavorably known: *a notorious gambler.*
2. publicly or generally known, as for a particular trait:
a newspaper that is notorious for its sensationalism.

- These trivial issues are normal. (تری وی یا: جزئی-ناقابل)

***trivial* –adjective**
1. of very little importance or value; insignificant: *Don't bother me with trivial matters.*
2. commonplace; ordinary.
3. *Biology.* (of names of organisms) specific, as distinguished from generic.
4. *Mathematics.*
a. noting a solution of an equation in which the value of every variable of the equation is equal to zero.
b. (of a theorem, proof, or the like) simple, transparent, or immediately evident.

- Although every project is different and has its peculiar[1] quirks[2]

1. (پِ کیو لیر:ویژه-مخصوص)
2. (کورکز:ابهام-حیله-کلک)

معانی یا بکار گیری لغات فوق در جملات دیگر:

peculiar –adjective
1. strange; queer; odd: *peculiar happenings.*
2. uncommon; unusual: *the peculiar hobby of stuffing and mounting bats.*
3. distinctive in nature or character from others.
4. belonging characteristically (usually fol. by *to*): *an expression peculiar to Canadians.*
5. belonging exclusively to some person, group, or thing:
the peculiar properties of a drug.
6. *Astronomy.* designating a star or galaxy with special properties that deviates from others of its spectral type or galaxy class.

quirk –noun

1. a peculiarity of action, behavior, or personality; mannerism:
He is full of strange quirks.
2. a shift, subterfuge, or evasion; quibble.
3. a sudden twist or turn: ***He lost his money by a quirk of fate.***
4. a flourish or showy stroke, as in writing.
5. *Architecture.*

- If you perceive that there are four possible ways in which a procedure can go wrong, circumvent it than a fifth way will promptly develop. (باحیله پیشدستی کردن بر- گول زدن-گیر انداختن)

circumvent –verb (used with object)
1. to go around or bypass: *to circumvent the lake; to circumvent the real issues.*
2. to avoid (defeat, failure, unpleasantness, etc.) by artfulness or deception; avoid by anticipating or outwitting: *He circumvented capture by anticipating their movements.*
3. to surround or encompass, as by stratagem; entrap: *to circumvent a body of enemy troops.*

- The difference can be subtle. (ساتل: زیرک-هوشیار-دقیق).

subtle *–adjective,* -tler, -tlest.
1. thin, tenuous, or rarefied, as a fluid or an odor.
2. fine or delicate in meaning or intent; difficult to perceive or understand: *subtle irony.*
3. delicate or faint and mysterious: *a subtle smile.*
4. requiring mental acuteness, penetration, or discernment: *a subtle philosophy.*
5. characterized by mental acuteness or penetration: *a subtle understanding.*
6. cunning, wily, or crafty: *a subtle liar.*
7. insidious in operation: *subtle poison.*
8. skillful, clever, or ingenious: *a subtle painter.*

- Prerogative an exclusive or special right or privilege

(پری راگ تیو :حق ویژه)

Something that is the prerogative of a particular person or group is a privilege or right that only they have; a formal word.
...luxuries which were considered the prerogative of the rich.

- *Insignificant*: *<Clinton Aide Says Richardson's endorsement is Insignificant>*

بی معنی- بی اهمیت- ناچیز-جزئی- ناقابل-حقیر- کم- پست

- Losses (لاسِس): the act of losing possession, Loses (لوزِس)

loss **–noun** :لاس زیان- ضرر- خسارت-فقدان- در جمع تلفات یا ضایعات
1. detriment, disadvantage, or deprivation from failure to keep, have, or get: *to bear the loss of a robbery.*
2. something that is lost: *The painting was the greatest loss from the robbery.*
3. an amount or number lost: *The loss of life increased each day.*
4. the state of being deprived of or of being without something that one has had: *the loss of old friends.*
5. death, or the fact of being dead: *to mourn the loss of a grandparent.*
6. the accidental or inadvertent losing of something dropped, misplaced, stolen, etc.: *to discover the loss of a document.*
7. a losing by defeat; failure to win: *the loss of a bet.*
8. failure to make good use of something, as time; waste.
9. failure to preserve or maintain: *loss of engine speed at high altitudes.*
10. destruction or ruin: *the loss of a ship by fire.*
11. a thing or a number of related things that are lost or destroyed to some extent: *Most buildings in the burned district were a total loss.*

lose **–verb (used with object)** : لُوز گم کردن- از دست دادن- تلف کردن- باختن- شکست خوردن
1. *I'm sure I've merely misplaced my hat, not lost it.*
2. to fail inadvertently to retain (something) in such a way that it cannot be immediately recovered: *I just lost a dime under this sofa.*
3. to suffer the deprivation of: to lose one's job; to lose one's life.

- I don't want speculate for that! (اِس پِ کِ لِیت فکر کردن-اندیشیدن)

speculate **–verb (used without object),-lat·ed, -lat·ing.**
1. to engage in thought or reflection; meditate (often fol. by *on, upon,* or a clause).
2. to indulge in conjectural thought.

- Doctor accuse of reviving 92 years old woman against her wishes.

revive **–verb (used with object)** (ر وایو : زنده کردن)
1. to activate, set in motion, or take up again; renew: *to revive old feuds.*
2. to restore to life or consciousness: *We revived him with artificial respiration.*
3. to put on or show (an old play or motion picture) again.
4. to make operative or valid again.
5. to bring back into notice, use, or currency: *to revive a subject of discussion.*
6. to quicken or renew in the mind; bring back: *to revive memories.*
7. to reanimate or cheer (the spirit, heart, etc., or a person).
8. *Chemistry.* to restore or reduce to the natural or uncombined state, as a metal.

- The decision to ration fuel.

ration ***–noun*** رَشِن: جیره بندی کردن
1. a fixed allowance of provisions or food, esp. for soldiers or sailors or for civilians during a shortage: *a daily ration of meat and bread.*
2. an allotted amount: *They finally saved up enough gas rations for the trip.*

- When two suicide bombers denoted themselves near a refreshment in …..

(دِ نُت : منفجر کردن- مشخص کردن، تفکیک کردن -علامت گذاردن)

denote–verb (used with object),**-not·ed, -not·ing.**
1. to be a mark or sign of; indicate: *A fever often denotes an infection.*

- US. worrier that making Kirkuk(کرکوک) part of an autonomous Kurdistan.

آ تا نِ مس: حکومت خودمختار

autonomous ***–adjective***
1. *Government.*
a. self-governing; independent; subject to its own laws only.
b. pertaining to an autonomy.
2. having autonomy; not subject to control from outside; independent: *a subsidiary that functioned as an autonomous unit.*

- Bush and Putin aim to revive friendship. (ر وایو: زنده کردن)

revive ***–verb (used with object)***
1. to activate, set in motion, or take up again; renew: *to revive old feuds.*
2. to restore to life or consciousness: *We revived him with artificial respiration.*
3. to bring back into notice, use, or currency: *to revive a subject of discussion.*

- Still many people are apprehensive (آپری هِن سیو: بیمناک)

apprehensive ***–adjective***

1. uneasy or fearful about something that might happen: *apprehensive for the safety of the mountain climbers.*
2. quick to learn or understand.
3. perceptive; discerning (usually fol. by *of*).

- This car had veered[1] off the Hwy-26 in Oregon. (v یِرد :تغییرجهت دادن).1

<the economy veered sharply downward>

Veer– v یِر **verb (used without object)**
1. to change direction or turn about or aside; shift, turn, or change from one course, position, inclination, etc., to another: *The speaker kept veering from his main topic.*
2. *The car veered off the road.*

- One of the world's most acclaimed (أكلِيم : تحسین کردن)
Controversial (مباحثه ای- جدال آمیز) novelists.

acclaim ***–verb (used with object)***
1. to welcome or salute with shouts or sounds of joy and approval; applaud: *to acclaim the conquering heroes.*
2. to announce or proclaim with enthusiastic approval: *to acclaim the new king.*
–verb (used without object)
3. to make acclamation; applaud.
–noun
4. acclamation defs. 1, 2.
acclaimed=applaud, praise, to declare by acclamation

controversial ***–adjective***
1. of, pertaining to, or characteristic of controversy; polemical: *a controversial book.*
2. subject to controversy; debatable: *a controversial decision.*
3. given to controversy; disputatious.

- This is sacred place to me. (سیک رِد: جای متبرک- مقدس- وقف- نثار)

<a fund sacred to charity>, *<a tree sacred to the gods>*

sacred ***–adjective*** سیک رِد

1. devoted or dedicated to a deity or to some religious purpose; consecrated.
2. entitled to veneration or religious respect by association with divinity or divine things; holy.
3. pertaining to or connected with religion (opposed to secular or profane): *sacred music; sacred books.*

- Nation of Afghanistan was mired in a helpless civil war.

(مایرد :گل و باتلاق- گرفتاری)

mire ***–noun*** مایرد :گل و باتلاق- گرفتاری
1. a tract or area of wet, swampy ground; bog; marsh.
2. ground of this kind, as wet, slimy soil of some depth or deep mud.
–verb (used with object)
–verb (used without object)
3. to sink in mire or mud; stick. <found themselves in a mire of debt>.

- Bush refused to explain clemency. کِ لِ مِن c : بخشش- نرم دلی

clemency ***–noun, plural*-cies.**
1. the quality of being clement; disposition to show forbearance, compassion, or forgiveness in judging or punishing; leniency; mercy.
2. an act or deed showing mercy or leniency.
3. (of the weather) mildness or temperateness.

- Your project will proceed[1] erratically[2].....

1.(پروسید: اقدام کردن- عمل کردن) 2. (E رَتیک لی : بطور نامنظم)

proceed–***verb (used without object)*** پروسید: اقدام کردن- عمل کردن
1. to move or go forward or onward, esp. after stopping.
2. to carry on or continue any action or process.
3. to go on to do something.
4. to continue one's discourse.
5. ***Law***.
a. to begin and carry on a legal action.
b. to take legal action (usually fol. by *against*).
6. to be carried on, as an action or process.
proceeds, *–noun*
a. something that results or accrues.
b. the total amount derived from a sale or other transaction: *The proceeds from the deal were divided equally among us.*
c. the profits or returns from a sale, investment, etc.

erratic ***–adjective*** E رَتیک لی : بطور نامنظم
1. deviating from the usual or proper course in conduct or opinion; eccentric; queer: *erratic behavior.*
2. having no certain or definite course; wandering; not fixed: *erratic winds.*
–noun

3. an erratic or eccentric person.

- In what respect? از چه لحاظ
- Arsonist: آدم آتش زن (arson تولید حریق)
- I shall be grateful if you will…. سپاسگزار خواهم شد اگر
- Grief is corrosive to man. غصه آدم را تمام میکند
- Going to a long ritual متضمن تشریفات
- Without a hitch بدون مانع یا گرفتاری

- Your prompt attention to this matter is appreciated.
از توجهٔ فوری شما به این موضوع قدردانی میشود

- Provocative پُرُواکِیتیو: انگیزه
<It was provocative of curiosity حس کنجکاوی فرد را تحریک می کند >

- You are insatiable man.

***insatiable* –adjective** این سِ شِ بِل : راضی نشو
not satiable; incapable of being satisfied or appeased:
<insatiable hunger for knowledge.>

- Ludicrous: (لودکراس :خنده آور- چرند), *<it is ludicrous to me! >*
(Richter scale (رکـ تر:میزان ریشتر زلزله)
(Absolute tyranny (حکومت استبداد مطلق)

- (At the very outset (در اولین وهله)
(In the last resort (در آخرین وهله)

- (Blasphemе, Blaspheming (بِ لَس فی مینگ کفر- بی احترامی به مقد سات)

- Explicit واضح- روشن *<explicit instruction>*, *<explicit books and films>*
Consensual sex= mutual consent sex کاً ن سِن چوآل : سکسی که با رضایت طرفین باشد

- Appurtenances *<the app. Of wealth>* ضمیمه- متعلقه- متعلقات
Appurtenant: (accessory, auxiliary) وابسته- متعلق

- Acquisition *(the act of acquiring something)* اکوازیشن : تحصیل
Accusation (اکیوزیشن: تهمت- ادعا)

- *Bar mitzvah*: *a Jewish boy who reaches his 13th birthday and attains (رسیدن- نائل شدن) the age of religious duty and responsibility.*
- *Bat mitzvah: a Jewish girl who at 12 or more years assumes religious responsibilities*

- Obsess : آب سِس : ازار دادن- اذیت کردن- ذهن کسیرا مشغول کردن

  < was obsessed with the idea>, <become obsessed with an idea>

  Obsession: (آب سِ شِن : ازار- اذیت :

  < an obsession with profits> 1.مجبورکردن- ناگزیرکردن

  <something that causes that obsession>

  Obsessive: (عقده ای) *(adj): tending cause obsession or excessive often to an unreasonable degree.*

  Obsessive, compulsive (اجباری), disorder [1] (1.(بی نظمی- بهم خوردگی مزاج

- A cognitive[1] scientist at University of Irvine in California…

  1. کاگ نتیو:مربوط به آگاهی و دانش یک دانشمند

  کاگ نیشن: بستگی و خویشاوند → cognation

  cognitive –adjective

  1. of or pertaining to cognition.
  2. of or pertaining to the mental processes of perception, memory, judgment, and reasoning, as contrasted with emotional and volitional processes.

- New law allows more eavesdropping without….

  eavesdrop → (E یوز دراپ : استراق سمع)

  eavesdropper → (E یوز دریر: استراق سمع کننده)

  eavesdrop–verb (used without object)
  To listen secretly to a private conversation.

- President signed legislation into law that broadly expands the government's authority to eavesdrop on the international telephone conversations and E-mail messages of American citizen without warrants.

  eavesdrop: to listen secretly to what is said in private.

- Bush and Hamid karzai said they agreed to make no concessions to the Taliban to win freedom for S. Koreans' hostages.

  کا ن سِ شِن : تسلیم-تن دردهی- اعطاء تسلیم- تن دردهی- اعطاء کردن کردن

هاس تیج : گروگان

concessions ***–noun*** کا ن س شِن

1. the act of conceding or yielding, as a right, a privilege, or a point or fact in an argument: *He made no concession to caution.*
2. the thing or point yielded: *Management offered a shorter workweek as a concession.*
3. something conceded by a government or a controlling authority, as a grant of land, a privilege, or a franchise.

Bush and Hamid Karzai agreed on much but differed on whether Iran is a help or hindrance in the effort to stabilize Afghanistan.

hindrance ***–noun*** این درنس :مانع- پاگیر

1. an impeding, stopping, preventing, or the like.
2. the state of being hindered.
3. a person or thing that hinders.

- "People aren't just cynical about politicians. They're pretty bloody angry. I'm sickened by what's happened in our politics."
  <You are taking a rather cynical view of marriage.>

cynical ***–adjective*** سی نیکا ل .: بدگمان نسبت به درستي ونيكوكاري بشر، غرغرو عيبجو

1. Someone who is cynical or who has a cynical attitude always thinks the worst of people or things.
2. like or characteristic of a cynic; distrusting or disparaging the motives of others.

- Which are burdened by religious rivalries and are not steady to take over defense duties from US troops?
  Rival= رای وِل: حریف- رقیب rivalry= رای ولری : چشم و همچشمی- رقاب

rivalry ***–noun, plural*-ries.**

1. the action, position, or relation of a rival or rivals; competition:
< *Rivalry between Yale and Harvard University.*>
2. an instance of this.

- Also heretofore unreported. (سابقا- قبلا- پیشتر)

heretofore ***---adverb***

before this time; until now و Up to the present time; before this; previously

---

- A copy of the document hereto is attached. If I had stayed 3 month longer, I would have been given a degree as a civil engineer.

hereto ***–adverb*** (باین نامه).
To this matter, document, subject, etc.; regarding this point:
<attached hereto; agreeable hereto.>

- Additional claims relating to property damage arising out of the aforesaid accident. (أفور سِد : مذکور- گفته شده در بالا)

aforesaid ***–adjective***
said or mentioned earlier or previously.

- Islamic party holds onto power in Turkey, but prime minister pledges to preserve secular traditions.

(سِ کیو لِر : دنیوی- مخالف آموزش تعلیم شرعیات)

secular ***–adjective***
1. of or pertaining to worldly things or to things that are not regarded as religious, spiritual, or sacred; temporal: *secular interests.*
2. not pertaining to or connected with religion (opposed to sacred): *secular music.*
3. (of education, a school, etc.) concerned with nonreligious subjects.

- Ruling party will have to face down the secularist military.

(sec·u·lar·ism سِک یو لاریزم) سِک یو لاریست: کسی که مخالف تعالیم دینی است

- I know him by sight but not by name. (سایت :قیافتاً- منظره)

sight ***–noun***
1. the power or faculty of seeing; perception of objects by use of the eyes; vision.
2. an act, fact, or instance of seeing.
3. one's range of vision on some specific occasion: *Land is in sight.*
4. a view; glimpse.
5. mental perception or regard; judgment.
6. something seen or worth seeing; spectacle: *the sights of London.*

–verb (used with object)
7. to see, glimpse, notice, or observe: *to sight a ship to the north.*
8. to take a sight or observation of (a stake, coastline, etc.), esp. with surveying or navigating instruments.

–verb (used without object)
9. to aim or observe through a sight.

10. to look carefully in a certain direction.
—Idioms
11. at first sight, at the first glimpse; at once: *It was love at first sight.*
12. *I know him by sight, but I know nothing about him*

- $2 million donation to museum from a private party will form the basis of a new endowment* fund for exhibition.

*(این دآ منت : بخشش- اعطاء- وقف)
endow: بخشیدن- اعطاء کردن- وقف کردن

endowment ***–noun*** **1.** the act of endowing.
2. the property, funds, etc., with which an institution or person is endowed.
3. Usually, **endowments.** An attribute of mind or body; a gift of nature.

- What make you dubious? (مشکوک)

dubious ***–adjective***
1. doubtful; marked by or occasioning doubt: *a dubious reply.*
2. of doubtful quality or propriety; questionable: *a dubious compliment; a dubious transaction.*
3. of uncertain outcome: *in dubious battle.*
4. wavering or hesitating in opinion; inclined to doubt.

- In Iran dissidents pay a higher price. (دیسی دِنت : مخالف عقیده عموم)

dissident–***noun***
1. a person who dissents.
–adjective
2. disagreeing or dissenting, as in opinion or attitude: *a ban on dissident magazines.*

- Israel often toppling into armed contract. (افتادن- واژگون شدن)

topple ***–verb (used without object)***
1. to fall forward, as from having too heavy a top; pitch; tumble down.
2. to lean over or jut, as if threatening to fall.
–verb (used with object)
3. to cause to topple.
4. to overthrow, as from a position of authority: *to topple the king.*

- *atrocity: the quality or state of being atrocious or an atrocious act, brutal, cruel, barbaric .* (آتروشس: بیرحمانه- شدید)
He should die for atrocities. (atrocity ← جمع).

- He wasn't apprehensive or anxious about it at all, اَپری هِن سیو : بیمناک- نگران

- This president has the audacity to ask for more patience, while our troops getting killed everyday policing a civil war.

(اَداسیتی: بی پروایی- گستاخی)

- insofar as: *to such and extend* تا حدی

She is the very image of his father → او شکل پدرش است

The proceeds hereof → عایدات از این

Clashing views نظرات مخالف

In distinction from ..... در مقابـل- در برابـر

patent aunt عمه (خواهر پدر), Maternal aunt خاله (خواهر مادر)

- This requires rigorous market research regarding the value of property.

(ریگُ رِس: بسیاردقیق)

rigorous ***–adjective***
1. characterized by rigor; rigidly severe or harsh, as people, rules, or discipline: *rigorous laws.*
2. severely exact or accurate; precise: *rigorous research.*

- Wildfires provoke federal changes.

(برانگیختن- تحریک کردن- در اینجا یعنی باعث شدن)

provoke–verb (used with object),**-voked, -vok·ing.**
1. to anger, enrage, exasperate,
2. to stir up, arouse, or call forth (feelings, desires, or activity):
The mishap provoked a hearty laugh.* (مِیس هَپ : بد، قضا، حادثه‌رویداد ناگوار، بدبختي)*
3. to incite or stimulate (a person, animal, etc.) to action.
4. to give rise to, induce, or bring about: *What could have provoked such an incident?*

- Attention Deficit Hyperactivity Disorder (ADHA) دِفِ سِیت : کمبود- کسری

deficit ***–noun*** دِفِ سِیت : کمبود- کسری
1. the amount by which a sum of money falls short of the required amount.
2. the amount by which expenditures or liabilities exceed income or assets.
3. a lack or shortage; deficiency.
4. a loss, as in the operation of a business.

- Today's religious procession of one million people is to be watched over by US. troops and 1800 Iraqi forces. پر سِ شِن: دسته دسته حرکت کردن

procession ***–noun***
1. the act of moving along or proceeding in orderly succession or in a formal and ceremonious manner, as a line of people, animals, vehicles, etc.
2. the line or body of persons or things moving along in such a manner.

- Police told to divulge documents. (d وُلج: افشاءکردن/ابراز کردن)

divulge ***–verb (used with object),*****-vulged, -vulg·ing.**
to disclose or reveal (something private, secret, or previously unknown).

- *foreclosure*: فورکِلو ژر : سلب حق فک رهن از خود
The act of foreclosing, especially a legal proceedi which a mortgage is foreclosed
- A major Shiite enclave in Baghdad sought to target a ring believed to be smuggling armor, piercing readied bombs for Iran.
N کِلیو : به ناحیه ای گفته می شود که کشور بیگانه دور آنرا گرفته باشد

P یِر سینگ : تیز، نافذ

enclave ***–noun*** : Nکِلیو
1. a country, or esp., an outlying portion of a country, entirely or mostly surrounded by the territory of another country.
2. any small, distinct area or group enclosed or isolated within a larger one: *a Chinese-speaking enclave in London.*
–verb (used with object)
3. to isolate or enclose (esp. territory) within a foreign or uncongenial environment; make an enclave of: *The desert enclaved the little settlement.*

- You are not at the mercy of[1] seller's unrealistic[2] asking price.
1.(در اختیار- دستخوش) 2.(غير واقعي، خيالي تصوري، واهي)

- America is the nation of immigrants. مهاجرین
- unilateral یکطرفه- یک جانبه
bilateral دوطرفه، دوجانبه
- decisive woman زن مصمم
- In this same regard در همین رابطه

- It is not protected by sanction.

sanction ***–noun*** سَنک شِن : جواز، تاييدرسمي، داراي مجوزقانوني دانستن - تصويب- تصويب كردن

1. authoritative permission or approval, as for an action.
2. something that serves to support an action, condition, etc.
3. something that gives binding force, as to an oath, rule of conduct, etc.
4. *Law.*
a. a provision of a law enacting a penalty for disobedience or a reward for obedience.
b. the penalty or reward.
5. *International Law.* action by one or more states toward another state calculated to force it to comply with legal obligations.

- I am just asking for little fairness and common decency.

decency **–noun, plural-cies.** د سِن c : شایستگی
1. the state or quality of being decent.
2. conformity to the recognized standard of propriety, good taste, modesty, etc.

- Afghanistan's heroin producing poppy crop set another record this season, despite intensified[1] eradication[2] effort. The US ambassador said Tuesday.

1.(سخت کردن- شدید کردن)- 2. (قلع و قمع کردن- از ریشه کندن)

intensify **–verb (used with object)**
1. to make intense or more intense.
2. to make more acute; strengthen or sharpen.

eradicate **–verb (used with object),-cat·ed, -cat·ing.**
1. to remove or destroy utterly; extirpate: *to eradicate smallpox throughout the world.*
2. to erase by rubbing or by means of a chemical solvent: *to eradicate a spot.*
3. to pull up by the roots: *to eradicate weeds.*

Many cities still refuse[1] to allow dispensaries[2] .

1. (امتناع کردن) 2.(دیس پنسری : پزشک خانه- طبابت در منزل)

refuse **–verb (used with object)**
1. to decline to accept (something offered): *to refuse an award.*
2. to decline to give; deny (a request, demand, etc.): *to refuse permission.*
3. to express a determination not to (do something): *to refuse to discuss the question.*
4. to decline to submit to.
–verb (used without object)
7. to decline acceptance, consent, or compliance.

dispensary **–noun, plural-ries.**
1. a place where something is dispensed, esp. medicines.
2. a charitable or public facility where medicines are furnished and free or inexpensive Medical advice is available.

- Mass protest overshadows[1] celebrations, tens of thousands gather to denounce[2] President Musharaf and call for a new leader.

1.(تاریک کردن، مسلط شدن بر تحت الشعاع قرار دادن، سایه افکندن بر)
2.(دِ نَ آنس : خبردادن از- اشاره کردن به- با تهدید اخطار کردنِ)

overshadow ***–verb (used with object)***
1. to be more important or significant by comparison:
For years he overshadowed his brother.
2. to cast a shadow over; cover with shadows, clouds, darkness, etc.; darken or obscure:
Clouds overshadowing the moon.

denounce ***–verb (used with object),*** **-nounced, -nounc·ing.**
1. to condemn or censure openly or publicly: *to denounce a politician as morally corrupt.*
2. to make a formal accusation against, as to the police or in a court.

- He is a megalomaniac : → (مِگالومِی نی اک:
کسی که به مرض خود بزرگ بینی مبتلا است

megalomania → مرض بزرگ پنداری - جنون گامهای بزرگ
A megalomaniac is someone who enjoys being powerful, or who believes that they are more powerful or important than they really are.

- Superiors choose compassion. (کام پَ شِن : رحم و شفقت و دلسوزی)

compassion ***–noun***
1. a feeling of deep sympathy and sorrow for another who is stricken by misfortune, accompanied by a strong desire to alleviate the suffering.
–verb (used with object)
2. *Archaic*. to compassionate. (*Archaic*→ کهنه، قدیمی، غیر مصطلح: آر کِه یک)

- The leader of notorious insurgent group. نُوتُوری اِس : انگشت نما- مشهوربه بدی

notorious ***–adjective*** نُوتُوری اِس
1. widely and unfavorably known: *a notorious gambler.*
2. publicly or generally known, as for a particular trait:
a newspaper that is notorious for its sensationalism.

- Becomes even more treacherous[1] Blackmail[2]

Treachery ترِه چِه ری : خیانت

1.(تِ رِچِرَس : خیانت آمیز-غیرقابل اطمینان)
2.(باج سبیل- باجی که به راه زنان داده میشود)

مَعانی یا بکار گیری لغات فوق در جملات دیگر:

treacherous ***–adjective*** تِ رِچِرِس

1. characterized by faithlessness or readiness to betray trust; traitorous.
2. deceptive, untrustworthy, or unreliable.

blackmail **–noun**

1. any payment extorted by intimidation, as by threats of injurious revelations or accusations.
2. the extortion of such payment:
He confessed rather than suffer the dishonor of blackmail

–verb (used with object)
4. to extort money from (a person) by the use of threats.

- Make it a daily ritual, (رِ یچوآل:مربوط به شعائر دینی- کارهایی که روزانه انجام میدهند)

ritual ***–noun*** رِ یچوآل

1. an established or prescribed procedure for a religious or other rite.
2. a system or collection of religious or other rites.
3. observance of set forms in public worship.

- Former Los Angeles Iranian-American architect sentenced for defying ban on export to Iran. (دِ فای : بی اعتنائی کردن)

defy ***–verb (used with object)***

1. to challenge the power of; resist boldly or openly: *to defy parental authority.*
2. to offer effective resistance to: *a fort that defies attack.*
3. to challenge (a person) to do something deemed impossible:
They defied him to dive off the bridge.
4. *Archaic.* to challenge to a combat or contest.
–noun **5.** a challenge; a defiance

- Some say the idea is absurd[1] Published cartoons lampooning[2] the prophet Mohammad… (لَم پُون :هجو کردن).2 (اَب سِرد: بی معنی- مزخرف- پوچ).1

absurd ***–adjective*** اَب سِرد: بی معنی- مزخرف- پوچ

1. utterly or obviously senseless, illogical, or untrue; contrary to all reason or common sense; laughably foolish or false: *an absurd explanation.*
–noun
2. the quality or condition of existing in a meaningless and irrational world.

lampoon ***–noun*** لَم پُون :هجو کردن

1. a sharp, often virulent satire directed against an individual or institution; a work of literature, art, or the like, ridiculing severely the character or behavior of a person, society, etc.

- Bush revives[1] interrogation[2] program.

1.(رِوایو : زنده کردن- دوباره معمولی کردن)
2. (اینِ تِ رِ گی شِن: پرسش- بازرسی- استنطاق)

<u>مَعانی یا بکار گیری لغات فوق در جملات دیگر</u>

revive **–verb (used with object)**
1. to activate, set in motion, or take up again; renew: *to revive old feuds.*
2. to restore to life or consciousness: *We revived him with artificial respiration.*
3. to bring back into notice, use, or currency: *to revive a subject of discussion.*
interrogation **–noun**
1. the act of interrogating; questioning.
2. an instance of being interrogated: *He seemed shaken after his interrogation.*
3. a question; inquiry.
4. a written list of questions.
5. an interrogation point; question mark.

- African get taste of bill Clinton as roving ambassador.→ سفیر

(رُوینگ : ولگردی کردن- پرسه زدن- آواره بودن)

roving **–adjective** رُوینگ
1. roaming or wandering.

- He reiterated: (ری ای تِ ریت : چندین بار گفتن) If you reiterate something, you say it again.
- chaos: (کِی آس) هرج و مرج the blackout cause chaos throughout the city
- proponent: پیشنهاد دهنده The proponent of a particular idea or course of action is someone who actively supports it; a formal word.
- During his tenure as president (10 یور: تصدی)
- Socratic dialogue, (سیک رَتیک: سقراطی)

- Fictitious[1]: conventionally[2] or hypothetically[3] assumed or accepted a fictitious concept of a name, false assumed…..

1.(فیک تی شی اِس : جعلی- ساختگی) 2. (برطبق رسوم- قراردادی- رسما)

3 .(های پُو تَ تیکال : بطور فرض)

مَعانی یا بکار گیری لغات فوق در جملات دیگر:

fictitious ---(This option registers a Fictitious Name Registration. You cannot use this option to renew your Fictitious Name or to form a Corporation, Limited Liability Company or Limited Partnership.) ... *Fictitious business n...*

conventional ***–adjective***
Conforming or adhering to accepted standards, as of conduct or taste: *conventional behavior.*

*hypothetical****–adjective*** Also, **hy·po·thet·ic** *for defs. 1–4.*
1. assumed by hypothesis; supposed: *a hypothetical case.*
2. of, pertaining to, involving, or characterized by hypothesis: *hypothetical reasoning.*
3. *–noun*
4. a hypothetical situation, instance, etc.:
The Secretary of Defense refused to discuss hypotheticals with the reporters.

- How much is your aggregate[1] indebtedness[2] ?

1.(اَگ ری گیت : مجموع- جمع امده) 2.(این دِ بِ ت نِس : مجموعه بدهکاری)

< *in the aggregate*: روی‌هم رفته بطور کلی>

aggregate ***–adjective***
1. formed by the conjunction or collection of particulars into a whole mass or sum; total; combined: *the aggregate amount of indebtedness.*

—Idiom
2. in the aggregate, taken or considered as a whole: *In the aggregate, our losses have been relatively small.*

indebtedness ***–noun***
1. the state of being indebted.
2. an amount owed.

- A project to eradicate graffiti. (قلع و قمع کردن- از ریشه کندن)

eradicate ***–verb (used with object),*** **-cat·ed, -cat·ing.**
1. to remove or destroy utterly; extirpate: *to eradicate smallpox throughout the world.*
2. to erase by rubbing or by means of a chemical solvent: *to eradicate a spot.*
3. to pull up by the roots: *to eradicate weeds.*

- If *I had stayed* three month longer *I would have been given* a degree as a civil engineer.
- Absolute tyranny (تی رنی): حکومت استبداد مطلق
- Vigorous debate مذاکره قوی و نیرومند

- Impudently asked him to leave, (بی شرمانه)
- Traitor to the country خائن به کشور
- Proprietary right: حق مالکیت

- Proprietor and proprietress: موجر و زنش
- Polygamy and monogamy: پُ لی گِ می: چند زنه / مِنا گِ می: یک زنه
- With a good grace با حسن نیت، قلبا
- In compliance with: برطبق، از لحاظ رعایت
- entrepreneur: آن تر پر نر این کلمه فرانسوی است
  similar terms include: *businessman, executive*
- grievance procedure: (گری ونس: شکایت)
  The female expression of a grievance is complaint شکایت، دادخواهي
- US. must leave this region in humiliation[1] and disgrace[2]

1.(هیو می لی ایشِن : تحقیر و پستی- احساس حقارت)

2.(دیس گِ ریس : رسوايي، خفت، فضاحت سيه رويي، بي ابرويي)

- You letting your hormones run your life. هورمن

***hormone*–noun**
Biochemistry. any of various internally secreted compounds, as insulin or thyroxine, formed in endocrine glands, that affect the functions of specifically receptive organs or tissues when transported to them by the body fluids.

- New York times says: this country is under absolute despotism.

***despotism* –noun** دِس پِ تی زیم: استبداد- حکومت خودسرانه یا استبدادی
1. the rule of a despot; the exercise of absolute authority.
2. absolute power or control; tyranny.
3. an absolute or autocratic government.
4. a country ruled by a despot.

- The principles of the constitution are; liberty (آزادی), equality (برابری) and justice (عدالت)

- **Thomas Jefferson** wrote the *Declaration of Independence* and was published July 4, 1776. دِکـ لِری شِن آو این دیپِن دِنس : اعلامیه استقلال

- **George Washington** made a penciled sketch of the design and Betsy Ross sews that flag with 13 stars on it.
- latent and patent defects: (لِ تِنت & پِ تِنت): خرابیهای اشکار و نهان

- The title of each section reflects a notion or a manifestation of the physical work. مَنی فِس تی شِن : اظهار - بیانیه

manifestation ***–noun*** اظهار - بیانیه مَنی فِس تی شِن
1. an act of manifesting.
2. the state of being manifested.

- caricature (کَری کاچِر: کاریکاتور)
Because of the graphic humor of the idioms in caricature.

- I shall not reply to such a scurrilous attack upon me, it is "beneath contempt". (اِس کُرْ لِس: بدهن- بدزبان)

scurrilous ***–adjective*** اِس کُرْ لِس
1. grossly or obscenely abusive: *a scurrilous attack on the mayor.*
2. characterized by or using low buffoonery; coarsely jocular or derisive: *a scurrilous jest.*

- President carter can't placate Rabbis who dislike his book. (پِ لِی کِیت آرام کردن- آشتی کردن)

placate ***–verb (used with object),*****-cat·ed, -cat·ing.**
to appease or pacify, esp. by concessions or conciliatory gestures:
to placate an outraged citizenry.

- Iraq as implacable[1] rival[2] : 1.(ایمْ پِ لَ کِ بِل : سنگدل- کینه توز)
2. رای وِل: حریف- رقیب

implacable ***–adjective***

not to be appeased, mollified, or pacified; inexorable: *an implacable enemy*

***rival* –noun**

1. a person who is competing for the same object or goal as another, or who tries to equal or outdo another; competitor.

2. a person or thing that is in a position to dispute another's preeminence or superiority: *a stadium without a rival.*

- *Iraq nearly autonomous Kurdish region.*

(آتانِمِس : مستقل دارای حکومت از خود)

***autonomous* –adjective**

1. *Government.*

a. self-governing; independent; subject to its own laws only.

b. pertaining to an autonomy.

2. having autonomy; not subject to control from outside; independent: *a subsidiary that functioned as an autonomous unit.*

- Speculation[1] has swirled[2] around Countrywide Co. since the lender said on August 9, that it could be hurt by unprecedented[3] disruptions[4] in the market to sell loans to Wall Street investors[5].

1. (اِس p-q لِی شِن : تفکر- اندیشه- تحقیقات نظری)
2. (سُو اِرل: چرخ زدن- پیچاندن)
3. (آن پِ رِسی دِن تِد : بي سابقه، بي مانند، جديد، بي نظير)
4. (ترکیدگی-جدائی- شکاف)
5. (سرمایه گذار)

<u>مَعانی یا بکار گیری لغات فوق در جملات دیگر:</u>

***swirl*–verb (used without object)** چرخ زدن- پیچاندن :سُو اِرل

1. to move around or along with a whirling motion; whirl; eddy.

***unprecedented* –adjective** بي سابقه، بي مانند، جديد، بي نظير : آن پِ رِسی دِن تِد

without previous instance; never before known or experienced; unexampled or unparalleled: *an unprecedented event.*

***disruption* –noun**

1. forcible separation or division into parts.

2. a disrupted condition: *The state was in disruption.*

***Investor*----noun**

An investor is a person who buys shares or who pays money into a bank in order to receive a profit.
The investor is entitled to a reasonable return on his money.... Investors sought to recover losses sustained earlier in the week.

- "Who had been bantering (شوخی کردن- کنایه) with his partner for most of the outing?" (گردش در بیرون شهر) said Anderson.

***banter*–noun**
1. an exchange of light, playful, teasing remarks; good-natured raillery.
–verb (used with object)
2. to address with banter; chaff.

- synonyms: (سی نو نیم- مترادف)→ Damp & Moist, pretty & Attractive
Words with similar meanings
- antonyms: (انتونیم – متضاد)→ Hot & Cold, Fast & Slow
Words with opposite meanings
- homonyms: (هامانیم- متشابه) → Hear & Here, Buy & By
Words that sounds alike but are spelled differently and have different meanings.

- Amid sagging sales, gap reports improved conditions at factories.
(سگینگ : افت- تنزل بها- فرونشستن ،ازوسط خم شدن فرو رفتگي شكم دادگي)

***sagging* –verb (used without object)**
1. to sink or bend downward by weight or pressure, esp. in the middle: *The roof sags.*
2. to hang down unevenly; droop: *Her skirt was sagging.*

- Recounted the saga of their family problems. (سا گا : حماسه)
A saga is a long and often complicated sequence of events.

All the reasons why I loathe Saga Magazine and the values it represents were vindicated last week with the publication of its.

لُوث : نفرت داشتن از، بیزار بودن، سبب بیزاري شدن
وین Dکیت : حمایت كردن از، پشتیباني كردن از، دفاع كردن از محقق كردن

1. a medieval Icelandic or Norse prose narrative of achievements and events in the history of a personage, family, etc.
2. any narrative or legend of heroic exploits.
3. Also called saga **novel.** a form of the novel in which the members or generations of a family or social group are chronicled in a long and leisurely narrative.

- podiatry – podiatric care پو دایت - re : علم امراض و معالجه پا
The branch of medicine that deals with the diagnosis, treatment, and prevention of diseases of the human foot.

- This document would seem to provide the smoking gun that may of Obama's detractors have been seeking. دی ترَک تُور : بدگو، نمام

detract–***verb (used without object)*** دی ترَک : بدگو، نمام
1. to take away a part, as from quality, value, or reputation (usually fol. by *from*).
–verb (used with object)
2. to draw away or divert; distract: *to detract another's attention from more important issues.*

- The appraiser[1] looks to determine[2] if the price you are paying for the home is justified[3] by recent scales of comparable[4] properties.
1. آپ ری زر **:** ارزیاب **2.** دی ترمِن **:** تصمیم گرفتن **3.** بحق دانستن- تصدیق کردن **4.** قابل مقایسه

<u>مَعانی یا بکار گیری لغات فوق در جملات دیگر:</u>

appraise ***–verb (used with object),*-praised, -prais·ing.** آپ ری زر **:** ارزیاب
1. to estimate the monetary value of; determine the worth of; assess: *We had an expert appraise the house before we bought it.*

determine–***verb (used with object)*** دی ترمِن **:** تصمیم گرفتن
To settle or decide (a dispute, question, etc.) by an authoritative or conclusive decision.

justify ***–verb (used with object)*** بحق دانستن- تصدیق کردن
1. to show (an act, claim, statement, etc.) to be just or right:
The end does not always justify the means.
2. to defend or uphold as warranted or well-grounded: *Don't try to justify his rudeness.*

comparable ***–adjective*** قابل مقایسه
1. capable of being compared; having features in common with something else to permit or suggest comparison: *He considered the Roman and British empires to be comparable.*
2. worthy of comparison: *shops comparable to those on Fifth Avenue.*

- Should your employee be precluded from returning to his usual occupation?
پری کلُود **:** جلوگیری کردن

preclude–***verb (used with object),*****-clud·ed, -clud·ing.** پری کلُود

1. to prevent the presence, existence, or occurrence of; make impossible: *The insufficiency of the evidence precludes a conviction.*

- Heterosexual person; *someone having a sexual orientation to persons of the opposite sex.* هترو سِک چو آل : علاقمند به جنس مخالف

Heterosexual ***–adjective***
1. of, pertaining to, or exhibiting heterosexuality.
2. *Biology*. pertaining to the opposite sex or to both sexes.
–noun
3. a heterosexual person.

- My lawyer (لاير يا لوُير) interested resurrect<u>ing</u> deed. رِزِرِکت : سند زنده کردن

resurrect–***verb (used with object)***
1. to raise from the dead; bring to life again.
2. to bring back into use, practice, etc.: *to resurrect an ancient custom.*
3. to rise from the dead.

- Voluntary health organization (اختیاری - افتخاری- داوطلبانه)
  Volunteer groups (وآلان‌آیر : داوطلب)

volunteer ***–noun***
1. a person who voluntarily offers himself or herself for a service or undertaking.
2. a person who performs a service willingly and without pay.

- Why do I always pick selfish, egotistical people to become friends with?
  E گو. تِس تیکال :خودپرستانه، ازروي خودبيني

egotistic–***adjective***
1. pertaining to or characterized by egotism.
2. given to talking about oneself; vain; boastful; opinionated.

- Some services subsidized by local or state government agencies may be offered free or low cost. ساب سی دایز: کمک هزینه/کمک خرج دادن

subsidize–***verb (used with object),*****-dized, -diz·ing.**
1. to furnish or aid with a subsidy.
2. to purchase the assistance of by the payment of a subsidy.

- The program vary significantly even in the name that is used. In a significant degree,
  < *the salaries differed significantly* >   سیگ نی فیکنت : قابل توجه

***significant* –adjective** سیگ نی فیکنت
1. important; of consequence.
2. having or expressing a meaning; indicative; suggestive: *a significant wink.*
3. *Statistics.* of or pertaining to observations that are unlikely to occur by chance and that therefore indicate a systematic cause.
–noun
4. something significant; a sign.

- Patients must agree to accept the allocation that is established for that service.   اَلِ کِی شِن : اختصاص- تخصیص

***allocation* –noun** اَلِ کِی شِن
1.the act of allocating; apportionment.   تعیین سهم و حصه
2. the state of being allocated.
3. the share or portion allocated.

- As we develop socially and intellectually[1], we tend[2] to associate with others who have similar interest and beliefs.

1. اینِ تِلِک چوُ آلی : بطور عقلا نی   2. کمک کردن- توجه- متمایل بودن به گرایش داشتن

***intellectual*–adjective**   < *Intellectual* playwrights >, < *intellectual* games>
1. appealing to or engaging the intellect: *intellectual pursuits.*
2. of or pertaining to the intellect or its use: *intellectual powers.*
3. possessing or showing intellect or mental capacity, esp. to a high degree:
an intellectual person.   *an intellectual way of speaking*
6. ***–noun*** : a person of superior intellect.

***tend*–verb (used without object)**   کمک کردن- توجه- متمایل بودن به گرایش داشتن
1. to be disposed or inclined in action, operation, or effect to do something:
The particles tend to unite.
2. to be disposed toward an idea, emotion, way of thinking, etc.: *He tends to be overly optimistic. Her religious philosophy tends toward pantheism.*

- Pakistan ravaged by flooding.   (رَوِج : ویرانی- خرابی)

***ravage*–verb (used with object)** رَوِج
1. to work havoc upon; damage or mar by ravages: *a face ravaged by grief.*

–verb (used without object)
2. to work havoc خرابي، غارت، ويران كردن ; do ruinous damage.
–noun
3. havoc; ruinous damage: *the ravages of war.*
4. devastating or destructive action.

- People who need help have a broad spectrum of social organization to choose from within the community اسپکترام : طیف

<a wide spectrum of interests>

spectrum **–noun, plural-, -trums.** اسپکترام : طیف
Physics.
An array of entities, as light waves or particles, ordered in accordance with the magnitudes of a common physical property, as wavelength or mass: comprising red, orange, yellow, green, blue, indigo, and violet.

- Not having a sectarian[1] character: *means not affiliate with or restricted to a particular religious group.*

< *Sectarian is a particular religious group*>
sectarian : فرقه ای- شیئی- عضوحزب

Nonsectarian organization such as... نان سکترین :آنهایی که جزو فرقه شیعه نیستند

- "To actually say that if diplomacy[1] fails the choice will be to accept a nuclear Iran or bomb Iraq , this is a diplomatic blockbuster[2] " (a very large high explosive[3] bomb)

1. *The art or practice of conducting international relations.* ديپلماسي، سياست سياستمداري

2. بمب داراي قدرت تخريبي زياد- شخص ياچيز خيلي موثر وسخت
A very large high explosive bomb also this word used for name of an American chain of DVD, Blu-ray, and video game rental stores.

3. *An explosive material is a substance that either is chemically or otherwise energetically unstable or produces a sudden expansion of the material after initiation,* (قابل انفجار explosive)

- But his debut[1] before his ambassador was marred[2] by a diplomatic imbroglio[3] involving his foreign minister.

1.(دِ ب یوُ : اغاز کار، نخستین مرحله دخول در بازي یا جامعه- شروع بکار کردن)

2.(مار: اسیب زدن)
3.(ایم بُرولی یوُ : gخوانده نمیشود- مساله غامض)

<u>مَعانی یا بکار گیری لغات فوق در جملات دیگر:</u>

debut **–noun** , *a formal entrance into society* دِ ب یوُ : اغاز کار، شروع بکار کردن
1. a first public appearance on a stage, on television, etc.
2. the first appearance of something, as a new product.

***mar–verb (used with object),*marred, mar·ring.** مار : اسیب زدن
To damage or spoil to a certain extent; render less perfect, attractive, useful, etc.; impair or spoil: *That billboard mars the view. The holiday was marred by bad weather.*

*imbro***g***lio* ***–noun, plural*-glios.** ایم بُرو یوُ : <u>جی خوانده نمیشود</u> - مساله غامض
1. a misunderstanding, disagreement, etc., of a complicated or bitter nature, as between persons or nations.
2. an intricate and perplexing state of affairs; a complicated or difficult situation.
3. a confused heap.

- Judge ordered self-described pedophile Jack-Mc to stay at least 10 yards from places where children congregate, including schools.

پدو فایل : لواط کار- بچه باز (کان گری گیت: جمع شدن- اجتماع کردن)

Pedophile: *one affected with pedophilia, it is a (Noun), A person who is sexually attracted to children*
<Judge orders pedophile to stay away from schools>, <pedophile to leave state>; <A self-described pedophile told a TV station he is leaving this state>

congregate ***–verb (used without object)*** کان گری گیت: جمع شدن- اجتماع کردن
1. to come together; assemble, esp. in large <u>numbers</u>: *People waiting for rooms congregated in the hotel lobby.*
–verb (used with object)
2. to bring together in a crowd, body, or mass; assemble; collect.
–adjective
3. congregated; assembled.
4. formed by collecting; collective.

- We wanted to have our employee's name inscribed on the award, but apparently there isn't enough room. اینس کِر ایب : نوشتن- نقش کردن
<The stones are inscribed with Kofi>. (*Inscription* کتیبه- نوشته)

inscribe **–verb (used with object),-scribed, -scrib·ing.** اینس کِر ایب : نوشتن- نقش کردن
1. to address or dedicate (a book, photograph, etc.) informally to a person, esp. by writing a brief personal note in or on it.
2. to mark (a surface) with words, characters, etc., esp. in a durable or conspicuous way.

- Medical examiner says forensic expert was wrong in saying his breathed after gunshot. فُ رِن سیک: وابسته به دادگاه
<A forensic expert called by prosecutors>. پراسی کیو تور: تعقیب کننده- وکیل عمومی

forensic **–adjective** فُ رِن سیک: وابسته به دادگاه
1. pertaining to, connected with, or used in courts of law or public discussion and debate.
2. adapted or suited to argumentation; rhetorical.

–noun
3. *forensics, (used with a singular or plural verb) the art or study of argumentation and formal debate.*

- Governor admonished to preserve rail money.
آدما نیش: نصیحت کردن- پند دادن

admonish **–verb (used with object) :**آدما نیش
1. to caution, advise, or counsel against something.
2. to reprove or scold, esp. in a mild and good-willed manner: *The teacher admonished him about excessive noise.*
3. to urge to a duty; remind: *to admonish them about their obligations.*

- Proponents[1] have four months to collect 4600 signature to get initiative[2] to oust[3] City of Fullerton's mayor on ballot.

1.(پُروپُونِنت: طرفدار-حامی- پشتیبان)
2.(اینِ شی- اِتیو: پیشقدمي، ابتکار، قریحه اغازي ، قدرت انجام عمل ابتکار عمل)
3.(اَست: خلع کردن)

<u>مَعانی یا بکار گیری لغات فوق در جملات دیگر:</u>

initiative –noun اینِ شی- اِتیو: پیشقدمي، ابتكار، قريحه اغازي ، قدرت انجام عمل ابتكار

1. an introductory act or step; leading action: *to take the initiative in making friends.*
2. readiness and ability in initiating action; enterprise: *to lack initiative.*
3. one's personal, responsible decision: *to act on one's own initiative.*

–adjective
4. of or pertaining to initiation; serving to initiate: *Initi-ative steps were taken to stop manufacture of the drug.*

oust–verb (used with object) اَست: خلع كردن
1. to expel or remove from a place or position occupied: *The bouncer ousted the drunk; to oust the Prime Minister in the next election.*
2. *Law.* to eject or evict; dispossess.

- estuary: a water passage where the tide meets a river current esp. an arm of the sea at the lower end of river.
  Estuaries) جمع ان← اِس چوا ری: خور- مصبی که خلیج شود
- 3000 birds seek temporary refuge in this richly endowed[1] sanctuary before continuing on to their ultimate destination, birders[2] flock[3] to these ungues are.

1.(اِن دا : بخشیدن به- دادن- وقف کردن)
2.(بِر بِر: شکارچیانی که برای فروش شکارمی کنن)
3.(فِ لاک : گله-گروه- جمع شدن)

مَعانی یا بکار گیری لغات فوق در جملات دیگر:

endow***–verb (used with object)*** اِن دا : بخشیدن به- دادن- وقف کردن

1. to provide with a permanent fund or source of income: *to endow a college.*

birder–noun بِر بِر: شکارچیانی که برای فروش شکارمی کنن
1. a person who raises birds. **2.** bird watcher.

- In Baghdad a security official blamed the lighting on al-Sadr's followers, saying that provoke the confrontations and shooting.

(پِرُوُک : انگیختن- تحریک کردن) کان فرآن تی شِن : مواجهه، مقابله

provoke ***–verb (used with object),-voked, -vok·ing.*** پِرُوُک : انگیختن- تحریک کردن
1. to anger, enrage, exasperate, or vex.

2. to stir up, arouse, or call forth (feelings, desires, or activity): *The mishap provoked a hearty laugh.* **3.** to incite or stimulate (a person, animal, etc.) to action.

- In a move that could further strain[1] US-Iranian relations. Bush sees progress and peril[2] .

1:(اِس ترِین : کشش- زور- فشار) 2.(پِ رول:خطر- مخاطره)

strain ***–verb (used with object)***
1. to draw tight or taut, esp. to the utmost tension; stretch to the full: *to strain a rope.*
2. to exert to the utmost: *to strain one's ears to catch a sound.*

peril ***–noun***
1. exposure to injury, loss, or destruction; grave risk; jeopardy; danger: *They faced the peril of falling rocks.*
2. something that causes or may cause injury, loss, or destruction.
–verb (used with object)
3. to expose to danger; imperil; risk.

- The Orange County Market for new homes is deflated to the core demand for sales. (دیفِ لیت : از قبل خالی کردن) - (کُر : ثقل)
At the core: از درون

*deflate****–verb (used with object)*** دیفِ لیت : از قبل خالی کردن
1. to release the air or gas from (something inflated, as a balloon): *They deflated the tires slightly to allow the truck to drive under the overpass.*
2. to depress or reduce (a person or a person's ego, hopes, spirits, etc.); puncture; dash: *Her rebuff thoroughly deflated me.*
3. to reduce (currency, prices, etc.) from an inflated condition; to affect with deflation.
–verb (used without object)
4. to become deflated.

- 5. 3 men accused of bilking 150 elderly investors.

(بیل کینگ: گول زدن- کلاه برداری کردن)

bilk***–verb (used with object)***
1. to defraud; cheat: *He bilked the government of almost a million dollars.*
2. to evade payment of (a debt). طفره زدن از، تجاهل کردن
–noun
5. a cheat; swindler.
6. a trick; fraud; deceit.

- California law-maker consider banning load ammunition where the birds (*condors*) forage … فوریج: جایی که این پرنده دنبال غذا می گردد- علف- علوفه

- State's health care prognosis in public eye.

***prognosis* –noun, plural-.** پراگ نو سِز: پیش بيني مرض، پیش بینی دوره ناخوشی
1. *Medicine/Medical.* a forecasting of the probable course and outcome of a disease, esp. of the chances of recovery.
2. a forecast or prognostication.

- Have you stayed abreast of all the new tax law changes?

***abreast* –adverb, adjective :** آ بِ رَست برابر- پهلو به پهلو

1. side by side; beside each other in a line: *They walked two abreast down the street.*
2. equal to or alongside in progress, attainment, or awareness (usually fol. by *of* or *with*): *to keep abreast of scientific developments; keeping abreast with the times.*

- Cuban gets 5 years for weapons stash, a Cuban exile who claimed that stashed more than 1500 guns and others weapons in his home as part of his plan to overthrow Fidel Castro.
  Stash: (S تَش) *To store in a usually secret place for future use.*

S تَش : انبار کردن، ذخیره کردن- (درمحل مخفي براي اينده) انباشتن، محبوس کردن پنهانگاه

- Officer was investigating complaints of lewd conduct in men's public restroom in Minneapolis.
  lewd: *evil, wicked, obscene, vulgar* (لود:هرزگی- شهوترانی)

- The birds (*condors*) sometimes ingest[1] lead when feeding on an animal carcass[2] (کارکِس : لاشه- مردار- لش- جسد).2 (اینجِست : به شکم فروبردن).1

- Early Tuesday crowds of angry pilgrims (زوار- مسافر) chanting (بطوریکنواخت سرودن) religious slogans surged (موج-موج زدن- اینسو آنسو رفتن) through the street attacking police and securities.
  <a ship surging in heavy seas>,<protesters were chanting outside>

<u>مَعانی یا بکار گیری لغات فوق در جملات دیگر:</u>

***pilgrim*–noun** پیل گِرَم : زوار- مسافر

1. a person who journeys, esp. a long distance, to some sacred place as an act of religious devotion: *pilgrims to the Holy Land.*
2. a traveler or wanderer, esp. in a foreign place.
3. a newcomer to a region or place, esp. to the western U.S.

chanting ***–noun*** چَن تینگ : بطوریکنواخت سرودن
1. a short, simple melody, esp. one characterized by single notes to which an indefinite number of syllables are intoned, used in singing psalms, canticles, etc., in church services.
2. a psalm, canticle, or the like, chanted or for chanting.
3. the singing or intoning of all or portions of a liturgical service.
4. any monotonous song.
–verb (used with object)
5. to sing to a chant, or in the manner of a chant, esp. in a church service.
6. to sing.

surge ***–noun*** سِرج : موج- موج زدن- اینسو آنسو رفتن
1. a strong, wavelike, forward movement, rush, or sweep: *the onward surge of an angry mob.*
2. a strong, swelling, wavelike volume or body of something: *a billowing surge of smoke.*
3. the rolling swell of the sea.
4. the swelling and rolling sea: *The surge crashed against the rocky coast.*

–verb (used without object)
5. (of a ship) to rise and fall, toss about, or move along on the waves: *to surge at anchor.*
6. to rise, roll, move, or swell forward in or like waves: *The sea surged against the shore. The crowd surged back and forth. Blood surged to his face*

- Surging energy demand pushes California toward a possible record today.

سِرج : موج زدن

- A Fullerton man who suffered an abrasion[1] to his face was arrested and charged, booked on one felony[2] count of burglary.
(Fullerton is the name of a beautiful city in Orange County, California)

1.(اَبریژِن : خراش- خراشیدگی) 2 .(فِلونی : تبهکاری- جنایت- گناه)

abrasion ***–noun*** اَبریژِن : خراش- خراشیدگی
1. a scraped spot or area; the result of rubbing or abrading: *abrasions on his leg caused by falling on the gravel.*
2. the act or process of abrading.

felony **–noun, plural-nies.** *Law.* فلونی : تبهکاری- جنایت- گناه
1. an offense, as murder or burglary, of graver character than those called misdemeanors, esp. those commonly punished in the U.S. by imprisonment for more than a year.
2. *Early English Law.* any crime punishable by death or mutilation and forfeiture of lands and goods. (offense گناه، تقصیر)

- Artist had a sense of whimsy; some were struck by his sense of whimsy, others by his striking good looks. (وُهمزی : بلهوسی- تلون)

whimsy **–noun, plural-sies.**
1. capricious humor or disposition; extravagant, fanciful, or excessively playful expression: *a play with lots of whimsy.*
2. an odd or fanciful notion.

- Hypnosis may ease pain from breast cancer surgery. (هیپ نو سِس: خواب مصنوعی)
- Re: Shiites 12th Emam راجع به امام دوازدهم- امام زمان
- Devote Shiites believe, he will return to earth to restore peace and harmony. (دیوُت : وقف کردن، اختصاص دادن فدا کردن)- (شی ات : شیعه)
- *devout*: *devoted to religion or to religious studies or exercises.* (بدون ed : وقف کردن- فداکردن/با اَتی دی فداکار-صمیمی)
- Pervert *To cause to turn aside or away from what is good or true or morally right→ corrupt* پر - ورت: شخص مرتد و گمراه
- That is a perversion ... (پروِرژِن : انحراف- گمراهی- برگشتگی)

perversion **–noun**
1. the act of perverting.
2. the state of being perverted.
3. a perverted form of something.
4. any of various means of obtaining sexual gratification that are generally regarded as being abnormal.

- The man was taken to trauma center and was in critical condition.

trauma **–noun, plural-mas, -ma·ta** ترا ما : مرکز زخمی ها- قسمت جراحی
1. *Pathology.*
a. a body wound or shock produced by sudden physical injury, as from violence or accident.

- President rebuts a panel's conclusion that killings could been prevented.

rebut–verb (used with object) ربات : رد کردن- تکذیب کردن

P & pp= rebutted ریباتد
1. to refute by evidence or argument.
2. to oppose by contrary proof.
–verb (used without object)
3. to provide some evidence or argument that refutes or opposes.

- Murder, learned hours before he was to executed Thursday that he had gotten a rare reprieve form Texas Governor Rick Perry.

reprieve ***–verb (used with object)*** ریپ ریو :مهلت دادن- به تعویق انداختن-حکم بخشش - تخفیف
1. to delay the impending punishment or sentence of (a condemned person).
2. to relieve temporarily from any evil.
–noun
3. a respite from impending punishment, as from execution of a sentence of death.

- Tehran also continues to defy the Security Council by building a plutonium producing reactor.

defy ***–verb used with object*** دِ فای : بی اعتناعی کردن- تحریک کردن به جنگ/رقابت یا مخالفت کردن

1. to challenge the power of; resist boldly or openly: *to defy parental authority.*
2. to offer effective resistance to: *a fort that defies attack.*
3. to challenge (a person) to do something deemed impossible: *They defied him to dive off the bridge.*

- A significant look: → سیگ نی فی کنت : یک نگاه پر معنی

significant ***–adjective***
1. important; of consequence.
2. having or expressing a meaning; indicative; suggestive: *a significant wink.*
–noun
3. something significant; a sign.

- The **g**ross **d**omestic **p**roduct (GDP) grew significantly[1] in the spring "the economy taken a significant blow from the turmoil[2] in financial markets and the housing down turn which is intensifying[3] "said chief economist.

1.(سیگ نِ فِکَنت: قابل توجه- پرمعنی)- 2.(تِرمُویل : آشوب و اضطراب)
3 .(این تِن سی فای : سخت کردن- شدیدکردن)

<u>مَعانی یا بکار گیری لغات فوق در جملات دیگر:</u>

significant ***–adjective*** سیگ نِ فِکَنت: قابل توجه- پرمعنی
1. important; of consequence.
2. having or expressing a meaning; indicative; suggestive: *a significant wink.*
3. *Statistics.* of or pertaining to observations that are unlikely to occur by chance and that therefore indicate a systematic cause.
–noun
4. something significant; a sign.

turmoil ***–noun*** تِرمُویل : آشوب و اضطراب
1. a state of great commotion, confusion, or disturbance; tumult; agitation; disquiet: *mental turmoil caused by difficult decisions.*

*intensify***–*verb (used with object)*** این تِن سی فای : سخت کردن- شدیدکردن
1. to make intense or more intense.
2. to make more acute; strengthen or sharpen.

- I lost my job because she is still having a difficult time coping[1] with my trauma[2]

1.(کُوپینگ : تحمل کردن- با چیزی ساختن- حریف شدن –از عهده بر امدن)
2.(تِرا ما : مرکز زخمی ها- قسمت جراحی- آسیب- ضربه-شوک روحی)

coping –noun کُوپینگ
1. to deal with and attempt to overcome problems and difficulties often used with *with* <learning to *cope with* the demands of her schedule>
2. a finishing or protective course or cap to an exterior masonry wall or the like.

trauma ***–noun, plural*-mas, -ma·ta** تِرا ما
1. *Pathology.*
a. a body wound or shock produced by sudden physical injury, as from violence or accident. **b.** the condition produced by this; traumatism.
2. *Psychiatry.* **a.** an experience that produces psychological injury or pain.
b. the psychological injury so caused.

- This item justifies the aforementioned office changes $16 per hour.

(جاس T فایز :حق دادن- تصدیق کردن- درستی کاری را معلوم کردن)- (أفورمِن شِن : مذبور، فوق الذکر)

justify **–verb (used with object)** جاس T فایز

1. to show (an act, claim, statement, etc.) to be just or right: *The end does not always justify the means.*
2. to defend or uphold as warranted or well-grounded: *Don't try to justify his rudeness.*

- F-22A Raptor called futuristic fighter. آخرین هواپیمای پیشرو جنگی مدل جدید
  (futuristic (مربوط به اینده، پیشرو)

- For him the differences go far beyond the political realm, (رِلم : حوزه)

realm **–noun** رِلم : حوزه
1. a royal domain; kingdom: *the realm of England.*
2. the region, sphere, or domain within which anything occurs, prevails, or dominates: *the realm of dreams.*
3. the special province or field of something or someone: the realm of physics; facts within the realm of political scientists.

- "you shouldn't be out to entrap people" He told the officer.
  Past: entrapped (اِن ترَپ : به تله انداختن- گول زدن)

entrap **–verb (used with object),-trapped, -trap·ping.**
1. to catch in or as in a trap; ensnare: *The hunters used nets to entrap the lion.*
2. to bring unawares into difficulty or danger: *He entrapped himself in the web of his own lies.*

- Justice to probe* whether he misled congress;

Misled: to lead in a wrong direction. *(پِرُب : خوب وارسی و آزمایش کردن)

probe **–verb (used with object)**
1. to search into or examine thoroughly; question closely: *to probe one's conscience.*
2. to examine or explore with a probe.
3. an investigation, esp. by a legislative committee, of suspected illegal activity.

- Gas guzzler regaining favor, as gas prices drop, consumers head back to hunting for SUV's. We have yet to see a sustained movement away from gas guzzlers.

(گازلِر: بنزین خور) (ساستِین : نگهداری کردن- متحمل شدن- تحمل کردن)

Sustain: < *sustained heavy losses*>, <*sustained by hope*>
SUV: *Sport Utility Vehicle*

- It is our understanding that you are alleging[1] nothing more than soft tissue and subjective[2] injuries as a result of the very minor impact to your vehicle. **1.**(ادعا کردن- اظهار داشتن) **2.**(ذهنی- تصوری یا نظری)

allege ***–verb (used with object),***-leged, -leg·ing. آلجینگ : ادعا کردن- اظهار داشتن

1. to assert without proof.
2. to declare with positiveness; affirm; assert: *to allege a fact.*
3. to declare before a court or elsewhere, as if under oath.

subjective ***–adjective*** ذهنی- تصوری یا نظری
1. existing in the mind; belonging to the thinking subject rather than to the object of thought (opposed to objective).
2. pertaining to or characteristic of an individual; personal; individual: *a subjective evaluation.*
3. placing excessive emphasis on one's own moods, attitudes, opinions, etc.; unduly egocentric.

- US Senator Grag will resign his seat[1] amid[2] a furor[3] over his guilty plea[4] in a police sex sting[5].

1.(سیت : جا، صندلي، صندلی حرفه ، مرکز مقر)
2.(أمید : درمیان، وسط)
3.(فی یو رُور:خشم زیاد یا عشق مفرط)

4.(پی لی : دادخواست- *(حقوق)* پاسخ دعوي، مدافعه، دفاع خوانده در برابر ادعاي خواهان)
5.(اس تینگ : نیش، زخم نیش، گزیدن، تیر کشیدن نیش زدن)

مَعانی یا بکار گیری لغات فوق در جملات دیگر

seat----**Noun** سیت : جا، صندلي، صندلی حرفه ، مرکز مقر
When someone is elected to parliament, you can say that they or their party have won a seat.
He won the seat at the last election with a majority of four thousand three hundred....
Mr. Smith says he will resign his seat at the next general election.

amid ***–preposition*** أمید : درمیان، وسط

1. in the middle of; surrounded by; among: *to stand weeping amid the ruins.*
2. during; in or throughout the course of.
Preposition
If something happens amid noises or events of some kind, it happens while they are occurring.

furor **–noun** فی یو رُور :خشم زیاد **یا** عشق مفرط

1. a general outburst of enthusiasm, excitement, controversy, or the like.
2. a prevailing fad, mania, or craze.
3. fury; rage; madness.

sting ***–verb (used with object)*** **V. stung** (stŭng), **sting·ing, stings**
اِس تینگ : نیش، زخم نیش، گزیدن، تیر کشیدن نیش زدن

1. to prick or wound with a sharp-pointed, often venom-bearing organ.
2. to affect painfully or irritatingly as a result of contact, as certain plants do: *to be stung by nettles.*
3. to cause to smart or to cause a sharp pain: *The blowing sand stung his eyes.*
4. to cause mental or moral anguish: *to be stung with remorse.*

- Al-Malike suggests denunciation from elsewhere may have sparked Karbala killings.

denunciation **–noun** دِ نان سی اِشن : اخطار تهدیدآمیز- بدگوئی- چغلی
1. an act or instance of denouncing; public censure or condemnation.
2. an accusation of crime before a public prosecutor or tribunal.

- Allavie's* 10 month tenure[1] in 2004 was masked by rampant[2] allegations[3] of corruption[4]. So other alternations[5] are being pondered[6].

1.(10 یور: تصرف- دوره تصدی)
2.(رَم پَ نت :شایع- متداول- بر دو پا ایستاده)
3.(اَل گی شِن : اظهار، ادعا، بهانه، تایید)
4.(کَ رَاپشِن : فساد، انحراف ، رشوه خواري)
5.(آل تِر نِی شِن : تناوب، نوبت، یک درمیاني - تغییر،تعویض)
6.(پا نْدِ ر : سنجیدن- اندیشه کردن)

*(Ayad Allavie was Head of Iraqi National Unity Movement)

<u>مَعانی یا بکار گیری لغات فوق در جملات دیگر:</u>

tenure **–noun** 10 یور: تصرف- دوره تصدی
1. the holding or possessing of anything: *the tenure of an office.*
2. the holding of property, esp. real property, of a superior in return for services to be rendered.
3. the period or term of holding something.

–verb (used with object)
4. to give tenure to: *After she served three years on probation, the committee tenured her.*

rampant ***–adjective*** رَم پَ نت : شایع- متداول- بر دو پا ایستاده
1. violent in action or spirit; raging; furious: *a rampant leopard.* پلنگ- گربه وحشي
2. in full sway; prevailing or unchecked: *a rampant rumor.* شایعه گفتن و یا پخش کردن

allegation **---noun** اَلِ گِی شِن : اظهار، ادعا، بهانه، تایید
1. Claim, charge, accusation, professing, declaration, statement, assertion, averment, avowal, deposition, plea, affirmation; **fml.** asseveration
2. An allegation is a statement suggesting that someone has done something wrong.

*Corruption***–noun** کَ رآپشِن : فساد، انحراف ، رشوه خواري
1. the act of corrupting or state of being corrupt.
2. moral perversion; depravity.
3. perversion of integrity.
4. The corruption in government offices . فساد در دستگاههاي دولتي
Anti – corruption campaign . مبارزه با فساد

alternation **–noun** آل تِرِ نِی شِن : تغییر،تعویض- تناوب، نوبت، یک درمیاني
1. the act or process of alternating or the state of being alternated.
2. alternate succession; repeated rotation: *the alternation of the seasons.*

*ponder***–verb (used without object)** پا ندِ ر : سنجیدن- اندیشه کردن
1. to consider something deeply and thoroughly; meditate (often fol. by *over* or *upon*).
–verb (used with object)
2. to weigh carefully in the mind; consider thoughtfully: *He pondered his next words thoroughly.*

- Federal lobbying[1] investigation doesn't deter[2] the Fullerton Republican.

1.(لابی : گذراندن لایحه با دیدن نمایندگان)
2.(d تِر : بازداشتن-چشم ترسیده کردن)

lobby–noun لابی : گذراندن لایحه با دیدن نمایندگان

1. an entrance hall, corridor, or vestibule, as in a public building, often serving as an anteroom; foyer.
2. a large public room or hall adjacent to a legislative chamber.
3. a group of persons who work or conduct a campaign to influence members of a legislature to vote according to the group's special interest.
–verb (used without object)
4. to solicit or try to influence the votes of members of a legislative body.
–verb (used with object)
5. to try to influence the actions of (public officials, esp. legislators).
6. to urge or procure the passage of (a bill), by lobbying.

deter –**verb** (used with object),-terred, -ter·ring. دیتر : بازداشتن-چشم ترسیده کردن
1. to discourage or restrain from acting or proceeding: The large dog deterred trespassers.
2. to prevent; check; arrest: timber treated with creosote to deter rot.

- This item justifies[1] aforementioned[2].

1.جاستی فای: حق دادن به- بجا دانستن-درستی کاری را معلوم کردن
2.أفور منشن: پیش گفته شده- مزبور

Justify–**verb** (used with object) جاستی فای: حق دادن به- بجا دانستن-درستی کاری را معلوم کردن
1. to show (an act, claim, statement, etc.) to be just or right: The end does not always justify the means.
2. to defend or uphold as warranted or well-grounded: Don't try to justify his rudeness.
3. Theology. to declare innocent or guiltless; absolve; acquit.

- Iran is a sovereign country in the world. ساو رن : والا رتبه- والامقام

- Astronomers[1] glimpse[2] evolving[3] planet[4].
  1. منجم 2 . باز شدن- ظاهر شدن 3. باز کردن- تکمیل کردن 4. سیاره

- When police began forcefully dispersing the crowd. پراکنده کردن- متفرق کردن

- Nonetheless (باوجود این- با این وصف), it is hard to fathom
  (پیمودن-رسیدن). :فِ تم ← (a unit of length =six feet)
  Fathom: خانم فضانورد که 38 سال پیش به فضا رفته بود از این لغت اشتفاده کرده

- "In the shadow of the moon", a documentary مستند that premieres this week in N.Y. and LA., tells the story of the Apollo program.
  Premiere: a first performance or exhibition, < *the premiere of the play*>
  نخستین نمایش یک نمایشنامه

- Financial market turbulence has noticeably hurt housing activity across the United States in 2009-2010. تُربی لانس: اغتشاش- شورش

turbulence ***–noun*** تُربی لانس: اغتشاش- شورش
1. the quality or state of being turbulent; violent disorder or commotion.
2. Hydraulics. the haphazard secondary motion caused by eddies within a moving fluid.

Type of sovereignty! ساوِ رِن تی : سلطه، حق حاکمیت، پادشاهي، پادشاهي و سلطنت

sovereign ***–noun*** ساوِ رِن

1. a monarch; a king, queen, or other supreme ruler.
2. a person who has sovereign power or authority.
3. a group or body of persons or a state having sovereign authority.
4. a gold coin of the United Kingdom, equal to one pound sterling: went out of circulation after 1914.

–adjective
5. belonging to or characteristic of a sovereign or sovereignty; royal.

sovereignty **–noun, plural-ties.** ساوِ رِن تی : پادشاهي و سلطنت وفرمانروايي
1. the quality or state of being sovereign.
2. the status, dominion, power, or authority of a sovereign; royalty.
3. supreme and independent power or authority in government as possessed or claimed by a state or community.
4. rightful status, independence, or prerogative.
5. a sovereign state, community, or political unit.

- *His complaint was not grounded* شکایت او بی اساس و بی مورد بود
When the agent defrauded the buyer. (گول زدن- کلاه برداری)

- The aircraft broke the sound barrier as they flew over Northern Syria and "dropped ammunitions" onto deserted area. آ میو نِ شِن : مهمات

ammunition–noun آ میو نِ شِن : مهمات
1. the material fired, scattered, dropped, or detonated from any weapon, as bombs or rockets, and esp. shot, shrapnel, bullets, or shells fired by guns.

- Against this flagrant[1] aggressive[2] act and retain the right to respond in an appropriate way, a Syrian military spokesman said.

1.(فِلا يِ گِرَنت: آشکار- برملا- وقيح و زشت)

2.(اَگرِ سیو : پرتکاپو- تجاوزکارانه)

مَعانی یا بکار گیری لغات فوق در جملات دیگر

flagrant –**adjective** فِلا یِ گِرَنت: آشکار- برملا- وقیح و زشت
1. shockingly noticeable or evident; obvious; glaring: a flagrant error.
2. notorious; scandalous: a flagrant crime; a flagrant offender. متخلف، تخطي كننده، متجاوز

***aggressive* –adjective** اَگرِ سیو : پرتكاپو- تجاوزكارانه
1. characterized by or tending toward *unprovoked* offensives(متجاوز، اهانت اور ، كريه), attacks, invasions, or the like; militantly forward or menacing: *aggressive acts against a neighboring country.*
unprovoked :بي جهت- بي داعي بيخود: *If you make an unprovoked attack, you attack someone who has not tried to harm you in any way.*
(***Provoke*** : تحریک کر دن - خشمگین کردن)
2. making an all-out effort to win or succeed; competitive: *an aggressive basketball player.*
3. vigorously energetic, esp. in the use of initiative and forcefulness: *an aggressive salesperson.* (**Vigorously**: (با قوت، با زور، شديدا)

- N.Y. Democrats tell colleagues to quit over bribery[1] probe[2].

1. رشوه دادن **2**.خوب وارسی و تحقیق کردن

bribery –**noun,plural-er·ies.** رشوه دادن
the act or practice of giving or accepting a bribe: Bribery of a public official is a felony.

***probe* –verb (used with object)** خوب وارسی و تحقیق کردن
1. to search into or examine thoroughly; question closely: *to probe one's conscience.*
2. to examine or explore with a probe.

- Police believe same bandit may have robbed gas station in Fullerton and Los Angeles. بَن دیت: دزد

bandit: a member of a band of marauders (مِرادِرز : غارتگران)
banditti: جمع آن←

bandit ***–noun, plural*** **ban·dits** دزد: بَن دیت

1. a robber, esp. a member of a gang or marauding band.
2. an outlaw or highwayman.
3. *Informal.*
a. a person who takes unfair advantage of others, as a merchant who overcharges; swindler; cheat.
b. a vendor, cab driver, etc., who operates a business or works without a required license or permit, and without observing the usual rules or practices.

- Former president Bush like predecessors is push through new ruler before having office. پِرِ دِ سِ سِر : شخص پیشین
  My predecessor: → متصدی پیش از من

predecessor–***noun*** پِرِ دِ سِ سِر : شخص پیشین
1. a person who precedes another in an office, position, etc.
2. something succeeded or replaced by something else: *The new monument in the park is more beautiful than its predecessor.*
3. *Archaic.* an ancestor; forefather. (*Archaic*→ کهنه، قدیمي، غیر مصطلح: آر کِه یک)

- Although the Makah tribe has subsistence fishing rights to kill whales. ساب سیس تِنس : زیست، وسیله امرار معاش
  Subsistence allowance حق معاش

  5 people thought to be members of Makah tribe shot and harpooned the whale Sat. morning.

harpoon–***noun*** هار پُون : بانیزه زدن یا کشتن
1. a barbed, spearlike missile attached to a rope, and thrown by hand or shot from a gun, used for killing and capturing whales and large fish.

–verb (used with object)
2. to strike, catch, or kill with or as if with a harpoon.

- To show bitter indignation : (این دیگ نِی شن: خشم و غیظ)

indignation ***–noun***
Strong displeasure at something considered unjust, offensive, insulting, or base; righteous anger.

- US. Will not concession.... امتیاز - تسلیم- تن دهی

concession ***–noun***
The act of conceding or yielding, as a right, a privilege, or a point or fact in an argument: *He made no concession to caution.*

- The law is not retroactive   رِتْرُ اَکتیو : قانون عطف به ماسبق نمی شود

retroactive ***–adjective***
1. operative with respect to past occurrences, as a statute; retrospective: *a retroactive law.*
2. pertaining to a pay raise effective as of a past date.

- It behooves you at least to try.   بی هوو: اقتضاء می کند- شایسته است
Behoove = it is necessary or To be necessary or proper for

behoove–**verb** (used with object) بی هوو

1. to be necessary or proper for, as for moral or ethical considerations; be incumbent on: *It behooves the court to weigh evidence impartially.*
2. to be worthwhile to, as for personal profit or advantage: It would behoove you to be nicer to those who could help you.

- Due to negligence and intentional disregard of….

نِگ لِ جِنس : قصور، اهمال، فراموشكاري- غفلت ، بي مبالاتي

Negligence is failure to do something that you ought to do.

The chairman of the Party had been dismissed for negligence.

- The hilarious comedy   هِلْ ری یَس : کمدی نشاط آور

hilarious ***–adjective*** هِلْ ری یَس
1. arousing great merriment; extremely funny: *a hilarious story; a hilarious old movie.*
2. boisterously merry or cheerful: *a hilarious celebration.*
3. merry; cheerful.

- Minor or inconsequential   این کانسی کوانشال : بی اهمیت- مهم نبود
- Notwithstanding the fact that   با وجود اینکه
- Responsibility in fulfilling all obligations and … انجام دادن- اجرا کردن
- Schools are rife with sexual harassment   رایف : شایع متداول فراوان
- Hypothetically   های پوثِ تیک لی : بطور فرضی
- How are you going remedy it?   درمان کردن- معالجه کردن- جبران

Looking at recent sale in an area and perceiving the average rate.

مشاهده کردن- دریافتن- دیدن- ملتفت شدن- فهمیدن

- Harnessing political star power former diplomatic offer presidential hopeful decades of experience. هار نِسینگ اسباب کار- در اینجا بکار انداختن- مورد استفاده قرار دادن

- File an interpleaded action in court

این تر پی لید: پیش از اقامه دعوا بر کسي باهم دعواي حقوقي را خاتمه دادن یا
محاکمه ای که بموجب آن دو نفر ناگزیر می شوند از اینکه پیش از اقامه دعوی دعاوی میان خودشان
را با نظر شخص ثالث خاتمه و حل و فصل نمایند. در نتیجه حکم(اینتر پی لیدر)
interpleader یعنی داور قوی تر از حاکم است (arbitrator) .

interplead–*verb (used without object)*,**-plead·ed, -plead·ing.**
Law.
1. to litigate with each other in order to determine which of two parties is the rightful claimant against a third party.
2. to bring two or more claimants before a court to determine which of them is entitled to a claim that a third party recognizes.

- It is an intricate[1] and elaborate[2] system.

1.(این 3 کِیت :بغرنج- پیچیده) 2.(انی ل بُو ریت : استادانه ساخته شده)

intricate –*adjective* این 3 کِیت :بغرنج- پیچیده

1. having many interrelated parts or facets; entangled or involved: *an intricate maze.*
2. complex; complicated; hard to understand, work, or make: *an intricate machine.*

elaborate –*adjective* انی ل بُو ریت : استادانه ساخته شده
1. worked out with great care and nicety of detail; executed with great minuteness: *elaborate preparations; elaborate care.*
2. marked by intricate and often excessive detail; complicated.
–verb (used with object)
3. to work out carefully or minutely; develop to perfection.

–verb (used without object) **4.** to add details in writing, speaking, etc.; give additional or fuller treatment (usually fol. by *on* or *upon*): *to elaborate upon a theme or an idea.*

- *raunchy* video رآنچی : پست تر از استاندارد یا میزان متعادل
- unilateral یونی لترال : یک طرفه
- bilateral بای لترال: دوطرفه

- Thank you in advance for your time and consideration.

consideration –**noun** کان بریشن : ملاحظه، رسيدگي، توجه
1. the act of considering; careful thought; meditation; deliberation: I will give your project full consideration.
2. something that is or is to be kept in mind in making a decision, evaluating facts, etc.:

—Idioms
3. in consideration of,
a. in view of.
b. in return or recompense for: She was offered money in consideration of her efforts.
4. take into consideration, to take into account; consider: We failed to take into consideration the large number of tourists attending the exhibition.

- During in his incumbency این کام بنسی : دوره تصدی او

incumbency –**noun**, plural-cies for 2–5.
1. the quality or state of being incumbent.
2. the position or term of an incumbent.

- This man is so pervasive . (پر وی سیو : نافذ)
< Bill Clinton is a pervasive man in USA>

pervasive –verb (used with object),-vad·ed, -vad·ing. پر وی سیو
to become spread throughout all parts of: Spring pervaded the air.
adj. Having the quality or tendency to pervade or permeate: *the* ***pervasive*** *odor of garlic.*

- Latent[1] and patent[2] defects:

1.(ل تنت : پنهان)
2.(پ تن : آشکار، حق امتيازمحفوظ مانده، داراي حق انحصاري، حق ثبت اختراع)

- I remember her for her fortitude[1] and strong pious[2] spirit

1.(فورتی تُود : شکیبایی- بردباری - پایمردی- شهامت) 2.(پایس : دیندار- پارسا- پرهیزکار)

fortitude –**noun** فورتی تُو : شکیبایی- بردباری
Mental and emotional strength in facing difficulty, adversity, danger, or temptation courageously: Never once did her fortitude waver during that long illness.

pious **---adjective** پایس : دیندار- پارسا- پرهیزکار
1. having or showing a dutiful spirit of reverence for god or an earnest wish to fulfill religious obligations.
2. characterized by a hypocritical concern with virtue or religious devotion; sanctimonious.

- Precision is key here. (پری 30 ژن : دقت و صراحت)

1. The Importance of Error, Accuracy, and **Precision** ... It is important to distinguish from the start a different between ***accuracy*** and ***precision***: Accuracy is the degree to which information on a map or in a digital database matches true or accepted values.

- You should from the outset understand أتسِت : از ابتدا

  Outset = beginning, start

- Technology marks milestone of our times.

  milestone –noun مایل اِستون : مرحله مهمی از زندگی- مرحله برجسته
  1. a stone functioning as a milepost.
  2. a significant event or stage in the life, progress, development, or the like of a person, nation, etc.: Her getting the job of supervisor was a milestone in her career.

- Your immediate attention to this matter is greatly appreciated.
  اِمی دی اِیت : بي درنگ، فوري، بلافاصله

  ***immediate*---Adjective**
  Something that is immediate happens without any delay.
  <They called for an immediate meeting of the Security Council.>

- surety شُوِر تی : ضامن- کفیل

  Personal surety: ← کفیل شخصی *<To stand surety for a person>.*

- Women intuition is real. (این تُو اِیشن : فهم و درک- شعور مستقیم)

  ***intuition* –noun**
  1. direct perception of truth, fact, etc., independent of any reasoning process; immediate apprehension.
  2. a fact, truth, etc., perceived in this way.

- With the proceeds[1] hereof[2] recovery hereunder[3] by the debtor shall not exceed amounts paid by the debtor. (پروسیدز : عایدات از آن).1
  (از این، متعلق باین، ازاینجا، در این خصوص).2 (هی یر آندر : در زیر، ذ یلا).3

<Some legal documents say "in the terms specified hereunder...", referring to the terms and guidelines of the arrangement......>

As hereunder و بشرح زیر *Named hereunder* نام برده در زیر

Recovery hereunder: *<to bring back to normal position or condition hereunder>.*

- Unearned increment (این کری منت : ترقی- افزایش)
افزایش بهای ملک در نتیجه آباد شدن محل و منطقه نه کوشش

increment ***–noun*** این کری منت
1. something added or gained; addition; increase.
2. profit; gain.
3. the act or process of increasing; growth.
4. an amount by which something increases or grows: a weekly increment of $25 in salary.

Patent definition: حق امتیاز محفوظ مانده، داراي حق انحصاري، حق ثبت اختراع

A government license that gives the holder exclusive rights to a process, design, or new invention for a designated period of time.

Investopedia Commentary: *In the United States most patents are valid for 17 years.*

patent ***–noun*** پ تنت : آشکار، حق امتیاز محفوظ مانده، داراي حق انحصاري، حق ثبت اختراع
1. the exclusive right granted by a government to an inventor to manufacture, use, or sell an invention for a certain number of years.
2. an invention or process protected by this right.

- To evade a question طفره رفتن – خودرا بکوچه علی چپ زدن

evade ***–verb (used with object)***
1. to escape from by trickery or cleverness: *to evade one's pursuers.*
2. to get around by trickery: *to evade rules.*
3. to avoid doing or fulfilling: *to evade an obligation.*
4. to avoid answering directly: *to evade a question.*
5. to elude; escape: *The solution evaded him.*
–verb (used without object)
6. to practice evasion.
7. to elude or get away from someone or something by craft or slyness; escape.

- He scorns to lying or lie ...→ او عار دارد دروغ بگوید

scorn ***–noun*** S کورن : اهانت- خواری
1. open or unqualified contempt; disdain: *His face and attitude showed the scorn he felt.*
–verb (used with object)
2. to treat or regard with contempt or disdain: *They scorned the old beggar.*

- On 2009 during Afghanistan War, Nicolas Sarkozy said that Iran could be attacked militarily if it did not live up to its obligations to curb its nuclear program.

curb ***–noun*** تحت کنترل دراوردن- جلوگیری کردن- فرونشاندن

1. a rim, esp. of joined stones or concrete, along a street or roadway, forming an edge for a sidewalk.
2. anything that restrains or controls; a restraint; check.
–verb (used with object)
3. to control as with a curb; restrain; check.

- Sarkozy stressed[1] that such an outcome[2] would be a disaster.

1.(اِس تِ رِس : فشار، تقلا ، تاکید کردن) 2.(برآمد- نتیجه)

stress ***–noun***
1. importance or significance attached to a thing; emphasis: *to lay stress upon good manners.* **2.** *Mechanics.*
The action on a body of any system of balanced forces whereby strain or deformation results.

outcome ***–noun*** برآمد- نتیجه
1. a final product or end result; consequence; issue.
2. a conclusion reached through a process of logical thinking.

- I call catastrophic: an Iranian bomb or the bombing of Iraq.

(کَ تَس تُرُفیک : مصیبت آمیز)

catastrophe ***–noun***
1. a sudden and widespread disaster: *the catastrophe of war.*
2. any misfortune, mishap, or failure; fiasco: *The play was so poor our whole evening was a catastrophe.*

- 35-year-old woman has given to rare idea identical quadruplets hospital official said. (کوادرا پلت: چهارقلو)

Quadruplets: *a combination four of a kind* بدون اس به معنی دوچرخه 4 نفره است

Quadruplet ***–noun***
1. any group or combination of four.
2. quadruplets, four children or offspring born of one pregnancy.
3. one of four such children or offspring.

- The babies were born about two month early and conceived without fertility drugs. فِر تِ لیتی :حاصل خیزی- پر باری

fertility ***–noun*** فِر تِ لیتی :حاصل خیزی- پر باری
1. the state or quality of being fertile.
2. *Biology*. the ability to produce offspring; power of reproduction:
the amazing fertility of rabbits.
3. the birthrate of a population.
4. (of soil) the capacity to supply nutrients in proper amounts for plant growth when other factors are favorable.

- Late summer and early fall can be great times for impromptu trip to Hawaii.

(ایم پرامتو *im promp tu* ← کاری را بدون مطالعه و به اقتضای وقت انجام دهند)
< an impromptu address to the unexpected crowds>, <an impromptu dinner>

- Investors should realize funds can get hit in a volatile market too.
<Rattle by stock volatility> وَالا تُو : بالا و پایین رفتن

volatile ***–adjective*** وَالا تُو : بالا و پایین رفتن
1. evaporating rapidly; passing off readily in the form of vapor:
Acetone is a volatile solvent.
2. tending or threatening to break out into open violence; explosive:
a volatile political situation.
3. changeable; mercurial; flighty: *a volatile disposition.*

- Cleavage[1] the depression[2] between a woman's breasts especially when made visible by a low-cut neckline.

1. (کِلِ وِج :چاک پستان) 2.(دیپرِ شِن : تو رفتگي، گود شدگي افسردگي، پريشاني- ركود، كسادي)
<Hillary Clinton, showing a little cleavage today!>

<u>مَعانی یا بکار گیری لغات فوق در جملات دیگر:</u>

depression ***–noun*** دیپرِ شِن : تو رفتگي، گود شدگي افسردگي، پريشاني- ركود، كسادي

1. the act of depressing. or the state of being depressed. Or sadness; gloom; dejection.
2. ***Psychiatry***. a condition of general emotional dejection and withdrawal; sadness greater and more prolonged than that warranted by any objective reason.Compare clinical depression.

3. dullness or inactivity, as of trade.
4. ***Economics***. a period during which business, employment, and stock-market values decline severely or remain at a very low level of activity.
5. the Depression. Great Depression.

- hype : → It is slang for two words:

  a. *a narcotics addict,*
  hypodermic is a French word for this, shortened and altered.
  <a drug addict, esp. one who uses a hypodermic needle.>

  b. hyperbolize مخفف hype (های پر بولایز) است یعنی مبالغه گفتن یا نوشتن- مبالغه امیز
  <She was hyped up at the thought of owning her own car.>,
  <Iran's critics refrained from perpetuating "hype" about a possible military attack, "we need not to hype the issue" he told reporters. >

  c. *hyperbolize*: To exaggerate to a hyperbolic degree, to indulge in hyperbole. e.g. The principal has a tendency to **hyperbolize** when discussing her school...

- He was alluding to a key US argument for invading Iraq in 2003 without Security Council approval. اَلود : اشاره کردن- اشاره داشتن

  ***allude*–verb (used without object),-lud·ed, -lud·ing.** اَلود
  1. to refer casually or indirectly; make an allusion (usually fol. by *to*): *He often alluded to his poverty.*
  2. to contain a casual or indirect reference (usually fol. by *to*): *The letter alludes to something now forgotten.*

- This is a concise definition of a condominium. کآن سایس : مختصر
  A condo is the same as a condominium; used in informal America English.
  Concisely به طور مختصر

- Erraticallyبطور نا منظم *<Erratically fluctuate>*:
  آخر هر دو لغت فوق (تیک لی) یکجور تلفظ میشود (Eرَ تیک لی : بطور نامنظم نوسان کردن)

- A lanky[1] stray[2] eludes[3] authorities for weeks.

  1.(لَن کی : دراز و زشت و لاغر) 2.(شخص یا حیوانی که گم شده و بی خبر پرسه می زند)
  3.(ائی لوُد : گریز زدن- طفره رفتن- غافل شدن)

مَعانی یا بکار گیری لغات فوق در جملات دیگر:

lanky **–*adjective,* lank·i·er, lank·i·est.**
ungracefully thin and rawboned; bony; gaunt: *a very tall and lanky man.*
Lanky, lankier lankiest دراز و زشت و لاغر
who says **lanky** is an insult? it's a compliment. most models are **lanky**: tall and skinny. a **lanky** walk, run, or dance is the best thing you could see...

stray **–*noun***
1. a domestic animal found wandering at large or without an owner.
2. any homeless or friendless person or animal.
3. a person or animal that strays: *the strays of a flock.*

elude **–*verb (used with object),* e·lud·ed, e·lud·ing.** ائی لُود
1. to avoid or escape by speed, cleverness, trickery, etc.; evade: *to elude capture.*
2. to escape the understanding, perception, or appreciation of: *The answer eludes me.*
(*To elude a person's observation.*) → از نظر کسی در رفتن - کسی راا‌غفال کردن
(*Elusion* گریز- طفره-اغفال) volatility

- Mr. Romny, the 2009 presidential candidate answered questions at Chapman University forum in California, including queries on Iran and constitutional law. [query: (کوائی ریز) پرسش- سئوال]

- How many respondents thought she was entitled to compensation for her alleged jail "defilement"? (دِفایل مِنت : ناپاک سازی- آلودگی)

defilement **–*verb (used with object),* -filed, -fil·ing.**
1. to make foul, dirty, or unclean; pollute; taint; debase.
2. to violate the chastity of.
3. to make impure for ceremonial use; desecrate.

- What if they were to put him away for life for burglary, wouldn't that be ironic? (آی رانیک : طعنه آمیز- طعنه زدن)

ironic **–*adjective***
1. containing or exemplifying irony: *an ironic novel; an ironic remark.*
2. ironical.
3. coincidental; unexpected: *It was ironic that I was seated next to my ex-husband at the dinner.*

- O.J. Simpson one of the sports memorabilia collectors involved in the alleged robbery. م مو رِ بِ لیا: چیزهای با ارزش جمع کردنی یا یادداشت کردنی

الِج : بی دلیل اظهار کردن، دلیل اوردن ارائه دادن

memorabilia:

Things that are remarkable and worthy of remembrance

1. mementos; souvenirs.
2. matters or events worthy to be remembered; points worthy of note.

allege–***verb (used with object),*-leged, -leg·ing.**
1. to assert without proof.
2. to declare with positiveness; affirm; assert: *to allege a fact.*
3. to declare before a court or elsewhere, as if under oath.

- Iranian American academic in a move seen as an effort to blunt criticism of the country's human rights record.

(بِ لانت : کند کردن- سست کردن)

blunt ***–adjective*** : بِ لانت کند کردن- سست کردن

1. having an obtuse, thick, or dull edge or point; rounded; not sharp: *a blunt pencil.*
2. abrupt in address or manner: *a blunt, ill-timed question.*

–verb (used with object)
4. to make blunt; hebetate: *He blunted the knife by using it to cut* ***linoleum***. لِ-no- لی یُم

linoleum **–noun** لِ -no- لی یُم
1. a hard, washable floor covering formed by coating burlap or canvas with linseed oil, powdered cork, and rosin, and adding pigments to create the desired colors and patterns.
2. any floor covering similar to this.

- He said he was being held in solitary[1] confinement[2].

1.(سالی تِری : تنها- مجرد)
2. (کان فاین منت : گرفتاری- توقیف- حبس)
Here is another ***word*** *Solidarity*[3] = (سالی دِرِتی : ضمانت یا مسئولیت مشترک).3

<u>مَعانی یا بکار گیری لغات فوق در جملات دیگر:</u>

solitary ***–adjective***

1. alone; without companions; unattended: *a solitary passer-by.*
2. living alone; avoiding the society of others: *a solitary existence.*
3. by itself; alone: *one solitary house.*

–noun
4. a person who lives alone or in solitude, or avoids the society of others.
5. a person who lives in solitude from religious motives.
6. solitary confinement. زندان انفرادی

confinement –noun کان فاین مِنت : گرفتاری- توقیف- حبس
1. the act of confining.
2. the state of being confined.
3. the lying-in of a woman in childbed; accouchement; childbirth.
4. *Military*. incarceration in a guardhouse or prison while awaiting trial or as a punishment (distinguished from arrest).

***Solidarity* –noun, *plural*-ties.** سالی دِرتی : ضمانت یا مسئولیت مشترک
1. union or fellowship arising from common responsibilities and interests, as between members of a group or between classes, peoples, etc.: *to promote solidarity among union members.*
2. community of responsibilities and interests.

- Police say vigilance act killed wife of man in porn case.

وی جولنس : مراقبت و هوشیار

vigilance –noun

1. state or quality of being vigilant; watchfulness:
Vigilance is required in the event of treachery. خیانت

2. *Pathology*. insomnia. بيخوابي ، مرض بيخوابي

- Religious freedom eroded in countries including Pakestan, Iran, Iraq, Egypt some Arab Countries and Eritrea during the past years.

erode–verb (used with object) (اِ رُد : فرسودن)

1. to eat into or away; destroy by slow consumption or disintegration: *Battery acid had eroded the engine. Inflation erodes the value of our money.*
2. to form (a gully, butte, or the like) by erosion.
–verb (used without object)
3. to become eroded.

- Ethiopians describe atrocities . (اَت رَا سی تی : بیرحمی- قساوت)

atrocity **–noun,plural-ties.**

1. the quality or state of being *atrocious.* بیرحم ستمگر، سبع
2. an atrocious act, thing, or circumstance.

- Interception[1] of Russian warplanes in NATO patrolled-air space has become increasingly common since the Kremlin ordered.

1. جداسازی- قطع- جلوگیری

Russian aircraft intercepted[2] again. 2. جلوگیری کردن

interceptor: → جداسازنده-حائل

- Professors and political activists battle over the rescinding of a job after to noted legal scholar Mr. Chemerisky, (رسیند : فسخ یا لغو کردن)

S کالر : پژوهشگر، دانش پژوه، محقق اهل تتبع

Mr. Chemerisky whose hiring was rescinded says he's willing to talk to UCI (**U**niversity of **C**alifornia in **I**rvine) chancellor about the law school dean ship.

rescinding ***–verb (used with object)***
1. to abrogate; annul; revoke; repeal.
2. to invalidate (an act, measure, etc.) by a later action or a higher authority.

scholar ***–noun*** S کالر : پژوهشگر، دانش پژوه، محقق اهل تتبع
1. a learned or erudite person, esp. one who has profound knowledge of a particular subject.
2. a student; pupil.
3. a student who has been awarded a scholarship.

- New report refines research on early puberty in girl.

(پیوبرتی : بلوغ- رسیدگی)

Age of puberty: سن بلوغ- سن تکلیف
pubescence: (پیو بِ سِنس و پیو بِ سِنت) بلوغ

puberty پیوبرتی***–nou***: زهاري شرمگاهي - بلوغ
the period or age at which a person is first capable of sexual reproduction of offspring: in common law, presumed to be 14 years in the male and 12 years in the female.

- To be especially zealous[1] in practicing charity[2] and consideration for others….

1.(زِلا س: با شوق و ذوق- با غیرت- غیور)

.2(چِر تی : دستگيري، صدقه، خيرات نيكوكاري)

zealous *–adjective* زِلاس
full of, characterized by, or due to zeal; ardently active, devoted, or diligent.

charity ***–noun,plural*-ties.** چِر تی : دستگيري، صدقه، خيرات نيكوكاري
1. generous actions or donations to aid the poor, ill, or helpless: *to devote one's life to charity.*
2. something given to a person or persons in need; alms: *She asked for work, not charity.*
3. a charitable act or work.

- Muslims are admonished[1] to avoid lies, slander.[2], denouncing[3] others behind their backs. False oaths[4] and every form of greed[5]

.1(آد ما نیش : نصیحت کردن- پند دادن) .2(اِس لَندر : بدگویی-افتراء- تهمت)

.3(دِ نَ آنس : عیب گرفتن از- متهم کردن)
.4 (سوگند) .5 (حرص- طمع)

<u>مَعانی یا بکار گیری لغات فوق در جملات دیگر:</u>

admonish **–verb (used with object)** آد ما نیش : نصیحت کردن- پند دادن
1. to caution, advise, or counsel against something.
2. to reprove or scold, esp. in a mild and good-willed manner: *The teacher admonished him about excessive noise.*

slander ***–noun*** اِس لَندر : بدگویی- افتراء- تهمت
1. defamation; calumny: *rumors full of slander.*
2. a malicious, false, and defamatory statement or report:
a slander against his good <u>name</u>.
3. *Law*. defamation by oral utterance rather than by writing, pictures, etc.

denounce –verb nounced, -nounc·ing. دِ نَ آنس : عیب گرفتن از- متهم کردن
1. to condemn or censure openly or publicly: *to denounce a politician as morally corrupt.*
2. to make a formal accusation against, as to the police or in a court.

- Fasting[1] is one of the line pillars.[2] of Islam. The others are: affirmation[3] of the faith[4], prayer, almsgiving.[5] and hajj or pilgrimage[6] of Mecca.

.1(فستینگ :روزه گرفتن)
.2(پی لِر : ستون-ارکان)

.3(اَفِر می شِن : اظهار قطعي، تصريح، تصديق اثبات، تاكيد)

4.(عقیده، ایمان، اعتقاد) 5.(آمزگی وینگ : خیرات- صدقه دادن)

6.(پیل گریمج : ز یارت اعتاب مقدسه ، زیارت رفتن)

مَعانی یا بکار گیری لغات فوق در جملات دیگر::

fasting **–verb (used without object)** فستینگ :روزه گرفتن
1. to abstain from all food.
2. to eat only sparingly or of certain kinds of food, esp. as a religious observance.

pillar **–noun** پی لِر : ستون-ارکان
1. an upright shaft or structure, of stone, brick, or other material, relatively slender in proportion to its height, and of any shape in section, used as a building support, or standing alone, as for a monument: *Gothic pillars; a pillar to commemorate Columbus.*
2. a natural formation resembling such a construction: *a pillar of rock; a pillar of smoke.*
3. any upright, supporting part; post: *the pillar of a table.*

—Idiom
Pillars of the state: ارکان دولت

*affirmation***–noun** اَفِر مِی شِن : اظهار قطعي، تصريح، تصديق اثبات، تاكيد
1. the act or an instance of affirming; state of being affirmed.
2. the assertion that something exists or is true.
3. something that is affirmed; a statement or proposition that is declared to be true.
4. confirmation or ratification of the truth or validity of a prior judgment, decision, etc.

almsgiving:**–noun** آمزگی وینگ : خیرات- صدقه دادن
a person who gives alms /charity.

pilgrimage **–noun** پیل گریمج : زیارت اعتاب مقدسه ، زیارت رفتن

1. a journey, esp. a long one, made to some sacred place as an act of religious devotion: *a pilgrimage to Lourdes.*
2. *Islam.* **a. the Pilgrimage,** hajj. **b.** ʿumrah.

- Perhaps adherents[1] of these two great world religious will use t coincidence[2] to reflect on what these children of Abraham have in common.

1.(اَدهی رِنت : هواخواهی- پیوستگی)
2. (کواین سی دِنس: تصادف- اتفاقی)

adherent **–noun** اَدهی رِنت

1. a person who follows or upholds a leader, cause, etc.; supporter; follower.
–adjective
2. sticking; clinging; adhering: *an adherent substance.*
3. bound by contract or other formal agreement: *the nations adherent to the Geneva Convention.*

coincidence ***–noun*** کواین سی دنس **:** تصادف- اتفاقی
1. a striking occurrence of two or more events at one time apparently by mere chance: *Our meeting in Venice was pure coincidence.*
2. the condition or fact of coinciding.
3. an instance of this.
<A striking occurrence of two or more events at one time apparently by mere chance: *Our meeting in Venice was pure coincidence.*>

- August aggravates[1] Orange County housing slump[2] .

1.(اگرویت : بدکردن- شدید کردن)
2.(اسلامپ : slang اسلنگ است- افت- یکبار پایین آمدن- رکود)

aggravate–***verb (used with object),-vat·ed, -vat·ing.*** اگرویت
1. to make worse or more severe; intensify, as anything evil, disorderly, or troublesome: *to aggravate a grievance; to aggravate an illness.*
2. to annoy; irritate; exasperate: *His questions aggravate her.*

slump ***–verb (used without object)*** اسلامپ : slang اسلنگ است- افت- یکبار پایین آمدن- رکود
1. to drop or fall heavily; collapse: *Suddenly she slumped to the floor.*
2. to assume a slouching, bowed, or bent position or posture: *Stand up straight and don't slump!*
3. to decrease or fall suddenly and markedly, as prices or the market.

- Oil prices set record, flirting with $80.00 a barrel.

(فلرت : لاس زدن -حرکت سبک وتند- تکان)

*flirt***ing** ***–verb (used without object)*** فلرت
1. to court triflingly or act amorously without serious intentions; play at love; coquet.
2. to trifle or toy, as with an idea: *She flirted with the notion of buying a sports car.*
3. to move with a jerk or jerks; dart about: *butterflies flirting from flower to flower.*
–verb (used with object)
4. Also, **flirter.** a person who is given to flirting.

- Put a halt to payday loan cycle. (هالت : مکث- توقف- ایست)

halt ***–verb (used without object)*** هالت
1. to stop; cease moving, operating, etc., either permanently or temporarily: *They halted for lunch and strolled about.*
–verb (used with object)
2. to cause to stop temporarily or permanently; bring to a stop: *They halted operations during contract negotiations.*
–noun
3. a temporary or permanent stop.

- Israel contemplates response to attack.

(کان تِم پِ لِیت : در نظر داشتن- در صدد بودن- اندیشه کردن)

<Bush contemplates to attack Iraq soon.>

contemplate ***–verb (used with object)*** کان تِم پِ لِیت
1. to look at or view with continued attention; observe or study thoughtfully: *to contemplate the stars.*
2. to consider thoroughly; think fully or deeply about: *to contemplate a difficult problem.*
3. to have as a purpose; intend.
4. to have in view as a future event: *to contemplate buying a new car.*
–verb (used without object)
5. to think studiously; meditate; consider deliberately.

- Returning to respect peers. (p یِر : برابر بودن- هم شان)

peer***–noun*** p یِر
1. a person of the same legal status: *a jury of one's peers.*
2. a person who is equal to another in abilities, qualifications, age, background, and social status.

- State ask extend Microsoft decree or to extend court oversight of Microsoft's business practice for five more years.

1.(دِ کری : امرکردن- حکم کردن یا دادن) 2.(اُور سایت : اشتباه نظری - از نظر افتادگی)

decree ***–noun*** دِ کری
1. a formal and authoritative order, esp. one having the force of law:
a presidential decree. *Decree: an order usually having the force of law*
2. *Law.* a judicial decision or order.

oversight ***–noun*** *oversight*: watchful and responsible care.اُور سایت
1. an omission or error due to carelessness: *My bank statement is full of oversights.*
2. unintentional failure to notice or consider; lack of proper attention: *Owing to my oversight, the letter was sent unsigned.*
3. supervision; watchful care: *a person responsible for the oversight of the organization.*

4. An oversight is something which you should have done but did not. *My oversight was in not remembering to inform the authorities.*

- The catholic diocese settles sex- abuse lawsuit for $5 million.

***Diocese*: (دای وسِس: اسقفیه)** → *The territorial jurisdiction of a bishop.*
<Is diocese hewing to covenant ? > (هیو: ضربت زدن- شکستن)

- New Jersey court decision avert[1] trial[2] on when life begins.

1.(اورت : دفع کردن- رد کردن) 2.(ترایال : محاکمه، دادرسي)

***avert* –verb (used with object)** اورت
1. to turn away or aside: *to avert one's eyes.*
2. to ward off; prevent: *to avert evil; to avert an accident*

trial --- ترایال In law, a **trial** is when parties to a dispute come together to present information (in the form of evidence) in a formal setting, usually a court, before a judge, jury, or other designated finder of ...

Rod **Blagojevich**, former Governor of Illinois, has been under investigation by the Federal Bureau of Investigation since 2005 for corruption. **...**
Blagojevich corruption (فساد، انحراف ، رشوه خواري) **trial** begins in Chicago

- *perennial* : پرنی یال *plant present at all seasons of year or persisting for several years.*

پر زیستینگ : ایستادگي -سماجت کردن، پافشاري کردن، اصرار کردن

- F. Castro relinquishing control for the first time since 1959 revolution.

(ریل نگوئیش : ترک کردن- رها کردن- ول کردن)

***relinquishing* –verb (used with object)**

1. to renounce or surrender (a possession, right, etc.): *to relinquish the throne.*
2. to give up; put aside or desist from: *to relinquish a plan.*
3. to let go; release: to relinquish one's hold.

- Orange County Sheriff Dept. was sued for allegedly violating her (*female Muslim*) religious right after she was arrested last fall, she suffered a defiling experience when deputies ordered to remove her hejab.

(دیفای لینگ : ناپاک کردن- بی عفت کردن)

Defile: دیفایل *< The countryside defile by billboards>*

- Two officers[1] tried to stop the altercation[2] and requested additional units.

1.(آفیسر : افسر، صاحب منصب، مامور) 2. (آل تر کِی شِن : ستیزه- مجادله)

altercation –*noun* : آل تر کِی شِن
a heated or angry dispute; noisy argument or controversy.
a noisy heated angry dispute

- Iranian woman miss Haleh Esf. Said Monday that she knew she had to be disciplined to survive in Iran's dreaded Tehran Evin prison. "I decided that I was not going to fall apart.

(دِ رَد : ترسناک)

dread–***verb (used with object)*** دِ رَد ترسناک
1. to fear greatly; be in extreme apprehension of: *to dread death.*
2. to be reluctant to do, meet, or experience: *I dread going to big parties.*

–noun **3.** a person or thing dreaded. **4.** *Informal.* a person who wears dreadlocks.

–adjective
5. greatly feared; frightful; terrible.

- If I was to avoid succumbing[1] to despair[2] I had to make the best of the conditions that were put at my disposal" said Miss Haleh Esfand.

1.(سه کام بینگ: از پای درامدن- تسلیم شدن- مردن)
2.(دیس پر : یاس- ناامیدی- نومید شدن)

succumb –verb (used without object) :سه کام بینگ
1. to give way to superior force; yield: *to succumb to despair.*
2. to yield to disease, wounds, old age, etc.; die.
succumbing: سه کام بینگ (to give way to superior force)

despair –noun دیس پر
1. loss of hope; hopelessness.
2. someone or something that causes hopelessness: *He is the despair of his mother.*

–verb (used without object)
3. to lose, give up, or be without hope (often fol. by *of*): *to despair of humanity.*

- To survive more than 100 days in solitary[1] confinement[2] in an Iranian prison is hard and painful.

1.(سالی تِری: تنها- مجرد) **2.**(کَان فاین مِنت : حبس- توقیف- گرفتاری)

solitary *–adjective* سالی تری: تنها- مجرد
1. alone; without companions; unattended: *a solitary passer-by.*
2. living alone; avoiding the society of others: *a solitary existence.*
3. by itself; alone: *one solitary house.*
4. solitary confinement. → زندان انفرادی

confinement *–noun* کان فاین منت : حبس- توقیف- گرفتاری
1. the act of confining.
2. the state of being confined.
3. the lying-in of a woman in childbed; accouchement; childbirth.

- Bin. Laden's visibility revived[1] Revival[2] and revivification

1.(ر وایو : زنده شدن- احیا کردن-زنده کردن)
2.(ری وای ول : احیا، تجدید، تمدید استقرارمجدد)

revive *–verb (used with object)* ر وایو
1. to activate, set in motion, or take up again; renew: *to revive old feuds.*
2. to restore to life or consciousness: *We revived him with artificial respiration.*
–verb (used without object)
3. to be quickened, restored, or renewed, as hope, confidence, suspicions, or memories.

(جملهٔ زیر در رابطه با گرفتاری و زندانی شدن علی- ش گفته شده است)

- He was not exactly sure about the reason for his incarceration generally they believed I was a threat to nation security.

(این کارسریت و این کارسریشن : حبس- توقیف-گرفتاری)

incarceration *–verb (used with object)* این کارسریشن
1. to imprison; confine.
2. to enclose; constrict closely.
–adjective, imprisoned.

- 1 to 5 snarls may get some relief. (S نارل :خرخرکردن)

snarl ***–verb (used without object)***
1. to growl threateningly or viciously, esp. with a raised upper lip to bare the teeth, as a dog.
2. to speak in a surly or threatening manner suggestive of a dog's snarl.
–verb (used with object)
3. to say by snarling: *to snarl a threat.*
–noun: **4.** the act of snarling. **5.** a snarling sound or utterance.

- Former mercenary who staged coups across Africa dies.

(مرسِ نری : مزدور- اجیرِ پول) (کوُ : کودتا - تغییر ناگهانی)

mercenary ***–adjective*** مِرسِنِری
1. working or acting merely for money or other reward; venal.
2. hired to serve in a foreign army, guerrilla organization, etc.
–noun
3. a professional soldier hired to serve in a foreign army.
4. any hireling.
Mercenary: one that serves merely for wages

Coup=**coup d'état.** کوُ : کودتا - تغییر ناگهانی
1. a highly successful, unexpected stroke, act, or move; a clever action or accomplishment.
2. coup d'état.

- **Napoleon**'s Own Account of His Coup d`Etat (10 November 1799) ... Napoleon glosses over the conspiracy to overthrow the Constitution of 1795 and the duly elected legislature.

  This conspiracy was organized in part by his younger brother Lucien. He does, however, admit that some of the deputies opposed his endeavor and... کو: یعنی کودتا- تغییر ناگهانی

coup–***noun, plural*****coups,** کوُ : کودتا - تغییر ناگهانی
—Idiom
1. . count coup, (among Plains Indians of North America)
a. to perform a coup.
b. to recount or relate the coups one has performed.

Due to Nationalize the Iranian oil in 1951 after 18 month oil crisis ended in the world, only after a joint operation by the CIA and British intelligence topple late prime minister M. Mossadegh in 1953 coup.

gloss ***–noun*** نرمي، صافي
1. a superficial luster or shine; glaze: *the gloss of satin.*
2. a false or deceptively good appearance.
3. Also, **glosser.** a cosmetic that adds sheen or luster, esp. one for the lips.
–verb (used with object)
4. to put a gloss upon.
5. to give a false or deceptively good appearance to: *to gloss over flaws in the woodwork.*

- *Messiah* [heb] م سا یا : مسیح- مسیحا

Word Origin & History

c.1300, meshiha and Heb. mashiah "anointed" → تدهین شده *(of the Lord), from mashiah "anoint." This is the word rendered in Septuagint as Gk. Khristos (see* **Christ***). In O.T. prophetic writing, it was used of an expected deliverer of the Jewish nation. The modern Eng. form represents an attempt to make the word look more Heb., and dates from the Geneva Bible (1560). Transf. sense of "an expected liberator or savior of a captive people" is attested from 1666.*

Messiah ***–noun***
1. the promised and expected deliverer of the Jewish people.
2. Jesus Christ, regarded by Christians as fulfilling this promise and expectation.
also **Mes·si·as** The anticipated savior of the Jews. also **Messias** *Christianity* Jesus.
Messiah One who is anticipated as, regarded as, or professes to be a savior or liberator

- *Gridlock*: as follows

  1. A traffic jam in which a grid of intersecting streets is so completely congested that no vehicular movement is possible.

  2. A situation resembling gridlock (as in congestion or lack of movement) , < *political gridlock* >

  3. A Democratic House and a Senate that is virtually tied -- that's the consensus of **political** analysts canvassed by ABC News, who also predict two years of confrontation and **gridlock**.

- Palestinians dedicate mausoleum to Arafat.

(ماس سیه لی یم):گورستان باشکوه یا مقبره عالی

mausoleum :a stately and magnificent tomb. ماس سیه لی یم

- I was very fortunate and did not feel any nausea[1] inkling[2] of any kind.

1. (نا زی یا : دل اشوب، حالت تهوع، حالت استفراغ)
2. (این کلینگ : اشاره-علامت)

nausea ***–noun*** نا زی یا
1. sickness at the stomach, esp. when accompanied by a loathing for food and an involuntary impulse to vomit.
2. extreme disgust; loathing; repugnance.

inkling ***–noun*** این کلینگ

a slight suggestion or indication; hint; intimation: *They hadn't given us an inkling of what was going to happen.*

- spay: to remove the ovaries[1] and uterus[2] of (a female animal)
Find out how much **a dog spay** or neuter should **cost**.
1.(اوُری : تخمدان) 2.(یوترس: زهدان، بچه دان، رحم)

The Huntington Beach City council of California will vote today on a new law that would require pet owners to spay or neuter and microchip their cats and dogs. (نُوتر: خنثی نه مذکر نه مونث)

- dredge:(درج): لاروب <*Dredging of harbor postponed.*> (لاروبی کردن)

<*We dredged up some old toys from the bottom of the trunk.*>
<*Dredging of harbor postponed.*> (لاروبی کردن)

- Edward, see an opportunity to erode[1] her/Hillary support among antiwar[2] activities. 2.(ان تی وار : مخالف جنگ) 1.(ائی رود: فرسودن)

anti : (ان تای) **anti-war:** (ان تی- وار)
Opposed to war or to a particular war: *antiwar protests; an antiwar candidate.*

- The parents didn't know of the teen's plans, but by virtue of her indulgence* she enabled him to get in his position.
Indulge: جلوگیری نکردن- آزاد گذاردن، مخالفت نکردن

*(این دال جنس : بخشیدن، لطف کردن، از راه افراط بخشیدن، ولخرجي كردن)

indulgence –noun این دال جنس
1. the act or practice of indulging; gratification of desire.
2. the state of being indulgent.
3. indulgent allowance or tolerance.
4. a catering to someone's mood or whim; humoring: *The sick man demanded indulgence as his due.*

- We congratulate Mr. Gore and hope its same personal consolation.
(کان سولیشن :دلداری- تسلیت)
(مطلب زیر در رابطه با زنی است که در حال دویدن ماشین به او زده)

<"I feel like it's a small consolation considering what we are gone through up until now and will continue to go through".>

consolation **–noun**
1. the act of consoling; comfort; solace.
2. the state of being consoled.
3. someone or something that consoles: *His faith was a consolation during his troubles. Her daughters are a consolation to her.*

- Ali Sh. spent 114 days of detention[1] at Tehran's Evin prison solitary[2] confinement[3], longing for conversation and human company and reading voraciously[4].

1.(دی تنشن: بازداشت- نگهداری) **2**.(سالی تری:تنها- مجرد)
3.(کان فاین منت:حبس- توقیف) **4**.(وُری شِس لی :حریسانه)

<u>مَعانی یا بکار گیری لغات فوق در جملات دیگر:</u>

detention **–noun–** دی تنشن: بازداشت- نگهداری

1. the act of detaining.
2. the state of being detained.
3. maintenance of a person in custody or confinement, esp. while awaiting a court decision.
4. of or pertaining to detention or used to detain: *the detention room of a police station.*

solitary **–adjective** سالی تری:تنها- مجرد
1. alone; without companions; unattended: *a solitary passer-by.*
2. living alone; avoiding the society of others: *a solitary existence.*
3. by itself; alone: *one solitary house.*
4. *a solitary journey. solitary chores. a solitary exception. a solitary cabin in the woods.*
5 solitary confinement. زندان انفرادی

confinement **–noun** کان فاین منت:حبس- توقیف
1. the act of confining.
2. the state of being confined.

*voracious***–adjective** وُری شِس لی :حریسانه
1. craving or consuming large quantities of food: *a voracious appetite.*
2. exceedingly eager or avid: *voracious readers; a voracious collector.*

- This subset[1] of medical marijuana[2] users is too small.

1.(ساب سِت: بخش یا قسمت)
2. مَر رُ وآ نا : ماري جوانا، کنف حشیش، شاهدانه)

subset **–noun** ساب سِت: بخش یا قسمت **Subset**=*division*=*portion*

1. a set that is a part of a larger set.
2. *Mathematics*. a set consisting of elements of a given set that can be the same as the given set or smaller.

marijuana **–noun** : مَر رُ وآ نا
1. hemp def.
2. the dried leaves and female flowers of the hemp plant, used in cigarette form as a narcotic or hallucinogen. Also, ma·ri·hua·na.

- Minimally invasive surgical procedures called laparoscopic surgery. (ایـن وِی سـیو : متجـاوز- مهـاجم)

invasive **–adjective** این وِی سیو

1. characterized by or involving invasion; offensive: *invasive war.*
2. invading, or tending to invade; intrusive. < *an invasive war* >
<*Of, engaging in, or given to armed aggression*: *an invasive military force.*>

- She appeared to be clean, healthy, and coherent.
Logically ordered to integrated, (کُوهی رِنت: دارای ارتباط منطقی)
<coherent style>, <a coherent argument

coherent **–adjective** کُوهی رِنت
1. logically connected; consistent: *a coherent argument.*
2. cohering; sticking together: *a coherent mass of sticky candies.*
3. having a natural or due agreement of parts; harmonious: *a coherent design.*

- Joggers and bikers should always be running toward traffic that way if you see some erratic driving you can alter your course.
(اِرَتیک : نامنظم- جابه جا شونده- ویراژ دهنده)

erratic **–adjective** اِرَتیک
1. deviating from the usual or proper course in conduct or opinion; eccentric; queer: *erratic behavior.*
2. having no certain or definite course; wandering; not fixed: *erratic winds.*

- A distraught man wearing what approved to be bomb walked into a Hillary Clinton campaign office and demanded to speak to the candidate.

(دیس ترات : پریشان حواس- شوریده- ناراحت)

distraught ***–adjective*** دیس ترات
1. distracted; deeply agitated.
2. mentally deranged; crazed.

- During train accident passengers were hurled into seat in front of them in the accident. (هرل:پرت شدن- انداختن)
(Hurl: to throw forcefully),

hurl ***–verb (used with object)*** هرل
1. to throw or fling with great force or vigor.
2. to throw or cast down.
–noun
6. a forcible or violent throw; fling.

- NASA after the last space shuttle flight and a flurry of work

(فـ لوری: سراسیمه- آشفتگی- تپش)

flurry ***–noun*** فـ لوری
1. a light, brief shower of snow.
2. sudden commotion, excitement, or confusion; nervous hurry:
There was a flurry of activity before the guests arrived.
3. *Stock Exchange.*
a. a brief rise or fall in prices. **b.** a brief, unusually heavy period of trading.

- 110-Room motel on west side of Anaheim, California, was too dilapidate to remodel for living quarters (د ل پ بیت: خراب کردن/شدن)
quarters: living accommodation, lodgings با اس یعنی خانه- منزل

dilapidate ***–verb (used with object)*** د ل پ بیت:خراب کردن/شدن
to cause or allow (a building, automobile, etc.) to fall into a state of disrepair, as by misuse or neglect (often used passively): *The house had been dilapidated by neglect.*

- Good humor, laughter, rest, happiness, these replenish health and bring long life. (ریله نیش : دوباره پرکردن- یا ذخیره کردن مجد د)

replenish ***–verb (used with object)***

1. to make full or complete again, as by supplying what is lacking, used up, etc.: *to replenish one's stock of food.*
2. to supply (a fire, stove, etc.) with fresh fuel.
3. to fill again or anew.

- *through fare* ثرو فر — راه عبور-شارع عام
- *Not through fare* — رفت و آمد ممنوع

- He was *affronted* by sheriff Lee Baca — بی حرمتی آشکار
- *through* — از میان-از وسط-از توی
- They prefer lamentation[1] gossip[2] and pessimism[3].

1.(لَ مِن تِی شِن : سوگواری- مرثیه خوانی) 2.(گاسپ : شایعات بي اساس، سخن چیني
3.(پِس مِی زِم : بدبیني، صفت بد، بدي مطلق- فلسفه بدبیني)

مَعانی یا بکار گیری لغات فوق در جملات دیگر:

Lamentation: the act of lamenting or expressing grief. لَ مِن تِی شِن

lamentation ***–noun***
1. the act of lamenting or expressing grief. **2.** a lament.
3. Lamentations, (*used with a singular verb*) a book of the Bible, traditionally ascribed to Jeremiah. *Abbreviation:* Lam.

pessimism ***–noun***
the tendency to see, anticipate, or emphasize only bad or undesirable outcomes, results, conditions, problems, etc.: *His pessimism about the future of our country depresses me.*

- It is the knowledge we have in and according to those commandments[1] we know that it is wrong being envious[2] to people. ... Lazy envious people...

1.(کامَند مِنت : ، دستور خدا، حکمفرمان) 2.(اِن وی یَس : رشک بر-حسود- غبطه خور)

commandment–noun کامَند مِنت
1. a command or mandate.
2. (*sometimes initial capital letter*) any of the ten commandments.
3. the act or power of commanding.

envious **----** اِن وی یَس About How to Deal With an **Envious** Friend. ... Steer away from **envious people**. They will not admit they are **envious** typically. Steer away fromthis person. Keep away until they confess and say sorry.

- Absolute[1] precision[2] → دقت مطلق

1.(اَبسو لوت: مطلق، غیر مشروط، مستقل استبدادي، خودراي، خالص)
2.(پر سی ژن : دقت، صراحت، درستي، صحت فرافت، دقیق)

absolute--- **Adjective** اَبسو لوت
1. means total and complete...*the necessity for absolute secrecy.... It is far easier to enforce absolute bans.*
2. You use absolute to emphasize what you are saying.
The script is an absolute mess.... The lights went out, and there was absolute chaos.
3. An absolute ruler has complete power and authority over his or her country.
An uprising in 1932 ended the system of absolute monarchy in Thailand.

precision ***–noun*** پر سی ژن : دقت، صراحت، درستي، صحت فرافت، دقیق
1. the state or quality of being precise.
2. accuracy; exactness: *to arrive at an estimate with precision.*

- Infrared cameras reveal superheated ash on ridge of silver canyon.

این فرد: وابسته به دستگاه اشعه و یا حرارت بدن- ماورای قرمز

What is infrared **communication** ? ... Remote controller of television or air-conditioner can turn on the switch and change the TV channel from the remote place. This is the infrared communication. ... Is infrared communication visible ?

- Here are some ways you can help revive[1] and boost[2] your metabolism[3]. Make sure you eat breakfast.; If you don't eat breakfast, you slow down your metabolism and send the body into "hoard mode," thinking it's starving because you're going a long period of time frequently 8 to 10 hours or more, without food.

1.(رِوآیو : زنده شدن، دوباره دایر شدن - نیروي تازه دادن، احیا کردن)
2.(بُوست : ترقي، بالارفتن، ترقي دادن جلوبردن، بالابردن، زیادکردن، کمک کردن)
3.(مِ تَا بُو لی زم : سوخت وساز، تحولات بدن موجود زنده براي حفظ حیات ، متابولیسم)

<u>مَعانی یا بکار گیری لغات فوق در جملات دیگر:</u>

revive ***–verb (used with object)*** رِوآیو : زنده شدن، دوباره دایر شدن
1. to activate, set in motion, or take up again; renew: *to revive old feuds.*
2. to restore to life or consciousness: *We revived him with artificial respiration.*

boost–***verb (used with object)*** بُوست ترقي، بالارفتن ، بالابردن، زیادکردن، کمک کردن
1. to lift or raise by pushing from behind or below.
2. to advance or aid by speaking well of; promote: *She always boosts her hometown.*
3. to increase; raise: *to boost prices; to boost the horsepower of the car by 20 percent.*

4. an increase; rise: *There's been a tremendous boost in food prices.* His pep talk was the boost our team needed.

boost: means increase, raise بُوست جلو بردن- تقویت کردن- تکان دادن

<A campaign to boost the new fashions>, *<Plans to boost production>*

- Middle portion of the small intestine...... (این تِس تین :روده)

***intestine* –noun** این تِس تین

1. Usually, **intestines.** the lower part of the alimentary canal, extending from the pylorus to the anus.

2. Also called **small intestine.** the narrow, longer part of the intestines, comprising the duodenum, jejunum, and ileum, that serves to digest and absorb nutrients.

–adjective

3. internal; domestic; civil: *intestine strife.*

- Going through a long ritual..... (مربوط به شعائر دینی- متضمن تشریفات)
ریچوآل : تشریفات مذهبي، ایین پرستش، تشریفات

***ritual* –noun** تشریفات مذهبي، ایین پرستش، تشریفات ریچوآ ل

1. an established or prescribed procedure for a religious or other rite.

2. a system or collection of religious or other rites.

3. observance of set forms in public worship.

4. *the ritual of the dead.*

–adjective; of the nature of or practiced as a rite or ritual: *a ritual dance. ritual laws.*

- The amendments[1] would allow the government to expropriate[2] private property to a court ruling.

1. (أ مِند مِنت : اصلاح - پیشنهاداصلاحي نمایندهٔ مجلس نسبت به لایحه یا طرح)
2. (اِکس پُرو پری اِیت : سلب مالکیت کردن از، از تملک در اوردن)

***amendment*–noun** أ مِند مِنت

1. the act of amending or the state of being amended.

2. an alteration of or addition to a motion, bill, constitution, etc.

***expropriate*–verb (used with object),-at·ed, -at·ing.**
اِکس پُرو پری اِیت : سلب مالکیت کردن از، از تملک در اوردن

1. to take possession of, esp. for public use by the right of eminent domain, thus divesting the title of the private owner: *The government expropriated the land for a recreation area.*

- Calling the reforms "unconstitutional", dissident lawmaker Ricardo G. rose against pro-Chavez congressmen for approving…

(د ی س ِ دنت : مخالف عقیده عموم)

Disagreeing or dissenting, as in opinion or attitude:
<a ban on dissident magazines.>, *< a person who dissidents.>*

***dissent*–verb (used without object)** د ی س ِ دنت : مخالف عقیده عموم
1. to differ in sentiment or opinion, esp. from the majority; withhold assent; disagree (often fol. by *from*): *Two of the justices dissented from the majority decision.*
2. to disagree with the methods, goals, etc., of a political party or government; take an opposing view.

- Some analysts argue that Iran would be deterred[1] – much as the Soviet Union and china were- by US. nuclear arsenal[2].

1.(دِتِر : ترساندن- چشم ترسیده کردن- بازداشتن)
2.(آرس نال : قورخانه، زرادخانه، انبار مهمات جنگي)

<u>مَعانی یا بکار گیری لغات فوق در جملات دیگر:</u>

deter —: دِ تِر **verb (used with object),-terred, -ter·ring.**
1. To deter someone from doing something means to make them unwilling to do it. *Such discrimination may deter more women from seeking work*

2. to discourage or restrain from acting or proceeding: *The large dog deterred trespassers.*
3. to prevent; check; arrest: *timber treated with creosote to deter rot.*

arsenal ***–noun*** آرس نال : قورخانه، زرادخانه، انبار مهمات جنگي
1. a place of storage or a magazine containing arms and military equipment for land or naval service.
2. a government establishment where military equipment or munitions are manufactured.
3. a collection or supply of weapons or munitions.
4. a collection or supply of anything; store: He came to the meeting with an impressive arsenal of new research data.

- A collector who was peddling[1] thousands of pieces of former US. football player Simpson's memorabilia[2]. The FBI would not absolve[3] OJ Simpson of any potential crime.

1.(پِدلینگ : ناچیز-جزئی)
2. (مِ مو رِ ب ِ لیا: چیزهای با ارزش جمع کردنی یا یادداشت کردنی)

3.(اَبزآلو : بخشیدن- عفو کردن-آزاد کردن)

<u>مَعانی یا بکار گیری لغات فوق در جملات دیگر:</u>

peddling –**adjective** پِد لینگ : ناچیز-جزئی

1. trifling; paltry; piddling.
2. Influence peddling- Definition:

memorabilia: مِ مو رِ بِ لیا: چیزهای با ارزش جمع کردنی یا یادداشت کردنی
things that are remarkable and worthy of remembrance

1. mementos; souvenirs.
2. matters or events worthy to be remembered; points worthy of note.

absolve–***verb (used with object),*-solved, -solv·ing.** اَبزآلو : بخشیدن- عفو کردن-آزاد کردن
1. to free from guilt or blame or their consequences: *The court absolved her of guilt in his death.*
2. to set free or release, as from some duty, obligation, or responsibility (usually fol. by *from*): *to be absolved from one's oath.*

- Grief[1] is corrosive[2] to man . غصه ادم راتمام میکند←

1.(گریف :غصه) 2.(کُرسیو : خورنده- تباه کنند)

grief is the normal response of sorrow, emotion, and confusion that comes from losing someone or something important to you. It is a natural part of life.

corrosive ***–adjective*** کُرسیو : خورنده- تباه کنند
1. having the quality of corroding or eating away; erosive.
2. harmful or destructive; deleterious: *the corrosive effect of poverty on their marriage.*

- Modern forensic technology allowed detective to link four bloody fingerprints found at the 1964 crime scene to Charles Faith.

(فورِن سیک :وابسته به دادگاه)

forensic ***–adjective*** فورِن سیک
1. pertaining to, connected with, or used in courts of law or public discussion and debate.
2. adapted or suited to argumentation; rhetorical.
–noun
3. forensics, (*used with a singular or plural verb*) the art or study of argumentation and formal debate.

- The agency much maligned[1] for its sluggish[2] response.

1.(ملاین: زبان آور- بدگویی کردن) 2. (اِس لا گیش : کند- آهسته)

malign–***verb (used with object)*** ملاین

1. to speak harmful untruths about; speak evil of; slander; defame: *to malign an honorable man.*

–adjective

2. evil in effect; pernicious; baleful; injurious: *The gloomy house had a malign influence upon her usually good mood.*

sluggish ***–adjective*** اِس لا گیش

1. indisposed to action or exertion; lacking in energy; lazy; indolent: *a sluggish disposition.*

2. not acting or working with full vigor, as bodily organs: *a sluggish liver.*

3. slow to act or respond: *a sluggish car engine.*

- The residential real estate industry's doldrums will affect jobs overall according to the UCLA forecast. Housing purchases stuck in doldrums. (دُل بِرآمز : سکوت- خمود)

doldrums ***–noun*** (*used with a plural verb*) دُل بِرآمز

1. a state of inactivity or stagnation, as in business or art: *August is a time of doldrums for many enterprises*

- Watchdog got whiff of money. (ویف: نسیم- باد مختصر- بو- رایحه)

whiff ***–noun*** ویف

1. a slight gust or puff of wind, air, vapor, smoke, or the like: *a whiff of fresh air.*

2. a slight trace of odor or smell: *a whiff of onions.*

3. a single inhalation or exhalation of air, tobacco smoke, or the like.

4. a trace or hint: *a whiff of scandal.*

- A helicopter makes a water drop Tuesday on a hot spot on a single overlooking Silverado Canyon, lighting the remnant of the Santiago fire. رِم نَنت : باقیمانده- در جمع بقایا/آثار

remnant ***–noun*** . رِم نَنت

1. a remaining, usually small part, quantity, number, or the like.

2. a fragment or scrap.

3. a small, unsold or unused piece of cloth, lace, etc., as at the end of a bolt.

4. a trace; vestige: *remnants of former greatness.*

–adjective
5. remaining; leftover.

- Firefighters work to extinguish the smoldering materials.

اِکس تین گو E ش : خاموش کردن، خفه کردن فرونشاندن، کشتن، منقرض کردن
اس مول دِرینگ : بی شعله واهسته سوختن ودود کردن

extinguish **–verb (used with object)** اِکس تین گو E ش
1 .to put out (a fire, light, etc.); put out the flame of (something burning or lighted): *to extinguish a candle.*
to put an end to or bring to an end; wipe out of existence; annihilate: *to extinguish hope.*

smolder–**verb (used without object)**بی شعله واهسته سوختن ودود کردن : اس مول دِرینگ
1. to burn without flame; undergo slow or suppressed combustion.
2. to exist or continue in a suppressed state or without outward demonstration: *Hatred smoldered beneath a polite surface.*
–noun; **4.** dense smoke resulting from slow or suppressed combustion.
5. a smoldering fire.

Smoldering: to burn sluggishly without flame and often with much smoke
Smoldering: to exist or continue in a suppressed state or without outward demonstration: *<Hatred smoldered beneath a polite surface.>*

- The most radical move yet in Chavez's. Push to transform Venezuela into a socialist state, threaten to spur[1] a new wave of upheaval[2] in this oil-rich country already deeply divided over Chavez's rule

1.(اِس پِر : انگیزه) 2.(آپ هی وِل : بالا آمدگی- تراکم)

<u>مَعانی یا بکار گیری لغات فوق در جملات دیگر:</u>

Spur---**verb (used with object)** اِس پِر
1. to prick with or as if with a spur or spurs; incite or urge on: *The rider spurred his mount ruthlessly. Appreciation spurs ambition.*
2. to strike or wound with the spur, as a gamecock.
3. to furnish with spurs or a spur. *We spurred onward through the night.*

upheaval ***–noun*** آپ هی وِل
1. strong or violent change or disturbance, as in a society: *the upheaval of war.*
2. an act of upheaving, esp. of a part of the earth's crust.

- *contempt* تحقیر - خواری
- *contempt of court* توهین به مقررات دادگاه

- When millions of children starve to death or perish from famine we are not doing our duty in the world, he said.

Famine: an extreme scarcity of food, starvation.

(فَ مِن: قحطی -گرسنگی)

famine ***–noun*** فَ مِن

1. extreme and general scarcity of food, as in a country or a large geographical area.
2. any extreme and general scarcity.
3. extreme hunger; starvation.

- Ban-Kimoon, former UN Secretary General said the world body needed its members' help facing "a daunting[1] array[2] of challenges".

1.(دان تینگ: ترساندن) 2. (اَ رِی : آراستن- در صف اوردن - صف آرایی کردن یک تروپ)

daunt–**verb (used with object)** دانت تینگ: ترساندن
1. to overcome with fear; intimidate: *to daunt one's adversaries.*
2. to lessen the courage of; dishearten:
Don't be daunted by the amount of work still to be done.

array–***verb (used with object)*** اَ رِی: آراستن- در صف اوردن
1. to place in proper or desired order; marshal: *Napoleon arrayed his troops for battle.*
2. to clothe with garments, esp. of an ornamental kind; dress up; deck out: *She arrayed herself in furs and diamonds.*
–noun; **3.** order or arrangement, as of troops drawn up for battle.
4. military force, esp. a body of troops. **5.** *He couldn't dismiss the array of facts.*

- inundated with letters پوشانیدن , کاغذ پیچ – غرق نامه
- *sacred* سیک رِد: وقف شده
- *centenarian* مربوط به قرن
- becoming Centenarian ادم صد ساله

- We need to pay less attention to rhetoric and more attention to results of getting things done. (رِ تِ ریک: علم معانی و بیان)

rhetor: ری تور: اموزگار علم بیان

rhetoric ***–noun*** رِ تِ ریک

1. (in writing or speech) the undue use of exaggeration or display; bombast.
2. the art or science of all specialized literary uses of language in prose or verse, including the figures of speech.

- Ban-kimoon former UN secretary general has not used his post as the world's top diplomat to exhort countries to live up to universal values of human rights.

(اِگ زُرت: نصیحت کردن- ترغیب کردن)

exhort ***–verb (used with object)*** اِگ زُرت
1. to urge, advise, or caution earnestly; admonish urgently.
–verb (used without object)
2. to give urgent advice, recommendations, or warnings.

- Soviet espionage chief dies…..

(اِس پی اُ ناژ : جاسوسی کردن به خصوص برای کشورخارجی)　(سُوی یِت : شوروی)

Soviet war in **Afghanistan**
The **Soviet** War in **Afghanistan** was a ten-year conflict involving the **Soviet** Union, supporting the Marxist government of the Democratic Republic of **Afghanistan** at their own request against the Islamism...

espionage ***–noun*** اِس پی اُ ناژ
1. the act or practice of spying.
2. the use of spies by a government to discover the military and political secrets of other nations.

- Fix could forestall foreclosures.

(فور اِستا ل : احتکارکردن- سلف خریدن- پیش از رسیدن به بازار خریدن)

forestall: to prevent, hinder, or thwart by action in advance:
<*to forestall a riot by deploying police.*>

- Costa Mesa to appeal[1] ruling in City Hall disruption[2] case.

1.(اَپی اِل : درخواست، التماس، استیناف دادن ، پژوهش، فرجام)
2.(دیس راپ شِن : ترکیدگی- شکاف-جدایی)

appeal ***–noun*** اَپی اِل: درخواست، التماس، استیناف دادن ، پژوهش، فرجام

1. an earnest request for aid, support, sympathy, mercy, etc.; entreaty; petition; plea.
2. a request or reference to some person or authority for a decision, corroboration, judgment, etc.

3. *Law.* **a.** an application or proceeding for review by a higher tribunal.
b. (in a legislative body or assembly) a formal question as to the correctness of a ruling by a presiding officer.

–verb (used with object)
4. *Law.* **a.** to apply for review of (a case) to a higher tribunal.
b. *Obsolete.* to charge with a crime before a tribunal.

disruption* *–noun دیس راپ شِن : ترکیدگی- شکاف-جدایی
1. forcible separation or division into parts.
2. a disrupted condition: The state was in disruption.

- Authority recorded 46,000 people returning to Iraq in Oct. 2007 attributed the large number to the "improving security situation".
(أتری بیوُت : نسبت دادن- نشان دادن)

attribute* *–verb (used with object) أتری بیوُت نسبت دادن- نشان دادن
1. to regard as resulting from a specified cause; consider as caused by something indicated (usually fol. by *to*): *She attributed his bad temper to ill health.*
2. to consider as a quality or characteristic of the person, thing, group, etc., indicated: *He attributed intelligence to his colleagues.*

- Soil erosion land slides and flooding are major concerns when rainfalls on hillsides weakened by fire. (ائی رُوژن : فرسایش- ساییدگی)

erosion* *–noun
1. the act or state of eroding; state of being eroded.
2. the process by which the surface of the earth is worn away by the action of water, glaciers, winds, waves, etc.

- After the Russian Chernobyl nuclear reactor exploded in 1986. French firm Novara has been hired to build a giant steel cover over the site of the world's west nuclear accident.
(شِرنوبِل : محل راکتورهای اتمي، هستهاي، مربوط به اتمي شوروی)

Chernobyl* *–noun شِرنوبِل
A city in N Ukraine, 80 mi. NW of Kiev: nuclear-plant accident 1986.

- The Stanford centennial campaign.
(سَن تِن نیال: صدمین سالگرد- صدمین سال)

centennial* *–adjective سَن تِن نیال

1. pertaining to, or marking the completion of, a period of 100 years.
2. pertaining to a 100th anniversary.
3. lasting 100 years.
4. 100 years old.
–noun **5.** a 100th anniversary or its celebration; centenary.

- Iran's defiant[1] stance[2] on its nuclear search program took center stage Tuesday.

1.(دِفا یِنت : جسورانه- بی اعتناء) 2.(اِس تَنس : وضع- حالت-ایستادن)

defiant ***–adjective*** دِفا یِنت
characterized by defiance; boldly resistant or challenging: *a defiant attitude*

stance ***–noun*** اِس تَنس
1. the position or bearing of the body while standing: *legs spread in a wide stance; the threatening stance of the bull.*
2. a mental or emotional position adopted with respect to something: *They assumed an increasingly hostile stance in their foreign policy.*

- She said that when she was not being interrogated she did stretching exercises on the floor.

(این تِ رِ گِیت : سئوال کردن-استنطاق کردن)

interrogate–***verb (used with object)*** این تِ رِ گِیت
1. to ask questions of (a person), sometimes to seek answers or information that the person questioned considers personal or secret.
2. to examine by questions; question formally: *The police captain interrogated the suspect.*
–verb (used without object)
3. to ask questions, esp. formally or officially: *the right to interrogate.*

- The arrogant powers have repeatedly accused Iran. (اَرگَن : متکبر-خودبین)

arrogant ***–adjective***
1. making claims or pretensions to superior importance or rights; overbearingly assuming; insolently proud: *an arrogant public official.*
2. characterized by or proceeding from arrogance: *arrogant claims.*

- Bush adopted a conciliatory[1] tone far from his confrontational[2] stance here five years ago when he argued his case against Iran.

1.(کان سی لی یِه توری: صلح آمیز)

2.(کان فِرآن تِی شِنال : مقابله ائی - رفتار همراه با اعتراض)

conciliatory –adjective کان سی لی یه توری

1.tending to conciliate: *a conciliatory manner; conciliatory comments.*
2.When you are conciliatory, you are willing to end a disagreement with someone. *The authorities were taking a conciliatory approach to the strikes.... He was both conciliatory and humble.*

confrontational –adjective مقابله ائی - رفتار همراه با اعتراض : کان فِرآن تِی شِنال
tending toward or ready for confrontation: *They came to the meeting with a confrontational attitude.*

- The president remarks, though[1] polarizing[2] found sympathizers[3] at the general assembly[4].

1.(ژُ :بهرحال، اگرچه ، باوجوداینکه ولو)
2.(پولورایزینگ: ذوقطبین- حالت ویژه جسمی نسبت به قطبهای مثبت و منفی ان- به دو طرف قضیه توجه داشتن)
3.(سیم پِ تای زِر:هم درد- جانبدار)
4.(اَسِم بِلی : مجمع، اجتماع انجمن، مجلس، هیئت قانون گذاري)

<u>مَعانی یا بکار گیری لغات فوق در جملات دیگر:</u>

though –conjunction ژُ :بهرحال، اگرچه ، باوجوداینکه- ولو
1. (used in introducing a subordinate clause, which is often marked by ellipsis) notwithstanding that; in spite of the fact that; although: *Though he tried very hard, he failed the course.* **2.** even if; granting that (often prec. by *even*).
–adverb **3.** for all that; however.
—Idiom **4. as though,** as if: *It seems as though the place is deserted.*

polarizing –verb (used with object) پولورایزینگ به دو طرف قضیه توجه داشتن
1. to cause polarization in.
2. to divide into sharply opposing factions, political groups, etc.: *The controversy has polarized voters into pro-abortion and antiabortion groups.*
3. to give polarity to.
–verb (used without object); to become polarized.

sympathizer–noun سیم پِ تای زِر:هم درد- جانبدار
1. a person who sympathizes.
2. *Ophthalmology*. an eye that exhibits ophthalmia because of disease or injury of the other.

assembly **–*noun*, *plural*-blies.** اَسِم بِلی : مجمع، اجتماع انجمن، مجلس، هیئت قانون گذاري

1. an assembling or coming together of a number of persons, usually for a particular purpose: *The principal will speak to all the students at Friday's assembly.*
2. a group of persons gathered together, usually for a particular purpose, whether religious, political, educational, or social. *a bill before the assembly*
3. *the New York State Assembly.* .

- The aggressor[1] said consolidate[2],

1.(اَگرِسِر : تجاوزکار- حمله)
2.(کان سالی دیت: یکپارچه کردن- یکی کردن- محکم کردن)

aggressor **–*noun*** اَگرِسِر
a person, group, or nation that attacks first or initiates hostilities; an assailant or invader.

consolidate **–*verb (used with object)*** کان سالی دیت
1. to bring together (separate parts) into a single or unified whole; unite; combine: *They consolidated their three companies.*
2. to discard the unused or unwanted items of and organize the remaining: *She consolidated her home library.*

- Demonstration against repression[1] and poverty under the junta's[2] leadership.

1.(رِپرِ شِن :جلوگیری کردن- فرونشاندن)
2.(هُونتا : شورای اداری یا دولتی در ایتالیا و اسپانیا)

repression –**noun** رِپرِ شِن
1. the act of repressing; state of being repressed.
2. **Psychoanalysis**. the rejection from consciousness of painful or disagreeable ideas, memories, feelings, or impulses.

junta –**noun** هُونتا: شورای اداری یا دولتی در ایتالیا و اسپانیا
1. a small group ruling a country, esp. immediately after a coup d'état = کودتا and before a legally constituted government has been instituted.
2. a council.
3. a deliberative or administrative council, esp. in Spain and Latin America.

- In the bludgeoning and slaying of Patricia who was nine when she die 1987. The bludgeoned body of Patricia was found by neighborhood children playing inside of feeder tunnel in Santa Ana river bed.

(بِلاجِن- بلاجِنینگ : کتک زدن)

bludgeon–***noun*** بِلاجِن- بلاجِنینگ : کتک زدن
1. a short, heavy club with one end weighted, or thicker and heavier than the other.

–verb (used with object)
2. to strike or knock down with a bludgeon.
3. to force into something; coerce; bully: The boss finally bludgeoned him into accepting responsibility.

- The question will be whether prosecutors[1] can build a strong enough case against OJ. Simpson on the words of his cohorts[2] or whether the testimony will be eroded[3] through contradiction[4] and cross-examination targeting the unsavory[5] background of his.

1.(پراسی کیو تِر: تعقیب کننده- تعقیب قانونی)
2.(کُو هُورت: گروه)

3.(اِرُد : فرسودن- فاسد کردن) 4.(کانترا دِکشِن : مغایرت- تناقض گوئی) 5.(آن سِی وِری: ناخوشایند)

<u>مَعانی یا بکار گیری لغات فوق در جملات دیگر:</u>

prosecutor **–noun** تعقیب کننده- تعقیب قانونی :پراسی کیو تِر
1. Law. **a**. prosecuting attorney. **b**. a person, as a complainant or chief witness, instigating prosecution in a criminal proceeding.
2. a person who prosecutes.

cohort–**noun,** < *A cohort of premedical students*>گروه :کُو هُورت
1. a group or company: She has a cohort of admirers.
2. a companion or associate.
3. one of the ten divisions in an ancient Roman legion, numbering from 300 to 600 soldiers.
4. any group of soldiers or warriors.

erode **–verb (used with object)** فرسودن- فاسد کردن : اِرُد
1. to eat into or away; destroy by slow consumption or disintegration: Battery acid had eroded the engine. Inflation erodes the value of our money.
2. to form (a gully, butte, or the like) by erosion.
–verb (used without object) 3. to become eroded.
Erode=to diminish or destroy by degrees

contradiction–**noun** مغایرت- تناقض گوئی : کانترا دِکشِن
1. the act of contradicting; gainsaying or opposition.
2. assertion of the contrary or opposite; denial.
3. a statement or proposition that contradicts or denies another or itself and is logically incongruous. 4. direct opposition between things compared; inconsistency. .

unsavory **–adjective** *An unsavory assignment* (آن سِی وِری: ناخوشایند)

1. not savory; tasteless or insipid: an unsavory meal.
2. unpleasant in taste or smell; distasteful.
3. unappealing or disagreeable, as a pursuit: Poor teachers can make education unsavory.
4. socially or morally objectionable or offensive: an unsavory past; an unsavory person.

- Posts tagged Pedophile at TV Squad ... A man in the UK who was raped along with his sister in the '70s (his younger brother was also molested) did not confront his abuser until 1995, attacking the alleged pedophile by punching him and stomping on him.
  Pedophile: (Noun) A person who is sexually attracted to children.
  Pedophile suspect

  Pedophile=one affected with pedophilia (sexual perversion in which children are the preferred sexual object).

- Pervert who groomed boy online still allowed to use internet, A mother has hit out at a decision to allow the internet pervert who groomed her disabled 12-year-old son to carry on working online.

1.(پر ورت : شخص مرتد و گمراه)

2.(گُرُم :داماد، تیمارکردن، اراستن، زیبا کردن داماد شدن)

per·vert **–verb (used with object)** پر ورت : شخص مرتد و گمراه

1. to affect with perversion. 2. to lead astray morally. 3. to turn away from the right course. 4. to lead into mental error or false judgment.

–noun; 5. a person who practices sexual perversion.
6. Pathology. a person affected with perversion.
7. a person who has been perverted, esp. to a religious belief regarded as erroneous.

groom–***noun*** گُرُم :داماد، تیمارکردن، اراستن، زیبا کردن داماد شدن
1. a bridegroom. 2. a man or boy in charge of horses or the stable.
3. any of several officers of the English royal household.

- On Tuesday night after the dinner one driver rammed police car and ran over two officers while trying to escape, authorities said.

رَم : کوبیدن- زدن

Verb with Object
If one vehicle rams another, it crashes into it with a lot of force. *The ship had been rammed by a British destroyer.*

- Police called for counterparts for backup, but before they could arrive….

کَ اَن تِر پارت : نقطه مقابل، همکار ، همتا- المثني

counterparts همکاران **–noun**
1. a person or thing closely resembling another, esp. in function: Our president is the counterpart of your prime minister.
2. a copy; duplicate.
3. Law. a duplicate or copy of an indenture.
4. one of two parts that fit, complete, or complement one another

---

- Senator say travelers were gouged with $97 passport fees.

گاج : بزورستاني - جبر، بزور ستاندن، گول زدن

gouge–***noun*** گاج بزورستاني - جبر، بزور ستاندن، گول زدن
1. a chisel having a partly cylindrical blade with the bevel on either the concave or the convex side. 2. an act of gouging. 3. a groove or hole made by gouging.

- Thousands flee in fences of huge Mexican deluge .....

(دِل یو ج: سیل و طوفان)

deluge ***–noun*** دِل یو ج: سیل و طوفان
1. a great flood of water; inundation; flood.
2. a drenching rain; downpour.
3. anything that overwhelms like a flood: a deluge of mail. 4. the Deluge. flood (def. 3).
–***verb*** (used with object) 5. to flood; inundate.
6. to overrun; overwhelm: She was deluged with congratulatory letters.

- People remain bunkered in many neighborhoods of west Baghdad.

بانکر : انبار ذغال در کشتی- پناه گاه

bunker–**noun** بانکر
1. a large bin or receptacle; a fixed chest or box: a coal bunker.
2. a fortification set mostly below the surface of the ground with overhead protection provided by logs and earth or by concrete and fitted with openings through which guns may be fired.

- Despite some camaraderie and good times کام راد ری : همراهي، همدمي، وفاداري رفاقت

camaraderie **–noun** کَم رادِ ری
comradeship; good-fellowship.
camaraderie= a spirit of friendly good fellowship
Uncount Noun
camaraderie is a feeling of trust and friendship among a group of people; a formal word.
...scenes of much heavy drinking, camaraderie and also bitter rivalry.... ...the camaraderie that exists among amateur astronomers

---

- Some property owners must be getting property antsy about their chances to sell a local home. (اَنستی)

antsy: restless, fidgety /antsy children/ apprehensive uneasy, or nervous: *<I'm a little antsy since hearing those storm warnings.>*, (نگران- بیمناک).

- Iran's former chief nuclear negotiation delivered an unusually sharp rebuke to President A.'s policies.

(رِب یُوک : توبیخ کردن، ملامت کردن، سرزنش کردن)

rebuke **–verb (used with object)** رِب یُوک

1. to express sharp, stern disapproval of; reprove; reprimand.
–noun; 2. sharp, stern disapproval; reproof; reprimand.

- The charges were built largely on forensic[1] evidence and in consistencies[2] in statements made by the suspects to investigators about what happened abroad.

1.(فُ رِن سیک : وابسطه به دادگاها) 2.(کان سیس تِن سی : سازگاری- توافق)

forensic **–adjective** فُ رِن سیک
1. pertaining to, connected with, or used in courts of law or public discussion and debate.
2. adapted or suited to argumentation; rhetorical.
–noun
3. forensics, (used with a singular or plural verb) the art or study of argumentation and formal debate.

consistency–***noun***, **plural-cies.** کان سیس تِن سی : سازگاری- توافق
1. a degree of density, firmness, viscosity, etc.: The liquid has the consistency of cream.
2. steadfast adherence to the same principles, course, form, etc.: There is consistency in his pattern of behavior. S تِد فَست : ثابت قدم ، استوار، پابرجاي خيره

3. agreement, harmony, or compatibility, esp. correspondence or uniformity among the parts of a complex thing: consistency of colors throughout the house.

- Sellers remember foreclosure must see inevitable to lender.

فُور کلوزر : سلب حق فک رهن از خود

این اِو بِتِ بِل : چاره نا پذیر- غیرقابل اجتناب- حتمی الوقوع

inevitable –adjective : این اِو بِتِ بِل
1. unable to be avoided, evaded, or escaped; certain; necessary: an inevitable conclusion.
2. sure to occur, happen, or come; unalterable: The inevitable end of human life is death.
–noun; 3. that which is unavoidable.

- Russian businessmen have flourished under former President Vladimir Putin with the number of millionaires rising sharply every year.

فلُوریش : رشد و نشو نما کردن- ترقی کرد

flourish–verb (used without object)
1. to be in a vigorous state; thrive: a period in which art flourished.
2. to be in its or in one's prime; be at the height of fame, excellence, influence, etc.
3. to be successful; prosper. 4. to grow luxuriantly, or thrive in growth, as a plant.

***–verb* (used with object)**
5. to brandish dramatically; gesticulate with: a conductor flourishing his baton for the crescendo.

- Calif. Senator Feinstein's maverick attitude may be isolating.

(مَ وِ ریک : تکرو شخص مستقلی که با گروه یا دسته ائی موافقت ندارد- مستقل)

maverick ***–noun*** مَ وِ ریک : تکرو شخص مستقلی که با گروه یا دسته ائی موافقت ندارد- مستقل
1. Southwestern U.S. an unbranded calf, cow, or steer, esp. an unbranded calf that is separated from its mother.
2. a lone dissenter, as an intellectual, an artist, or a politician, who takes an independent stand apart from his or her associates.

- Miss Haheh Esf. knew she had to be disciplined[1] to survive in Iran's dreaded[2] Evin prison.

1.(دِ سیپ لین: انضباط، تحت نظم و ترتیب دراوردن، تادیب کردن)
2.(دِرید: ترس- ترسیدن از)
I dread to do that → از انجام ان کار ترس دارم
Dreadful → ترسناک- مخوف

<u>مَعانی یا بکار گیری لغات فوق در جملات دیگر:</u>

disciplined **–adjective** سیپ لین d

1. having or exhibiting discipline; rigorous: paintings characterized by a disciplined technique.
2. Discipline is the practice of making people obey rules and punishing them when they do not.
She was a harsh mother and imposed severe discipline.

dread **–verb (used with object)** درِید: ترس- ترسیدن از d
1. to fear greatly; be in extreme apprehension of: to dread death.
2. to be reluctant to do, meet, or experience: I dread going to big parties.
–noun; 5. terror or apprehension as to something in the future; great fear.

- Novelist was an innovator and provocateur.

اینو وِی تور : مبتکر، بدعت گذار پُرواکِتور :برانگیزنده- تحریک کننده

provocateur **–noun, plural-teurs** پُرواکِتور
1. A person who provokes trouble, causes dissension, or the like; agitator.
2. Provocation is a deliberate attempt to make someone react angrily.
She has a tantrum at the least provocation.... They must not react to this provocation.

innovator ***–verb (used without object)***
1. to introduce something new; make changes in anything established.
–verb (used with object)
2. to introduce (something new) for or as if for the first time: *to innovate a computer operating system.*

- From 2000 to 2006, we witnessed irrational[1] exuberance[2] in the OC. Cal. Real Estate market.

1.(E رَش نال : نامعقول- غیرمنطقی) 2. (اِگزِ بِ رِنس: فراوانی-بسیار-وفور)

exuberance: an instance of this: *His pranks are youthful exuberances.*

Irrational: not in accordance with reason; utterly illogical:
< *Irrational arguments*> نامعقول- غیرمنطقی

- Potential flooding or dam inundation* are or tsunami inundation area.

*(این آن دی شِن: سیل- طیغان)

inundate: *to cover with flood, overflow* (این آن دِیت : سیل زده کردن)

tsunami: *an unusually large sea wave produced by a seaquake undersea volcanic eruption. Also called Seismic sea wave.*

- The numbers coincide with efforts by Syria and Jordan.
(کُ این ساید : منطبق شدن- تصادف کردن)

coincide **–verb (used without object)**,-cid·ed, -cid·ing. کُ این ساید
to occupy the same place in space, the same point or period in time, or the same relative position: The centers of concentric circles coincide.
Our vacations coincided this year.

- Study abstinence only. (اَبس تِ نِنس: پرهیزکاری- خودداری- امساک- ریاضت)

abstinence ***–noun*** اَبس تِ نِنس
1. forbearance from any indulgence of appetite, esp. from the use of alcoholic beverages: *total abstinence.*
2. any self-restraint, self-denial, or forbearance.
3. Economics. the conserving of current income in order to build up capital or savings.
4. the state of being without a drug, as alcohol or heroin, on which one is dependent.

- Women may face death penalty in Los Angeles brawl case.
(بِراُل : داد و بیداد کردن-قیل و قال کردن-نزاع کردن)

brawl **–noun-- *Drunken brawl*:** عربده بِراُل

1. a noisy quarrel, squabble, or fight.
2. a bubbling or roaring noise; a clamor.
3. Slang. a large, noisy party.
–verb (used without object); 4. to quarrel angrily and noisily; wrangle.
5. to make a bubbling or roaring noise, as water flowing over a rocky bed.

- Cyrus stutters → ِ اِس تا تِر سیروس لکنت زبان دارد
- Slurry* a watery mixture of insoluble[1] matter (as mud, lime, or plaster of pare).
1. (این سالِ بِل: حل نشدنی)

*slurry** (اِس لـری) : **–noun**
1. a thin mixture of an insoluble substance, as cement, clay, or coal, with a liquid, as water or oil.
2. Ceramics . a thin slip.
–verb (used with object); 3. to prepare a suspension of (a solid in a liquid).
–adjective; 4. of or pertaining to such a suspension.

insoluble: not soluble, این سالِ بِل: حل نشدنی
fat is insoluble in water چربی در آب حل نمی شود

- The buyer of property must also be prepared for a protracted time period to conclude the purchase of property.

(پرُ ترَکت : طولانی شدن- طول داده)

Protracted: delay, defer

Protract–**verb (used with object)** پرُ ترَکت
1. to draw out or lengthen, esp. in time; extend the duration of; prolong.
2. Anatomy . to extend or protrude.

- Flow of money to Mexico stagnates (S تَگ نیت : راکد ماندن)

stagnate–***verb*** (used without object) S تَگ نیت
1. to cease to run or flow, as water, air, etc.
2. to be or become stale or foul from standing, as a pool of water.
3. to stop developing, growing, progressing, or advancing:
My mind is stagnating from too much TV.

the show started to stagnate.
–**verb (used with object);** 5. to make stagnant.

- Seller has some element of control over the losses being incurred.

(این کرِ : متحمل شدن- مواجه شدن)

incur–verb (used with object), -curred, -cur·ring. این کرِ
1. to come into or acquire (some consequence, usually undesirable or injurious): to incur a huge number of debts.

- The process began with a tentative exploration a first meeting, e g: tentative plans . (10تِی تیو: آزمایشی)

tentative –adjective 10تِی تیو
1. of the nature of or made or done as a trial, experiment, or attempt; experimental: a tentative report on her findings.
2. unsure; uncertain; not definite or positive; hesitant: a tentative smile on his face.

- From the group who want to perpetuate the cycle of being helpful and helping. (پر پِ چُو 8 : دائمی کردن- همیشگی کردن)

Perpetuate –**verb (used with object), -at·ed, -at·ing.** پر پِ چُو 8
1. to make perpetual. Or to make perpetuate or cause to last indefinitely.
2. to preserve from extinction or oblivion: to perpetuate one's name.

- For those helpers who had, organized, reach out to others, and bolster[1] to group's morale[2] by their own example, reward comes in seeing the progress of others. 2. (مُرَل : دلگرمی- روحیه)

1.(بُل ستِر: بالش، تیری که بطور عمودی زیرپایه گذارده شود ، تقویت کردن، در اینجا یعنی تکیه دادن)

bolster **–noun** :بُل ستِر

1. a long, often cylindrical, cushion or pillow for a bed, sofa, etc.
2. anything resembling this in form or in use as a support. **3**. any pillow, cushion, or pad.
–verb (used with object); 4. to support with or as with a pillow or cushion.

morale: مُرَل : دلگرمی- روحیه
the mental and emotional condition (as of enthusiasm, confidence, or loyalty) of an individual or group with regard to the function or talks at hand.
< the *morale of the troops.* >

- Adjusting to a long convalescence becomes the greater challenge.

(کان ولِ سنس: نقاهت- بهبود)
convalescent → (بهبودیافته- دارای نقاهت)
convalesce → (کان ولِس): بدون nt بهبود یافتن

convalescence **–noun** کان ولِ سنس: نقاهت- بهبود
1. the gradual recovery of health and strength after illness.
2. the period during which one is convalescing.

- For both, the practical problems of everyday life can be overwhelming[1] in particular those who have a mental or emotional[2] illness.

overwhelm → مستغرق دراندیشه شدن، دست پاچه کردن، سراسر پوشاندن

1.(اُور ولِمینگ : فشارآور- سخت- زیاد از سر در رونده- طاقت فرسا)

2.(E مُشِ نال : هیجانی احساساتی، مهیج)

overwhelming **–adjective** اُور ولِمینگ
1. that overwhelms; overpowering: The temptation to despair may become overwhelming.
2. so great as to render resistance or opposition useless: an overwhelming majority.

emotional **–adjective** E مُشِ نال : هیجانی احساساتی، مهیج
1. pertaining to or involving emotion or the emotions.

2. subject to or easily affected by emotion: We are an emotional family, given to demonstrations of affection.
3. appealing to the emotions: an emotional request for contributions.

- Overtime, those have tended to be less money available for medical and … (تِند : منجر شدن- متمایل بودن به گرایش داشتن، گراییدن، میل کردن)

<As we develop socially and intellectually, we tend to associate with others who have similar interests and beliefs.>

tend–**verb (used without object)** تِند در اینجا به معنی وسایل چیزی را فراهم کردن-کمک کردن
1. to be disposed or inclined in action, operation, or effect to do something: The particles tend to unite.
2. to be disposed toward an idea, emotion, way of thinking, etc.: He tends to be overly optimistic. Her religious philosophy tends toward pantheism.

- Civic and fraternal organizations and social clubs. (فِرَ تِر نال : برادرانه- برادروار)

fraternal –**adjective**
1. of or befitting a brother or brothers; brotherly.
2. of or being a society of men associated in brotherly union, as for mutual aid or benefit: a fraternal order; a fraternal association

---

- People today are apt to live in more than one home and have series of jobs. (مستعد-آماده)

Apt to: having a tendency, ex: < *plants apt to suffer from drought* >

apt –**adjective**

1. inclined; disposed; given; prone: too apt to slander others.
2. likely: Am I apt to find him at home?
3. unusually intelligent; able to learn quickly and easily: an apt pupil.
4. suited to the purpose or occasion; appropriate: an apt metaphor; a few apt remarks on world peace.

- The emotional and practical support they gave is no longer available and may not be forthcoming from new neighbors and friends. (فورث کامینگ : درآینده- آماده برای ارائه کردن)

forthcoming –**adjective** فورث کامینگ : درآینده- آماده برای ارائه کردن
1. coming forth, or about to come forth; about to appear; approaching in time: the forthcoming concert.

2. ready or available when required or expected: He assured us that payment would be forthcoming. <The forthcoming holidays>, <your forthcoming novel>, *<funds are forthcoming>, <a forthcoming and courteous man>*

- Group disapproval of those who stumble in the march toward recovery is rare because everyone knows how difficult it can be.

Sتام بُل : لغزش خوردن

Stumble: to fall into sin or waywardness[1], to make an error: (blunder[2])
<Stumble onto the truth> 2. اشتباه بزرگ 1.خودسری

stumble **–verb (used without object)** Sتام بُل : لغزش خوردن
1. to strike the foot against something, as in walking or running, so as to stagger or fall; trip.
2. to walk or go unsteadily: to stumble down a dark passage.
3. to make a slip, mistake, or blunder, esp. a sinful one: to stumble over a question; to stumble and fall from grace.
–**verb (used with object)** 4. to cause to stumble; trip.
5. to give pause to; puzzle or perplex.
–noun 6. the act of stumbling. 7. a moral lapse or error. 8. a slip or blunder.

- If your voice is hoarse, it sounds rough and unclear, and you can hardly speak *(درمورد صدا)* خشن، گرفته، خرخري

<a hoarse voice> *(horse اسب ← a بدون)*

- U.S. troops capture or kill 25 suspected al-Qaida members after a web posting mentions a revolt. (رِوُلت: شورش- ظغیان)

***revolt* –verb (used without object)** رِوُلت (*Revolted*متمرد- یاغی)
1. to break away from or rise against constituted authority, as by open rebellion; cast off allegiance
or subjection to those in authority; rebel; mutiny: *to revolt against the present government.*
2. to turn away in mental rebellion, utter disgust, or abhorrence (usually fol. by *from*): *He revolts from eating meat.*

- A suicide bomber driving an explosive-laden trick filled with sand struck a police station. (لِی دِ ن: بارگیری کردن)

بدون n تلفظش مثل laid است یعنی بارگیري کردن خالي کردن

laden **–adjective** لِی دِ ن: بارگیری کردن
1. burdened; loaded down.
–verb (used with object)
2. to lade.

lade ***–verb (used with object)***
1. to put (something) on or in, as a burden, load, or cargo; load.
2. to load oppressively; burden (used chiefly in the passive):
laden with many responsibilities.

- The driver detonated[1] his payload[2], after the driver told the guards he was delivering the sand to a construction site inside. The driver detonated his payload when two policemen approached him as he hired to enter a parking lot, police said.

1.(دِ ت نی تِد : باصدا منفجر شدن)
2.(پِلی لُود : حداکثر بار، حداکثر قابلیت حمل بار، بازده خودرو)

detonate: دِ ت نیت) < to explode with sudden violence, < detonate a bom>

detonate ***–verb (used without object)*** باصدا منفجر شدن : دِ ت نی تِد
1. to explode with suddenness and violence.
–verb (used with object)
2. to cause (something explosive) to explode.

payload ***–noun*** پِلی لُود : حداکثر بار، حداکثر قابلیت حمل بار، بازده خودرو
1. the part of a cargo producing revenue or income, usually expressed in weight.
2. the number of paying passengers, as on an airplane.
3. *Aerospace, Military* .
the bomb load, warhead, cargo, or passengers of an aircraft, a rocket, missile, etc., for delivery at a target or destination.

- The blast sent shards of glass flying through the air.

(شاردز : خرده شیشه یا تکه های کوچک از← *scrap*)

shard–noun; شارد → A fragment, esp. of broken earthenware.

- Violence has been unrelenting[1] in northern Iraq as insurgents[2] fight a US-Iraqi security crackdown and a ground-swell[3] of public opinion that has turned.

1.(سخت- سنگدل- بی رحم) 2.(این سِر جِنت : یاغي، شورشي)
3.(سوِال: باد کردن- بزرگ شدن-از نظر سایز و حجم بزرگ شدن)

***unrelenting* –adjective** سخت- سنگدل- بی رحم
Not relenting; not yielding or swerving in determination or resolution, as of or from opinions, convictions, ambitions, ideals, etc.; inflexible: *an unrelenting opponent of the Equal Rights Amendment.*

***insurgents* –noun** این سر جنت : یاغي، شورشي
1. a person who rises in forcible opposition to lawful authority, esp. a person who engages in armed resistance to a government or to the execution of its laws; rebel.
2. a member of a section of a political party that revolts against the methods or policies of the party.

- "I couldn't do this" he said about the crimes. This is so ruthless.

ruth : رحم- شفقت (رُث لِس : بی رحم- سنگدل- ستمگر)

ruthless –adjective; Without pity or compassion; cruel; merciless: *a ruthless tyrant.*

- After a contentious agreement that security responsibilities to Afghan elders.

(کان تِن شِس : مورد نزاع)

***contentious* –adjective** کان تِن شِس (*Contention:* مشاجره- مجادله)
1. tending to argument or strife; quarrelsome: *a contentious crew.*
2. causing, involving, or characterized by argument or controversy: *contentious issues.*
3. *Law* . pertaining to causes between contending parties.

- Reducing the number and intensity of bombings.

(این تِن سیتی : سختی- شدت)

intensify سخت- شدید کردن

***intensity* –noun, plural** -ties. سختی- شدت :این تِن سیتی
1. the quality or condition of being intense.
2. great energy, strength, concentration, vehemence, etc., as of activity, thought, or feeling: *He went at the job with great intensity.*
3. a high or extreme degree, as of cold or heat.
4. the degree or extent to which something is intense.

- The foreign intelligence surveillance[1] court said the public has no right to view the documents because they deal with the clandestine[2] workings of national security agencies.

Secular: دنیوی- غیرروحانی- مخالف اموزش شرعیات
Secularism : مخالف با تعلیم شرعیات و مطالب دینی
Secularity: دنیویت- دنیوی
<A secular shitte >

1.(سِر ویل لِنس : نظارت، مراقبت، پاییدن مبصري، تجسس بررسي كردن، زیر نظرداشتن، دید باني)
2.(کِلِن دِستِن: پنهانی)

surveillance **–noun** سِر ویل لِنس
1. a watch kept over a person, group, etc., esp. over a suspect, prisoner, or the like: *The suspects were under police surveillance.*
2. supervision or superintendence.

- One of the sheriff's deputies killed during a bungled robbery attempt was convicted, Tuesday of murder.

(بان گِل : سرهم بندی کردن- سنبل کردن)

bungle–**verb (used with object)** بان گِل < *bungle a job*>
1. to do clumsily and awkwardly; botch: < *bungled the job.* >
–verb (used without object)
2. to perform or work clumsily or inadequately: *He is a fool who bungles consistently.*
–noun
3. that which has been done clumsily or inadequately.

- Opera's political cachet she is supporting Obama,

(کَش: مهر- نشان مشخص)

cachet ***–noun, plural*** ca·chets کَش
1. an official seal, as on a letter or document.
2. a distinguishing mark or feature; stamp: *Courtesy is the cachet of good breeding.*
3. a sign or expression of approval, esp. from a person who has a great deal of prestige.

- They sold off stocks furiously. (فیوری یِس لی: با خشم زیاد-دیوانه وار)

furious ***–adjective*** فیوری یِس خشمناک، اتشي، عصباني متلاطم، متعصب
1. full of fury, violent passion, or rage; extremely angry; enraged: *He was furious about the accident.*
2. intensely violent, as wind or storms.

- US house described the Ir. people resistance's "profound[1] Popular and religious roots within Ir…'s people" as "the best impediment[2] to the Ir…. regime's abuse of popular religious sentiments".

1. (پِرُ فَ آند :عمیق- مفرط -زیاد)
2.(ایم پِ دِ مِنت : مانع-اشکال- گیر)

profound ***–adjective*** پِرُ فَ آند
1. penetrating or entering deeply into subjects of thought or knowledge; having deep insight or understanding: *a profound thinker.*

2. originating in or penetrating to the depths of one's being; *profound grief.*
3. *profound insight. a profound book. a profound silence.*

impediment ***–noun*** ایم پِ دِ مِن : مانع- اشکال- گیر
1. obstruction; hindrance; obstacle.
2. any physical defect that impedes normal or easy speech; a speech disorder.
3. *Chiefly Ecclesiastical Law* . a bar, usually of blood or affinity, to marriage: *a diriment*

- The option could viably transform American's current strategic shift into a matured policy with the enviable and peaceful prospects.

(وای ابلی : بطوررزنده) اِن وای ابل: غبطه آور

Envy : رشک و حسد

viable ---**adjective** وای ابل
1. capable of living.
2. Physiology
3. Botany . able to live and grow.

enviable –**adjective**
worthy of envy; very desirable: an enviable position

- A new US report on weapons work will boost chances for diplomacy

(بُوست :ترقي، بالارفتن، ترقي دادن جلوبردن، بالابردن، زيادكردن، کمک کردن)

Boost: Increase, raise.
<Plans to boost production>, <an extra holiday to boost moral>.

- Vindicate[1] to free from allegation or blame or to protect from attack or encroachment[2].

1.(وین دی کیت : دفاع کردن از- بجادانستن- حمایت کردن از)

2.(Nکرُوچ منت: دست اندازی- تخطی- تجاوز تدریجی)

vindicate: وین دی کیت : دفاع کردن از- بجادانستن- حمایت کردن از
1. to clear, as from an accusation, imputation, suspicion, or the like: to vindicate someone's honor.; **2**. to afford justification for; justify: Subsequent events **vindicated** his policy.; **3**. to uphold or justify by argument or evidence: to **vindicate** a claim.;

encroachment ***–noun*** N کرُوچ مِنت : دست اندازی- تخطی- تجاوز تدریجی
1. an act or instance of encroaching.
2. anything taken by encroaching.
3.Something (as a structure) that encroaches on another's land *encroachment*

- UN atomic watchdog agency said Wednesday that Iran had been "somewhat vindicated" by the US review and expressed hopes it would give a push to negotiations.
  Iran touted[1] the assessment as a vindication[2] for his refusal to cave in[3] to the west's demands that Iran *suspend uranium enrichment* and….

1.(تائِد : مشتري جلب كردن) **2**.(حمايت- دفاع) **3**. (تن در دادن)

tout: to spay (عقیم کردن) on ←(تَ آت: مشتری جو

(*Suspend uranium enrichment*: به تعلیق دراوردن غنی سازی اورانیوم)

tout **–verb (used with object)** تَ آت

1. to solicit support for importunately. 2. to describe or advertise boastfully; publicize or promote; praise extravagantly: a highly touted nightclub.

- But the space of texting appears to have resumed[1] after widespread[2] criticism in the media of such a policy.

1.(رِزُوم: دوباره بدست آوردن)

2.(همه جامنتشر-کاملا گسترده- وسیع)

Resumed: reoccupy, < resumed his seat by the fire.>

resume **–verb (used with object)** رِزُوم

1. to take up or go on with again after interruption; continue: to resume a journey.
2. to take or occupy again: to resume one's seat.
3. to resume her maiden name. to resume the title to a property.

- At least, it appears that nothing is safe from criticism or ridicule.

(ریدی کی یُول : دست انداختن- استهزاء- ریشخند- مسخره کردن)

ridicule **–noun**

1. speech or action intended to cause contemptuous laughter at a person or thing; derision.

–verb (used with object) 2. to deride; make fun of.

ridiculous **–adjective** ریدی کیلاس:مسخره- مضحک

Causing or worthy of ridicule or derision; absurd; preposterous; laughable: a ridiculous plan.

- To expend and replenish their machinery of war and suppression coupled with their accelerated quest for much weapons, constitutes a necessary step towards a peaceful and democratic Middle East.

(ریپلِ نیش: دوباره پرکردن- جایگزین کردن) (ساپ رِشِن : فرونشانی- جلوگیری)
(کواست: طلب- جستجو کردن)

<u>مَعانی یا بکار گیری لغات فوق در جملات دیگر:</u>

replenish **–verb (used with object)** ریپلِ نیش: دوباره پرکردن- جایگزین کردن
1. to make full or complete again, as by supplying what is lacking, used up, etc.: to replenish one's stock of food. 2. to supply (a fire, stove, etc.) with fresh fuel.
3. to fill again or anew.

suppression **–noun** ساپ رِشِن : فرونشانی- جلوگیری
1. the act of suppressing. 2. the state of being suppressed.
3. Psychoanalysis . conscious inhibition of an impulse.

quest **–noun** کواست: طلب- جستجو کردن
A search or pursuit made in order to find or obtain something: a quest for uranium mines; a quest for knowledge.

- American's strategic shift with respect to Tehran must also attain a viable focus.

(اَتِین : نائل شدن-رسیدن به) (وآی اِبل: زنده ماندنی) (فوکس : مرکزتوجه، متمرکز کردن توجه)

attain –verb (used with object)
1. to reach, achieve, or accomplish; gain; obtain: to attain one's goals.
2. to come to or arrive at, esp. after some labor or tedium; reach: to attain the age of 96; to attain the mountain peak.
–verb (used without object)
3. to attain to knowledge. These trees attain to remarkable height.

- how to lobby - Start by making posters about the topic you are interested in *lobbying* for. Most people picket courthouses or political ... How does someone make a challenge *lobby*?

(*lobby* لابی هتل → lobbies: جمع ان)

(ولی در سیاست یعنی لایحه ائی را بوسیله دیدن نمایندگان با خواهش و اصرار گذراندن)
مثل جمله زیر: <To lobby a bill through U.S.>

lobby :
The Legal Term * **Lobby** * Defined & Explained ... The definition of a **lobby** and the activity of **lobbying** is a matter of differing interpretation. By some definitions, **lobbying** is limited to direct attempts to influence lawmakers through personal interviews and persuasion.

- People with mild cognitive[1] impairment[2] can have difficulties with language.

1.(کاگ نِ تیو: مربوط به آگاهی یا دانش)
2.(ایم پیر مِنت :خراب سازی- لطمه- آسیب زنی)

<u>مَعانی یا بکار گیری لغات فوق در جملات دیگر:</u>

cognitive **–adjective** کاگ نِ تیو
1. of or pertaining to cognition.
2. of or pertaining to the mental processes of perception, memory, judgment, and reasoning, as contrasted with emotional and volitional processes.

impair :آسیب زدن **–verb (used with object)** ایم پیر مِنت
1. to make or cause to become worse; diminish in ability, value, excellence, etc.; weaken or damage: to impair one's health; to impair negotiations.

- New Jersey's senate voted Monday repeal the death penalty. (رِپیل : لغوکردن)

repeal **–verb (used with object)** رِپیل : لغوکردن
1. to revoke or withdraw formally or officially: to repeal a grant.
2. to revoke or annul (a law, tax, duty, etc.) by express legislative enactment; abrogate.
–noun
3. the act of repealing; revocation; abrogation.

- Click on Map to View all Used Concession Trailers for Sale By Owner in Your Area Buy Your Trailer Now to Start Working this Season!

کان سِه شِن: امتیاز-واگذاری- تن دردهی- تسلیم

- "For someone to commit a crime like that in the freeway shows he's brazen and dangerous" said sheriff.

(بریزن: بی شرمانه اجراکردن)

brazen **–adjective** بریزن
1. shameless or impudent: brazen presumption.
2. made of brass. 3. like brass, as in sound, color, or strength.

–verb (used with object) 4. to make brazen or bold.
—**Verb phrase** 5. brazen out / through, to face boldly or shamelessly: He prefers to brazen it out rather than admit defea

---

- Businessmen in Orange County can get mentoring.

(مِنتُور : رایزنی خردمندانه- مربی)

mentor–**noun** مِنتُور
1. a wise and trusted counselor or teacher.
2. an influential senior sponsor or supporter.

- The troops "are fortifying their positions as they continue with their cleanup operation", he said

(فُورتی فای : سنگربندی کردن- مستحکم کردن- تقویت کردن)

fortify–**verb (used with object)** فُورتی فای
1. to protect or strengthen against attack; surround or provide with defensive military works.
2. to furnish with a means of resisting force or standing strain or wear: to fortify cotton with nylon.
3.To fortify oneself with a good breakfast. To fortify a diet with vitamins; To fortify a lotion with lanolin. To be fortified by religious faith. To fortify an accusation with facts.

- More moderate opponents at home are hopping the assessments conclusion that Tehran shelved its effort to develop.

(اپانِنت : مخالف، ضد، حریف طرف، خصم) (شلود : کنارگذاشتن)

opponent–**noun** اپانِنت
1. a person who is on an opposing side in a game, contest, controversy, or the like; adversary.
–adjective
2. being opposite, as in position. 3. opposing; adverse; antagonistic.
4. Anatomy . bringing parts together or into opposition, as a muscle.
Shelved: کنارگذاشتن : شلود to put off or aside <shelve a project>

- The political rivalry in Tehran could have important implications for what happens next in this dispute over Iran's nuclear program.

(رایوَل re :همچشمی- رقابت) (ایم پلی کِی شِن : استنباط- مفهوم ضمنی- اشاره ضمنی)

rival: هم چشمی و رقابت کردند با

rivalry **–noun, plural -ries.** رقابت -همچشمی: رایوُل re
1. the action, position, or relation of a rival or rivals; competition: rivalry between Yale and Harvard university. 2. an instance of this.

implication–**noun** ایم پلی کِی شِن : استنباط- مفهوم ضمنی- اشاره ضمنی
1. something implied or suggested as naturally to be inferred or understood: to resent an implication of dishonesty.
2. the act of implying: His implication of immediate changes surprised us.
3. the state of being implied: to know only by implication.
4. We heard of his implication in a conspiracy.
5. Usually, implications. relationships of a close or intimate nature; involvements: the religious implications of ancient astrology.

- UN sanctions and the possibility of military action,

(سَنک شِن : فرمان، تصدیق مجازات اقتصادي- تصويب يا تصويب كردن)

<It is not protected by sanction> ضمانت اجرایی ندارد

sanction--- A sanction is a severe course of action which is intended to make people obey the law. *The ultimate sanction of the government is the withdrawal of funds.*
Plura Noun----Sanctions are measures taken by countries to restrict trade and official contact with a country that has broken international law.
The UN would impose economic sanctions against the offending nation.... The international community reacted with trade sanctions.

- One of the most onerous decisions US. Defense Secretary Robert Gates made to. (آنِرِس:سنگین- دشوار- پرخرج)

onerous **–adjective** آنِرِس
1. burdensome, oppressive, or troublesome; causing hardship: onerous duties.
2. having or involving obligations or responsibilities, esp. legal ones, that outweigh the advantages: an onerous agreement. Ex:< *an onerous contract or an onerous task*>

- Campaign watching Shirley erupted[1] with indignations[2] at the fine levied[3] against supervisor Janet N. last week and fired back with...

1.(E رایپت: منفجرشدن-درآمدن دندان)
2.(این دیگ نی شِن: خشم و غضب-اوقات تلخی)
3.(وصول کردن- بزور گرفتن- مالیات بندی)

<u>مَعانی یا بکار گیری لغات فوق در جملات دیگر:</u>

erupt–**verb (used without object)** E رایپت: منفجرشدن- درآمدن دندان

1. to burst forth: Molten lava erupted from the top of the volcano.
2. (of a volcano, geyser, etc.) to eject matter.
3. to break out of a pent-up state, usually in a sudden and violent manner: Words of anger erupted from her.
4. to break out in a skin rash: Hives erupted all over his face and hands.
–**verb (used with object)**; She erupted angry words.

indignation–**noun** این دیگ نی شِن: خشم و غضب-اوقات تلخی
strong displeasure at something considered unjust, offensive, insulting, or base; righteous anger.

- *totalitarianism*: تُوتالیتِ ری یَن نیزم اختیارداری دولت بر کلیه شئون زندگی اجتماعی و ثروت ملی

- levy, levied (لِ وی : مالیات بندي ، وصول مالیات، مالیات بستن بر جمع اوري کردن)
<They levied the sum on his property> آن مبلغ را از محل ملک یا دارایی او تامین کردند

levy definition : *To collect or assess money that is due.*

An example of levying is the government assessing how much tax you owe, or a regulatory agency fining you for not paying what you owe.

- He told the world he wants to kill all infidels. (این فیدِل : کافر - بی ایمان)

*infidel---**noun*** این فیدِل
1. *Religion* . **a.** a person who does not accept a particular faith, esp. Christianity.
b. (in Christian use) an unbeliever, esp. a Muslim.
c. (in Muslim use) a person who does not accept the Islamic faith; kaffir.
2. a person who has no religious faith; unbeliever.
–adjective **3.** not accepting a particular faith, esp. Christianity or Islam; heathen.
4. without religious faith.

- He was unaware that an insidious cancer was consuming him.
Pope Benedict : "*Gay marriage is insidious and dangerous*" . On his visit to Fatima, Portugal called *abortion and same-sex marriage some of the most insidious and dangerous" threats facing the world today.*

Insidious باسروصدا- موذی
Insidiously موذیانه-خائنانه- بی سروصدا
Insidiousness موذیگری-خیانت-حیله گری

- insinuate (8 این سی نیو) — به اشاره فهماندن، بطور ضمني فهماندن
  insinuator: (این سی نیو اِی تور: خود شیرینی کننده-چاپلوس
  کسیکه خود را پیش از دیگری طرف توجه قرار میدهد)

To bring or introduce into a position or relation by indirect or artful methods: *<to insinuate oneself into favor.>*

Insinuation: an indirect or covert suggestion or hint, esp. of a derogatory nature: *<She made nasty insinuations about her rivals.>*

- mutilate, mutilated, mutilating, mutilation — میو تی لی شِن: قطع کردن اعضاء بدن
  mutilate: To cut up or alter radically so as to make imperfection.
  <The child mutilated the book with scissors.>

- *defamatory*[1] *statements* that disparage a company's goods or services are called trade libel[2]. Trade libel protects property rights, not reputations. While you can't damage a company's "reputation," you can damage the company by disparaging its goods or services.

1.(دی فَ مِ توری: بدنام کننده- رسواکننده) 2.(لای بِل : افترا، تهمت، توهین، هجو افترا زدن)

containing defamation; injurious to reputation; slanderous or libelous:
< She claimed that the article in the magazine was defamatory.>

<u>مَعانی یا بکار گیری لغات فوق در جملات دیگر:</u>

libel ***–noun*** لای بِل : افترا، تهمت، توهین، هجو افترا زدن

1. *Law .*
a. defamation by written or printed words, pictures, or in any form other than by spoken words or gestures. **b.** the act or crime of publishing it.
c. a formal written declaration or statement, as one containing the allegations of a plaintiff or the grounds of a charge.
2. anything that is defamatory or that maliciously or damagingly misrepresents.
–verb (used with object) **3.** to institute suit against by a libel, as in an admiralty court.

- Impersonator[1] the act of defaming[2] another.

1.(ایم پرسونی تُور : شخصیت دهنده) 2.(دِ فِیم اینگ: بدنام کردن)

defaming: *To damage the reputation, character, or good name of by slander*

defame–verb (used with object), -famed, -fam·ing.

1. to attack the good name or reputation of, as by uttering or publishing maliciously or falsely anything injurious; slander or libel; calumniate: *The newspaper editorial defamed the politician.*

- Water swirls around him (سوارل: چرخ زدن)
  swirl=eddy (ادی),
  commercial/industrial proximity .... (نزدیکی- هم جواری)
  proximity of blood . → خویشاوندی

- Liquefaction zone area. لی کوافکشِن: آبگونه شدن
  Liquefaction: The process of liquefying.

  Commonage : کام نیج: زمین یا ملک مشاع
  Unilateral یونی لَترال : یکطرفه ***Bilateral*** بای لَترال : دوطرفه

- He is not afraid to milk sacred cows . (سیکرِد:مقدس)

***sacred* -adjective** سیکرِد
1. devoted or dedicated to a deity or to some religious purpose; consecrated.
2. entitled to veneration or religious respect by association with divinity or divine things; holy.
3. pertaining to or connected with religion (opposed to secular or profane): *sacred music; sacred books. a morning hour sacred to study. the sacred memory of a dead hero.*

- You will find my demeanor[1] and customer service skills to be unsurpassed[2].
  1.(دِ می نِر: رفتار- سلوک- وضع)
  2.(آن سرپس : بدون un در شروع کلمه یعنی پیش افتادن از- عقب نیفتادن)

***demeanor* -noun** دِ می نِر
1. conduct; behavior; deportment.
2. facial appearance; mien.

***surpass* -verb (used with object)** سرپس
1. to go beyond in amount, extent, or degree; be greater than; exceed.
2. to go beyond in excellence or achievement; be superior to; excel: *He surpassed his brother in sports.*
3. to be beyond the range or capacity of; transcend: *misery that surpasses description.*

- After a peal for leniency by his paralyzed victims.

(لی نی یِن سی: نرمی- مدارا- ملایمت- آسان گیر)

(پیل :صداي پیوسته، طنین متناوب، صداي گوشخراش دادن)

leniency ***–noun, plural*** -cies. لی نی یِن سی
1. the quality or state of being lenient. **2.** a lenient act. Also, le·ni·ence.

peal—**Verb**
When bells peal, they ring one after the other, making a musical sound. Verb here but can also be used as a count noun. e.g. The peals can be overwhelming for people living nearby. *Nearby church bells pealed across the quiet city.*

- Angry youth shoot at police in new strife outside Paris.

(اِس تِرایف : نزاع-دعوا- ستیزه)

strife –noun اِس تِرایف
1. vigorous or bitter conflict, discord, or antagonism: to be at strife.
2. a quarrel, struggle, or clash: armed strife.
3. competition or rivalry: the strife of the marketplace.

- 31-year-old man was working on a palm tree in Cerritos, California when a cluster of fronds fell, pinning him in the tree.

(فِران: یک برگ بسیاربزرگ درختِ پام با شاخه های اطرافش)

- City delays decision on new rectory garden at mission.

(رِکتوری: خانه کشیش- کشیش بخش یا رئیس دانشکده)

Rectory ***–noun, plural*** -ries. رِکتوری
1. a rector's house; parsonage.
2. *British* . a benefice held by a rector. <*a benefice* held by a rector.*> (درامد کلیسائی)*

- It is misconception that you can't prosecute a murder case without with the body. (میس کان سِپ شِن : تصورغلط)

Misconceive تصورغلط کردن- درست نفهمیدن

misconception:**–noun** (میس کان سِپ شِن : تصورغلط)
an erroneous conception; mistaken notion.
(to conceive or interpret wrongly; misunderstand.)

- As the holiday shopping season wanes. (وِین : روبکاهش یا زوال گذاشتن)

wane **–verb (used without object)** وِین

1. to decrease in strength, intensity, etc.: Daylight waned, and night came on. Her enthusiasm for the cause is waning.
2. to decline in power, importance, prosperity, etc.: Colonialism began to wane after World War II.
3. to draw to a close; approach an end: Summer is waning.
–noun
4. the waning of the moon. a period of waning.
—Idiom
9. on the wane, decreasing; diminishing: The popularity of that song is on the wane

---

- Which candidate will back elimination of farm subsidies?

subsidy (ساب سه دی)= a grant or gift of money as: *sum of money formerly granted by the British parliament to the crown and raised by special taxation.*
subside: فروکش کردن- موقوف شدن (ساب ساید) to sink to a low or lower level.

- If abortion[1] is outlawed[2]: 1.(اَبور شِن : کورتاژ) 2.(از حقوق بی بهره کردن)
A lawless person or habitual criminal, esp. one who is a fugitive from the law.
He was waterbording! (Torture), Did he Break the Law by waterbording?

- Not for unit cohesion (کُ هی ژن : پیوستگی- چسبندگی)

cohesion **----noun** کُ هی ژن
1. the act or state of cohering, uniting, or sticking together.
2. Physics . the molecular force between particles within a body or substance that acts to unite them

---

- *tramp stamp* (خالکوبی بالای باسن دختر)
- America to embrace Islam. (ایم بریس : در آغوش گرفتن- اختیارکردن)
- newsmonger : (نوز مانگر: سخن چین- خبر بر)
A person who spreads gossip or idle talk; a gossip or gossipmonger.

- US officials consider eavesdropping: (عیوز دراپ -eev-zdrop)استراق سمع
<Probably back-formation from eavesdropper, one who eavesdrops, from Middle English eavesdropper>

- Buttressed[1] by think-tankers[2] outside government… 1(شمع پشتیبان دیوار)

Think-tank[2]: a research institute or organization employed to solve complex problems or predict or plan future developments, as in military, political, or social areas.

- It seems to represent a forceful push back against the small cadre of mostly neoconservative officials

(کَ دری: کادر - لغت فرانسوی است مثل کادر افسران)

neoconservative نیو کان سِر وِتیو : *forme liberal espousing political conservatism.*

conservatism **–noun** نیو کان سِر وِتی زِم :
moderate political conservatism espoused or advocated by former liberals or socialists.

- Destructions[4] of a ruling tyranny[1] does not mean that peace, contentment[2] and all parties joining hands to work in concert together follows inevitably[3]

1.(تِ رنی : حکومت استبداد و جور و ستم) 2.(کان تِنت مِنت : خرسندی و قناعت)
3.(این اِ وِتِ بِلی : ناچار- به ناچار) 4.(دیس تِراکشِن : ویرانی- هلاکی- تخریب)

destruction: the act of destroying: <wanton *destruction of a town.*>

- It's likely this estimate was presented more meticulously than previous reports. (مِتِ کیلا سلی : بادقت زیاد- باریک بین، خیلي دقیق وسواسي)

meticulous---adjective مِتِ کیلا سلی
1. taking or showing extreme care about minute details; precise; thorough: *a meticulous craftsman; meticulous personal appearance.*
2. finicky; fussy: meticulous adherence to technicalities.

- One month before Iowa's leadoff[1] caucuses[2] the presidential candidates stood together in welcoming the report's assessment.

1.(لید آف : آغاز- شروع- پیش قدمی)
2.(کاکِ سِس: دیدار یک گروه نزدیک بهم که در یک حزب باشند)

caucus–noun کاکِس
1. *U.S. Politics* .
a. a meeting of party leaders to select candidates, elect convention delegates, etc.
b. a meeting of party members within a legislative body to select leaders and determine strategy. **c.** (*often initial capital letter*) a faction within a legislative body that pursues its interests through the legislative process: *the Women's Caucus; the Black Caucus.*
2. any group or meeting organized to further a special interest or cause.
–verb (used without object) **3.** to hold or meet in a caucus

---

- Iran on Tuesday touted a new US. intelligence report as vindication that its nuclear program is peaceful (وندیکیشن : حمایت- دفاع)

tout: to say on or watch → تات : مشتری بخود جلب کرد

vindication **-noun** (وندیکیشن : حمایت- دفاع)

1. the act of vindicating.
2. the state of being vindicated.
3. defense; excuse; justification: *Poverty was a vindication for his thievery.*
4. something that vindicates: *Subsequent events were her vindication.*

- "As far as we know, it has probably since revived it", Obama said. (روآیو : دوباره زنده کردن- دوباره از سرگرفتن- احیاء کردن)

***revive*-verb (used with object)** روآیو

1. to activate, set in motion, or take up again; renew: *to revive old feuds.*
2. to restore to life or consciousness: *We revived him with artificial respiration.*
3. to put on or show (an old play or motion picture) again.
4. to make operative or valid again. *to revive a subject of discussion. to revive memories.*

- I think we all start from the presumption that now things have changed. (پری زامشن : فرض- استنباط)

***presumption* -noun** پری زامشن

1. the act of presuming. **2.** assumption of something as true.
3. something that is presumed; an assumption.

- Flow of weapons from ...?... to Iraqi shitte militias appeared to have been curtailed. (کرتیل: موقوف- کوتاه کردن)

- You can't help but wonder what treasure trove of intelligence gathered on the Iranian nuclear program... تُرُو چیز پیدا شده، گنجینه، تحفه

trove:**-noun** تُرُو چیز پیدا شده، گنجینه، تحفه

A collection of objects. Also, the seller attested that these were no defects affecting the house not otherwise disclosed to buyers.

اَتِست : گواهی دادن- تصدیق کردن

***attest*-verb (used with object)** : اَتِست

1. to bear witness to; certify; declare to be correct, true, or genuine; declare the truth of, in words or writing, esp. affirm in an official capacity: *to attest the truth of a statement.*
2. to give proof or evidence of; manifest: *His works attest his industry.*

3. to put on oath.
–verb (used without object)
4. to testify or bear witness (often fol. by *to*): *to attest to the reliability of an employee.*

- Hobby city gets reprieve.

(رِپ ریو : مهلت دادن- حکم بخشش یا تخفیف - مجازات کسي را بتعويق انداختن،)

***reprieve* –verb (used with object)** رِپ ریو
1. to delay the impending punishment or sentence of (a condemned person).
2. to relieve temporarily from any evil.

- When the mortgage brokers originated the loans, it was done in accordance with the bank's guidelines for those specific programs.

(سرچشمه- بوجودآمدن)

- In a significant manner. (پرمعنی- قابل توجه- مهم)
<To a significant degree>, < the salaries differed significantly. >

- Trio[1] of kitten siblings[2]: (one of two or more individuals having one common parent).

1.(تِرِیُو: یک قطعه موسیقی 3نفره- یا چیز مربوط به 3 نفر)
2. (سی بلینگ : هم نیا، هم نژاد، برادر یاخواهر)

- He has had endure racial comments because he is Muslim. (این دُور: تحمل کردن)
<I can't endure to see that. → طاقت یا تحمل دیدن آن را ندارم >

- It seems buyers/sellers are skeptical[1] of commission amount and the veracity[2] of agents.

1.(اِس کِپ تی کال: شکاک ، مشکوک ، ادم شکاک در دین وعقاید مذهبي)
2.(وِرَسیتی: راستگویی- صحت)

skeptical –adjective اِس کِپ تی کال
1. inclined to skepticism; having doubt: a skeptical young woman.
2. showing doubt: a skeptical smile.

veracity: devotion to the truth: truthfulness وِرَسیتی: راستگویی- صحت

- As technology has developed, so have the complexity regulation, requirements and procedures facing real estate buyers and sellers.

(درهمی- پیچیدگی- آشفتگی)

- Why Ir…'s leadership decided to halt the covert effort. Specially the covert nuclear weapons program.

(هالت : ایست کردن- مکث کردن) (کوورت: پوشیده و پنهان)

- Ultimately, the notes and deliberations were corroborated by other intelligence, the officials said, including intercepted conversations among Iranian officials

(دلِ بریشن : برسی- شور) (کرابِ ریت: تایید یا ثابت کردن) (این تر سپت : قطع کردن- جداشدن)

deliberation: –noun دلِ بریشن

1. careful consideration before decision.
2. formal consultation or discussion.
3. deliberate quality; leisureliness of movement or action; slowness.

corroborate: کرابِ ریت to make more certain; confirm:
<He corroborated my account of the accident>
careful consideration before decision

- Several news organization have reported that the reversal[1] was promoted in past by intercepts[2] of conservations involving Ir.....n officials.

1.(رِوِرسال: نقص- برگشت)
2. (این تر سپت : قطع کردن-جداشدن)

- Highly classified operation, which led to one of the biggest reversals in the history of US nuclear intelligence. On Tuesday termed a great discovery that led to the reversal.

رِوِرسال : نقض، برگشت، واژگون سازي واژگوني

- There is no any record of any violence or physical altercations with any members of the staff. (ستیزه- مجادله- مباحثه)

(Altercate: ستیزه کردن- مجادله/مباحثه کرد)

- One inmate died after being subdued: with a stun gun, while the other was killed by fellow prisoners. (ساب do: مطیع یا مقهور ساختن)

subdue–verb (used with object), -dued, -du·ing.
1. to conquer and bring into subjection: Rome subdued Gaul.

2. to overpower by superior force; overcome.

- As estimated 2.38 million people were incarcerated[1] in state and Federal facilities. 1.(این کارسریت : زندانی کردن- توقیف کردن- نگاه داشتن)

  Detention[2] : 2.(بازداشت)

  (detention facilities بازداشتگاه)

  <Immigration detention facilities had the greatest growth rate last year.>

  ***incarcerate*–verb (used with object)** این کارسریت

  1. to imprison; confine. 2. to enclose; constrict closely.

- The date reflects deep racial disparities in the nation's correctional institutions. (دیس پَرتی : تفاوت کلی- بی شباهتی جمع واژه disparity)

  ***disparity*–noun, plural -ties.** دیس پَرتی

  lack of similarity or equality; inequality; difference: a disparity in age; disparity in rank.

- Police officials- as two shitte factions the Mehdi Army and Badr organization دسته بندی- گروه هواخواهان- تیم هوادار یکدیگر

- Terrorism that would surely followed any attack that did not destroy the regime utterly. (آتِر لی : کاملا- بطورکلی)

- Moratorium would freeze interest rates for final years. Only loans for owner-occupied homes would be eligible. (مُورا تو ری یوم : مهلت قانونی)

- We also need to be absolutely resolved in our desire to see the nascent sign of hope across Iraq. نَ سِنت: زائیده شونده- نوظهور

  <Her nascent singing career or a nascent middle class >

  Nascency : نوظهوری- آغاز پیدایش یا رشد

  ***nascent* –adjective,** beginning to exist or develop: the nascent republic.

- Head of the city said Mr. Gates' visit probably spurred the attack. (اس پِرد: مهمیز- سیخ- انگیزه- تحریک کردن)

  <Wearing spur>,<Having one or more spurs>

- UCI physic professor Roger to be an absentminded[1] tinkerer[2]

  1. (اَب سِنت مایند د: فراموشکار، حواس پرت) ,2.(تین کِرِر: بندزن- تعمیرکار)

absentminded **–adjective** <*Always tinkering with his car.*>
so lost in thought that one does not realize what one is doing, what is happening, etc.; preoccupied to the extent of being unaware of one's immediate surroundings.
UCI : *University of California in Irvine*

- Typical ownership tenure of losses was two years.

tenure: the act, right manner or (تن یور: تصرف- نگهداری- مدت اجار ه)

- Obama evoked the memory of President Kennedy and his Peace Corps volunteers. (احضار کردن- در حقوق یعنی به دادگاه بالاتر بردن)

evoke: conjure, evoke evil spirits, to create imaginatively, to bring to mind or recollection. <*this place evoke memories*>

- When the mortgage brokers originated the loans, it was done in accordance with the bank's guidelines.(اُری جی نیت : بوجودآوردن- موجب شدن)

- Instead of assimilating me to the system, they are alienating me. (اَسِی می لیت : یکسان و شبیه کردن) (اِ لیه نت : بیگانه کردن)

alien: بیگانه-اجنبی

alienate : To cause to become withdrawn or unresponsive; isolate or dissociate emotionally: <*The numbing labor tended to alienate workers.*>

- I believe the big banks need to look in the mirror to see who the real culprits are with the mortgage loan debacle.

(کال پرِت: مقصر- متهم) (دی بَکِل: مصیبت بزرگ)

debacle: دی بَکِل a great disaster, a complete failure
<*Please do so but only on the actual culprits and not on mortgage broker as a whole.*>

- Cuban police said church to expel[1] . dissidents[2]

1.(اِکس پِل : بیرون کردن- خارج کردن) 2. (دِیسی دِنت : مخالف عقیده عموم)

expel **–verb (used with object)**, -pelled, -pel·ling.
1. to drive or force out or away; discharge or eject: to expel air from the lungs; to expel an invader from a country.

2. to cut off from membership or relations: to expel a student from a college.

***dissident*–noun** دیسی دِنت : مخالف عقیده عموم
1. a person who dissents.
–adjective
2. disagreeing or dissenting, as in opinion or attitude: a ban on dissident magazines.

- Every night millions of young new generation are engaged in subversive[1] and in some case Scandalous[2] activity.

1.(سابِرِ سیو : واژگون سازنده) 2 . (اس کَن دِلِس: افتضاح آور- ننگ آور- تهمت آمیز)

***scandalous* –adjective** اس کَن دِلِس (*Subversion*=انهدام-واژگون سازی)
1. disgraceful; shameful or shocking; improper: scandalous behavior in public.
2. defamatory or libelous, as a speech or writing.
3. attracted to or preoccupied with scandal, as a person: a scandalous, vicious gossip.
scandalous: libelous, defamatory <*scandalous allegation*>

- ***defamatory***: <*a libellous statement* افترا آمیز- بدنام کننده>

libelous :لای بِ لِس با دو ال LL هم صحیح است یعنی افترآمیز-بدنام کننده

- It's become the preferred way to conduct political and cultural discourse[1]. filling the gap left by the dearth[2] . of free and independent media.

1.(: کمیابی- گرانی) 2 (دِرث : سخنرانی کردن- اداکردن- درس گفتن)

dearth: An inadequate supply; scarcity; lack: <*There is a dearth of good engineers.*>

- One government intended to launch a campaign to make young women adhere[1] strictly[2] to the Islamic dress code.

1.(پیوستن- طرفدار یا هواخواه بودن)
2.(اکیدا"، سخت، دقیقا)

- One false report, claiming that gasoline rationing had been postponed for a day, led to mile-long lines of vehicles at service stations across the country. (رَشنینگ : جیره بندی کردن)

- Because the violation was inadvertent and had been corrected.

(این اِدوِرتِنت : غیر عمدی- بی ملاحظه)

inadvertently: سهوا- بطورغیرعمدی

inadvertent **–adjective** این اِدورتنت
1. unintentional: an inadvertent insult.
2. not attentive; heedless.

- This notion of brokers being responsible is purely idiotic =foolish

(ادی‌اُ یا تیک : سبک مغز-ابلهانه)

Idiotic= showing complete back of thought or common sense.

idiotic **–adjective** اِدی‌اُ یا تیک
1. of, pertaining to, or characteristic of an idiot.
2. senselessly foolish or stupid: an idiotic remark.

- Be suspicious; be leery of email with requests for personal identifying information. (لِری: ناقلا- مواظب- باهوش و با احتیاط)

Often used with *of* → <*leery of strangers*

- Clinton cranks up rhetoric (کرَنک : پیچ خوردن- وسواس داشتن در سخنرانی)

(رِ تو رِک : علم معانی و بیان) or → (The act of speaking or writing effectively)

rhetoric ***–noun*** رِ تو رِک : علم معانی و بیان
1. (in writing or speech) the undue use of exaggeration or display; bombast.
2. the art or science of all specialized literary uses of language in prose or verse, including the figures of speech. **3.** the study of the effective use of language.

- An immigrant rights groups is the latest in a flurry of challenges filed against US citizenship and immigration services.

(فلوری : گردباد- آشفتگی- سراسیمگی)

- Nelson: plea deal accepted to spare victims from ordeal.

(اسپِر : چشم پوشی کردن- بخشیدن) (اُرِ دیل : زمایش سخت-امتحان با عذاب جسمی)

ordeal ***–noun*** اُرِ دیل :
1. any extremely severe or trying test, experience, or trial.
2. a primitive form of trial to determine guilt or innocence by subjecting the accused person to fire, poison, or other serious danger, the result being regarded as a divine or preternatural judgment.

- "It hasn't culminated yet" he said. (کال م نیت : به اوج رسیدن- منجرشدن)

culminate–verb (used without object) کال م نیت
1. to reach the highest point, summit, or highest development (usually fol. by *in*).

2. to end or arrive at a final stage (usually fol. by *in*):
The argument culminated in a fistfight.
3. to rise to or form an apex; terminate (usually fol. by *in*):
The tower culminates in a tall spire. **4.** *A rock song culminates the performance.*

- How to grow snap dragon flowers? گل میمون
- Defying a threat of a presidential vote. بی اعتنایی/مخالفت/مقاومت کردن
- defy: تحریک به جنگ- مخالفت کردن

propagate → زیاد کردن- تکثیر کردن- در گیاه قلمه زدن
propagation تکثیر- افزایش (نوع جانور یا گیاه)

- In the resulting political atmosphere which rests atop* a general antipathy to war. (اَن تی پَ تی: تنفر طبیعی)

atop*= on, to, at the top :(اِتاپ)
antipathy: opposition in feeling اَن تی پَ تی: تنفر طبیعی

- In broad terms, one line of policy considers perpetuating[1] the Iraqi regime in power by continuing with the policy of appeasement.[2]

The consequence of appeasing Hitler was not peace, but World War II. The indisputable[3] fact after three decades of appeasement[2] in that regime in ..?...

1.(پِر پِ چُو 8 : ابدی کردن- دائمی کردن) **2.**(اَپیز مِنت : فرونشانی- تسکین)

3.(این دیس پیو تِبِل : بی چون و چرا، بطور غیر قابل بحث)

- Rather, a prolonged policy of appeasement would ultimately and inevitably drag the world into another war because leniency

(اَپیز مِنت : فرونشانی- تسکین) (لی نی یَن سی : آسان گیری- نرمی- مدارا)

- In the face of provocative acts renders diplomacy ineffective and paves the way for war. (پُرو وُکی تیو : محرک- انگیزه)
(رِندِر : نمودن- بجاآوردن- ثابت کردن)

<To render assistance > همراهی کردن

- I looked at my trembling legs, I couldn't go forward. (ترِ مبِل: لرزنده)

- Therefore the idea that the west would evade the risk of going into war with Iran (*The Regime*) by adopting a conciliatory approach is nothing but a chimera.

(E ویِد : طفره رفتن- گریززدن- خود را به کوچه علی چپ زدن)
(کان سی لیِه توری : صلح آمیز) (کای مِرا: قسمی جانورافسانه ای- لولو- وهم)

- New York Times: The most realistic option for the Iranian dilemma is new elections for presidency. (دِ لِ ما : مسئله غامض، وضع دشوار)

A dilemma is a difficult situation in which you have to choose between two or more alternatives. < *It put me in a difficult moral dilemma.*>

- It's most palatable version is propounded by advocates* of the democratic Iranian resistance. (پَ لِ تبِل: پسندیده-خوش آیند)
(ورژن : ترجمه زبان دیگر) (پْروپاند : مطرح/پیشنهاد/ارائه کردن)

*(اَد وُ کیت : طرفداري كردن حامي، طرفدار)

version: *a form or variant of a type or original,*
<An experimental version of the airplane>

- However, the tangible consequences of heeding their recommendation render it anything but peaceful, for two main reasons.

(تن جِ بل : قابل لمس، محسوس)
(هید : اعتناء- محل گذاشتن- توجه کردن به) (رِندِر : انجام دادن- ارائه دادن)

a. (*To pay attention*), **b**. (*Take heed of what you say*: ملتفت باشید چه می گویید)
Account rendered (بموجب صورت حسابی که قبلا داده شده)

- One could nonetheless→ (*same as* ***never****theless*) discern a striking resemblance between the 21st century Iraq dilemma and Europe's Nazi predicament of the 1930s.

(نان دِ لِس : باوجود اینکه- با این وصف- معهذا) (دی سِرن : تشخیص دادن- درک کردن- باچشم دیدن)
(پیری دِکِ منت : حالت ناگوار- وضع بد)

< *Discern* right from wrong>

***predicament* ---noun** پیری دِکِ منت
An unpleasantly difficult, perplexing, or dangerous situation.

- Thank to Robert for his discerning critique and the excellent work of his wife Nancy. (دی سر نینگ: تشخیص دادن)

***discerning* -adjective** دی سر نینگ:تشخیص دادن
showing good or outstanding judgment and understanding:
a discerning critic of French poetry.

- Because there is nothing worse than bitterness and vengeance.
(ون جنس: کینه جویی-انتقام)

<*To take vengeance on a person* از کسی انتقام کشیدن >

- I smelled my grandma's bosom it smelled good. I will never forget it. (بوزَم: آغوش- بغل)

- The ideas, procedures and suggestions in this book are not intended to replace the services of trained health professional.
(بدون انی دی: قصدداشتن-خیال داشتن)

- Depriving[1] us all of the rich experience of interacting[2] with other generations

1. (محروم کردن) 2 . (در میان هم کارکردن)
Interact: آنتراک- فاصله میان دو پرده

- National alliances of soviet citizens (NASC) goals are accomplished through lobbing in congress making sure member's voices are heard on key issues concerning them.
(لاَب : لایحه ای که با اسرار نمایندگان پس کنند)

lobbying (also Lobby) is a form of advocacy with the intention of influencing decisions made by legislators and officials in the government by individuals, other legislators, constituents, or advo...

- My natural optimism[1] just leads me to be skeptical[2].
1.(آپ تِ می زم : خوش بین) 2 .(اِس کِپ تی کال: ادم شکاک)

***skeptical* -adjective** اِس کِپ تی کال: ادم شکاک
1. inclined to skepticism; having doubt: *a skeptical young woman.*
2. showing doubt: *a skeptical smile.*

3. denying or questioning the tenets of a religion: *a skeptical approach to the nature of miracles.*

- Some people more circumspect took the shelter in the basement of big hotels well-known for their safety. (سِر کامْ S پِکت: ملاحظه کار- باملاحظه)

circumspect ***–adjective*** : سِر کام S پکت

1. watchful and discreet; cautious; prudent: *circumspect behavior.*
2. well-considered: *circumspect ambition.*

- The 10 predicaments→ pre دیکِ منت : مقولات ده گانه ارسطو
There are **ten predicaments** or categories: *substance, quantity, relation, quality, action, passion, time, place, posture, habiliment.* **...**

- Saturday is the Jewish Sabbath. سَبث
(این روزی است که کلیمی ها ازجمعه تا عصر شنبه را برای استراحت و عبادت در نظرگرفته)

- When their home was completely destroyed by boom, I could feel that she was discreetly pulling me away. (دیس کِریتلی : محتاطانه- بصیرانه)
discreet: → باالحتیاط-باخرد
- *aggression*: *on that commits (مرتکب شدن) or practices aggression**
*(تجاوز-تخطی)

<Aggression upon others' rights تجاوز به حقوق دیگران >
aggressor: تجاوزکار- حمله کننده
aggress: تجاوز کردن- تعرض کردن

- bureaucrat : a member of a bureaucracy
بی یو - راکْ- راسی: رعایت تشریفات اداري بحدافراط ، کاغذ پراني
(بی یو ری کِرَت: کسی که می خواهد به نفوذ و اهمیت اداره خود بیفزاید)

- Traditionally, when a girl gets married, the husband is supposed to pay her a dowry. (دَاری : جهیزیه)

A woman's dowry is the money or goods which her family give to the man that she marries. *Excessive dowry demands can have tragic results for young brides.*

- Hitting the principal was a veritable crime.. (وِری تِ بِل : واقعی- حسابی ، بحقیقت)

veritable ***–adjective*** وِری تِ بِل

1. being truly or very much so: *a veritable triumph.*
2. *Obsolete* . true, as a statement or tale.

- If you wear neckties that dreaded symbol of the west.
  dread: *to fear greatly….* (دِرِد: ترسیدن)
- Showing off her Buffy thighs to them. (تایز: رانها)
- ***stingray*** **=large sharp barbed dorsal* (پـشتـی) *spines* (برآمدگی تیز)
  *(یک نوع ماهی پهن با برآمدگی تیز پشتی)
- cauterize: (کاتورایز :داغ کردن- سوزاندن زخم), *<Cauterize a wound>*

- *Fundamentalist: a movement or attitude stressing strict and literal adherence to a set of basic principles.* *<name any religion fundamentalism>*

فاند مِن تآ لیست : کسیکه نسبت بکتاب مقدس واصول دین پروتستان طرفدارعقایدکهنه است

As for her fundamentalist husband who drank himself into a stupor[1] every night, now he uses mouthwash every time he utters[2] the word "alcohol". 1.(اس توپر: کرختی- گیجی) 2.(آتِر: اداکردن- گفتن)
<A drunken stupor>

utter** --- **verb (used with object) آتِر
1. to give audible expression to; speak or pronounce: *unable to utter her feelings; Words were uttered in my hearing.*
2. to give forth (cries, notes, etc.) with the voice: *to utter a sigh.*

- We are overwhelmed. (مستغرق در فکر- درفکر فرورفتن- دست پاچه شدن)
  <Overwhelm with reflection> (انعکاس- بازتاب- تفکر)
  overwhelming فشارآور- سخت- زیاد-از سردر رونده
  Have you seen all the casualties ? (کَژُالتیز: قضا و بلا در جمع تلافات و زخمی ها)

- The streets are packed with nuptial*(نَپ شال) chambers.**
  *(نکاحی- یا چیزهای مربوط به مراسم ازدواج)
  **(اتاق- خوابگاه)
- In August 11 my wife abruptly planned a vacation. (ناگهانی)
  abrupt =تند- ناگهان

- The dead man can symbolically attain carnal knowledge. (کارنال: شهوانی)
  با knowledge به معنی بغل خوابی و جماع است

سیم بالیک لی :نمادي ، حاکي، دال بر

Marked by sexuality <carnal love>, worldly <a carnal mind>, For unlawful carnal...

- I remember my initiation* it was the first day of class after summer vacation. ..
*(آغاز- شروع- آشناسازی)

Initiate تازه وارد کردن- آغاز کردن- شروع کردن
Initiator پیشقدم- مبتکر
Initiative پیشقدمی- نخستین قدم- قوه ابتکار

- hypnotize (هیپنو تایز): *to induce[1] hypnosis[2] in........*
induce = to move by persuasion or influence
1 . (این دُس : یعنی اغوا کردن- وادارکردن) 2.(هیپ نوسِس : هیپنوتیسم، خواب مصنوعي)

پرسوُ ای ژن : قانع سازي- تشويق، تحريک

- Hitting yourself is one of the country's rituals[1] during certain religious ceremonies, some people flagellated[2] themselves brutally[3].
< Pertaining to or caused by flagellates>

1.(ریچو آل : مراسم عبادت)
2.(فِل جی لِیت : شلاق زدن)
3.(برُتلی : وحشیانه)

- A glimpse* of what goes on in our house would be enough for them to denounce** us.
*(نگاه آنی- نظر اجمالی)
** (خبردادن از- اشاره کردن)

At a glimpse : → به یک نظر به یک اشاره

- To be an unmarried mother in this country you will be shunned(شانْد), life will be hell.
(شان: پرهیز کردن از- دوری کردن)

- The proletarian shall rule! پرولِتِرین: مربوط به گروه رنجبران- کارگر- مزدور - فقیر
proletarian: *a member of the proletariat.*

- You really are an enigma to me! (اِ نیگما: معما- رمز)
Enigmatic or enigmatical معمائی- مبهم
enigma: *an obscure speech or writing sometimes hard to understand or explain*

- We are the deliverer of divine justice! (دی واین: خدائی- الهی- مقدس)

- Later on we learned they crossed the border hidden among a flock of sheep. (یک گله گوسفند).

- I decided to go home, I got a false passport and disguised myself.
  disguise = disfigure (دیس گایز : لباس مبدل- تغییر قیافه)

- My great dream *went up in smoke*. I wouldn't be able to go to USA.

- Man who waits for roast duck to fly into mouth must wait very very long time. *Chinese Proverb*

- The educational system and what is written in school books at levels, are decadent.
  decadent. دِکِدِنت :زایل شونده- پس رونده
  decadence : دِکِدِنس : زوال- فساد

- ***ludicrous***: *amusing or laughable through obvious absurdity incongruity), exaggeration or*
  (اَبسِر دِ تی :حرف محال- حرف نامربوط), (این کان گُرو اِتی : ناجوری- ناشایستی- ناسازگاری- بی تناسبی)
  (اِگزَ جِری شِن : اغراق- مبالغه)
  جمع این چهار کلمه با ies است

  (اِک سِن 3 سیتی:گار غریب- در هندسه دوری یا خروج از مرکز. *eccentricity*)
  (اغراق امیز- گزاف گو- مبالغه کننده *exaggerative*)

- Women's hair emanates rays that excite man.
  (اِم نی تس: ناشی شدن - سرچشمه گرفتن)

  اگر emanate از یک منبع درآید مثل جمله بالا معنی سرچشمه گرفتن میدهد
  <A sweet scent emanating from the blossoms.>

- Dynasties have succeeded each other but the kings always kept their promises. (دای نِستیز : سلسله- دودمان)
  dynasty مفرد کلمهء فوق ←

- He is another martyr شهید :مارتِر

martyr: a person who willingly suffers death rather than renounce* his or her religion. *(انکار کردن، سرزنش یا متهم کردن)

- cummerbund or kamarband تلفظ هر دو کامِر باند است یعنی : کمربند

cummerbund ***-noun***
A wide sash worn at the waist, esp. a horizontally pleated one worn with a tuxedo.

- I went to his clandestine (*marked by*) looking with my mother.
  <*A clandestine love affair.* > (کِ لَن دِستِن:پنهانی- زیرجلی)

- surreptitious (سه رِپ تی شِس : پنهانی- محرمانه) = done, made, or acquired
  stealth : (اِس تِلث)حرکت دزدانه یا پنهانی

surreptitious ***-adjective*** سه رِپ تی شِس
1. obtained, done, made, etc., by stealth; secret or unauthorized; clandestine: *a surreptitious glance.* **2.** acting in a stealthy way. **3.** obtained by subreption; subreptitious.

- Shah and Sadam's statues[1] were torn down, and then their effigies were burned.

1.(اِس تَ چی اوس: مجسمه) (اِف جی : پیکر)

status (اِس تِ تِس): The candidation of a person or thing in the eye of the law,
< *the status of the negotiations*>

statues & status اسپل اینها بسیار شبیه به هم است اما متفاوت تلفظ می شوند.←
statute → <*Statue* اِس تَ چی اوُت *of limitations* قانون مرور زمان>

- expatriate: banish, exile (x پی تِ ریت : به کشور دیگری تبعید کردن)
  <To expatriate oneself ترک تابعیت کردن >

- Satrap the governor of a provenance in ancient Persia
  (سی تِرَپ :فرماندار یک محدوده از ایران را سارتراپ می گویند)

پُر اوِ نِنس : منشاء، اصل، حد منطقه قدرت- محدوده

provenance ***-noun*** پُر اوِ نِنس
place or source of origin: *The provenance of the ancient manuscript has never been determined.*

- But my mother arrived in the middle of our euphoria[1] .

It means a feeling of well-being or elation[2].
Elate :پرباد-مغرور سربلند، بالا بردن

1.(یوفوریا : رضامندي، خوشي، خوشحالي رضايت)
2.(الی شِن : بالابري، رفعت، ترفيع سرفرازي شادي)

***elate*-- verb**, to make very happy or proud: news to elate the hearer.

- His crime was: wrote subversive articles in the newspaper

subversive: واژگون سازنده
Subvert: واژگون ساختن- برانداختن
Subversion: انهدام- سرنگونی

- Time is irretrievable: (E ری 3 و بِل : برنگشتنی-غیرقابل استرداد-جبران ناپذیر)

irretrievable –adjective , not retrievable; irrecoverable; irreparable.

- He always had cyanide on him in case he was arrested.

(سایو نایِد: قرص سیا نور)

- *Don't be a wimp*: weak, cowardly or ineffectual person.

- Idiotic showing complete lack of thought or common sense: *foolish*
(ای دی یا تیک : سفیه- احمق- سبک مغز), < *an idiotic remark*>
- As a member of the guerillas he suffered hell. (جنگ غیررسمی یا نظامی)

- The next morning I was so tormented. (تورمنت: عذاب دادن- زجر- آزاردادن)

- The most realistic option for the Iraqi dilemma is regime change. It's most palatable* version is propounded** by advocates*** of the democratic Iraqi resistance. *Propounder*: → مطرح کننده

*(پَ لِ تَ بِل: خوش آیند-پسندیده) **(مطرح کردن- ارائه دادن) ***(حمایت کردن)

celestial light : (سه لِس شال: نور آسمانی یا بهشتی)

<*The sun, moon, and stars are celestial bodies*>
<*Yes you are celestial light* . > نورآسمانی یا بهشتی

- I will be your first disciple . (دی سای پُل: شاگرد-زید)

nonetheless = nevertheless, نانذ لِس: باوجود این- با این وصف-معهذا

I want to be justice, love and wrath of god all in one. راث: خشم و غضب

wrath: strong vengeful anger or indignation or retribution punishment for an offense or crime
wrathful خشمگین-غضب ناک

- *vengeful*: ونج فول : کینه جو
  Desiring or seeking vengeance; vindictive: <*a vengeful attitude.*>

- 2500 years of tyranny* and submission**
  *(حکومت ستمگری- ظلم و جور و استبداد) **(فرمانبرداری و اطاعت- تسلیم- واگذاری)

- Once he was sidetracked* from his princely destiny, he began to meet intellectuals. *(دوراهی- روی خط فرعی افتادن)
  Since his entourage was uneducated. (آن توراژ: اطرافیان- همراه)
  <*The opera singer traveled with an entourage of 20 people.*>

entourage **–noun** آن توراژ
1. a group of attendants or associates, as of a person of rank or importance: The opera singer traveled with an entourage of 20 people.
2. surroundings; environment: a house with a charming entourage of trees and flowers.
3. Architecture . the landscaping and other nearby environmental features shown on a rendering of a building.

- *destiny:* A predetermined course of events considered as something beyond human power or control: <*"Marriage and hanging go by destiny"*>

- It disgusts* me that people are condemned** to a bleak*** future by their social class.
  *(متنفر یا بیزار کردن), ** (محکوم کردن) ***(سرد و بی پناه),

---

- Orange County man makes him reality-television debut under the direction of the self-proclaimed world's first supermodel: a formal entrance into society.
  (دیب یو: آغاز کار- نخستین مرحله دخول در بازی یا جامعه شروع بکار کردن)

debut: دیب یو a first public appearance on a stage, on television, etc.
debutant (دیب یو تانت): <*Debutante ball*>, < *How to become a debutant*>
دختری که برای اولین بار وارد جامعه شده- تازه کار

- It stipulates that if consent is not obtained by that time either party will be entitled to cancel the agreement. (اِس تی پیو لِیت : شرط / قید کردن)

- The profoundly* deaf may require auditory assistance and physical therapy following cochlear** implant surgery. *(گود- عمیق- سنگین)
**(کوک لی یر: یک لوله خالی داخل گوش)

To evade a question → خود را به کوچه علی چپ زدن

- There was another cadaver an old man carried out on a stretcher.
(کَدوِر:لاشه- نعش-مرده)

- Therefore the idea that the west would evade[1] the risk of going into war with mullah regime by adopting a conciliatory[2] approach is nothing but a chimera[3]

1 (اِنی وید : طفره زدن از) 2(کَان سی لیه توری: استمالت امیز- صلح آمز
3.(کای مِی را: قسمی جانور افسانه ای- لولو- وهم)

evade ***–verb (used with object)*** اِنی وید : طفره زدن از
1. to escape from by trickery or cleverness: *to evade one's pursuers.*
2. to get around by trickery: *to evade rules.*
3. to avoid doing or fulfilling: *to evade an obligation.*
4. *to evade a question. The solution evaded him.* to practice evasion.

chimera **–noun**, plural -ras. کای مِی را: قسمی جانور افسانه ای- لولو- وهم
A horrible or unreal creature of the imagination; a vain or idle fancy: He is far different from the chimera your fears have made of him.

- Rather a prolonged policy of appeasement would ultimately and inevitably drag the world into another war because leniency in the face of provocative acts renders diplomacy infective and paves the way for war.
(اَپیز مِنت : فرونشانی- تسکین) (این اِ وِتِ بِلی : بناچار- ناچار) (لی نی n -c : نرمی- ملایمت- مدارا)

(پُرو وُکِ تیو : محرک، برانگیزنده، عصباني کننده) (رِندِر : نمودن- بجاآوردن- ثابت کردن)
(این فِکتیو : آلوده یا عفونی کننده) (پیوز :ش کردن- جاده را مساعد کردن)

- Holiday hustle→ (جلوانداختن- عجله-شتاب), Hustler: → کلاه بردار- اغواکننده

<Hustling up new customers>, <hustling the suckers>,
<hustling new products>

hustle: to make strenuous efforts to obtain money or business, or to obtain money by fraud or deception. (اس ترَن یو اِس: با حرارت-مصر)

strenuous ---**adjective** :اس ترَن یو اِس
1. characterized by vigorous exertion, as action, efforts, life, etc.: a strenuous afternoon of hunting.
2. demanding or requiring vigorous exertion; laborious:
To think deeply is a strenuou task.

- righteous: acting in accord with divine or moral law. Free from guilt or sin,
  <*a righteous decision*>, رای چس : نیکوکار- عادل – صالح
  <*"She was a righteous victim and I left bad for her".*>
  <*righteous indignation* خشم- غیظ- اظهار تنفر- اوقات تلخی : این دیگ نی شِن >

- Prosecutors* said they had no recourse** but to close the most notorious*** missing person case in the Los Angeles.
  *(تعقیب کننده- وکیل عمومی) , **(توسل- مراجعه) ,***(بدنام-رسوا)
  public prosecutor: داد ستان- مدعی العموم
  notoriety: انگشت نمایی- رسوایی- بدنامی

- It was an overwhelming experience. She was emotionally overwhelm.
  (فشار آوردن- زیاد از سر رونده - مستغرق کردن)

- The basic three major monotheistic religions. (مانو تی ایستیک: مبنی بر توحید)
  monotheistic: the doctrine or belief that there is but one God
  monotheism: یکتاپرستی- توحید

- Forest Service argument rebutted. بر گرداندن، جواب متقابل دادن ، تکذیب کردن : re بات

  rebut---**Verb with Object**
  If you rebut a charge or criticism that is made against you, you say or write something which proves that it is not true; a formal word.
  I am writing this letter to rebut the suggestion that I have failed in my duty.

- US navy accuse Iran of provocation . (تحریک- برانگیختن- انگیزش : پرُ وُکی شِن

- Already heralded by *departure magazine* as the luxury hotel for park city.
  (جِرولد د: آگاهی-خبرداده شده)

- They frantically worked all day on necessary patch. (دیوانه وار- به شدت)

- The Disney architectural explosion erupting* from the desert can seem surreal** . *(منفجرشدن) معنی دیگر آن درآمدن دندان

**(سُو رِیِل : باورنکردنی - وابسته به سوررئالیسم یا فرا راستي گرايي ، عجیب و غریب، اوهامي)

surreal = fantastic

The second meaning of surrealistic in relation with *Surrealism* = having a strange dreamlike atmosphere or quality like that of a surrealist painting surrealistically.

**(سُو رِیِل : باورنکردنی - وابسته به سوررئالیسم یا فرا راستي گرايي ، عجیب و غریب، اوهامي)

- Don't try to be omnipotent: آم نی پوتِنت: قادر مطلق

  <*an omnipotent ruler*>

- Commission abatement program ... اَبیت مِنت : تخفیف

  An amount deducted or subtracted, as from the usual price or the full tax.
- We were appalled by his behavior.

  appall= dismay-shock آپـــا ل : ترساندن- متوحش کردن

  <I was appalled at the lack of due professional care in this transaction.>

- In particular, my Cosmic posting philosophy will be precisely the same as my Preposterous posting philosophy has been……

  Pre پاس تِرِس: نامعقول- مضحک- افتضاح

  Preposterous means contrary to nature

  <*When I reviewed there documents I noted that she had been charged for rent back which was preposterous.*>

- I am not compelled to take responsibility for incident as there was no prior knowledge of the circumstances.

  کام پِل : مجبور کردن- وادار کردن

  ***compel*–verb** (used with object)

  1. to force or drive, esp. to a course of action: His disregard of the rules compels us to dismiss him.
  2. to secure or bring about by force. 3. to force to submit; subdue. 4. to overpower.

- Real estate would be the economic linchpins of the future.

  (لینچ پِن: میخ یا محور)

- These trellis designs will beautify your garden like no other structure can!
  Patio ترلیس : در منزل داربست یا مثل

- Information which is suppressed for third party users..
  (ساپ رس: متوقف کردن- بند آوردن- جلوگیری کردن)

- What Iraq is doing is pure vanity (بطالت- بیهودگی- خودبینی- باد دماغ)
  lack of real value; hollowness; worthlessness: the vanity of a selfish life.

معانی و روش بکار گیری

Take for granted or Taking for granted :

Grant: دادن بخشیدن، اهداء، بخشش، عطا، امتیاز اجازه واگذاري رسمي، کمک هزینه تحصیلي،اعطا کردن، تصدیق کردن، مسلم گرفتن، موافقت کردن

Grant –**verb** (used with object)
1. to bestow or confer, esp. by a formal act: to grant a charter.
2. to give or accord: to grant permission.
3. to agree or accede to: to grant a request.
4. to admit or concede; accept for the sake of argument: I grant that point.
5. to transfer or convey, esp. by deed or writing: to grant property.
–noun
6. something granted, as a privilege or right, a sum of money, or a tract of land: Several major foundations made large grants to fund the research project.
7. the act of granting.
8. Law . a transfer of property.
9. a geographical unit in Vermont, Maine, and New Hampshire, originally a grant of land to a person or group of people.

- **idiom:** Take for granted,

  a. to accept without question or objection; assume:
  <Your loyalty to the cause is taken for granted.>
  b. to use, accept, or treat in a careless or indifferent manner:
  c. *<A marriage can be headed for trouble if either spouse begins to take the other for granted>*

- *Taking something for granted*, **Ex:**
  < upon losing my home, I realized I had taken my assets and estate's value for granted.>

  Things we **take for granted** Just Talk ...
  I was thinking about the many things that we tend to **take for granted** that many people don't have in this world.
  Hot running water; TV; Radio; Lots of food available; Homes; Good transportation;
  That's just a few things that we tend to **take for granted** there are also things we no...

- take for granted:
  assume something is a certain way or is correct
  I took it for granted that you knew him. Otherwise I would have introduced you. تقلید از چیزی

  take someone or something for granted:

  to expect someone or something to be always available to serve in some way without thanks or recognition; to value someone or something too lightly.
  I wish you didn't take me for granted. I guess that I take a lot of things for granted.

- **take somebody for granted**
  to not show that you are grateful to someone for helping you or that you are happy they are with you, often because they have helped you or been with you so often *One of the problems with relationships is that after a while you begin to take each other for granted.*

- **take something for granted** to expect something to be available all the time and forget that you are lucky to have it *We take so many things for granted in this country - like having hot water whenever we need it.*

- **take somebody for granted**
  to fail to appreciate someone *When your own children are growing up, you tend to take them for granted, and then, suddenly, they are grown up. Politicians seem to take voters for granted, except when they face a serious challenge.*

Usage notes: usually said about someone who is not appreciated because you think they will always be available.

- **take something for granted** to fail to appreciate the value of something *So many of us take clean water for granted* to accept something as true without questioning or testing it *We take it for granted that our children will be better off than we are.* Opposite of: not *take anything for granted*

- **Idiom Definitions for 'Take for granted'** *If you take something for granted, you don't worry or think about it because you assume you will always have it. If you take someone for granted, you don't show your appreciation to them*

Hi, I could not get the meaning and function of "by definition and *take for granted, taken for granted*", please help me thanks in advance

By definition:

Immigrants are seemed to be regarded by definition as a burden on society, but his could not be further from the truth.
In other words some people seem to think of all immigrants to be like this without looking at individual cases. They refuse to think of individuals when it comes to immigrants and think they are all alike.

taken for granted:

Sometimes I feel taken for granted when I get no thanks for being a volunteer at this organization.
In other words you don't feel you are being appreciated for working there and people are just using you.

<My son takes for granted that I will allow him unlimited use of the computer>
In other words my son believes that he has the right to use the computer any time he wants and I should not interfere.

- Could you fix light in hallway! It's been flickering for a week now.
< Candle flicking in the window> (فـ لِ کِـرینگ : سوسوکننده- لرزش)

flicker **–verb** (used without object)
1. to burn unsteadily; shine with a wavering light: The candle flickered in the wind and went out.
2. to move to and fro; vibrate; quiver: The long grasses flickered in the wind. **3**. to flutter.
–verb (used with object); **4**. to cause to flicker.
–noun **5**. an unsteady flame or light. a flickering movement.

- He is as giddy* as two-year old son Tomas, who's frolicking** on the private beach of the family's palatial*** new-residence.

* (گی دی : گیج کردن- گیج شدن) ,**(فِرالیک : خوشی- شادمانی)
*** (پِ لِی شال: کاخ مانند- باشکوه)

frolick **–noun** : فِرالیک
1. merry play; merriment; gaiety; fun. **2.** a merrymaking or party.
3. playful behavior or action; prank.
–verb (used without object); **4.** to gambol merrily; to play in a frisky, light-spirited manner; romp: *The children were frolicking in the snow.*

- He moved into 5000 square foot, three weeks earlier and remain exchanged by serenity* of their cosmopolitan** community.

*(سِرِ نِ تی : آرامش- سکوت و صفا) **(کازما پالی تَن : وابسته به همه جای جهان)

serenity ----**noun**, plural -ties. سِرِ نِ تی
1. the state or quality of being serene, calm, or tranquil; sereneness.
2. (usually initial capital letter) a title of honor, respect, or reverence, used in speaking of or to certain members of royalty (usually prec. by his, your, etc.).

cosmopolitan –**adjective** کازما پالی تَن : وابسته به همه جای جهان
1. free from local, provincial, or national ideas, prejudices, or attachments; at home all over the world. **2**. of or characteristic of a cosmopolite.
3. belonging to all the world; not limited to just one part of the world.
–noun 4. a person who is free from local, provincial, or national bias or attachment; citizen of the world; cosmopolite.

- Addendum* to purchase contract for structural investigation and fortification ** work. *(ضمیمه), **(استحکام- تقویت)

- All information necessary for buyer to complete the transaction contemplated by the purchase contract has been provided to buyer satisfaction. در نظر داشتن – اندیشه کردن

- You may be aware of volatility in the mortgage market, وا لاتی لی تی فرار- سبک
Volatility means unexpectable change, <*A volatile (وآلاتو) market*>

volatile **–adjective** وا لاتی لی تی فرار- سبک
1. evaporating rapidly; passing off readily in the form of vapor: Acetone is a volatile solvent.

2. tending or threatening to break out into open violence; explosive: a volatile political situation.
3. changeable; mercurial; flighty: a volatile disposition.
4. volatile market conditions., volatile beauty., able to fly or flying.
–noun 5. a volatile substance, as a gas or solvent.

- It is imperative that you complete the continuing education courses you are currently enrolled in prior to February.

(امری- آمرانه- ضروری- اجباری)

---

hoarse, hoarseness.

تلفظ آن درست مثل اسب است با گرفتگی صدا و سینه با اسپل بدون a

Having a vocal tone characterized by weakness of intensity and excessive breathiness; husky: *<the hoarse voice of the auctioneer.>*

- Syria in archenemy of the USA. آر که نمی : دشمن بزرگ

archenemy **–noun**, plural -mies.
1. a chief enemy. **2**. Satan; the Devil.
<Archenemy means principle enemy.>

- Business cards not adhering to Tarbell Realtors sign specifications herein are subject to confiscation. (اَد هی یر : هواه خواه یا تابع)

adhere ----**verb** (used without object) اَد هی یر
to stay attached; stick fast; cleave; cling (usually fol. by to):
The mud adhered to his shoes.
Adherence to the following sign specification is mandatory.

اَد هی رنس : هواخواهی- پیوستگی- در اینجا یعنی تابع

adherence ***–noun*** اَد هی رنس : هواخواهی- پیوستگی- در اینجا یعنی تابع
1. the quality of adhering; steady devotion, support, allegiance, or attachment: *adherence to a party; rigid adherence to rules.*
2. the act or state of adhering; adhesion.

- Clay soil probably causes more consternation among gardeners than any other soil type. کانس تر نی شِن: آشفتگی

- Well aerated soil. اِ ریت د: خاک خوب هوا داده شده

Aerated or aerating = to supply or impregnate* (*as the soil or a liquid*) with air. (*انیم پرِگ نِنت : ابستن کردن، لقاح کردن اشباع کردن - بارور کردن)

impregnate---If you impregnate something with a substance, you make the substance pass into it and spread through it.
...paper that has been impregnated with chemicals.

- Who knows what kind of maniacs there buyers are! Who knows what kind of maniac this buyer is. (مِی نی اِک : آدم دیوانه/مفرد)

- In Russia Mr. Kasparov* says the Kremlin finessed** him out of presidential race. *(اسم رقیب پوتین), **(فِ نِس: زیرکی- حیله و زرنگی)

- An even formidable power broker in Iraq. فُور میدِبِل : سنگین- مهیب- نیرومند
  <A *formidable lion* شیر نیرومند>

- Former Vice President Al Gore blames US for Bali stalemate, a drawing position in chess in which a player is not in checkmate but has no longer legal move to play. (s تِیل مِیت : پات کردن)
- In USA, On Dec. 15, 1791 the Bill of Right went into effect after ratification by Virginia. تصویب- تصدیق
  ratify: تصویب/تصدیق کردن

- A real estate career can be lucrative however it is not good for everyone! لُوک رِ تیو : پرسود
- "Every one that knows me knows I couldn't be capable of such a heinous crime" he said. (هی نِس: زشت- شنیع- ظالم)
  Heinously = بطور شنیع- شریرانه

- Congregations in Orange County have volunteer guards, some of them armed.
  (کان گِ رِ گی شن: جماعت- گروه- گردآمدگی)
  Congregate: جمع شدن- جمع کردن

- Surgery achieved with only small incisions. این سِ ژن : برش- بریدگی- چاک
  incise : (این سایز : بریدن- چاک دادن- کندوکاو کردن)
  In the email, Bhutto بوتو said P. Musharraf should be held complicit in her death due to his refusal to meet safety requests she had made.

(complicity: همدستی در جرم) (کام پ لِ سیت : شریک جرم)

complicit –adjective
choosing to be involved in an illegal or questionable act, esp. with others; having complicity.
complicit: association or participation in or as if in a wrongful act

---

- "Criminals should stop their despicable activities, otherwise they will have to face serious consequences" interior minister said.
  < Despicable behavior> , (دیس پ کَ بِل: پست- نکوهش پذیر)

- Argentina's new president rebukes* US and reacted furiously**
  rebuke: to criticize sharply

  *(رِب یوک: سرزنش کردن- توبیخ کردن)
  **(باخشم زیاد- دیوانه وار)

- The development is engulfed in a dispute that has dragged on for more than a year. (این گالف : غوطه ور ساختن)

- Bombers' lives were colored by despair. دیس پر : مایوس کردن- نومیدی- یاس

despair –noun دیس پر : مایوس کردن- نومیدی- یاس
1. loss of hope; hopelessness.
2. someone or something that causes hopelessness: *He is the despair of his mother.*
–verb (used without object)
3. to lose, give up, or be without hope (often fol. by *of*): *to despair of humanity.*

- Hajj begins and millions of pilgrims will descend* on Mecca to circumambulate** to Kaaba.

  *(اطاعت و تمکین کردن)
  **(سِر کام ام بی یو لِیت: دورچیزی گشتن- طواف کردن)

circumambulation → طواف

- It is demonstration of both solidarity* of Muslims and their Submission** to Allah. *(اتحاد و همبستگی- مسئولیت مشترک)
  **(تسلیم-اطاعت-فرمانبرداری)
- Driver's license is sacred. (سِیک رِد: مصون- محترم- مقدس)

- Slump will continue despite Federal expert says.

(ڈلامپ : افت- تنزل فاحش- یکباره پایین آمدن یا افتادن)

- He acknowledges that public support is lacking for increasing Afghan deployment.

(آرایش قشون یا نیرو / در نظام معنی تفرقه هم دارد)

- Radio city revives spirits. (احیاء کردن- نیروی تازه دادن)

  reviver: احیاء کننده

- "but though the increase has been dramatic[1], the market continues to recognize the propensity* for ongoing security issues and output** volatility***.

  1.(دُرُ مَ تیک : چشمگیر، نمایشي) *(تمایل طبیعی- رغبت- گرایش)

  (محصول- بازده) , *(فرار- سبک)

- House would ban waterboarding in interrogations.

  Waterboarding: is a form of torture that consists of immobilizing the victim on his or her back with the head inclined downwards, and then pouring water over the face and into the breathing passages, ...

  interrogation **–noun**

  1. the act of interrogating; questioning.

  2. an instance of being interrogated: *He seemed shaken after his interrogation.*

- Australia seen as profitable market for meth $C_{10}H_{15}N$, bought in Canada.

  meth:(*meth/am/phe/ta/mine)use for treatment of obesity* أبی سیتی : چاقی

- Red Crescent trucks were pulled up in front of hospital. کراسانت: هلال احمر

در اینجا منظورش همان هلال یا آمبولانسهای هلال احمر است که شکل کراسنت دارند

- We are terribly* strapped** at the moment.

  *(ترسناک وار- بطور مخوف) **,(با نیرو و تسمه نگهداشتن)

- He found his house ransacked. (رَن سَکد: خوب جستجو کردن)

- My brothers were in prison together during the reign of the Shah. رِین: سلطنت

***reign* –noun** رِین : سلطنت
1. the period during which a sovereign occupies the throne.
2. royal rule or authority; sovereignty. .

- Tell me the truth, are you hypocrite: (هی پو کرِت: آدم ریاکار)
hypocritically (هی پو کرِ تیک لی : ریاکارانه- از روی دو رویی)
hypocritical→ ریاکارانه- دورو

- What do I see here? Michael Jackson! That symbol of decadence[1] (دِک دِنس : زوال- فساد- تنزل).1

decadence = *the process of becoming decadent, the quality or estate of being decadent*[2] . (دِک دِنت : زایل شونده- پس رونده).2

***decadence* –noun** دِک دِنس : زوال- فساد- تنزل
The act or process of falling into an inferior condition or state; deterioration; decay: *Some historians hold that the fall of Rome can be attributed to internal decadence.*

- Opt (آپت): *to make a choice especially to decide in favor of something,*
*opt***ed** : گذشته آن آپتِد است <*opted for tax increase*>

<To keep us from forgetting that we were at war, Iraq opted for a new strategy…>
Synonyms: *select, pick, elect, prefer.*

- My uncle was a vintner, he had built a genuine wine-making lab in his basement. (وی نت نِر: عمده فروش شراب)
vintner: *a wine merchant or a person who makes wine.*

- No one dared say a word (جرات کردن)
< He did not dare to go او جرات نکرد برود >

- Naturally the regime becomes more repressive.
(رپِر سیو : جلوگیری- فرونشانی)

repressive –adjective رپِر سیو

Tending or serving to repress: *repressive laws.,* The regime's repression.

- The walls were suddenly covered with belligerent slogans.
(بِل لِ جِرِنت : جنگ دارنده- متحارب- دولت متحارب)

belligerent ***–adjective*** بِل لِ جِرِنت

1. warlike; given to waging war.
2. of warlike character; aggressively hostile; bellicose: *a belligerent tone.*
3. *a peace treaty between belligerent powers. belligerent rights.*

- The one that struck me most by its gory* imagery** was "to die a martyr is to inject blood into the veins of society"

*(GO ری :پوشیده از خون بسته)   **(E م ج re : شبیه سازی- تصورات)

- Anyone showing the slightest resistance to the regime was persecuted.

پرسه کیو ت : آزار کردن- زجر دادن- اذیت کردن
persecution : شکنجه، ازار، اذیت ، تعقیب

- She invoke her country, her family etc, etc. (این وُک : دعا کردن- طلبیدن)

invoke— این وُک ***Verb with Object***
If you invoke a law, you use it to justify what you are doing; a formal word.
The Government invoked the Emergency Powers Act.

- Sometimes it scares me how blunt she is. (بِلانت :کند- سست)

blunt **–adjective** بِلانت
1. having an obtuse, thick, or dull edge or point; rounded; not sharp: *a blunt pencil.*
2. abrupt in address or manner: *a blunt, ill-timed question.*
3. slow in perception or understanding; obtuse: *His isolation has made him blunt about the feelings of others.*

–verb (used with object)
4. to make blunt; hebetate: *He blunted the knife by using it to cut linoleum.*
5. *Wine first excites, then blunts the imagination.*

- Nuclear disarmament*   *(دیس آر مامِنت : خلع سلاحد)

disarmament: the reduction or limitation of the size, equipment, armament, etc., of the army, navy, or air force of a country.

disarm: *to deprive*[1] *of a means of attack or defense for example* <*disarm a ship*>, or <*disarm a bomb*>,
<*To deprive someone of access.*>, (deprive معزول کردن - بي بهره کردن، محروم کردن).1

- catamite*: *a boy kept by a pederast***

*(کَ تِمایت: کونی - بی ریش- ابون) , **(پِد اِ رَست: بچه باز-لواط گر)

pederast: one who practice and intercourse esp. with a boy

- As seniors ourselves we came to realize that problem become less formidable if we educate ourselves on the many conditions we face as we grew older. (دشوار- سنگین- قوی و نیرومند), *<A formidable line>*

- As we age, the waning life force along with the enemies of life presents significantly different physical problems.

wane (وین)/ *waning* (وِی نینگ) → روبکاهش و زوال گذاشتن

- Often it is traumatic to move from a secure home to a retirement community. (تْرُمَ تیک : زخمی- جراحی- ولی در اینجا معنی مرهم می دهد)

traumatic ***–adjective***
1. of, pertaining to, or produced by a trauma or wound.
2. adapted to the cure of wounds. **3.** psychologically painful.

- When we become frail (سست- کم زور- فانی- ضعیف)

- *Biennial: occurring every 2-year continuing or lasting for two years.*
(بای اِنی یال: دوسال یکبار- گیاه دوسالانه)

- We digested[1] the data, exclude much of the chaff[2].
1.(دای جست : هضم کردن ، هضم شدن، خلاصه کردن و شدن خلاصه) **2**.(شَف: کاه- پوشال- چیز بی بها)

- We hope you will find happiness and fulfillment* in spite of the adversities** of life. (بدبختی و فلاکت)** , (انجام – تکمیل- اجرا) *

adversity→ مفرد کلمه است

fulfillment: the act or state of fulfilling;
<to witness the fulfillment of a dream>, < to achieve fulfillment of one's hopes.>

- Older Woman's League has played a key leadership role in instituting public initiatives[1] around pension[2] reform.

1. (اینی شی اِی تیو : پیشقدمی- ابتکار- نخستین قدم)
2. (حقوق بازشنستگي، مقرري پانسيون، پانسيون شدن)

initiator: پیشقدم- مبتکر

***initiative*–noun** اینی شی اِی تیو: پیشقدمی- ابتکار- نخستین قدم
1. an introductory act or step; leading action: *to take the initiative in making friends.*
2. readiness and ability in initiating action; enterprise: *to lack initiative.*
3. one's personal, responsible decision: *to act on one's own initiative.*

pension ---A pension is a regular sum of money paid to someone who is old, retired, widowed, or disabled.

She and her disabled husband are currently living off a pension of just 100ه a week.... ...an old age pension.

- If you are in real estate business, it's time to develop a real business strategy.
  (دراینجا روش- فن - در جنگ :علم لشکرکشی- یا سوق الجیشی)

strategy--- A plan, method, or series of maneuvers or stratagems for obtaining a specific goal or result:
<a strategy for getting ahead in the world.

- Penalties for retailers who violate food stamp regulations may involve the forfeiture of the bond they have posted.
  (ری تی لِر : خرده فروش) (فور فی چر: جریمه- تاوان در اثر نقض تعهدات)

***forfeiture* –noun** فور فی چر
1. an act of forfeiting.
2. something that is forfeited; fine;

- To implement the program in towns and cities across the country..
  (ایم پی لی مِنت : انجام دادن- اجرا کردن)
- Agricultural implements, war implements (آلت و افزار- در جمع ساز و برگ)
- I am sympathetic to their plight given the short they were in the home prior to this unfortunate event. (پِ لایت: مخمصه- گرفتاری)
- I was disappointed by your client's assertion that I willfully withheld this information from them during the transaction.
  (اَسِر شِن : اظهارمثبت- ادعا- اثبات)
- *Proximity* (نزدیکی-جوار) <*proximity of blood* خویشاوندی-قرابت>

<Commercial/industrial proximity>

- *Methamphetamine* = *meth/am/phe/ta/mine*
  a central nervous system stimulant, $c_{10}\,h_{15}\,n$ used clinically in the treatment of narcolepsy, and for blood pressure also widely used as an illicit drug.

- protecting your mail and serving as a deterrent. (دی تِ رِنت: بازدارنده- مانع)
  <A deterrent effort or a deterrent vein of punishment>

- Steps you can take to deter detect and defend yourself against identity theft. (بازداشتن- چشم ترسیده کردن)

- Report will satisfy the statutory* obligations of the seller (قانونی)*

- For many people whose conditions are somewhat less sever, however, a variety of services are available. (قدری- تااندازه ای)

- It is the least disruptive option, *<agitators trying to disrupt the meeting>* to interrupt (in/ter/rupt) the normal course of unity... شکستگی
- I was inundated with phone calls. (سیل- طغیان)

- *Respite: a period of temporary delay or an interval of rest or relief .*
  <Some communities offer volunteer or pail respite services that provide short-term temporary care for an impaired older person. >*
  (رِس پیت: مهلت- استراحت) ,*(آسیب زدن- لطمه زدن)

  respite: Temporary suspension of the execution of a person condemned to death; reprieve.

- These services are for the chronically* ill or incapacitated**
  *(کرُآ نیک لی:دائمی-همیشگی) , **(فاقد صلاحیت)

- *Chore services: the regular or daily light work of a householder or farm, or a routine task or job.*

- Adult day care center are for elderly persons who are ambulatory but who need supervision during the delay. (اَم بی یو لِ توری: گردشی- سیار)

- *Synagogue* or synagoug : *a Jewish congregation* (جماعت- گروه)
  <*congregation meals*>

- There are orders that are infrequently used. (بندرت- کم کم- گاه گاهی)
- An attorney had been hired to represent *Sara Palin* in a state probe* into whether she'd forced a commissioner into resigning because he'd refused to fine a trooper**! (سپاهی- نظامی)**, (خوب وارسی کردن)*

- The market dealt in commodities such as wheat and tobacco.
  <*commodity memory chip*> (کاما دِ تی: جنس- کالا)

  commodity ***–noun, plural*** -ties. کاما دِ تی
  1. an article of trade or commerce, esp. a product as distinguished from a service.
  2. something of use, advantage, or value.
  3. *Stock Exchange* . any unprocessed or partially processed good, as grain, fruits, and vegetables, or precious metals.
  4. *Obsolete* . a quantity of goods.
- To build a resource network that effectively keeps an eye on elderly and disable patrons register in the program.
  مشتری پابرجا- معنی دیگر مشوق و حامی یا پشتیبان)

- The mayor was forced to resign because of his unscrupulous business dealings. آن اس کرو پی ل : بی همه چیز- بی مرام- فاقد اصول یا مرام اخلاقی
  scrupulous: s کُرُم p لاس : محتاط، وسواسي، ناشي ازوسواس يا دقت زياد

  Not scrupulous: Means unprincipled or without moral principles, unprincipled .
  <*An unscrupulous scoundrel.*> (اس گن دِرول: آدم پست و رذل)

- He sued the talk show host for defamation, claiming he falsely suggested…
  (دِ فِ مِی شِن : افترا- بدنامی - رسوائی- تهمت)

- I am flattered* that former Alaska Governor Sara Palin has chosen to cite** me as a source of wisdom.
  (سایت : ذکر کردن، اتخاذ سند کردن گفتن)**, (اغفال کردن- پی زر لای پالان گذاشتن)*

- Your friend will be the head of his class when he is incarcerated .
  (این کار سِه ریت : زندانی/حبس شدن)

***incarcerate*–verb (used with object)**
1. to imprison; confine.
2. to enclose; constrict closely.
–adjective **3.** imprisoned.

- The constituency* is outrageous**
  *(کانستی چُو اِنسی : هیات موسسان یک حوزه) , **(بی حرمتی و جسارت آمیز - قبیح)

  <outrageous manners>, <outrageous language>,
  <An outrageous disregard of human rights>

  constituency **–noun, plural** -cies. کانستی چُو اِنسی
  1. a body of constituents; the voters or residents in a district represented by an elective officer. **2.** the district itself. **3.** any body of supporters, customers, etc.; clientele.

- There are many orders that are infrequently used (بندرتا- کم کم - گاه گاهی)
- Terminally ill persons. (بطور نهایی)
- ***maverick***: *an independent individual who does not go along with a group or party.* ***Network***: a group or system. < *A network of hotels*>

- You will find there are four groups whose cooperation is indispensible.
  (این دیس پن سِبل :حتمی- ضروری-لازم الاجرا)
- Longevity for older American is increasing, thanks to advancement in medical technology and improved health care. (لان ج و تی: درازی عمر- عمر زیاد)
  longevity: *a long duration of individual life*
- ***network***: a group or system. < *A network of hotels*>
- As we enter our eighties, the chance increase considerably that we will face health problems or frailty and we need assistance.
  (فِ ریل تی: سستی- ضعیفی- از کار افتادگی)
- ***frailty***: *a fault due to weakness esp. of moral character, or a physical or intellectual imperfection or imprisonment.*
  frail = *fragile*

- Nursing and social service over a prolonged period of time, this can also be called "chronic care", as distinct* from more intensive medical treatment for a short-term illness. Called "acute care."
  <An acute patient>, *<acute hospital>* * (جدا- مجزا)

  chronic, *chronic care*, *chronic illness*, or *<suffering from chronic disease>*
  <an inauspicious start> (کُرانیک : مزمن- کهنه- نحس- شوم)

- Distinguished as not being the same; not identical;
  Distinguishing or perceiving clearly: *<distinct vision.>*

- Those ongoing problems do not signify* a failure on part of professional caretakers.... *(دلالت کردن بر- حاکی بودن از- معنی دادن)
  caretaker : *a person who takes care of another.*

- Same programs are mandated by the federal government and are available in all states. (به قیومیت واگذار کردن)
  <The older American act has mandated all state units on aging to establish….>
- Full retroactive* services for those who require institutional care including a comprehensive array** of community based long-term care services.
  *(عطف بما سبق- معطوف به گذشته), **(آراستن- صف آرایی کردن- صف)

  disarray : بی نظمی-درهم پاشیدگی- قاطی پاتی
  <The room was in disarray>

  disarray **---verb (used with object)**
  1. to put out of array or order; throw into disorder. **2.** to undress.
  –noun
  3. disorder; confusion: *The army retreated in disarray.* **4.** disorder of apparel.

- Benefits from research designed to sustain and improve health and happiness. (تقویت- نگهداری کردن- طاقت چیزی را داشتن)

- Potent توانا- قوی- پرزور , (Impotent ناتوان- ضعیف- سست کمر)
  (Impotently از روی ناتوانی), utterly unable to do something.

- Hysterectomy درآوردن زهدان
- Mastectomy درآوردن قسمتی از پستان

- Heir (وارث- بمیراث گذاردن) / heirs (ورثه- وراث)
تلفظ اینها به ترتیب مثل air و airs می باشد

Arthritis (ورم مفاصل) can produce pain that limits sexual activity.

- *mastectomy* (مَس تِک تومی): *surgical removal of all or part of the breast and sometimes associated lymph-nodes (غدد لنفاوی) and muscles*

- republic — جمهوری
republican — جمهوریخواه- یا طرفدار آن حزب

- *democracy* — حکومت ملی- حکومت دموکراسی
democratic — طرفدار حکومت ملی- وابسته به حکومت ملی یاملت
democrat — طرفدار حزب دموکرات

- Sex in the young is fast and furious, (فیو ری یِس: پرتلاطم- متلاطم)
Find new vista* of sexual satisfaction. *(منظره باریک- دورنما)

- That will compensate for the deficits (دِفِ سیت : کمبود-کسری)

- If your quandary is window treatments we will solve it.
(کو آن دِری: سرگردانی- معما- گیجی)

- According to the experts, marital ardor* declines as couples age, both for biological reasons and because society frowns**
on grandma and grandpa having sex. *(آردِر: گرمی- سوز- شوق)
**(فِ ران: اخم کردن- ترشرویی کردن- با اخم ساکت کردن- یامانع شدن)

- Much less the chaos and confusion we find it in today.
Chaotic, chaotically (کِ یاس: هرج و مرج- بی نظمی)

- Ironically under this system. (بطور طعنه آمیز)
Ironical — طعنه آمیز- طعنه زدن

- Insurance companies accept your wager وِی جِر (premium) betting either (e ذِر یا آی ذِر) that the event (fire or accident) won't happen for a significant period of time (death).

- "Failure to thrive*" is how pediatrician** describe developmental delay in children. *(ثِ رایو: پیشرفت- ترقی کردن)
Pediatrician: *a physician who specialize in pediatrics.*
**(d-p-اَت ریشِن : دکتر اطفال)
pediatric : → (علم امراض و بهداشت کودکان)

- Dissecting the debate (d سِکت : . پاره کردن- تشریح کردن- در اینجا موشکافی)

dissect: *To examine, analyze, or criticize in minute detail, dissected the plan afterward to learn why it had failed.* See Synonyms at analyze.
dissection: *the act or process of dissecting.* کالبد شکافی- قطع

- Frustration of parents whose adult-children are failing to thrive.

پیشرفت کردن، رونق یافتن کامیاب شد

- You can also involve your state insurance commissioner's office they may intervene for you. (پادر میان گذاردن- مداخله کردن)

- Buying insurance is like placing a wager* something on which bets are laid : (gamble شرط بندی or betting). *(وِی جِر: شرط بستن)

- Federal authorities are investigating in an effort to find the culprit.
(کال پِرِت: متهم- مقصر)

- The birds fly form perch (پِرچ) to perch.
محل فرود نشستن پرندگان مثل لب بام یا سر تیرهای برق و غیره

- The index slumps* 200 points despite** a half point rate cut.
*(افت- یکباره پایین افتادن یا آمدن) **(،با وجود، بااینکه لج- کینه-عداوت)
Slump= ایـــن کلمـــه اســـلنگ اســـت

despite--**Preposition**
You use despite to introduce a fact which makes the other part of the sentence surprising. *Despite the difference in their ages they were close friends.... The programme was broadcast despite government pressure to stop it being screened.* Despite: the feeling or attitude of despising: contemp

—Idiom
In despite of, **in spite of**; notwithstanding:
<He was tolerant in despite of his background and education.>
Despise: (دیس پایز) to regard with contempt, distaste, disgust, or disdain; scorn; loathe

- *spite*: لج- کینه و غرض
  <He has a spite against me> با من لج دارد- با من کینه دارد
  <**In spite of**= in despite of> با وجود- علیرغم
  In spite of (با وجود اینکه) *the fact that....*

- Her rewards are in heaven! (heaven forbid خدانکنه)
  It is heaven's will خواست خداست
  Would to heaven.... کاش- خدامیکرد
  توجه شود (هی ون) *haven* یعنی بندرگاه- لنگرگاه با (هون **heaven** یعنی بهشت اشتباه نشود

heaven ***---noun***
1. the abode of god, the angels, and the spirits of the righteous after death; the place or state of existence of the blessed after the mortal life.
2. (*initial capital letter*) Often, Heavens. the celestial powers; God.
3. *For heaven's sake!* **4.** heavens,

- *Maverick: an independent individual who does not go along with a group or party, or* به معنی دیگر آن : بچه گاو یا گوساله ای که مادرش را از دست داده

  <As a team of maverick>, <He has been a maverick in some education...>
  <I think we to send maverick to senate (سِ نِت)*>*

- Partisan or partizan : با هر دو اسپل صحیح است (پار تی زن:طرفدار-هواخواه حزبی
  <By partisan effort>, < I have clear record of bipartisanship>

*partisan: an **adherent** or supporter of a person, group, party, or cause, esp. a person who shows a biased, emotional allegiance.*
اَد hé رِنت : تابع پیرو، هواخواه، طرفدار، بهم چسبیده

- You can get a lot of answers, it can be deceptive. فریبنده- اغفال کننده
  <*He is guilty as deception*. فریب- حیله>

- Should health care be treated as a commodity? کالا- جنس- متاع

- The magnitude of the problem is overwhelming!
  سخت- فشار آور- زیاد از سر در رونده

- By actuaries who consider every possible relevant factor.
  (اَک چو آری :آمارگر، دبیر، منشي، کارشناس بیمه)
  actuary: It means: clerk, register, a person who calculates insurance and annuity premiums.

- They are expected to treat the interests of a policy holder on a par with their own interests.
  در یک تراز روی هم رفته- ولی (پار) به تنهایی یعنی برابری- تعادل
  (ورزشی) حساب امتیاز استاندارد براي هر بخش از بازي گلف
  par --- If one thing is on a par with another, the two things are equally good or equally bad. *Forcing a child to learn is on a par with forcing a man to adopt a religion.*

  At par برابر- بی صرف
  Above par باصرف
  Below par باکسر

- Enthralled[1] by cults[2] or *gurus*, enmeshed[3] in abusive relationship.
  1.(این ترال: بنده- اسیر- گرفتار کردن) 2.(کالت : پرستش- آئین دینی) 3.(n مَش گرفتار کردن- در دام نهادن)

  guru (گ رو): *a personal religious teacher and spiritual guide in Hinduism.*
  <Deeply enmeshed in the plot>
  enmesh-***verb (used with object)*** (n مَش گرفتار کردن- در دام نهادن)

  To catch, as in a net; entangle: < *He was enmeshed by financial difficulties.*>

- As we always do, we ask our peers: p یِر: برابر بردن- هم شان بردنی

Peerless : → p پیر لِس: بی مانند- بی نظیر- بی همتا

peer–**noun**

1. a person of the same legal status: < *a jury of one's peers.* >
2. a person who is equal to another in abilities, qualifications, age, background, and social status.
3. something of equal worth or quality: < *a sky-scraper without peer.*>
4. a nobleman.

- atrocity (اَت را سی تی): *an atrocious act, objector situation*
(اَت را شِس: شریر- بی رحم- بی رحمانه)
<*the quality or state of being atrocious*>

خانم قاضی در مورد زنی که بچه اش را در ماکروفر گذاشته و سوزانده و کشته بود گفت:

"No adjective exist to adequately describe this heinous atrocity" Mary Wiseman said. "The act is shocking and utterly abhorrent* for a civilized society". *(متنفر- منزجر- شنیع- مغایر)

abhorrent: *strongly opposed, feeling or showing abhorrence*

heinous : هی نِس (زشت- شنیع)
heinous: *hatefully or chokingly evil.*

heinously : هی نِس لی بطور شنیع- بطور زشت و شریرانه)

- ***noxious*** (زیان آور- مضر): *physically harmful or destructive to living beings* <noxious waste> *or constituting a harmful influence on mind or behavior esp. morally corrupting.*
Noxious or slyness → موذی گری

- Obnoxious or obnoxiously بد- زیان آور- نفرت انگیز
<*Noxious gases*> or <*it is noxious to health*>

- My best friend was one of those super organized parents who pushed her kids to excel and one of them is a drug addict.
(برتری داشتن- بهتربودن از- پیشی جستن از)

- Obama is too articulate said former president Bush.

(T-R کی لیت : شمرده سخن گفتن، ماهر در صحبت)

articulate **–adjective**

1. uttered clearly in distinct syllables.
2. capable of speech; not speechless.
3. using language easily and fluently; having facility with words: *an articulate speaker.*

- Achilles (أکِ لی ز): *the greatest warrior among the Greeks*
  <*What is your real Achilles heel as a V.P. candidate?*>

  An **Achilles' heel** is a fatal weakness in spite of overall strength that can actually or potentially lead to downfall.

- According to the Los Angeles times, Iraq is a serious threat a league of democracy اتحادیه- مجمع, <*league of nations*> مجمع اتفاق ملل
  In league هم پیمان

- I don't have stomach for genocide when they come for Darfur.
  Genocide: the deliberate and systematic destruction of a racial, political or cultural group. <*When a country engaging in genocide*>

- Why the economy is trumping race? (خال- آتو **یا** برگ برنده)
  این مطلب روی مجله تایمز موقع انتخابات رئیس جمهوری Obama و McCain نوشته شده بود.

- What is the difference between a harangue and homework?
  Harangue*: a ranting speech or writing.*
  (هَرَنگ: سخنرانی بلند- سخنرانی که در مجلس .... می شود)

- He makes him the agent of a devious plot that could just about same the world. (دی وی اِس: گمراه- منحرف- غیرمستقیم)

- So ***the body of lies*** film hopscotches the globe. هابس کاچز: بازی اکردوکر
  Hopscotches: *to jump or leap from one place to another*:
  <*Small birds hopscotched on the lawn.*>

- At the behest of gay rights organizations..... بی هِست: دستور-امر
  behest*: an authoritative order or command*
  <*called at the behest of my friends*>

- His estate descended to his son. دارایی او به پسرش به ارث رسید

- To passé out who she is and who she might become.
(پَ سِه : تشریح یا تجزیه کردن)

- Government can compel people, مجبور کردن
Public opinion compelled him to sign the bill,
<Hunger compelled him to eat>

- Cumulative services should be considered tests and ... جمع شده-یکجا
<Cumulative evidence> قرائن یا مدارک اضافی

- Budget deficit in 2008 surges to all-time high.
موج زدن- این سو و آنسو رفتن- جنبیدن
اگر به آخر surge یک on اضافه کنیم می شود جراح

- For lawyer, trial was tribulation... (تری بیولی شن: آزمایش سخت)...
Tribulation: distress or suffering resulting from oppression or persecution***
*(ستم- ظلم- تعدی), **(زجر- آزار- تعقیب به منظور آزار دادن)

- The fumbling bumbling clown dancing. سرهمبندی کردن

- The chairman rapped* his gavel ** on second time.
*(به صدا درآوردن- ضربه زدن)
**(چکش چوبی که در حراجی بکار می برند)

- Turmoil[1] (ترمویل): a state or condition of extreme condition agitation[2] or commotion[3]. [1](آشوب - اضطراب)
[2](آشوب کن- تولید کننده هیجان عمومی- همزن) [3](آشوب - اضطراب- اغتشاش- شلوق- هیجان)
<Market turmoil rattles Europeans!>

- Furious* flutter** over project. *(فیو ری یس:آتشی- خشمگین)
**(درجا بال زدن- پرپرزدن- به این سو و آنسو رفتن)

- He was apparently roused by the suspects, who jumped a fence in his back yard around 1:30 AM. (رآزد: بیداد کردن- رم دادن)

- Petitioner's claim would, if meritorious affect (a) *title to*, or *the right to possession of specific real property.* (مِرِ توُ ری یَس : شایسته-لایق- مستحق)
Meritoriously = meritorious by→ از روی شایستگی

Meritorious: *deserving of honor or esteem* (اس تیم:ارزش-قدر)
<Assuring you of our highest esteem> با احترامات فائقه
<He is highly esteemed by me> در نزد من بسیار ارجمند است

***meritorious* –adjective** مِرِ توُ ری یَس : شایسته-لایق- مستحق
deserving praise, reward, esteem, etc.; praiseworthy: *to receive a gift for meritorious service.*

- Does temperament matter? مزاج- حالت- طبیعت
Does temperament have a rule?
What kind of temperament is best?
This is why temperament descends* easily into caricature**
*(پایین آمدن- به ارث رسیدن- تمکین کردن)
**(کَ ری کَ چِر : کاریکاتور)

descend: *to pass from a higher place or level to lower one*
<*Descend from a noble family* بزرگزاده >
<*His estate descended to his son* دارایی او به پسرش رسید >

توضیح: عکس 3 سگ در یک مقاله نشان داده شده بود که دارای 3 رنگ بودند و این مطلب نوشته شده بود:

Any dog breeds[1] will tell you temperament[2] is a crucial aspect of breeding. Why should it mean anything less for a president?

1. بی رید : *(زیستشناسي)* نسل پروردن ، جنس) 2.(تِم پِر مِنت : مزاج- حالت- طبیعت)

- Prosecutors say, while defense says informants lied. (خبررسان - مخبر)
<It was clear that she had lied>
Informant: *a person who gives information as informer*

- He was booked at Los Angeles Jail on suspicious of lewd (لُود) acts with minor.
lewd: *evil, ricked, sexually unchaste or licentious* obscene, vulgar***
*(لای سِن شِس:هرزه- شهوت ران) **(وِل گِر : در اینجا یعنی پست)

- An author who claims US comedian jerry Seinfeld's wife plagiarized her cookbook.. پلی ج رایزد: دزدید

plagiarize–**verb (used with object)**
1. to take and use by plagiarism.
2. to take and use ideas, passages, etc., from (another's work) by plagiarism.
–verb (used without object)
3. to commit plagiarism.

- City of Fullerton a lovely place with strong sense of community and an enviable quality of life. ان وی ایبل: غبطه آور
Enviable= highly desirable

- Prime Minister Maliki proposed series of amendments in an effort to make the deal more palatable.
پ ل ِت ِبل: خوشمزه- مطبوع- در اینجا یعنی پسندیده

- Customer reported that their account had been comprised. دربرداشتن ، شامل بودن
<Confidential information was compromised>
Compromise: to reveal or expose an authorized person and esp. to an enemy

---

- Police say he barred* a door, poured gas on garden G. home.
<*a barred feather*> , <barred by statute> *(بار : بستن- سد کردن)

- Robert 34 is facing torture mayhem* and sexual assault charges stemming** from an incident…
*(مـی جـم) (حقـوق) ضـرب وشـتم، جـرح (حقـوق) فلـج کـردن، چـلاق کـردن نـاقص العـضو کـردن
**(إسـتم : ریـشه لغـت قطـع کـردن، ریـشه اصـل، سـاقه دار کـردن)

- *mayhem: willful and permanent deprivation* of a bodily member resulting in the impairment of a person's fighting ability.* *(اشتقاق-کلمه مشتق-اقتباس)

stem **–verb (used with object)**
1. to stop, check, or restrain.
2. to dam up; stop the flow of (a stream, river, or the like).

- *privation*: *lack of the usual comforts or necessaries of life:*
  < *His life of privation began to affect his health. ..*>
  (پُو رای وی شن: فقدان- عدم- محرومیت)
  توجه: این کلمه با private به معنی خصوصی فرق دارد

- May you live to see your grand children!
  انشاءاله زنده باشید که نوه های خود را ببینید

- An Orange Country judge who was admonished* for failing to be patient, dignified** and courteous on the bench has resigned.

  *(اَد ما نیش : تنبیه- نصیحت شدن) ,**(باوقار- بزرگ)

- Lavish = Expanding *or* bestowing* profusely . (پِراف یوسلی): زیاد -مسرفانه
  prodigal: ولخرج- مسرف : (پُرا دی گِل) , *(بخشیدن- ارزانی داشتن)

- 72% expected to see changes needed to revive* the ailing** economy
  *(زنده شدن- احیا کردن- دوباره رونق دادن) , ** (ناخوش- رنجور- علیل)

- In the meantime, which Obama concentrate on building a cabinet and assembling an array of advices on a range of issue..
  <*to array a troop* صف آرایی کردن>, array: (آراستن- صف)

- We expected weather temperature to give way today to another blustery* jolt**
  *(صدای باد) ,**(تکان خوردن- تق تق کردن- بالا پایین انداختن)

- Thereby (بموجب- بدان وسیله- در نتیجه آن) fueling (فیولینگ: سوخت) job losses in the construction industry already exacerbated (اگزَسِربیت: سخت تر/بدتر کردن) by the slow down in single family home construction.

  exacerbation = اِگزَ سِر بِی شن: تشدید- سختی- شدت =
  Leaders failed to organize a visible and vigorous defense of same-sex marriage. (وِگِرِس : پرزور- شدید- قوی), *vigorously*= شدیدا- قویا

  ***vigorous* –adjective**
  1. full of or characterized by vigor: *a vigorous effort.*
  2. strong; active; robust: *a vigorous youngster.*
  3. energetic; forceful: *vigorous steps; a vigorous personality.*

4. powerful in action or effect: *vigorous law enforcement.*
5. growing well, as a plant.

- Sometimes clashing* with police and snarling** traffic .

*(درق- صدای بهم خوردگی و شکستگی) ** (s نارل : پیچ افتادن-گره خوردن)

Snarl=tangle

- Night is long and murky تاریک و غلیظ
- During Nixon's tenure (تن یور: دوره تصدی)

- In Feb. 2006, he was publically admonished for using his court room clerk to help with secretarial tasks involved in the day-to-day management of two rental properties he owned, the commission said.

(نصیحت کردن- پند دادن - تنبیه کردن)

Admonisher: ناصح- مشاور

- With the presidential election a day away, the candidates hurled (هارلد) themselves into a grueling tour of suing states.

hurl هارلد : *rush* (گرُ ارلینگ: تنبیه شدن- شکست خوردن)

Support a ticket: لیست کاندیدها و کسانیکه برای انتخابات معرفی شده اند

<*Hurled myself over the fence*>, <*hurled the manuscript into the fire*>
grueling= trying or taxing to the point of exhaustion, punishing.
<*a grueling race*>, <*to have or get one's gruel*>

- The fight and classic civil rights struggle marked by bigotry (تعصب)

<bigot = شخص متعصب > *Bigotries* ← جمع کلمه

- Doesn't even require a major undertaking.

(تقبل- تعهد- کسیکه مسئولیت کاری رابعهده میگیرد)

- The recent surge in populating of Sara Palin. (موج-موج زدن)

Sara Palin: She was former Alaska Governor

- California has become the central battle ground in ferocious culture war.

(فروشَس : وحشی- درنده- ستمگر)

Battleground=*battlefield*
<*A ferocious predator* (غارتگر وحشی)> (*predator*→ غارتگر)

ferocious ***–adjective***
1. savagely fierce, as a wild beast, person, action, or aspect; violently cruel: *a ferocious beating.*
2. extreme or intense: *a ferocious thirst.*

- It's unthinkable in the 21st century to eliminate rights already bestowed upon a group. (بِس تُ : بخشیدن- امانت گذاردن)

bestow-- ***verb (used with object)*** بِس تُ
1. to present as a gift; give; confer (usually fol. by *on* or *upon*): *The trophy was bestowed upon the winner.*
2. to put to some use; apply: *Time spent in study is time well bestowed*

- Candidates sprint for the finish line. (دویدن دوی کوتاه و تند)
sprint.: to run or go at top speed for a short distance.

- At the same rate that their speed subtly slows. (ساتِلی: از روی دقت و موشکافی)

- Fire doused in vacant unit. (دَاس د: با شتاب پایین آوردن)
<If you douse a fire or light, you stop it burning or shining.>

- The home had been ransacked and deputies found evidence that some one had tried but failed to set the home on fire in an effort to destroy evidence. (رَنسَک : خوب جستجو کردن)
ransack: to search thoroughly, to examine closely and carefully

---

- The crime scene was shielded from the view of a freeway by dense bush and tangled tree limbs. (انبوه - تراکم)

- Agents need to be wary when handling short sales.

wary = caution, *<to be wary of …>* (وِری: محتاط - ملاحظه کار)

- Spector ranted* against women, music producer was ejected** form two of the star's X-Mas parties for brandishing*** a gun and declaring that all women should be shot.

*(لفاظی کردن), **(بیرون انداختن), ***(تاب/حرکت دادن)

X-Mas= Christmas, Brandish= swing سوئینگ ← (مترادف آن)

rant: *to talk in a noisy, excited or declamatory manner*

(رَنت : رفتار فصیحانه یا میخته به تصنع)

(دِکلِمِ توُری : وابسته به دکلمه، مربوط به قرائت مطلبي باصداي بلند وغرا)

- The act or action of receding: *withdrawal*,
  receding= *to make back or away*

- People across America and around the world scooped up copies of our commemorative election issue to observe the occasion. It has already become a collector's item. (S کوپ : ملاقه-در اینجا یعنی خالی کردن)

- Pacific pianist a smooth collaborator. (کُو لَ بُو ری تُور : همکار- همدست)

- Kevin Costner indulges* passion** with a root-rock CD
  *(این دالج : آزاد گذاشتن- جلوگیری نکردن), **(پَ شِن :شور و هیجان اشتیاق و علاقه شدید-)

  <Let us indulge in a little daydreaming...>.
  <If you indulge someone, you let them have or do whatever they want, even if this is not good for them.>

- Burglar ransack home as teens hide...... (رَن سَک :خوب جستجو کردن- غارت کردن)
  ransack = *to search thoroughly, to examine closely and carefully*
  <to search through to commit robbery>

- To overlook a fault. نادیده گرفتن- صرفنظر کردن
  overlook= neglect چشم پوشی کردن- نادیده گرفتن ، مسلط یا مشرف بودن بر

- She combines integrity, dedication; shrewd negotiations skills and the latest technology to her clients achieve their real estate goals. (شُورُود :زیرک- باهوش)

  A shrewd operator...
  <Shrewd people are able to understand and judge situations quickly.>,
  <He is a shrewd and sometimes ruthless adversary.>

- *unscrupulous*: (آن کروپی لس) without moral, principles, unprincipled,
  <an unscrupulous scoundrel >
  <A scoundrel is someone who cheats and deceives people> (اس کَن دِرِل: آدم پست و رذل)

- The incoming and out coming second couples behave cordially.
  (کورجولی: قلبا- بامودت)

  well-behaved → خوش رفتار- باادب
  bad-behaved → بدرفتار- بی ادب

- Experts urge President Obama to tread lightly with Iran. (ت رِد: گام برداشتن)
  <To walk or proceed along>, *<to stop or walk on or over>*

  ***tread* –verb (used without object)** ت رِد: گام برداشتن
  1. to set down the foot or feet in walking; step; walk.
  2. to step, walk, or trample so as to press, crush, or injure something (usually fol. by *on* or *upon*): *to tread on a person's foot.*

- Don't bother to wield* economic or military threats**
  *(ویلد:گرداندن- اداره کردن) **(ت رِت: تهدید کردن)

- A disreputable person: *rascal* دیس- re -P- U تِ بِل : بدنام ، بي اعتبار مايه رسوايي

- His parlor revives* nostalgia. *(زنده شدن- نیروی تازه گرفتن- احیاء کردن)
  parlor: *a room used primarily for conversation or reception of guests.*
  nostalgia: *homesickness* (ناس تَل جا : دلتنگی برای میهن)

- Louisiana senator, cruised to victory in a primary last week and is expected to easily win re-election کُروزد : گشت زدن - سفر دريايي
  <cruise over to her house to see if she's home>

- Since the arm shipment allegations become public 14 months ago, black water, state dept. ready to fine blackwater ….
  اَلِ گِی شِن : اظهار، ادعا، بهانه ، تایید
  blackwater: *any of several disease (as blackwater fever) characterized by dark-colored urine.*

- A man reads a spoof* copy of New York Times with the headline that Iraq war has ended Wednesday in N.Y. about 1.2 million copies of the parody** were handed out nationwide.

*(اس پُوف: تقلبی- دروغی- کلک) و **(پَ رِ دی: بصورت هزل درآوردن)

spoof: *deceive, hoax, <N.Y.T spoof distributed >*
parody: *a feeble or ridiculous imitation = caricature*

- Long-term-care ombudsman (آم بادز مَن) program.

Ombudsman: (آم بادز مَن) *A government official that investigates reported complaints (as from students or consumers) against abuses or ....*

- capricious* act of public officials. *(کاپ ریشِس : دمد می- بالهوس- متلون)

capricious **–adjective** کاپ ریشِس
1. subject to, led by, or indicative of caprice or whim; erratic: *He's such a capricious boss I never know how he'll react.*
2. *Obsolete* . fanciful or witty.
3. A capricious person often changes their mind unexpectedly. *Authoritarian rulers are typically capricious.*

- Help you implement your financial plan. (انجام دادن-اجرا کردن-تکمیل کردن)
- ***Megabyte*** (MB)**:** *an amount of computer memory equal to* 2^{20}*= 1024 kilobytes. One megabyte can store more than one million characters.*

- Respite care/respite care registration. (رِس پیت : مهلت- مهلت دادن- بتعویق انداختن)

- Services also include nutrition education, nutrition counseling (Normal and therapeutic nutrition. (ثِ رَا پیو تیک: علم درمان شناسی)
<All that fresh air is very therapeutic.>

- But it is an investment that can pay substantial* dividend's** in the long run.
*(ذاتی- واقعی- اساسی- قابل توجه)
**(سودسهام- بهره- مقسوم در بخش کردن)

- What credentials do you have to practice financial planning?
Credential: (credential letters استوارنامه)
<Your credentials are your previous achievements, training, and general background, which indicate that you are qualified to do something.>

- It is up to you to make your grievance known. If your grievance can not be resolved at these levels go to the organization or licensing authority that oversee the planner.

(شکایت- گله- نگرانی)

- Thumping[1] bed springs and sensual[2], sweating*, moaning[3] young bodies that turn intimacy[4] into an athletic.

[1](مشت زدن- ضربه زدن), [2](سن چوآل: شهوانی- جسمانی- نفس پرست)
[3](مونی اینگ: ناله کردن- یا زاری کردن برای)
[4](صمیمیت- رابطه نامشروع جنسی)
*(عرق کردن، عرق ریزي، مشقت کشیدن)

(sensualism نفس پرستی), (moanful نالان)

- It can be done very quietly without much hubbub.

(هَباب: شلوغی و هیاهو)

Hubbub: *noise, uproar, confusion, turmoil*

- Diabetes is one of the few diseases that can cause impotence* once diabetes is diagnosed and controlled, however, potency** in most cases may be restored.

*(ایم پوتِنس: ناتوانی جنسي در مرد - ضعف- سستی کمر) , **(توانایی- نیرو- زور)

impotence or *impotency*
potence or *potency*

- rationing on horizon.... (رَشِن نینگ : جیره بندی کردن خوار و بار یا جیره)
rational عاقل- معقول
rationalistic: رَشِنِ نالیس تیک : مبنی بر اصول معقول و عقلی

- Bail out could turn tables on oligarchs*.

(آلی گارک: عضو یک حکومت متنفذین یا مشتی از مردم)

- Do you enjoy risky ventures? (جرات- اقدام به کارمخاطره آمیز)

- For a hypothetical election for the presidency. های پُ تَ تیکال : فرضی

hypothetical – های پُ تَ تیکال ***adjective*** Also, hy·po·thet·ic *for defs..*
1. assumed by hypothesis; supposed: *a hypothetical case.*

2. of, pertaining to, involving, or characterized by hypothesis: *hypothetical reasoning.*
3. given to making hypotheses.
4. *Logic* .
a. (of a proposition) highly conjectural; not well supported by available evidence.
b. (of a proposition or syllogism) conditional.
–noun
5. a hypothetical situation, instance, etc.: *The Secretary of Defense refused to discuss hypotheticals with the reporters.*

- If you specify something, you state it precisely. The report specified seven areas where the Government had a responsibility.... The landlord can specify that rent should be paid in cash.
(specify C-p-s قاید : معین/معلوم کردن), (specified معین- مذکور)

- Great park housing plan elicits comments . E له سیت : استخراج کردن- بیرون کشیدن

If you elicit a response or a reaction, you do something which makes other people respond or react; a formal word.
<Threats to reinstate the tax elicited jeers from the opposition.>
<hypnotism elicited his hidden fears>

- I had enough of my psoriasis so I could asked my dermatologist about…

(سُ رای- سِز : مرض مزمن پوستی قرمز رنگ پوشیده با وایت اسکیلز)

psoriasis ***–noun*** *Pathology* .
A common chronic, inflammatory skin disease characterized by scaly patches.

- I sat in cold balcony and eavesdropping madly, realized that my neighbors at every one of the adjoining tables were consumed by the vagaries (وِی- گِری ز)* of appointive politics

(ایوز- دارایپنگ : استراق سمع) *(وِی- گِری ز :خیالپرستي، تخیلات)
eavesdropping.: : (ایوز - دارایپنگ)
To listen secretly to the private conversation of others.

appointive: *of relating to, or filled by appointment.*
<An *appointive office*>
vagary, vagaries = caprice (کپ ریس: بوالهوسی- هوس، تمایل فکري)

- Warmed by the cheers of thousands and sticking to the issues they think will sway waffling voters. سُوای : این سو و آنسو رفتن

- On many issues, the presidential candidates problem-solving strategies diverge. (دِیورج: از هم دور شدن)

diverge: *to move or extend in different directions from a common point.*
US Senator John McCain favors unspecified boost in US forces.
(بُوست :جلوبردن- تکان دادن- این کلمه آمریکایی است)

- Pledged not to raise taxes, then equivocated saying nothing can be rule out in negotiating compromises to keep social security solvent.
Equivocate: to use equivocal language esp. with intent to deceive
(e کُو-e وی کِیت : دو پهلو حرف زدن)

- Nonpartisan (نان پار تی زن) Tax policy Center estimates tax break $325 for the middle class ……...
partisan: هواخواه-هوادار-حزبی
<*nonpartisan ballot*>, <*a nonpartisan blood*>,
- I learned from anger management classes but has been stigmatized
s تیگ م تایز : بی آبرو کردن

stigmatize **–verb (used with object),** -tized, -tiz·ing.
1. to set some mark of disgrace or infamy upon:
The crime of the father stigmatized the whole family.
2. to mark with a stigma or brand.
3. to produce stigmata, marks, spots, or the like, on.

- As race ends, volunteers barrage* voter and candidates hopscotch** the states.
*(بِ راج: سربندی) ,**(هاپ اسکاچ: بازی اکر دوکر)

- hoax (شوخی- فریب آمیز-حقه)
<*Feared that the deal was a sham*>

sham **–noun**

1. something that is not what it purports to be; a spurious imitation; fraud or hoax.
2. a person who shams; shammer.
3. a cover or the like for giving a thing a different outward appearance: *a pillow sham.*

- He was apprehended after a chance. (هراسیدن‌داشتن، بیمکردن، توقیفکردن‌درک)

)

- About 300 turn out at Saddleback church on Saturday to denounce* passage** of measure that bans gay marriage.
  *(خبردادن از- اشاره کردن بر- متهم کردن- باتهدید خطاب کردن) , **(گذرگاه، راهرو، تصویب)
  <*to denounce a person as a traitor.*> (کسی را به خیانت متهم یا محکوم کردن)

- Civil rights concerns as well as attempts to cast a shadow on both Obama & Islam eclipsed* affronts** by the Obama campaign.
  *(خسوف- کسوف- تحت الشعاع قراردادن) , **(توهین آشکار- آشکارا توهین کردن به)

affronter: توهین کننده- هتاک
affrontive : توهین آمیز- دشنام آمیز

- In an ironic manner, Its ironic, curious, or surprising
  ironically: (آی رانیک لی: بطعنه- از روی کنایه)
  ironical (آرانی کال : طعنه امیز- طعنه زدن)

- Did anyone notice the hypocrisy[1] of seeing Reverent Jackson bawling[2] his eyes out in a show of emotion at Obama's victory speech?
  [1](هی پاک راسی: دورویی- ریا و ریاکاری)
  [2](بالینگ: دادزدن- فریاد- بلند گفتن)

hypocrite هی پوکرت : آدم ریاکار و دورو
hypocritically : هی پوکرتک لی: ریاکارانه- از روی دورویی
bawling: *to cry out loudly and unrestrainedly* .

- It is time for **three** dissemblers like Jessie Jackson, Al Sharpton and Lui Farrakhan.... (دیس سمبلرز: ریاکار، دورو)
  dissembler: *to hide under a false appearance*

- Prognostic پیش گویی از روی علائم

Prognosticate پیش بینی کردن از روی علائم- حاکی بودن از

- California's gay-right movement has been beset* by infighting** and finger-pointing since the ... *(بِ سِت : آزارکردن- به ستوه آوردن)
**(مشت بازی از نزدیک-جنگ دست و پنجه)

- None of us would find ourselves in our present predicament because even if we didn't do all "right" things we certainly didn't do all the "wrong" ones. *<dilemma >* (Pری دِکِ مِنت : وضع بد- ناگوار)

predicament **–noun** Pری دِکِ مِنت : وضع بد- ناگوار
1. an unpleasantly difficult, perplexing, or dangerous situation.
2. a class or category of logical or philosophical predication.
3. *Archaic* . a particular state, condition, or situation.
<Stranded in a strange city without money, he was in a predicament. >

- Occasionally our troubled kids are ready to absolve us of blame or guilt even before we are. (اَب زالو : بخشیدن- آمرزیدن- عفو کردن)

absolve : *to set free from an obligation or the consequence of guilt.*

- Two kind of letter conclusion or complimentary sample:

1. *I look forward to meeting you personally.*
   Kindest regards,
   Your name

2. *I look forward to seeing you on Tuesday Sept. 8 at 11 AM.*
   See you soon,
   Your name

- session سِه شِن : جلسه
in session منعقد- دایر
Live in session جلسه زنده در حال اجرا
The house went into secret session مجلس جلسه خصوصی تشکیل داد

- He also on trial in alleged memorabilia* heist** .
*(مِ مُو رِ بی لی یا :چیزهای یادداشت کردنی- خاطرات)
**(های سْت: اقدام به دزدی مسلحانه کردن)

memorabilia are things that you collect because they are connected with a person, organization, and so on in which you are interested.
<He had a large collection of war memorabilia.>

- The usual benefit from such a company is to receive dividends. (سود سهام)

- This litany of our sins of commission or omission… لیتنی: دعا- مناجات

- If your agent is young and has had a short tenure there is a far chance that person may not be around for long. تن یور: دوره تصدی- تصرف

- A man made reef designed to grow into a self-sustaining 175 acre keep forest. ریف : تپه دریایی

- Former US. Vice president Candidate Sara Palin was so tenacious as a high school basketball point guard. (تِ نِی شِس : محکم نگهدارنده- مصر- چسبیده)
  < a tenacious mental > or < a tenacious memory >

- She is very well-versed on this issues, US. President candidate John McCain obviously found her to be very intelligent and very well-versed on the issues. (متبحر- بااطلاع- زبردست)

- Mrs. Palin responded to the clamor with characteristic confidence and common sense. (کِ لَمر: فریاد زدن- فریاد کردن)
  <They clamored him down دادزدند تا خاموش شد >

- Speculation* has centered on the telegenic Mrs. Sara Palin despite her tumultuous** two months on the national political scene.
  *(تفکر- اندیشه- تحقیقات نظری)
  **(تومول چو اس: پرآشوب- آشوبگر)

  ***speculation**: a transaction involving such SP.*
  ***telegenic**: well-suited to the medium of television esp. having an appearance and manner that are markedly attractive to TV viewers.*

- Nancy Regan gets Obama apology for séance (سه یانس) remark.
  این کلمه دو معنی دارد:
  1.همان سانس فرانسوی یا سه ئِنْ 2. معنی دیگری به جمله زیر مراجعه شود

séance **:** *a spiritualist meeting to receive spirit communications*
<I didn't want to get into a Nancy Regan thing about doing any séances>

- However, if your payment is dishonored or rejected by the payor / payer bank or financial institution, this continuation of coverage notice is invalid and hereby rescinded.

(ریسَندِ د: فسخ یا لغو کردن)

- 19-year-old city council (کَان سِل) enjoyed a standing ovation from 250 cheering classmates. (اُوِی شِن : ستایش- استقبال عمومی) کَان سِل: شورا- انجمن

Please contact your academic counselor at your campus.

Counselor=counselor

(کَان سِلِر: مشاور) هردو اِسپل صحیح است

Town council انجمن شهرداری

council -- **noun** کَان سِل: شورا- انجمن
1. an assembly of persons summoned or convened for consultation, deliberation, or advice.
2. a body of persons specially designated or selected to act in an advisory, administrative, or legislative capacity: *the governor's council on housing.*
3. (in certain British colonies or dependencies) an executive or legislative body assisting the governor.

- ***statute***[1]: *a law enacted by the legislative branch of a government.*

1.(اس تَت چُوت: قانون (مجلس)

statutory[2] of or relating to statutes*. **2.**(اس تَ چِ تورِی: قانونی- مقرر)

* (اس تَت چُو تس): **statutes**

statute of limitations قانون مرور زمان

<a statutory age limit>

statuary اس تَ چو اِری: مجسمه ساز- مجسمه سازی-مجسمه
statuaries ← *Pl.*
statute (اس تَ چو: مجسمه)

- A scorched[1] fire hose lay frayed[2] and abandoned on the blackened earth just out side of the green river neighborhood.

1.(S کُرچ :سوزاندن) 2.(فِرِی :سائیده)

- Spurred* in part by some fresh US. concessions** as well as by threats[1] to suspend all operations in Iraq if..

*(اِس پر : تحریک کردن) , **(کان سه شِن : امتیاز- واگذاری- تن دردهی) ,
[1](تِرِت : تهدید، تهدید کردن، ترساندن)

- One of the fatally plunging a knife into the man's chest during the brawl police said.

(بِرال: داد و بیداد کردن- قیل و قال و دعوا کردن)

brawl= to quarrel or fight noisily: wrangle, <*drunken brawl* عربده کشیدن>

- The chief of staff of the court-appointed receiver over seeing the revamping of the inmate health care system makes it clear that…

revamping: *remark, revise, renovate, reconstruction*

(ری وَمپ : دوباره رویه انداختن، دوباره وصله یا سرهم بندي کردن نو نما کردن)

revamping –verb (used with object) ری وَمپ

1. to renovate, redo, or revise: *We've decided to revamp the entire show.*

–noun

2. an act or instance of restructuring, reordering, or revising something; overhaul: *a revamp of the nation's foreign policy.*

- Recession may force reduction in endowment and federal grants.

(این دآمِنت: بخشش- اعطا- وقف)

<*may reduce fed. Grants and the school's substantial endowment*>

Endow بخشیدن به- اعطا کردن

Harvard's endowment posted an 6% return and grew to 36% billion

<*Unprecedented endowment losses and plan.*>

<*Harvard's is the nation's largest university endowment.*>

- In foreign affairs essay, Clinton harshly criticized the Bush administrations refuse to engage with adversaries[1] such as Iran." true statesmanship requires that we engage with our adversaries, not for the sake of taking but for because robust[2] diplomacy is prerequisite to achieving our aims",

[1](دشمن- مخالف- حریف- رقیب), [2](رُباست: قوی- تنومند)

- She wrote if Iran launched a nuclear strike on Israel, she said she would "totally obliterate them"(آب لی تریت: پاک/محو کردن- از بین بردن)

- More however might be as urgent or treacherous[1] as Iran. Continue to enrich uranium that could be used to fuel a nuclear weapon, in defiance of[2] the UN and has stymied[3] international inspection .

[1](بِت رَ چِرِس: غیرقابل اطمینان) , [2](بی اعتنائی – مقاومت -علیرغم)
[3](اس تای می د :مانع شدن، گیر کردن)

defiant → بی اعتنا-جسور- دعوت به جنگ و مبارزه- بی اعتنایی- مقاومت

stymie: to present an obstacle to: stand in the way of , <stymied by red tape>

- Volunteers mobilize to help residents of fire-ravaged.

(رَوِج: خرابی- ویرانگری)

Ravagement, *<a country ravaged by war.>*
Ravager, *Devastate= ravage*

- Jurors listen to more excerpts[1] of ex-sheriff's talk with Haidl, the judge presiding[2] over the public corruption trial of former OC. Sheriff chastised[3] Crona's defense team.

1(اکس سرپتس: اقتباس کردن)
2(پری زایدینگ: ریاست کردن- سرپرستی کردن)
3 (چِس تای زد: گوشمالی دادن- زدن- تنبیه کردن)

excerption: x سرپشِن : اقتباس- انتخاب و استخراج- مواد اقتباس شده

excerpt–**noun** اکس سرپت: اقتباس کردن
1. a passage or quotation taken or selected from a book, document, film, or the like; extract.
–verb (used with object)
2. to take or select (a passage) from a book, film, or the like; extract.
3. to take or select passages from (a book, film, or the like); abridge by choosing representative sections.

- Arizona governor, who is well-versed in immigration issues, is reported to be Homeland Security choice. متبحر- زبردست- بااطلاع

- Poorer areas bear subprime brunt .. (برانت : ضربه- سختی- لطمه)

brunt **---noun** : برانت
the main force or impact, as of an attack or blow: *His arm took the brunt of the blow.*

- Lawmaker will juggle congress and motherhood. جاگل: چشم بندی کردن

*juggle --To alter or manipulate in order to deceive, as by subterfuge**or
<.*to juggle the business accounts; to juggle the facts.* > *طفره، گریز، ، عذر، بهانه
To manage or alternate the requirements of (two or more tasks, responsibilities, activities, etc.)
So as to handle each adequately: *to juggle the obligations of job and school.*

- Judge collapsed during a speech and was rushed to a hospital after losing consciousness[1]. Now he is conscious[2], conversant[3] and alert.

1.(کان شس نس:آگاهی و هوشیاری), **2**.(آگاه و هوشیار)
3.(کان ورسنت: آگاه و بصیر)

- Commuter, freight trains collide. (فریت: کرایه بار)

commuter: a small airline that carries passengers relating short distance on a regular schedule.
freight: the compensation paid for the transportation of goods.

- cordially (کور جلی): *of or relating to the heart; or sincerely or deeply felt,*
cordial (کورجوال : قلبي، صميمي)، <cordial relation>
Synonym see gracious

- An insurance claim is a business negotiation. You have to be assertive[1] we call it polite assertiveness[2].

1(مثبت- قطعی) 2 .(روانشناسي) جرات

assertive ***--adjective***
1. confidently aggressive or self-assured; positive: aggressive; dogmatic: *He is too assertive as a salesman.*
2. having a distinctive or pronounced taste or aroma.
<learn assertiveness skills for managers and supervisors for one day>

- Obama has shown a knack for symbolism in this case following the thanksgiving tradition of helping the poor. (نک: فَن- لِم- فوت کاسه و کوزه گری)

- California Senator Feinstein recalls day of infamy.

(این فَ مي) روز بدنامی و رسوائی- روز محرومیت از حقوق مدنی
Synonyms see disgrace → رسوايي ، خفت ، ننگ ، فضاحت ، بي ابرويي

- Exphaty[1] or not, Senator John Kerry's backslap[2] marked Senator J. McCain's induction[3] into an unofficial bipartisan caucus[4] of .....

1.(صریحا- بوضوح), **2**.(تظاهر بصمیمیت کردن چاخان کردن)
3.(استدلال- قیاس از جزء به کل) , **4**.(کاکِس :نمایندگان حزب کارگر درپارلمان یا انجمن نمایندگان)

backslap: to display excessive cordiality or goodwill. (بَک اِسلَپ)
***caucus**: a close meeting of a group of persons belonging to the same political party or faction ... to select candidates or to decide on policy.*

- City of Anaheim Hills educators lauded[1] by john Glen who stuttered[2] .

1.(لاَد : ستایش- تمجید) **2**.(اِس تا تِر: با لکنتِ زبان صحبت کردن- زبان گرفتگی)

laud: praise, extol, or If you laud someone, you praise and admire them; an old-fashioned word.

stutter–verb (used with object), verb (used without object) اِس تا تِر
1. to speak in such a way that the rhythm is interrupted by repetitions, blocks or spasms, or prolongations of sounds or syllables, sometimes accompanied by contortions of the face and body.
–noun
2. distorted speech characterized principally by blocks or spasms interrupting the rhythm.

- Another Mideast menace....

(مِ نِیس: تهدید- تهدید کردن)
این مطلب را جلوی یکی از عکس های هیلاری نوشته بودند

menacingly= مِنِسینگ لی : از روی تهدید

- A sad procession[1] of residents returned Monday after burning their homes to see for themselves the devastation wrought[2] by a wind-drive wildfire.

1.(حرکت دسته جمعي ، اجتماع), 2.(رآت : بشکل در آمده- تشکیل شده- ساخته)

- The house is gone, it's twisted metal. It's totally charred*. There is no hope at all.

* (چار :برگشتن- تبدیل به ذغال شدن)

charred: *to convert to charcoal or carbon, burn.*

char---verb (used with object)
1. to burn or reduce to charcoal: *The fire charred the paper.*
2. to burn slightly; scorch: *The flame charred the steak.*
–verb (used without object); **3.** to become charred.

–noun **4.** a charred material or surface., charcoal.

- As the last evacuees return home. *evacuees: an evacuated person*

E وَ کیو- E : فراري یا پناهندهاي که درموقع جنگ محل خودراتخلیه میکند

evacuee ***–noun*** E وَ کیو- E
A person who is withdrawn or removed from a place of danger, a disaster area, etc.

- My sincere gratitude[1] goes out to all of the firefighters who braved such harrowing[2] conditions to save my parents home.

1.(حق شناسی- نمک شناسی- قدردانی) 2.(هَرو اینگ: جان آزار- د لخراش)
harrowing : *pillage, plunder*

- Presidential contender[1] resumes[2] duties with no fanfare[3].

1.(کان تِندِر : برنده احتمالي، مدعي دربرابر قهرمان)
2.(رِزوم زَ :از سرگرفتن) , 3.(فَن فِر: آهنگ کوتاه)

contender: کان تندر *A competitor for a championship or high honor.*
< A heavy weight title contender.>
مشتقات آن → [resumes (رِزوم), and resuming (رِزومینگ)]
ولی اگر با تلفظ رِزم وبدون اس بیان شودمعنی خلاصه- مختصر
[Resume (رِزِم)]

fanfare ***–noun***
1. a flourish or short air played on trumpets or the like.
2. an ostentatious display or flourish.
3. publicity or advertising.

- Some one face was still smudged[1] with soot[2] and ash as he helped load boxes into the back of a pickup.

1.(اس ماجد: لک لکه- آتش و دود در هوای آزاد)
2. (سوت: دوده ای کردن- دوده)

Smudge, smudging, smudged

- A firefighter shoveled through a pile of soot سوت دوده and debris (دِبری) on the bedroom floor and pried open a closet.

(پِر اید: بادقت نگاه کردن-کاوش یا جستجو کردن)

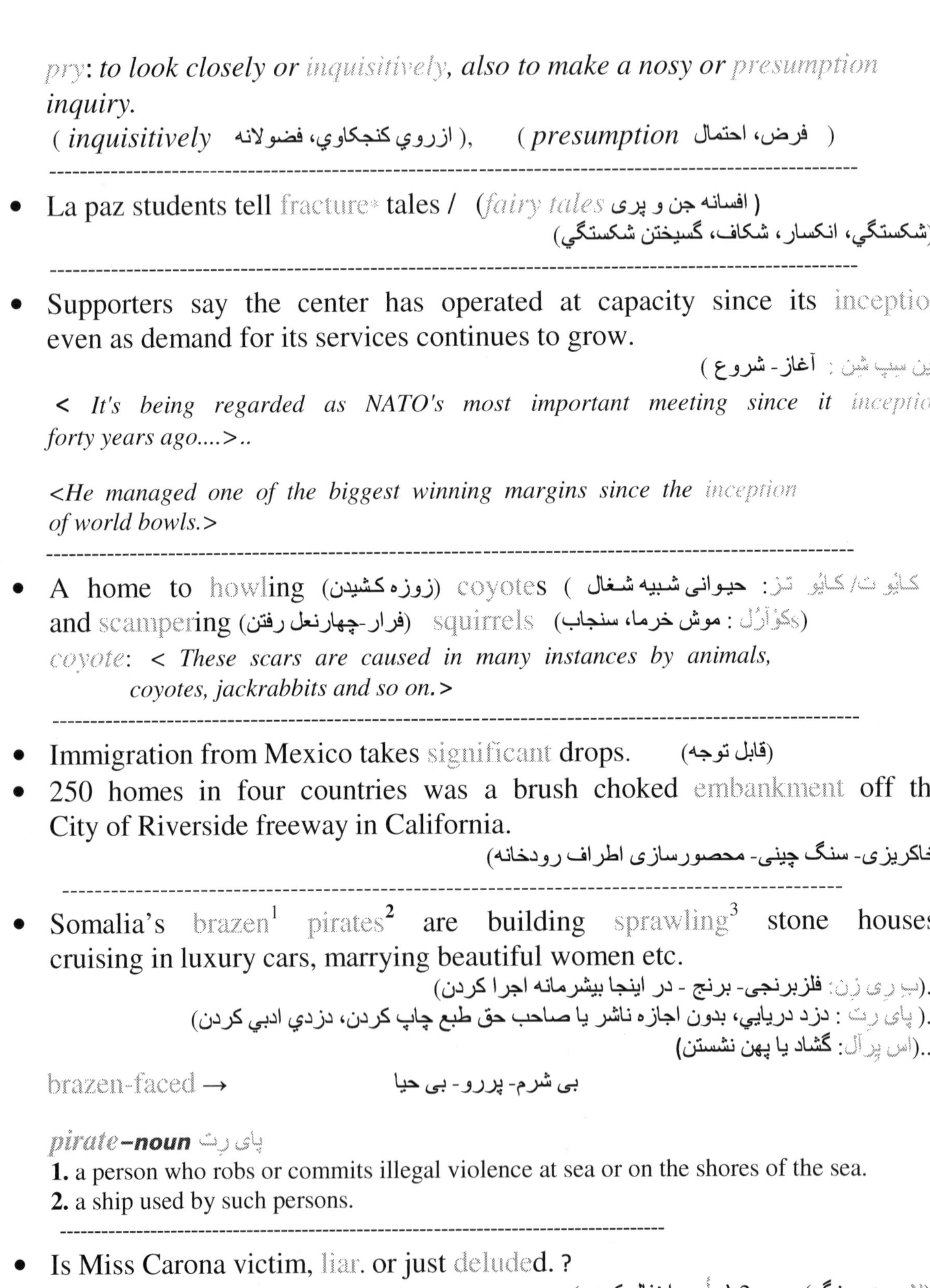

pry: to look closely or inquisitively, also to make a nosy or presumption inquiry.
(*inquisitively* ازروي كنجكاوي، فضولانه), (*presumption* فرض، احتمال)

- La paz students tell fracture* tales / (*fairy tales* افسانه جن و پری)
*(شکستگي، انکسار، شکاف، گسیختن شکستگي)

- Supporters say the center has operated at capacity since its inception even as demand for its services continues to grow.
(این سیپ شِن : آغاز- شروع)

< It's being regarded as NATO's most important meeting since it inception forty years ago....>..

<He managed one of the biggest winning margins since the inception of world bowls.>

- A home to howling (زوزه کشیدن) coyotes (کایوت/ کایو تز: حیوانی شبیه شغال) and scampering (فرار-چهارنعل رفتن) squirrels (سکوآرل : موش خرما، سنجاب)
coyote: *< These scars are caused in many instances by animals, coyotes, jackrabbits and so on.>*

- Immigration from Mexico takes significant drops. (قابل توجه)
- 250 homes in four countries was a brush choked embankment off the City of Riverside freeway in California.
(خاکریزی- سنگ چینی- محصورسازی اطراف رودخانه)

- Somalia's brazen[1] pirates[2] are building sprawling[3] stone houses, cruising in luxury cars, marrying beautiful women etc.
1.(بِ ری زن: فلزبرنجی- برنج - در اینجا بیشرمانه اجرا کردن)
2.(پای رِت : دزد دریايي، بدون اجازه ناشر یا صاحب حق طبع چاپ کردن، دزدي ادبي کردن)
3..(اس پِرآل: گشاد یا پهن نشستن)

brazen-faced → بی شرم- پررو- بی حیا

***pirate*-noun** پای رِت
1. a person who robs or commits illegal violence at sea or on the shores of the sea.
2. a ship used by such persons.

- Is Miss Carona victim, liar. or just deluded. ?
1(لایر: دروغگو), 2.(دِ لود: اغفال کردن)

delude: *to mislead the mind or judgment of deceive, trick*
delusion: ← (فریب-اغفال) (فریبنده → Delusive)

- It can be approved by a two-thirds vote, and then ratified by voters.
(تصویب/تصدیق کردن)
- Orange County Fire Authority says day hydrants hindered crews efforts.
(ممانعت/جلوگیری کردن- عقب انداختن)
- She told police she holds no ill will toward the person who hit her.
ایل ویل : دشمني، سوء نیت
- The revelation comes as residents and city officials continue to demand answers for why ... (آشکارسازی- افشاء)

- God bless those affected by the fires….. my heart goes out to them.

- Bill Clinton's trysts (تی رست) * with his secretary Miss Monica Lewensky at the white house....
*(گذاشتن، نامزدی، قرار ملاقات، میعادگاه قرار ملاقات)

tryst: 1. An agreement (as between lovers) to meet,
2. An appointed meeting or meeting place

- According to your representatives, this fee is related to a procedure having been performed by a "specialist" and may have been averted if performed by a "dentist". (برگرداندن، گردانیدن، دفع کردن،)

کلمه زیر را دکتر لورا دکتر مشگلات خانوادگی به کسی می گفت که با زنش از لحاظ سکس وضع درستی نداشت .

- Do slurping: it means to make a sucking noise while eating or drinking
s لُرپ : صداي مکیدن دراوردن ، باصدا خوردن یا اشامیدن هش هش

- Military leaders: repeal don't ask don't tell policy.
ر پیل: لغو کردن- ملغی ساختن
توضیح راجع به جمله‌ء فوق : در زمان کلینتون در ارتش آمریکا مقرر شد که هم جنس بازان راجع به منحرف بودنشان **قانون چیزی بهم نگویند و نپرسند** را پیشه گیرند.

- Insurance scammer kills himself. s کمر : کلاهبرداري کردن

scam: s کم :deceive, defraud or to obtain (as money) by a scam.

- glowing* embers** took the fire south of the freeway to Anaheim Hills. *(گلو اینگ : فروزان- برافروخته), **(آمبر :جرقه)
- A house on Alder street was hit by flying embers and destroyed Saturday pm. (اَم بِر: اخگر- جرقه روشن)

- Fashion designer sexually assaulting[1] seven girls and women some of them aspiring[2]. models lured[3] with promises of job and stays at luxury hotels.

1.(اَسالتینگ :حمله - یورش کردن) **2**.(اَس پایه رینگ: آرزو داشتن) **3**.(لُرد: بدام انداختن- تطمیع کردن)

- He sued the talk show host for defamation claiming he falsely suggested .... دِفِ مِی شِن : افترا- تهمت- بدنامی- رسوایی

- Also he was guilty of multiple counts of committing a lewd[1] act on a child, attempted forcible[2] oral copulation[3]

1.(لُود یا لود: هرزه، ناشي از هرزگي شهوت پرست) 2.(اجباري- عدواني) 3.(کاپیو لِیشِن : جماع

copulation ***–noun***
1. sexual intercourse.
2. a joining together or coupling.

- *lewd*: evil, wicked[1] sexually *unchaste[2] or licentious[3] obscene, vulgar[4] .*

1.(وی کِد: شریر- بدکار- گنهکار)
2.(آن چیست: متضاد پاکدامن و عفیف) - **3**.(لای سِن شِس: هرزه-شهوتران), **4**.(وُل گِر:پست)

licentiously لای سِن شِسلی : از روی هرزگی
copulation کاپیولی شن*: copulate, copulating: to engage in sexual intercourse*

wicked: *morally very bad, evil*

- I am flattered[1] that former Alaska governor Sara Palin has chosen to cite[2] as a source of wisdom.

1.(فِلَتِر: خرسند – مسرور) **2**.(ذکر کردن، اتخاذ سند کردن گفتن- احضار کردن)

flattered-- If you are flattered by something, you are pleased because it makes you feel important
flatter ---verb (used with object)

1. to try to please by complimentary remarks or attention.

2. to praise or compliment insincerely, effusively, or excessively: *She flatters him by constantly praising his books.*
3. to represent favorably; gratify by falsification: *The portrait flatters her.*

cite: to call upon officially or authoritatively to appear

- Firefighters continued to stamp out the smoldering[1] remain of sprawling[2] freeway complex wildlife Thursday.

1.(اس مول دریینگ: سوختن ودودکردن، بي اتش سوختن خاموش کرد)
2.(اس پرال: پهن نشستن، گشاد نشستن ، بي پروا درازکشیدن یا نشستن)

smolder **–verb (used without object)**
1. to burn without flame; undergo slow or suppressed combustion.
2. to exist or continue in a suppressed state or without outward demonstration: *Hatred smoldered beneath a polite surface.*
3. to display repressed feelings, as of indignation, anger, or the like: *to smolder with rage.*
–noun
4. dense smoke resulting from slow or suppressed combustion. **5.** a smoldering fire.
*smolde***ring**: *to burn sluggishly* بکندی *without flame often with much smoke.* <to burn sluggishly>

- *He says the tiger grabbed the girl's hand, then spooked* ترساندن *and bit her when a visitor jumped over a fence to help.*

spook: ghost, specter, an undercover agent: spy
spookish: is adjective
A spook is a ghost that is thought to appear and haunt a place; an informal word.

- In USA State's new law ban[1] on same sex marriage but referred to allow gay couples to resume[2] marriage pending a decision. The California Supreme Court accepted three law suits seeking to nullify[3] proposition #8.

1.(قدغن/تحریم/لعن کردن)

2.(رزوم:از سرگرفتن- دوباره بدست آوردن), 3.(نولی فای : لغو/ملغی کردن)

nullify: to make null; esp. to make legally null and void

What was proposition # 8 in California (Nov. 2008)?

ان بود که به آرای عمومی گذاشته شده بود اگر ازدواج باید بین یک زن و مرد باشد رای بدهید بله، در غیر اینصورت نه. که در زمان اوباما مورد قبول قرار گرفت

- To return to or begin again after interruption. < *resumed her work*>

resumed, resuming → مشتقات *resume* می باشند

resume این لغت اسپلش شبیه به رزمِه فرانسوی است یعنی خلاصه .

همان چیزی که موقع شغل پیدا کردن بطور خلاصه دربارهٔ خودت می نویسی و جویای کار می شوی.

- The democrat had faced increasing pressure to step down and possible expulsion by her senate colleagues since she was arrested last month.

اکس پال ژِن: اخراج/بیرون کردن

expulsion: the act of expelling: the state of being expelled

- Someone attached a cab driver with a machete in a road rage incident. Hebegan whacking the cab-driver on the leg with the flat side.

(ماشِT: کارد بزرگ و سنگین) (وَ کینگ:کتک زدن)

ماشِتی: چاقوی بزرگ و سنگین که با آن شاخه های درختان را قطع می کنند

machete (ماشِT): *a large heavy knife used for cutting sugar cane and underbrush* ماشِT کارد بزرگ و سنگین

- Laura Bush is planning a memoir[1] and has met with publishers. She collaborate[2] with daughter on a children's book published last year.

1.(مِمْ آر: یادداشت- تاریخچه- ترجمه احوال)

2.(همکاری- تشریک مساعی)

memoir: R مِمْ *an official note or report; memorandum or a narrative composed from personal experience*

Mentor devotes years to helping a boy grow up.

(رایزن- خردمند-امین/ناصح- مربی)

- Obama no socialist, but is a meddler (مِ دِ لِر:فضول- آدم فضول)

(Meddle فضولی کردن)

To meddle in or with an affair در کاری فضولی کردن

- Work a good distraction for Madonna . (پریشانی- آشفتگی- آشوب)

- Afghan teacher seeks retribution. (ریتری بیو شِن : کیفر- تلافی)

- California's clout in congress growing. (کِلات: قاب دستمال یا رگ - نفوذ سیاسی)

<Political clout نفوذ سیاسی >   ولی در سیاست معنی نفوذ میدهد←

- US TV star Oprah wants a court to dismiss or order arbitration[1] in a defamation[2] lawsuit filed by the ex-head mistress of her girl's school in South Africa.

(داوري ، راي بطريق حكميت : آربی تری شِن) 1.   (افترا- تهمت : دِفِ می شِن) 2.

arbitration is the judging of a dispute between people or groups by someone who is not involved.
<...arbitration between employers and unions.>

- A strobe light can guide ambulance.
strobe : a device that utilized a flash tube for light speed illumination (as in photography), stroboscope.
<The police helicopter circled above flashing strobe lights>.
(اس تُو- رؤب : *(کامپیوتر)* سیگنالي که بیان میکند آدرس معتبر در باس آدرس قرار دارد)

- Slain man had scientology ties.   (کشتن- به قتل رساندن) *PP.* of slay
Slay, slew (اِس لُو), slain   ←   سه قسمت لغت
scientology: *is the study and handling of the spirit in relationship to itself,*
slay—Verb with Object
To slay someone means to kill them; a literary word.
Samson performed incredible feats of strength such as slaying 1,000 Philistines with the jawbone of an ass....< Two visitors were brutally slain yesterday.>

- What is the difference between a plebiscite and a **referendum**? My experience in Canada, having actively participated in both, is that a **referendum** is a non-binding expression of the opinion of the electorate, whereas the result of a plebiscite is binding on the...
(پِلِ بِ سایت: آراء عمومی- رای عموم اهالی)

A plebiscite is a vote in which all the people in a country or region are asked whether they agree or disagree with a particular policy, for example a policy of unification with another country.

- A woman was arrested Friday on suspicion of swindling a bank out of $25000. It was unclear if anyone else was involved in the scheme?

(سُوُ اِن دِ لینگ : گول زدن- گوش بری کردن)

swindling: to obtain money or property by fraud or deceit.

cheat=swindle

- Shippers urge naval blockade[1], shipper called for a military blockade along Somalia's coast to intercept[2] pirate vessels heading out to sea.

1.(بِلا کِید : راه بند- سد- محاصره کردن) , **2.**(این تِر سِپت : قطع/جلوگیری کردن- بریدن)

blockade **-noun** بِلا کِید

1. the isolating, closing off, or surrounding of a place, as a port, harbor, or city, by hostile ships or troops to prevent entrance or exit.

intercept **-verb (used with object)** قطع/جلوگیری کردن- بریدن : (این تِر سِپت.)

1. to take, seize, or halt (someone or something on the way from one place to another); cut off from an intended destination: *to intercept a messenger.*

2. to see or overhear (a message, transmission, etc., meant for another): *We intercepted the enemy's battle plan.*

3. to stop or check (passage, travel, etc.): *to intercept the traitor's escape.*

4. *Sports* . to take possession of (a ball or puck) during an attempted pass by an opposing team. **5.** to stop or interrupt the course, progress, or transmission of.

- Nationwide sales of existing homes fell more than expected last month as economic fears made buyers leery (even though prices plunged to the lowest level).

(لِی ری: اسلنگ است یعنی ناقلا/در اینجا تهی- خالی)

leery often used with ***of*** → <*leery* ***of*** *stranger*>

- Cal State University in Fullerton event designed to demystify (D میس تی فای) hunger, homelessness…

demystify: to eliminate the mystifying features of demystification.

(Dمیس تی فای : سر چیزي را برطرف کردن- گیج کردن- دست انداختن- رمزی کردن)

- The 49-year-old distinct was under heavy scrutiny Tuesday as officials tried to explain why pressure died in some areas.

(S کُروتِنی: رسیدگی دقیق- امتحان کردن)

scrutiny: a searching study, inquiry, or inspections

- She watched old footage showing flames devouring brush in the Santa Ana Canyon. (دِوَ اور: دریدن- خوردن- بلعیدن)

devouring: to eat up greedily or ravenously for: ..... (رَوِنِس لی) حریصانه
<Lines devouring their prey> (پِرِی: شکار-صید)

- The hot air and faint whiff (V ف) of smoke were the only signs in old town of Yorba Linda that …

V ف: باد مختصر- آهسته وزیدن- در اینجا بوی دود

whiff **-noun**
1. a slight gust or puff of wind, air, vapor, smoke, or the like: *<a whiff of fresh air.>*
2. a slight trace of odor or smell: *<a whiff of onions.>*
3. a single inhalation or exhalation of air, tobacco smoke, or the like.

- Insurance scanner kills himself. The judge there was set sentence Brown to as many as five years in prison and $250,000 fine for helping to con (کان)* a number of companies out of more than $100 million by selling phony workers compensation insurance.

scanner is noun, to obtain (as money) by a scam (see below for meaning)
scamming, deceive, defraud

scam: کلاهبرداري، گوشبري، شيادي ، کلاهبرداري کردن، گوش بريدن، شيادي کردن
con: to commit to memory or to study or examine closely
*con**ned**, con**ning*** ← مشتقات کان
*(اعتماد، گول زدن، مخالف پیشوند confidence از بر کردن، دانستن، مخفف کلمه عامیانه)

- Masked commandos rappelled from a helicopter to rooftop of the building.

رَپل: از یک نقطه بلند خود را با طناب به نقطه پایین تر رساندن
*Rappel, rappel**ling**, rappel**led*** ← مشتقات آن

- Indian forces fired a racket at the building. Soon after elated[1] commandos ran out with rifles raised in a sign of triumph[2].

1.(E لیت: مغرور- مغرور کردن) 2.(تری آمف : پیروزي، فتح، غالب امدن پیروزشدن)

- Shrapnel kills man in Irvine, he died after apparently hit with shrapnel during an industrial accident. (شِرَپ نِل: گلوله نارنجکی)

stalemate پات کردن: *deadlock, a drawing position in chess in which a player is not checkmate but has no legal move play.*

- Violence stated when more than a dozen assailant attacked to sites across the city. (أ سِی لِنت: حمله کننده- مهاجم)
  Assail, assailer (حمله کردن، هجوم اوردن بر) assailable, assailant ← مشتقات

- Taj-Mahal Hotel was struck for hours by intermittent gunfire and explosions. (این تِرمی تِنت: متناوب- نوبتی)

intermittent: :این تِرمی تِنت *coming and going at intervals, not continuous,* <*Intermittent rain*> also <occasional>, <*intermittent trips abroad*>, <*intermittent fever*> تب نوبه ایی

- "You can not put him on a pedestal[1] and wrap him in cellophane [2]so that people will fall down and worship him. It is not fair to expect someone swoop[3] down and save you"

1.(پایه ستون، پایه مجسمه شالوده، محور، روي پایه قرار دادن، بلند کردن ترفیع دادن)
2.(سِه لِفین:به معنی انگلیسی آن مراجعه شود)
3.(سُوپ:ناگهان فرود آمدن)

cellophane **--noun** سِه لِفین

1. a transparent, paper like product of viscose, impervious to moisture, germs, etc., used to wrap and package food, tobacco, etc.
–adjective: **2.** of, made of, or resembling cellophane.
Cellophane is a trademark. <*Drugs wrapped in cellophane.*>

- "There is no question it will have a ripple effect, because of power of the position". (رِپِل: موج کوچک- پخش شدن هم می تواند باشد)
  موج دار شدن، داراي سطح ناهموار، بطور موجي حرکت کردن

ripple effect: spread <*the news ripple outwards*>

- Obama was destined to be president. (دِس تین : در نظر گرفتن-عازم بسوی مقصدی)

destine دِس تین**–verb (used with object),** -tined, -tin·ing.
1. to set apart for a particular use, purpose, etc.; design; intend.
2. to appoint or ordain beforehand, as by divine decree; foreordain; predetermine.

Another benefit to fall transplanting is that most plants and trees are entering a period of dormancy[1] rather than continuing to transfer energy into new foliage[2] and above-ground growth. (*Dormant*خوابیده- بی حرکت)

1.(دُرمَنسی: خوابیدگی- ایست- وقفه) 2.(فولی یج: برگ درختان ، شاخ وبرگ)

- Plants growing below grade can easily succumb to root rot or disease.

(سِه کام: ازپادرآمدن- مردن- تسلیم شدن)

succumb **–verb (used without object)** سِه کام
1. to give way to superior force; yield: *to succumb to despair** . نومیدي، یاس، مایوس شدن*
2. to yield to disease, wounds, old age, etc.; die.

- Have you ever heard of the expression "dig a $10 hole for a $1 plan" ? This means making the planting hole two to three times wider than the current root ball. But don't make the hole any deeper than the plant was growing in its previous environment.

(این وای رِ مِنت : محیط، اطراف، احاطه، دور وبر)

- Extending the stay of U.S. forces could impinge[1] on Iraq's sovereignty[2] they warn.

1.(ایم پِن ج: برخورد کردن- اینجا یعنی تجاوز کردن)
2.(ساو رِن تی: پادشاهی- اقتدار- اینجا یعنی حاکمیت)

impinge **–verb (used without object)**
1. to make an impression; have an effect or impact (usually fol. by ***on*** or ***upon***); *to impinge upon the imagination; social pressures that impinge upon one's daily life.*
2. to encroach; infringe (usually fol. by ***on*** or ***upon***): *to impinge on another's rights.*
3. to strike; dash; collide (usually fol. by ***on, upon,*** or ***against***): *rays of light impinging on the eye.*
sovereignty ***–noun, plural*** -ties. ساو رِن تی: پادشاهی- اقتدار- اینجا یعنی حاکمیت
1. the quality or state of being sovereign.
2. the status, dominion, power, or authority of a sovereign; royalty.
3. a sovereign state, community, or political unit.

- Futility[1] the quality or state of being futile[2] **use**lessness.

1. (فیو تی لیتی : بیهودگی- بی فایدگی) 2. (فیو تِل : بیهوده- عبث- بی فایده)

- The pressure from the clerics show cases the precarious position of Iraqi Nouri al Maliki reject the deal.

(پِر کَ ری آس: ناپایدار- چند روزه- متزلزل)

precarious **–adjective** پِر کَ ری آس
1. dependent on circumstances beyond one's control; uncertain; unstable; insecure: *a precarious livelihood.*
2. dependent on the will or pleasure of another; liable to be withdrawn or lost at the will of another: *He held a precarious tenure under an arbitrary administration.*

- As lawmakers craft[1] their Iraq strategy, they could be entering either a constitutional minefield[2] or an exercise in futility[3]

.3) .1.(پیشه) 2.(ماین فیلد : ناحیه مین گذاری شده- اینجا یعنی چیزی که باید خیلی احتیاط کرد) بیهودگی- بی فایدگی)

minefield **–noun** Military, Naval . ماین فیلد

An area of land or water throughout which explosive mines have been laid.
<*A political minefield*>

- I don't see same bizarre[1] aberrations[2]

1.(بزار: غریب ناشی از هوس)
2.(گمراهی- انحراف- در فیزیک عدم تمرکز به یک کانون- خبط دماغ)

bizarre: بزار *syn.*→ fantastic.

bizarre → *adj*, ***bizarrely***→ *adv*, ***bizarreness*** →*noun*

bizarreness: غريب وعجيب، غير مانوس ناشي از هوس، خيالي وهمي

- Officer taken on harrowing[1] ride gunmen stole a police van but failed to see the constable[2] in the black seat.

1.(جان آزار- دلخراش) ,2.(افسر ارتش، پاسبان، ضابط)

<*Constable Steven Hanson led passengers to safety.*>

- "At first, I thought it was a going-away prank Andrew said".

(پرَنک : شوخی- فریب- حرکت نامنظم)

prank: *Trick, a malicious act, a mildly, mischievous act, as ludicrous act*

- They scoffed when they saw police officers in bullet proof vest had been killed. (اس کاف: تمسخر - طعنه- استهزاء)

scoff–verb (used without object) :اس کاف

1. to speak derisively; mock; jeer (often fol. by *at*): *If you can't do any better, don't scoff. Their efforts toward a peaceful settlement are not to be scoffed at.*

–verb (used with object); **2.** to mock at; deride.

- The gunmen opened the doors and dumped five slumped officers' bodies into the streets.

(S لامپ : یکباره فرو ریختن سقوط کردن، خمیده شد ن - افت- تنزل فاحش- پایین افتادن)

- slump: *to drop or slide down suddenly: collapse,* <*Slump to the floor*>

He selected a luxurious house; the selected property sets or returns the value of the selected attribute of an option.

(اَتری b یُوت: نسبت دادن- اسناد کردن –حمل کردن بر)

attribute **–verb (used with object)** اَتری b یُوت

1. to regard as resulting from a specified cause; consider as caused by something indicated (usually fol. by ***to***): *She attributed his bad temper to ill health.*
2. to consider as a quality or characteristic of the person, thing, group, etc., indicated: *He attributed intelligence to his colleagues. to attribute a painting to an artist.*
–noun: **4.** something attributed as belonging to a person, thing, group, etc.; *Sensitivity is one of his attributes.* In *the red house, red* is an attribute of *house.*

- Obama selections include longtime advisers and political foes[1] alike, most notably democratic primacy[2] rival Hillary Clinton.

1.(فُ : دشمن- مخالف) 2.(پرای مِسی : برتري، تقدم)

foe: one who has personal enmity for another, (اِن می تی :دشمني، خصومت)

foe: <an enmity in war>, adversary, opponent, or one who opposes on principle

foe **–noun** فُ

1. a person who feels enmity, hatred, or malice toward another; enemy: *a bitter foe.*
2. a military enemy; hostile army. **3.** a person belonging to a hostile army or nation.
4. an opponent in a game or contest; adversary: *a political foe.*

- The democratic officials disclosed the plans Sunday on condition of anonymity because they were not authorized for public release ahead of the news conference. اَنْ نی م تی: بدناتمی- گمراهی

anonym → اَنُونیم: شخص بی نام- نویسنده گمنام

- Sound processing may be autism (آتـی زم) key. Scientists said they found a common brain wave pattern in children with autism that they think represent a delay in processing sound.

(اَتی زم : خیال پرستي، عدم توجه بعالم مادي، وهم گرايي , *(روانشناسي)* در خود ماندگي [اوتيسم]

- He is been coy in some of his answers but has said he will remain in office until the end of his team in Jan 2011. (شرم رو- کناره گیر)

<using coy trick to attract attention> , *Synonym: shy*

- Three weeks ago, a cleric close to Iran's president gloated publicly that the world financial crisis was God's punishment on United States.
  (گِ لُوت: چشم چرانی کردن- اینجا یعنی نگاه با حسرت)

- Will California's governor share the stage with former US vice president AL-Gore as a global environmental crusader promote green technology for an Obama administration? (سرباز جنگ صلیبی- مجاهد)

crusade: *any of the military expeditions undertaken by the Christians of Europe in the 11th, 12th, and 13th centuries for the recovery of the Holy Land from the Muslims.*

- He didn't make his getaway (گریز) before an ethnicity related .
  (اِت نِ سیتی : نژاد- قومیت)

ethnicity-- ***noun, plural*** -ties. اِت نِ سیتی
1. ethnic traits, background, allegiance, or association.
2. an ethnic group: *Representatives of several ethnicities were present.*
<*to make one's getaway* گریختن- دررفتن >

ethnic نژادی-قومی / ethnically مربوط به نژاد
<*Ethnic quality or affiliation* >, <*aspects of ethnicity*>
<*Students of diverse ethnicities*>, (دای وِرس : گوناگون، مختلف)

- He starting to rise up, assert himself. (اظهار/ادعا کردن)
  (*To assert oneself.*) → حق خود را اعاده یا مطالبه کردن

- To look or glance admiringly or amorously . (آموِرِس: عاشقانه- شیفته وار)

- Are you dreading going to work today? (ترسیدن- بیم داشتن)

- Iran plunged this week into a bitter storm of political recrimination. largely directed at Iran's president . (بدگویی در مقابل بدگویی)
  Recriminate متقابلا بدگویی کردن

- blab- **verb**
  If you blab, you reveal a secret; an informal word. *I wonder who blabbed.... He's been blabbing to the Press.*

blab فضولی کردن- فضول- وراجي کردن
blabber آدم بی چاک و دهن-فضول

- Critics say he was squandered[1] Iran's oil windfall[2] on costly, subsidized[3] imports, from fruit and other goods.

1. (s گو آندِر : برباد دادن ، تلف کردن ، ولخرجي ، اسراف)
2. (ویند فال : میوه باد انداخته، ثروت باداورده - برباد دادن)

3. (ساب سی دایز: کمک هزینه دادن، کمک خرج دادن)

(squanderer شخص ولخرج- مصرف)

squander **–verb (used with object)** : s گو آندِر

1. to spend or use (money, time, etc.) extravagantly or wastefully (often fol. by *away*).
2. to scatter.
–noun; **3.** extravagant or wasteful expenditure.

subsidize **–verb**), -dized, -diz·ing. ساب سی دایز: کمک هزینه دادن، کمک خرج دادن

1. to furnish or aid with a subsidy.
2. to purchase the assistance of by the payment of a subsidy.
3. to secure the cooperation of by bribery; buy over.

- To spend extravagantly or foolishly.

extravagant اکس ترا وگنت: نامعقول- مفرط

extravagant **–adjective**
1. spending much more than is necessary or wise; wasteful: *an extravagant shopper.*
2. excessively high: *extravagant expenses; extravagant prices.*
<*extravagant praise*>. <extravagant or wasteful expenditure.>

- Both candidates said the long wait has been agonizing. Asking for a recount was a difficult decision for me, he said.

(اگ نایزینگ : بخودپیچیدن- غذاب دادن- درد کشیدن- تقلا کردن)

***agonizing* –adjective** اگ نایزینگ
accompanied by, filled with, or resulting in agony or distress: <We spent an agonizing hour waiting to hear if the accident had been serious or not.>

- The government hopes creating jobs and spurring the economy out of recession. (s پر : مهمیز/سیخ زدن- انگیزه)

- The revelation came as senior US. official said India received a warning form the United States. (رِو لِی شِن : آشکارسازی-افشاء)

revelation **–noun** رِو لِی شِن آشکارسازی-افشاء
1. the act of revealing or disclosing; disclosure.
2. something revealed or disclosed, esp. a striking disclosure, as of something not before realized.

- California governor Arnold Sh. flanks Alaska governor Sara P. on Tues. At national governors association meeting.
پهلو- طرف- درکنارچیزی واقع شدن

- President Obama has more leeway to change US. Cuba policy.
(لی وِی : انحراف-عقب افتادگی راه گریز),
معنی دیگر آن یکبرشدگی کشتی به آن سویی که از باد در امان باشد

leeway **–noun** راه گریز انحراف-عقب افتادگی : لی وِی
1. extra time, space, materials, or the like, within which to operate; margin: *With ten minutes' leeway we can catch the train.*
2. a degree of freedom of action or thought: *His instructions gave us plenty of leeway.*

- Legal claims are often precursors to lawsuits. پیشرو- منادی : p ری- کِرسِرز

(precursory : مقدماتی-از پیش)
precursors **–noun** پیشرو- منادی : pری- کِرسِرز
1. a person or thing that precedes, as in a job, a method, etc.; predecessor.
2. a person, animal, or thing that goes before and indicates the approach of someone or something else; harbinger: *The first robin is a precursor of spring.*

- Prosecution contends killers wanted victim's vehicle to chop it for parts.
ستیزه کردن، ، ادعا کردن, مجادله/کشمکش کردن

<A list with the personal info of 1200 people a group contends are illegal immigrants has been mailed around Utah,>

- Family of trampled man sues Wal-mart Store. The family of worker trampled to death in a **Black Friday** (*day after Thanksgiving Day*).

(تِ رَم پِل: پایمال کردن-زیرپا له کردن)
مطلب فوق درباره کارمندی است که روز بعد ازتعطیلات شکر گزاری در اثر حمله خریداران به داخل فروشگاه کشته شده.

- Egyptian President **Hosni Mubarak** travels to Camp David Friday, with an urgent appeal to President Bush for the U.S. to set a timetable for the establishment of In 1977, **Mubarak's** predecessor, the late **Anwar Sadat**, flew to Jerusalem in a dramatic gesture that resulted in a peace treaty with Israel two years later.

(Pری دِس سُر : شخص پیشین- متصدی پیش از من- در جمع پیشی نیان)

Predecessor-- ***noun*** P ری دِس سُر
1. a person who precedes another in an office, position, etc.
2. something succeeded or replaced by something else: *The new monument in the park is more beautiful than its predecessor.*

- cutting-edge: a sharp effect or quality, the foremost* part or place: vanguard**. * (جلوترین) ,**(جلودار- طلایه- پیش قراول- واحد مقدم)

vanguard ***–noun***
1. the foremost division or the front part of an army; advance guard; van.
2. the forefront in any movement, field, activity, or the like.
3. the leaders of any intellectual or political movement.

- Poor Greek man who was trampled to death at a Wal-mart store in New York. (تِ رَم پِل: پایمال کردن-زیرپا له کردن)

trample → *verb*
trample and trampling are→ *intransitive verb*
trample and trampler are → *noun*

- In addition to immense[1] amount of respect deemed[2] from her esteemed[3] colleagues[4], … *<I deem it my duty to…* وظیفه خود میدانم که >

1.(بی اندازه- خیلی زیاد- بطوروسیع) **2**.(دانستن- فرض کردن) **3**.(محترم شمردن-لایق دانستن)

4.(هم کار، هم قطار ***–noun*** *an associate.*)

- Murder trial veers (V یِرز) toward hung jury and back again. Veer (وِر), veers (وی یِرز) , (Vیرز : تغییرجهت/تغییر رای دادن)

- But some Latin are grumbling the appointment *is not enough* after all the support they gave him in campaign. (قرقر/شکایت کردن)
این مطلب در رابطه با انتخاب فرماندار نیومکزیکوبسمت وزیر بازرگانی بوسیله اوباما که از طرف مردم لاتین کاندید شده بود .

- A Boston red sox fan was convicted of battery[1] for assaulating[2] an angels fan.
1.(بَ تِ-re : ضربه/کتک زدن), 2.(حمله کردن-یورش بردن)

battery **–noun, plural** -ter·ies. بَ تِ-re
1. *Electricity* .
a. Also called galvanic battery, voltaic battery. a combination of two or more cells electrically connected to work together to produce electric energy.
2. any large group or series of related things: *a battery of questions.*
the act of beating or battering.
3. *Law* . an unlawful attack upon another person by beating or wounding, or by touching in an offensive manner.

assault **–noun**
1. a sudden, violent attack; onslaught: *an assault on tradition.*
2. *Law* . an unlawful physical attack upon another; an attempt or offer to do violence to another, with or without battery, as by holding a stone or club in a threatening manner.
3. *Military* . the stage of close combat in an attack.
4. Rape . A violent physical or verbal attack
–verb (used with object) **5.** to make an assault upon; attack; assail.

- Mr. Corona sought illicit donation ex-lawyer says. E لِ سیت**:** ممنوع- قاچاق
illicitly→ *adv.* از راه قاچاق
illicitness→ *noun* ممنوعیت- قاچاقی بودن

illicit **–adjective** E لِ سیت**:** ممنوع- قاچاق
1. not legally permitted or authorized; unlicensed; unlawful.
2. disapproved of or not permitted for moral or ethical reasons.

- Circumstantial evidence → مدرک دارای جزئیات
Other evidence may be slight and need only be enough to support a reasonable inference that someone's criminal conduct caused an injury, loss, or harm. (این فِرنس : استنباط- نتیجه)

- The school assembly started with a stern[1] warning from the police chief that truancy[2] and gang activity will not be tolerated and could result in jail.

1.(اس ترن : سخت- سخت گیر) , 2.(ترو ان سی: فرار از آموزشگاه)

stern اس ترن**–*adjective,*** -er, -est.
1. firm, strict, or uncompromising: *stern discipline.*
2. hard, harsh, or severe: *a stern reprimand.*
3. rigorous or austere; of an unpleasantly serious character: *stern times.*
4. grim or forbidding in aspect: *a stern face.*
truancy ترو ان سی **–*noun, plural*** -cies.
1. the act or state of being truant.
2. an instance of being truant: *His parents were questioned about his many truancies.*
<*an act or instance of playing truant the state of being truant*>
(ترو انت: بچه مکتب گریز- آدم طفره رو یا تنبل)
<*To play the truant* از آموزشگاه فرار کردن >

- The terms application of force and apply force mean to touch in harmful or offensive[1] manner. The slightest[2] touch can be enough if it is done in a rude[3] or angry way.

Offense=offence

1.(متهاجم- متجاوز- اهانت آمیز) ,
2.(مقدار ناچیز، شخص بي اهميت) **3.**(رُود : خشن، جسور)

offensively بطور اهانت امیز- از راه تهاجم
<*To take the offensive*> حالت تهاجمی به خود گرفتن

- The defendant personally inflicted great bodily injury on. این فلیکت: وارد آوردن

<*To inflict a stroke upon* (بر) *a person*>
<*To inflict a loss on someone*> به کسي ضرر زدن (رساندن) ؟
<*If you inflict something unpleasant on someone, you make them suffer it.*>

- He was in imminent danger of suffering bodily injury.

إمی ننت : تهدید کننده- قریب الوقوع

imminence نزدیکی- مشرف بودن

کلمه *Imminence* از نظر دستوری اسم است و معنی خطر مشرف و تهدید کننده هم میدهد

- A soldier's story from a day of infamy*. (رسوایی- بدنامی- محرومیت از حقوق مدنی)*

(infamy * : این فمی) (Infamous → این فِ مِس : رسوا- بدنام- محروم از حقوق مدنی)

- To pursue an assailant* until the danger of bodily injury has passed. (*A person who attacks.* ← (حمله کننده- مهاجم)*

assail هجوم آوردن بر- حمله بردن بر
assailment یورش- حمله (اسم است)
<He was assailed in the press....>
<He has been assailed with death threats and obscene phone calls.>

- He is charged with one felony[1] count of lewd[2] acts upon a child

1 . (فِلو نی : تبه کار- جنایتکار- بدکاری-خیانت)
2 . (لُـو د : ناشی از هرزگی: هرزه- شهوت پرستی)

(lewdness → هرزگی- شهوت پرستی)

- Male nursing assistant accused of sexual assault. حمله کردن- یورش بردن بر
<An assault by an army is a strong attack made against an enemy.>

- Supreme court will hear enemy combatant . (جنگ کننده- مبارز)
combative جنگجو

- Police said gardener and his co-defendants decide to kill white woman as retribution for slavery. (کیفر- مکافات-تلافی)

- We are besieged with such advertisements. (بسیج : محاصره کردن)

***besiege*–verb (used with object),** -sieged, -sieg·ing. بسیج
1. to lay siege to.
2. to crowd around; crowd in upon; surround: *Vacationers besieged the travel office.*

- A tribute to their lady. (3 بی یوُت : احترام- ستایش- پیش کشی)
<Military pays tribute at Pearl Harbor>, *<To pay tribute to* ستایش کردن >
< *Floral tributes* گل پیش کشی شده یا نثار شده >

***tribute* –noun** 3 بی یوُت احترام- ستایش- پیش کشی
1. a gift, testimonial, compliment, or the like, given as due or in acknowledgment of gratitude or esteem. **2.** a stated sum or other valuable consideration paid by one sovereign or state to another in acknowledgment of subjugation or as the price of peace, security, protection, or the like.

- Palestinian political squabbling[1] has kept thousands of would-be pilgrims from traveling to Mecca. Bank have run out of currency, depriving[2] thousands of civil servants of salaries.→ (سَلِ ریز)

1.(اس کُوا بِ لینگ: داد و بیداد- نزاع کردن- بهم ریختن)
2.(دیپ رآیو : محروم کردن- معزول کردن)

Squabble, squabbled, squabbler -- ***noun*** ← مشتقات

squabble-- verb (used without object)→ *to engage in a petty quarrel.* :اس کُوا بِل

- We are fervent in our belief that we all have a role to play in building a healthy, prosperous investment community.

فِرونت: با حرارت و اشتیاق

(fervently → باحالت حرارتی و التهاب)

fervent ***–adjective*** **فِرونت:** با حرارت و اشتیاق
1. having or showing great warmth or intensity of spirit, feeling, enthusiasm, etc.; ardent: *a fervent admirer; a fervent plea.* **2.** hot; burning; glowing.

- A letter-writer of city of Brea expressed concern over influence peddling[1] by former president Clinton aided and abetted[2] by his spouse.

1.(دوره گردی/خرده فروشی کردن- بیهوده وقت گذرانی کردن) 2.(اَبِت: تقویت/تشویق کردن)

abet–***verb (used with object),*** a·bet·ted, a·bet·ting.
to encourage, support, or countenance by aid or approval, usually in wrongdoing:
<to abet a swindler; to abet a crime.>

- Parole eligibility after five years. → (پِ رُل : اِلتزام- کلمه- قول شرف- گفته)
(اِل ج بِل تی : شایستگي- واجد شرایط بودن

By parole در حقوق (زبانی- شفاهی)
To release parole باگرفتن قول شرف آزاد کردن
parolee (پارولی): → *noun,* one release on parole
<A parolee was arrested in connection with a strong-arm robbery.>
<Parolees at large>, <Parolee rule and regulations>

Baby boomer[1] gloom[2] looms[3]

1.(ترقی فاحش و ناگهانی) ,**2.**(تیره تاریک- افسرده) **3.**(از دورنمودار شدن)

- There are publications that evaluate policies that are offered in such profusion. (پِر فیو ژِن : وفور- فراوانی-سرشاری)

(profuse پرف — u س : فراوان- بسیار)
<*The quality or state of being profuse*>, <*snow falling in profusion*>

profusion **–noun** پر فیو ژن : وفور- فراوانی-سرشاری
1. abundance; abundant quantity.
2. a great quantity or amount (often fol. by *of*).
3. lavish spending; extravagance.

The thought of calling an agent and sitting through a session of deductibles, exclusions, riders, or other insurance jargon[1] can seem intimidating[2].

1. (جارگن: سخن نامفهوم- دست و پاشکسته) , 2.(این تی می دِی تینگ: تشرزدن- ترساندن)

jargon **–noun** جارگن
1. the language, esp. the vocabulary, peculiar to a particular trade, profession, or group: *medical jargon.*
2. unintelligible or meaningless talk or writing; gibberish.
3. any talk or writing that one does not understand.

intimidate **–verb (used with object),** -dat·ed, -dat·ing. این تی می دِیت
1. to make timid; fill with fear.
2. to overawe or cow, as through the force of personality or by superior display of wealth, talent, etc.
3. to force into or deter from some action by inducing fear: *to intimidate a voter into staying away from the polls.*

- While the disparity in your financial means is a sensitive issue for you please consider this….. (دیس پَرتی : تفاوت کلی- بی شباهتی)

disparity **–noun, plural** -ties. دیس پَرتی
lack of similarity or equality; inequality; difference: *a disparity in age; disparity in rank.*

- My wife had been nagging[1] me all week to get a lottery ticket , so when I saw the lotto sign … I sprinted[2] in to get the ticket before they closed
1.(نَگینگ : مرتبا گوشزد کردن ، نق نقو- خرده گیري)
2.(دوسرعت، با حداکثر سرعت دویدن –دوی کوتاه و تند)

- Despite exhortation[1] to stimulate[2] the economy by consuming, we
1.(اِگ- زُرتی شِن: نصیحت- وادارسازی- ترغیب- اصرار)

2.(s- امی u لیت تحریک کردن، تهییج کردن انگیختن)

exhortation **–noun** اِگ- زُرتی شِن

1. the act or process of exhorting.
2. an utterance, discourse, or address conveying urgent advice or recommendations.

stimulate **–verb (used with object)**
1. to rouse to action or effort, as by encouragement or pressure; spur on; incite: *to stimulate his interest in mathematics.*
2. to invigorate (a person) by a food or beverage containing a stimulant, as coffee, tea, or alcoholic liquor.
–verb (used without object) **3.** to act as a stimulus or stimulant.

- Requiring community services is arrogant[1] and bigoted[2] .....

1.(اروگنت:متکبر - خودبین)
2.بدون ائی دی: بی گت-- (بی گیرتد: شخص متعصب)

bigotry→ تعصب (بی گ بتری)

arrogant **–adjective**
1. making claims or pretensions to superior importance or rights; overbearingly assuming; insolently proud: *an arrogant public official.*
2. characterized by or proceeding from arrogance: *arrogant claims.*

bigoted **–adjective**
1. utterly intolerant of any creed, belief, or opinion that differs from one's own.
2. Someone who is bigoted has strong and often unreasonable opinions and will not change them, even when they are proved to be wrong.
<*He was a bigoted, narrow-minded fanatic*>.
Synonyms→: narrow-mindedness, bias, discrimination

- He said the trio who are expected in court Tuesday are accused of follow-home robberies in city of Lake Forest. (3 یو: گروه 3 چیز)

- A claim is often a precursor to a lawsuit .....(پری کرسر: پیشرو - منادی)

Precursory (با Y یعنی مقدماتی- از پیش خبر دهنده)←

precursor **–noun**
1. a person or thing that precedes, as in a job, a method, etc.; predecessor.
2. a person, animal, or thing that goes before and indicates the approach of someone or something else; harbinger: *The first robin is a precursor of spring.*

- Bush's Secretary foreign minister Ms. Rice said she was still really appalled* at the inability of the international community to deal with tyrants**.

**(تای رِنت:حاکم ستمگر یا مستبد)

tyranny — حکومت ستمگرانه
appall*=appal → — اَپال: ترساندن
appalled, appalling → — ترسناک
<we were appalled his behavior>

- Police attribute rise in cold cases to more drug and gang killings.

(اَت ری بیوُت : نسبت دادن- اسناد کردن- حمل کردن بر)

- Sara Palin lost the election, but she's a winner to a connoisseur[1] of quotations[2]. 1.(کانِ آ سر:خبره) 2.(نقل قول)

Connoisseur means expert esp. one that enjoys with discrimination and appreciation of subtleties ساتِل- تی ز: باریک بینی- موشکافی

subtle — زیرک- هوشیار
subtly — از روی زیرکی
subtlety — باریک بینی- موشکافی

connoisseur: کانِ آ سر *A person who is especially competent to pass critical judgments in an art, particularly one of the fine arts, or in matters of taste: <A connoisseur of modern art.>*

- You have opted for ticket collection at your local Emirates office.

(آپت : برگزیدن- انتخاب کردن)

***opt*–verb (used without object)** آپت
1. to make a choice; choose (usually fol. by *for*).
—Verb phrase
2. opt out, to decide to leave or withdraw: *to opt out of the urban rat race and move to the countryside.*

- Mumbai massacre invokes memories. (احضار/استناد کردن)

- Further insurance protection is an intangible benefit. (لمس ناپذیر-نامحسوس)
- Mesmerize means hypnotist. مِزمُورایز : هیپنوتیزم کردن یا شدن

hypnotize هیپ نُ تایز

- I was so dumbfounded I could only laugh. گیج و مبهوت
  با این اسپل dumfound هم درست است

- Slavery database * débuts دِ ب یو :نخستین مرحله کار-شروع بکار کردن-وارد اجتماع شدن

* (در کامپیوتر): مجموعه پیچیده از فایل ها یا دادههاي ذخیره شده به صورت ساخت یافته در یک حافظه بزرگ که توسط یک یا چند کاربر در ترمینالهاي مختلف قابل دستیابي است، **پایگاه داده ها**

A first appearance, A formal entrance into society
<made her singing début>

- Accused say they do not trust authorities to mete our justice.
  (می ت: حد)

meted, meting ←مشتقات

- Muslims give meat to the poor and splurge on clothes and other gifts for friends and family.
  (اس پ لرج: شادی و تفریح و ولخرجی کردن)

Splurge is a noun & verb
If verb: splurged, splurging
<*To make a splurge* به رخ دیگران کشیدن >, <*splurge on a new dress*>

- To include oneself extravagantly often use with on.
  (اکس ترا وگنت لی: بطور نامعقول- به افراط)

***extravagant*–adjective**
1. spending much more than is necessary or wise; wasteful: *an extravagant shopper.*
2. excessively high: *extravagant expenses; extravagant prices.*
3. exceeding the bounds of reason, as actions, demands, opinions, or passions.

- Transitive verb: *to spend extravagantly or ostentatiously.*
  (اس تن طی شس لی: از روی خودنمایی)

***ostentatious*–adjective** اس تن طی شس
1. characterized by or given to pretentious or conspicuous show in an attempt to impress others: *an ostentatious dresser.*
2. (of actions, manner, qualities exhibited, etc.) intended to attract notice: *Lady Bountiful's ostentatious charity.*

- As Bush hailed progress in the war that defines his presidency,

تگرگ، طوفان تگرگ- تگرگ باریدن

Hailed: *1. <To precipitate hail /it was hailing hard>,*
2. <To pour down or strike like hail>

- The scuffle injured White House press secretary Dana Prino's eye.

(اِس کا فُل : نزاع- جنجا ل- غوغا- کشمکش)

scuffle ***–verb (used without object)*** اِس کا فُل
1. to struggle or fight in a rough, confused manner.
2. to go or move in hurried confusion.
3. to move or go with a shuffle; scuff.

- You mentioned they are your "longtime friends", it is surprising that you had not noticed the husband's boorish behavior before?

(بُوریش : بی تربیت- روستایی- دهاتی)

(مطلب فوق درباره زن و شوهری بودکه به مهمانی رفته بودند و شوهر خیلی بی تربیت و از خود راضی بود)

boorish ***--adjective*** بُوریش
of or like a boor; unmannered; crude; insensitive.

- "when she had the stroke the effect on him was horrendous"

(ها رِن دِز : ترسناک)

horrendous*: horrible, dreadful, <the tax rate was horrendous> or <horrendous crimes>*

- Needless to say احتیاج به گفتن نیست
New Port Beach Mayor renowned for his job performance,
(Renown آوازه - نام- معروفیت), (of great renown → مشهور- معروف)

- But recent attention to President Obama's on-and-off smoking habit has pinned a new kind of audacious hop to him.

(اُدِی شِس: بی پروا- بی باکانه)

<Audacious mountain climber>
hop*: To make a short, bouncing leap; move by leaping with all feet off the ground.*

audacious ***–adjective*** اُدِی شِس: بی پروا- بی باکانه
1. extremely bold or daring; recklessly brave; fearless: *an audacious explorer.*

2. extremely original; without restriction to prior ideas; highly inventive: *an audacious vision of the city's bright future.*

- City of Fullerton resident might have been surprised at plummeting metal prices. He may not have known scrap metal prices have plummeted in the past month. (پلامیتینگ: گلوله سربی-وزنه شاقول)

plummeting: to fall perpendicularly / birds plummeted or to drop sharply and abruptly <prices plummeted>

plummet--**noun** پلا مِت
1. Also called **plumb bob.** a piece of lead or some other weight attached to a line, used for determining perpendicularity, for sounding, etc.; the bob of a plumb line.
2. something that weighs down or depresses.
–verb (used without object) **3.** to plunge.

- Attempt to rescue barge stuck in bay gets messy.

(بارج : یک نوع کشتی جادار و صاف)

A barge collecting big piles of sediment[1] for a New-Port Harbor dredging[2] (دِرج اینگ) project got stuck in the bay muck[3] ...

1.(لای نشست، تەنشینته)

2.(دِرج اینگ :عمران- لاروبي- (علوم نظامي) لاروبي، كشيدن لنگر به كف دريا -(معماري) خاكبرداري زير ابي
3.(: کودتازه- کثافت)

dredge: to dig, gather, or pull out with or as if with a dredge. (often used with up) .
dredging: *Buy the right dredge for your dredging project.*
sediment : The matter that settles to the bottom of a liquid; lees; dregs.

- Sheriff's officials secretly disparaged speakers at a meeting on permits.

(دیس پَرِجد: انکار فضیلت چیزی/بی قدر کردن)

<sheriff's officials traded disparaging texts>
If you disparage someone or something, you talk about them with disapproval or lack of respect; a formal word.

- Our interest gratification society. .... (گَرَا تی فی کِی شِن: خوشی و لذت)*<He did it for his own gratification*! <برای خوشایند خودش این کار را کرد

gratification **–noun** گرَاتی فی کِی شِن: خوشی و لذت
1. the state of being gratified; great satisfaction.
2. something that gratifies; source of pleasure or satisfaction. **3.** the act of gratifying

- Orange County Animal care center euthanized 23% of dogs at the shelter. یوثِ نایز: فراهم کردن وسایل راحت مردن

euthanize--**verb (used with object),** -nized, -niz·ing. یوثِ نایز
to subject to euthanasia: *to euthanize injured animals.*

- A doctor after receiving treatment for sex addiction after he was accused of groping[1] a woman, he gave her a hug and caressed[2] her breast.

1.(گروپینگ : کورمال دستمالی کردن- کورمال پیدا کردن)
2.(کورِسد: نوازش کردن)

groping: Showing or reflecting a desire to understand, esp. something that proves puzzling:< a groping scrutiny; a groping expression.>

(*To caress (fondle) someone →* کسي را ناز ونوازش کردن)

Caress: *fondness or affection*

caress **–noun** کورِس: نوازش کردن
1. an act or gesture expressing affection, as an embrace or kiss, esp. a light stroking or touching.
–verb (used with object)
2. to touch or pat gently to show affection.
3. to touch, stroke, etc., lightly, as if in affection: *The breeze caressed the trees.*

- State officially revoked his license for "flagrant[1] sexual misconduct" toward female patient, colleagues[2] and staff, "As soon as I saw his hand on my breast, I pushed it away" she said.

1.(فِ لِی گِرَنت : آشکار- برملا) ,**2.**(کالیگز: همقطار و همکار)

colleague → همقطار colleagueship→ همقطاری

- The number of Orange County homes that sold for $1 million or more plummeted 45.3 percent last year vs. 2007.

پلا مِت : گلوله سربي، وزنه شاقول ، سرازيرشدن

plummeted*= to fall perpendicularly* پلا مِت
<Birds plummeted down> or *<to drop sharply and abruptly>,*
<Prices plummeted>

- He (18-year-boy) flaunts[1] his body on almost every occasion. He struts[2] around going from room to room, all the while his pants shipping even lower.

1.(فلانت : جولان دادن- نمایش دادن) , 2.(S ترآت : قدم زني-خراميد ن)

Flauntingly: خودفروشانه-خرامان

Strutted : *p & pp*. of *strut*

flaunt–**verb (used without object)** فلانت : جولان دادن- نمایش دادن

1. to parade or display oneself conspicuously, defiantly, or boldly.
2. to wave conspicuously in the air.
–verb (used with object)
3. to parade or display ostentatiously: *to flaunt one's wealth.*
4. to ignore or treat with disdain: *He was expelled for flaunting military regulations.*
–noun **5.** the act of flaunting.

strut–**verb (used without object)** Sترآت : قدم زني-خراميد ن

1. to walk with a vain, pompous bearing, as with head erect and chest thrown out, as if expecting to impress observers.
–noun **2.** the act of strutting. **3.** a strutting walk or gait.
—Idiom **4.** strut one's stuff, to dress, behave, perform, etc., one's best in order to impress others; show off.

- *bootlegger* بوت لگر: کسی که مشروبهای ممنوعه را قاچاقی می فروشد

bootleg: to carry (alcoholic liquor) on one's person illegally

---

- Can dogs be barred from a Condo.? (بازداشتن ممنوع کردن، مسدود)

A condominium is a block of flats in which each flat is owned by the person who lives there. It is also used to refer to one of the flats; used in American English.

- He gave police a full report –and the video tape that showed his assailant. (أسی لنت : حمله کننده-مهاجم)

assailant **–noun** أسی لنت : حمله کننده-مهاجم

1. a person who attacks.
–adjective
2. *Archaic* . assailing; attacking; hostile. (*Archaic*→ آر که یک :کهنه، قديمي، غير مصطلح)

- Actor Simpson stumbles through act. (لغزش خوردن- گیرکردن- اشتباه کردن)

stumble–**verb (used without object)**

1. to strike the foot against something, as in walking or running, so as to stagger or fall; trip.
2. to walk or go unsteadily: *to stumble down a dark passage.*
3. to make a slip, mistake, or blunder, esp. a sinful one: *to stumble over a question; to stumble and fall from grace.*

- He may be picking upon your ambivalence which is why he says you don't love him as much as he loves you and become "offended" when you try to discuss your feelings.

آمبی وَلِنس : توجه ناگهاني و دلسردي ناگهاني نسبت بشخص ياچيزي، دمدمي مزاجي

ambivalence: آمبی وَلِنس *continual fluctuation (as between one thing and its opposite or uncertainty as to which approach to follow). or The coexistence of opposing attitudes or feelings, such as love and hate, toward a person, object, or idea.*
Ambivalent → *adj* , Ambivalently→ *adv.*

- To suppresses any appetite (کاهش دادن- فرونشاندن)
Suppress a mutation (میو تیشِن : تغيير کلی جهش، انقلاب، شورش، تغييرناگهاني)
<*Suppress a cough, Suppress her anger, Suppress the best result*>

suppressible : (ساپرِسه بِل: فرونشاندنی-قابل جلوگيری-خواباندنی)
Suppressibility→ (noun)

- Gun carrier arrested, "I will be vindicated of this" said arrested man of Orange County. (وِن دِ کيت : حمايت کردن از- دفاع کردن از)
vindication → حمايت- دفاع- اثبات

***vindicate*–verb (used with object),** -cat·ed, -cat·ing. وِن دِ کيت
1. to clear, as from an accusation, imputation, suspicion, or the like: *to vindicate someone's honor.*
2. to afford justification for; justify: *Subsequent events vindicated his policy.*
3. to uphold or justify by argument or evidence: *to vindicate a claim.*
—*Synonyms*. exonerate.., support.

- China defends revival paln. (رِ وای وِل : احيا- تجديد- برقراری مجدد)

***revival* –noun** رِ- وای وِل

1. restoration to life, consciousness, vigor, strength, etc.
2. restoration to use, acceptance, or currency: *the revival of old customs.*
3. a new production of an old play.

- Iceman signs memoir in Harbor Beach. ممو آر: یادداشت- مقاله علمی- تاریخچه

memoir: *A memoir is a book or article that you write about someone who you have known well.*

- President announces combat troops will leave before September 2010.
(کام بَت : رزمی- جنگی)

<President sets end to combat mission.>

combat ***–verb (used with object)***
1. to fight or contend against; oppose vigorously: *to combat crime.*
–verb (used without object)
2. to battle; contend: *to combat with disease.*
–noun
3. *Military* . active, armed fighting with enemy forces.
4. a fight, struggle, or controversy, as between two persons, teams, or ideas.

- Israel sought to rebut the report, providing evidence to US intelligence officials that....
(ری بات: رد/تکذیب کردن- برگرداندن)

- Grim[1] times, gloomy[2] nation.
1.(گریم : ترسناک- شوم- سخت)
2.(گو لوُ مي : تیره- تاریک- افسرده- دلتنگ کننده)

Gloom → تاریکی- تیرگی- دلتنگی

gloomy ***--adjective,*** gloom·i·er, gloom·i·est. گو لوُ مي : تیره- تاریک- افسرده- دلتنگ کننده
1. dark or dim; deeply shaded: *gloomy skies.*
2. causing gloom; dismal or depressing: *a gloomy prospect.*
3. filled with or showing gloom; sad, dejected, or melancholy.
4. hopeless or despairing; pessimistic: *a gloomy view of the future.*

- A jury recommended the death penalty for an accomplice[1] convicted of helping a man murder a couple on their yacht[2] in 2004 .
1.(آکام پ لِس :شریک جرم- همدست) **2.**(یات : کرجي بادي)

accomplice **--noun** : آکام پ لِس

1. A person who knowingly helps another in a crime or wrongdoing, often as a subordinate. **2.** An accomplice is a person who helps to commit a crime.
<He then jumped out of the car and ran back inside the flats to warn his accomplice.>

yacht : *A yacht is a boat with sails or a motor, used for racing or for pleasure trips.* *They were forced to remain on board the yacht.... ...fur coats, fancy motor cars and private yachts.... ...a yacht race between Spain and England.*

- Re discrimination law suit, witness Friday described a culture of homophobia[1] at New port Beach, California public department and how it could have hindered[2] the serpent's[3] attempts to move up the ranks.

1.(هوموفوبی یا: *Fear of or contempt[4] for lesbians and gay men..*)
2.(بازداشتن- ممانعت کردن- عقب انداختن) 3.(سر پنت: مار، ماربزرگ، ابلیس)

4.(کان تمپت : تحقیر ، اهانت، خفت، خواري، *(حقوق)* اخلال در نظم دادگاه)

phobia → به تنهایی در روانشناسی یعنی هراس و ترس

- US pledges to thwart Iran's aims. (سُورت:خنثی/باطل کردن)

thwart **–verb (used with object)** سُورت
1. to oppose successfully; prevent from accomplishing a purpose.
2. to frustrate or baffle (a plan, purpose, etc.). **3.**To prevent the occurrence, realization, or attainment of: *They thwarted her plans.* **4.**To oppose and defeat the efforts, plans, or ambitions of

- Now lenders are back to hawking their delinquent portfolios.
(هاکینگ: دوره گردی- در اینجا یعنی دست فروشی)

- The US "will seek an end to Iran's ambition to acquire & illicit nuclear capacity and its support for ....." US Sec. Ms. Rice told.
آم بیشِن : جاه طلبي، بلند پروازي (E لی سیت: ممنوع- قاچاقی- غیر مجاز)

ambition ***–noun*** جاه طلبي، بلند پروازي : آم بیشِن
1. an earnest desire for some type of achievement or distinction, as power, honor, fame, or wealth, and the willingness to strive for its attainment: *Too much ambition caused him to be disliked by his colleagues.*
2. the object, state, or result desired or sought after: *The crown was his ambition.*
3. desire for work or activity; energy: *I awoke feeling tired and utterly lacking in ambition.*
–verb (used with object) **4.** to seek after earnestly; aspire to.

- The setback[1] came when a US appeals court rejected the justice department's request for a stay in case involving a defunct[2] Islamic charity, lawyers for the defunct charity said the papers showed illegal wire tapping by the national **s**ecurity **a**dministration (NSA)

  1 .(عقب نشاندن، عقب نشستن، لگدزدن تفنگ) ,2.(مرحوم- از رده خارج- روبه زوال- منسوخ)

- He must repudiate his views if he wants to be a Roman Catholic clergyman.

  (کلِر جی مَن : کشیش، روحاني ، شيخ) (رِ پیو d - 8 : تکذیب/انکار کردن)

repudiate ***–verb (used with object),*** -at·ed, -at·ing.

1. to reject as having no authority or binding force: *to repudiate a claim.*
2. to cast off or disown: *to repudiate a son.*
3. to reject with disapproval or condemnation: *to repudiate a new doctrine.*
4. to reject with denial: *to repudiate a charge as untrue.*

clergyman ***–noun, plural*** -men. کشیش، روحاني ، شيخ : کلِر جی مَن

1. a member of the clergy.
2. an ordained Christian minister.

- Re pregnant student: I needed to get prenatal care, she said.

  (پری نی تال: پیش از تولد رخ دادن)

prenatal ***–adjective***

previous to birth or to giving birth: *prenatal care for mothers.*

- Bodies found at mutiny[1] site, guard uncovered the results of the forces two-day muting-dozens of senior officers massacred[3], their bodies hurriedly dumped into shallow graves and sewers[2].

  1.(میُوت نی: شورش، ياغي گري، تمرد سرکشي، شورش کردن ياغي شدن)
  2.(سو اِر: گنداب، مجراي فاضل اب، اگو)
  3.(قتل عام کردن، کشتار)

  4.(ها رید لی : از روي شتاب، از روي دست پاچگ

*massacre**d*** --A massacre is the killing of many people in a violent and cruel way. Count or uncount noun here but can also be used as a verb. e.g. The police had massacred crowds of people.

...the massacre of twelve thousand soldiers.... Enmity between them runs very deep, resulting often in bloodshed and massacre.

- Regarding Iranian uranium enrichment program, the top US. military official said Iran has enough fissile material for a nuclear weapon declaring any Tehran progress toward a bomb .... (فِس سُل: قابل انشقاق)

fissile **–adjective** فِس سُل: قابل انشقاق
1. capable of being split or divided; cleavable.
2. *Physics* . **a. fissionable**. **b.** (of a nuclide) capable of undergoing fission induced by low-energy neutrons, as uranium 233 and 235.

fis·sion·a·ble **– adjective *Physics*** . فی شِن اِبل
capable of or possessing a nucleus or nuclei capable of undergoing fission: *a fissionable nucleus; fissionable material.*

- Man says he was informant[1] on Arabs, ex-convict claims he infiltrated[2] Irvine mosque in service of ......

1.(این فور منت**:** خبرچین،، خبر رسان مخبر، شکل دهنده- آگاهی دهنده)
2.(این فیل ترِیت : از صافی رد کردن- نفوذ کردن- رخنه کردن)

- The first family seems unlikely to pick a congregation before Easter.

(کان گری گِی شِن : جماعت- گروه- گردآمدگی)
1. an assembly of persons brought together for common religious worship. **2.** the act of congregating or the state of being congregated. **3.** a gathered or assembled body; assemblage. ...
4. A congregation *is a large gathering of people, often for the purpose of worship*

- Letters she wrote to the boy in August while jailed on earlier charges stemming from their relationship

(S تِم :جلوگیری کردن از- روبرو شدن با- بند کردن- سد کردن)
مطلب فوق در رابطه با خانم معلمی که به شاگرد پسر 16 ساله اش تجاوز کرده بود نوشته شده است.

stem--**noun, verb** S تِم :جلوگیری کردن از- روبرو شدن با- بند کردن- سد کردن
1. the ascending axis of a plant, whether above or below ground, which ordinarily grows in an opposite direction to the root or descending axis.
2. the stalk that supports a leaf, flower, or fruit.
3. the main body of that portion of a tree, shrub, or other plant which is above ground; trunk; stalk. **4.** a cut flower: *We bought roses at the flower market for 50¢ a stem.*

- "This case is all about challenging on assertion of power by the executive branch which is extra ordinary".

(أسر شِن :اعلامیه، بیانیه اگهي، اعلان تاکید- اصرار- پافشاری)

- Some couple has a higher capability quotient than others.

(کُوشِنت: (اقتصاد) کسر، نسبت (روانشناسي) بهر، خارج قسمت)

- Politicians, celebrities[1] flaunt[2] scientific illiteracyبیسوادي deciding how to vote in November election was excruciatingly[3] difficult.

1.(سه لِب رِ تی: شهرت، شخص نامدار)

2 .(فلانت : خرامیدن- جلوه دادن- نمایش دادن)

3.(اِ کس کرو شی اِی تینگ : بطور آزاردهنده- اذیت کننده)

excruciation: → (اکس کرو شی یشن: شکنجه- آزار)

flaunt **–verb (used without object)** فِلانت : خرامیدن- جلوه دادن- نمایش دادن

1. to parade or display oneself conspicuously, defiantly, or boldly.
2. to wave conspicuously in the air.
–verb (used with object)
3. to parade or display ostentatiously: *to flaunt one's wealth.*
4. to ignore or treat with disdain: *He was expelled for flaunting military regulations.*
–noun
5. the act of flaunting.
6. *Obsolete* . something flaunted.

- One witness said the man even bragged of maiming (مِی مینگ) and killing people...........→ اصل لغت maim است یعنی فلج و چلاق کردن

- Ex-football player calls verdict a vindication "it was vindication" he said. How I can just go on with my life and relax.

وِر دیکت : راي، راي هیئت منصفه فتوي، نظر، قضاوت

وِن دِ کِی شِن حمایت، دفاع، اثبات بیگناهي توجیه، خونخواهي

Vindicative → وِن دِ کِ تیـو :حمایـت آمیـز- دفـاعی- اثبـات کننـده)

vindication **–noun** وِن دِ کِی شِن

1. the act of vindicating.
2. the state of being vindicated.
3. defense; excuse; justification: *Poverty was a vindication for his thievery.*
4. something that vindicates: Subsequent events were her vindication.

- CPR: **C**ardio **P**ulmonary (پُل م نِری) **R**esuscitation (رِسا س- c تِی شِن)

pulmonary: (مربوط به ریه و قلب) *of or relating to the heart and lungs,*
resuscitation: *to revive from apparent death or unconsciousness,*

Cardio Pulmonary*: of or relating to the heart and lungs,*
cardiovascular: (مربوط به قلب و عروق) of or relating to, or involving the heart and blood vessels

---

- An arrest warrant[1] was issued for an imprisoned man in 2001 killing of a federal intern[2], Miss Chandra Levy, whose disappearance ....

1. (وارنت: گواهي حكم- تعهد كردن- ضمانت كردن كسي، تضمين حكم *(بازرگاني)* ضمانت)

2.(این ترن : داخل شدن در، کار ورز *(طب)* انترن پزشک مقیم بیمارستان)

a. *If something warrants a particular action, it makes the action seem necessary; a formal use.* ***b****. The case warrants further investigation*
A warrant is an official document signed by a judge or magistrate, which gives the police special permission to do something such as arrest someone or search their house. Grenoble has issued a warrant for the arrest of the former Mayor of Nice.

***intern* –verb (used with object)**انترن پزشک مقیم بیمارستان :این ترن
1. to restrict to or confine within prescribed limits, as prisoners of war, enemy aliens, or combat troops who take refuge in a neutral country.
2. a person who is or has been interned; internee.

- The initial investigation was bungled because police missed leads and even searched the wrong part of the park for Miss Levy's body.

(بان گل : سر هم بندی/سنبل کردن)

bungle: *worked clumsily and awkwardly,* *<bungle a job>*

***bungle*—Verb with Object or [GC]Verb** بان گل
If you bungle something, you fail to do it properly, because you make mistakes or are clumsy. *They bungled the whole operation.... The costs have been high in Britain only because the politicians bungled.*

- Captivate: *To attract and hold the attention or interest of, as by beauty or excellence; enchant:* *<Her blue eyes and red hair captivated him.>*

captivated the country. (شیفتن- اسیرکردن- مجذوب کردن)
captivating فریبنده- د لربا
captivation عمل فریفتن- د لربایی

- It's ok for an average citizen to ask President Barak Obama for his autograph. But member of congress need to show some decorum.
(دِکورَم: ادب- شایستگی)

- Celebrity trainer helps sorority with 15 freshmen.
(سو را ر ت : خواهري، انجمنهاي خيريه يا كلوب نسوان)

sorority ***–noun, plural*** -ties. A society or club of women or girls, esp. in a college.

- Chrysler is offering up to $ 6,000 worth of incentive on its 2009 cars and trucks. (این سن تیو : محرک- انگیزه)
Synonym:→ *motion, stimulating*

- I hope this will bring the Mr. Joe's family some closure knowing her murder has admitted being responsible in … (کِلو ژِر : بستن- خاتمه دادن)

puberty: ***Puberty in Boys***; *Introduction; Around the time a child reaches the teenage years, puberty or sexual development occurs. Part of the normal check-up of pre-adolescents is making sure that puberty develops normally. ... During puberty, significant growth occurs as well, usually peaking about one year after the beginning...* u-p بِر t : بلوغ، رسیدگي، سن بلوغ

puberty ***–noun*** u-p بِر t : بلوغ، رسیدگي، سن بلوغ
the period or age at which a person is first capable of sexual reproduction of offspring: in common law, presumed to be 14 years in the male and 12 years in the female.

Your body is changing - During puberty you begin to see changes in your body, these are normal. Find out what changes you should expect during puberty and when you need to talk to a trusted adult. From body hair to breast development, puberty can be mind-boggling. <*Age of puberty* بلوغ- سال بلوغ>

- He took the gospel (گاس پل : انجیل), All their creeds[1] were an abomination[2] in his right.. 1.(کرید: کشیش-عقیده-اعتقاد) 2.(اَبا می نی شِن: کراهت-زشتی)

creed***–noun*** کرید (Creedless→ بی دین-بی عقیده)

1. any system, doctrine, or formula of religious belief, as of a denomination.
2. any system or codification of belief or of opinion.

Abomination: *something abominable or extreme disgust and hatred* loathing[3] or detestation[4]

3 .(لُوزینگ : بیزاری - تنفر، نفرت) 4 .(بیمیلي، بیزاري، نفرت، تنفر)

- I screwed up , In the side of inclusion[1] not exclusion[2]

1.(دربرداري) .2(دفع، استثناء، اخراج، محروم سازي، ممانعت، محرومیت)

inclusion ***–noun***
1. the act of including.
2. the state of being included. **3.** something that is included.

exclusion ***–noun***
1. an act or instance of excluding. **2.** the state of being excluded.
3. *Physiology* . a keeping apart; blocking of an entrance.

- ***subsidiary*** (ساب d-c اِ ری): *see subsidy* (ساب d–c)→ سُوب سید : کمک مالی دولتی furnishing aid or support: ***auxiliary***
<Subsidiary details>, <a subsidiary stream> or <a subsidiary payment to..>

- When an escrow case does not close in a timely manner and the contingencies[1] were never remove, albeit [2] the seller's agent .

1.(کاَن تِن جِنسی : شرطي شدن - پیش امد ، محتمل الوقوع، احتمال
.2(آل b اِت : اگرچه، ولواینکه)

contingency ***–noun, plural*** -cies. کاَن تِن جِنسی
1. dependence on chance or on the fulfillment of a condition; uncertainty; fortuitousness: *Nothing was left to contingency.*
2. a contingent event; a chance, accident, or possibility conditional on something uncertain: *He was prepared for every contingency.*
3. something incidental to a thing.
albeit ***–conjunction***
although; even if: *a peaceful, albeit brief retirement.*

- Three people were tied up while bandits[1] ransacked[2] their house Wednesday.

1.(بندت: راه زن) , **2.**(رَن سَکد :خوب جستجو کردن- غارت کردن)

- interrogate بازرسی- استنطاق کردن- سوال پرسیدن از
  interrogation استنطاق- بازرسی
  Interrogator → بازپرس
  <The journey into the CIA's most extreme interrogation program began in darkness> , *<No torture charges for interrogators>*

---

*(مطلب زیر در رابطه با زنی است که بچه دو ساله اش را می کشد و بعد گیر می افتد)

- She later recanted her story to sheriff's deputies and helps them locate the child's body in the bush beside a road in Sylmar Road High Way.
  رِکَنت : انکار کردن ، گفته خود را تکذیب کردن، بخطاي خود اعتراف کردن- حرف خود را پس گرفتن

  recant–verb (used with object) رِکَنت

  1. to withdraw or disavow (a statement, opinion, etc.), esp. formally; retract.
  –verb (used without object)
  2. to withdraw or disavow a statement, opinion, etc., esp. formally.
  3. If a witness who has completed his or her **testimony** requests the opportunity to appear before the grand jury to **recant testimony**, the prosecutor should grant the request, provided it is timely and in keeping with the promotion of truthful **testimony**.

- Irvine woman conned out of $75K, authorities say two men scammed an Irvine woman out of $60k in cash and more than $16k in jewelry this week. کان : گول زدن
  *The **k** stands for each 1000, 1000=1k, 50.000 = 50k.*

  ***Scam**: a fraudulent or deceptive act or operation.* *<An insurance scam>*
  Scam: *deceive, defraud, to obtain (as money) by a scam*
  scammed, scamming, scammer (*noun*)

- Mexican president Calderon insists Mexico intact. اینْ تکت دست نخورده- بی عیب

- His left hand was bandaged from a skirmish* on broad**. (پهن، عریض، گشاد) **
  <They skirmished with the police.> (کشمکش- زد و خورد)*

- Shelter facility expect an influx of kittens by May's end. (اینْ فلاکس: جریان)
  Influx: a coming in *<an influx of tourists>*

- *cushy* (کُوشی): *entailing little hardship or difficulty.*
  <a cushy job – with a high salary>, <a pirate's life has gotten pretty cushy>

  *<**Cushy Tushy** makes your toilet seat feel warm and comfortable without the use of expensive electronics.>* *Cushily*→ (adverb)

- Attention is increasingly focused on two of the world's apparently insoluble[1] yet related problems involving Afghanistan and illicit[2] drugs.

  1.(این سالِ بِل: حل نشدنی- آب نشدنی-لاینحل)
  2.(اِ لِ سیت: ممنوع، قاچاق، نا مشروع- مخالف مقررات)

  <fat is insoluble I water>
  ***illicit**: not permitted, unlawful*
  Insolubleness= insolubility , *illicitly*→(*adverb*)

- Distraught[1] means: *agitated*[2] *with doubt or mental conflict or pain,*
  1.(دیس تِرآت : پریشان حواس- شوریده- ناراحت) , 2.(اَجی تِیت : آشفتن- سراسیمه کردن)
  <distraught mourners>
  The other meaning: *mentally deranged: crazed*
  < As if thou wert distraught and mad with terror-shake>*(آشفتن-سراسیمه)*

- When a mailman notices any changes in routine that may mean a customer is in distress:..... (پریشانی- گرفتاری- دلتنگی)
  distress پریشانی- اندوه- محنت زده کردن
  distressful اندوه ناک- پریشان

- His name was jerry 42 of N.Y. but that was believed to be an alias a law enforcement official said. (اِ لی اس:اسم عاریه)
  alias::اِ لی اس *otherwise known as........*

- The man believed to have carried out the attack was found dead with a self-inflected[1] gunshot wound in an office, a satchel[2] with ammunition slung[3] around his neck, authorities said.

  1.(بسمت خود برگرداندن)
  2.(سَ چِل یعنی کیف کوچک با بند بلند که به روی شانه میاندازند.)
  3 .(قسمت دوم کلمه sling است یعنی پرتاب کردن)

- The brawl (بِرآل) happened just before bar closing time.
  drawl : (بِرآل داد و بیداد- قیل و قال کردن- نزاع کردن)
  drunken brawl→ عربده

- Afghanistan does the largest share of the nation population use opiates. (o -p اِیت : مخدر تکسین دهنده - افیون زن)

opiate–**noun** (o -p اِیت : مخدر تکسین دهنده - افیون زن)

1. a drug containing opium or its derivatives, used in medicine for inducing sleep and relieving pain.
2. any sedative, soporific, or narcotic.
3. anything that causes dullness or inaction or that soothes the feelings.
–adjective **4.** mixed or prepared with opium. **5.** inducing sleep; soporific; narcotic.
–verb (used with object) **7.** to subject to an opiate; stupefy. **8.** to dull or deaden.

opiate: *a drug (as morphine or codeine), Containing or derived from opium and tending to induce sleep and alleviate pain, which is a kind of narcotics...*

- If you qualify and wish to opt out see your supervisor.
opt: *to make a choice*, (اَپت : انتخاب کردن), <*opted for tax insurance*>

opt **–verb (used without object)**
1. to make a choice; choose (usually fol. by *for*).
—Verb phrase **2.** opt out, to decide to leave or withdraw: *to opt out of the urban rat race and move to the countryside.*

- Repentant (ری پن تِنت) synonym penitent* (پِ نِ تِنت)
Repent, repented, repenting → توبه کردن- پشیمان شدن
repenter → توبه کار
repentant , penitent هر دو یعنی تائب- کسی که توبه میکند- پشیمان شدن

- Chambers asked for maximum sentence, saying smuggler (اس مـاگ لِر) had been unrepentant (آن-ری پن تِنت) and accused authorities of lying.

- Penitent (پِ نِ تِنت): *feeling or expressing humble or regretful pain or sorrow for sins or offenses: repentant.*
Penitently→ (*adverb*) Penitent → (*adjective*)

- Medicare will scrutinize[1] the private plan's bids for year 2010 to eliminate offerings that only tweak[2] a basic plan.

1. (s کُرُ to نایز : مورد مداقه قرار دادن)
2. (نیشگان گرفتن و کشیدن- پیچ دادن، در اینجا معنی زیر را دارد)

Tweak : to make usually small adjustments *in* or *to*: <*tweak the controls*>

- Talking with Iranian official were promising but not substantive.

(اساسی- ذاتی- مستقل)

- Flood inflict[1] fiscal[2] soaking.

1.(وارد آوردن-زدن-تحمیل کردن) و 2.(مالی-مالیاتی)

<To inflict a stroke upon a person>, <To inflict one's views on the public>

Inflict able وارد آوردنی-تحمیل کردنی

Strip, stripped *also* stript

این لغت بغیر از معنی لخت شدن معنی لخت کردن هم میدهد- معنی دیگر آن یعنی

Stript: *to deprive of possessions .* (محروم کردن)

*to divest of honors*دای وِست بی بهره کردن- محروم کردن- سخت کردن

- With a housing market gone berserk[1], bank is running headlong[2] into the mortgage business.

1.(بِر سِرکَ:شوریده- آشفته) 2.(با کله جلو رفتن- شتابزده- دستپاچه- بی پروا)

- Bank sees opportunity springing from calamity

(کَ لَ مِ تی: مصیبت- بلا- فاجعه- آفت)

<calamities of nature>, <an economic calamity>

- If Iran going to err, I am going to err on the side of caution.

(غلط- نادرست - خطاکردن، بغلط قضاوت کردن)

To err is human بشر جایزالخطاست

If you err, you make a mistake; a formal use.

<Undoubtedly we have erred in giving such low status to our nurses.>

- US. dissident[1] political faction[2] that nominated former president T. Roosevelt for presidency in 1912…

1.(d - c - دِنت: مخالف عقیده عموم)، 2.(دسته بندی- گروه هواخواهان)

dissident ***–noun*** d - c دِنت

1. a person who dissents.

–adjective

2. disagreeing or dissenting, as in opinion or attitude: *a ban on dissident magazines.*

faction ***--noun***

1. a group or clique within a larger group, party, government, organization, or the like: *a faction in favor of big business.*

2. party strife and intrigue; dissension: *an era of faction and treason.*

- Prices are dropping because of the anomaly that occurred during the market boom. (آنام لی: خلاف قاعده)
  Anomalous → غیرعادی- خلاف قاعده
  Anomaly: someone or something anomalous.
  <With his quiet nature, he was an anomaly in his exuberant family.>

- deviation* from common rule, such as irregularity.
  *(انحراف، انحراف جنسي)
  deviation is a difference in behavior or belief from what people consider to be normal or acceptable.
  <There had been a number of deviations from army regulations.>

- Severance: *The act or process of severing, the state of being severed*
  سه ورنس: تفکیک- جدایی

- When the market is strong people's purchases quickly increase in value, which leads to euphoria[1] which can lead to rush decision making.
  euphoria: a feeling of well-being or elation [2]
  1.(يوفوريا : رضامندي، خوشي، خوشحالي رضايت، مشاط) 2. (باد- غرور)
  Euphoric, يوفوريک, euphorically ←(مشتقات)
  <from euphoria states a downward cycle>
  <the point of maximum risk for any investment is during the euphoria stage>

- Immigration vies with other priorities. (وايز/بدون اس:(وای)
  vied وايد , vying همچشمی/رقابت کردن
  <Swimmers from many nations were vying for the title.>
  synonyms: compete, contest, and struggle.

- Is there anything in the stimulus act that will affect my 2008 tax return? (اس تی میُولس: انگیزه- محرک)
  <stimulus grant employers ID leeway. (لی وی: انحراف)>
  <clash over stimulus option>*
  *(بصدا درآمدن در اثر تصادف- درق صدا کردن- مخالف بودن)

- *collusion*[1]: *secret agreement or cooperation esp. for an illegal or deceitful*[2] *purpose*
  1.(کلوژن:سازش- ساخت و پاخت-تبانی) 2.(متقلب- کلاهبردار- فریب امیز)

- Economic contrarian* (کان تِرَ ری یَن) plots move.

موقع خریدفروش استاک *آن کسیکه وقتی همه می خرند او می فروشدو وقتی همه میفروشنداو میخرد

contrarian: A person who takes an opposing view, esp. one who rejects the majority opinion, as in economic matters. <*Contrarian* investor>

- A woman avoids prison after reconciling with husband, which asks judge for leniency .

لی نی c- n : نرمی- ملایمت- ارفاق- تخفیف- آسان گیری- ارفاق- مدارا

leniency ***–noun, plural*** -cies. c- n لی نی
1. the quality or state of being lenient.
2. a lenient act.

- Price are dropping because of the anomaly that occurred during the market boom. (اَنام لی:خلاف قاعده)

anomaly ***–noun, plural*** -lies.
1. a deviation from the common rule, type, arrangement, or form.
2. someone or something anomalous: *With his quiet nature, he was an anomaly in his exuberant family.*

- Although there are no steadfast rules to determine future pricing.

(اِستِد فَست: ثابت قدم)

steadfast ***–adjective*** اِستِد فَست : ثابت قدم
1. fixed in direction; steadily directed: *a steadfast gaze.*
2. firm in purpose, resolution, faith, attachment, etc., as a person: *a steadfast friend.*

<The refugees remained steadfast.... ...steadfast loyalty.>

مطلب زیر درباره مرد ایرانی است که زن و مادرزنش را با چاقو می کشد و در وان حمام قرار میدهد

- He quizzed[1] him about the whereabouts of the two women, he was contemplating suicide. Police officer subdued[2] him with ruler bullets and discovered the women's bodies in the bathtub.

1.(دست انداختن و با کنجکاوی نگاه کردن)
2.(مطیع یا مقهور ساختن-رام کردن-ملایم کردن← (رنگ یا صدا)

subdued: Someone who is subdued is quiet, often because they are sad or worried about something.

<The General appeared more subdued than in previous appearances.... The assembly murmured in subdued agreement.... Only some fifty thousand joined the march and the atmosphere appeared subdued compared with earlier protests.>

- Satisfied with things as they are; content: a contented expression on the child's face.
  he contended ...... او مجادله داشت- کشمکش داشت
  Contending → مجادله کننده

contend–**verb (used without object)**
1. to struggle in opposition: *to contend with the enemy for control of the port.*
2. to strive in rivalry; compete; vie: *to contend for first prize.*
3. to strive in debate; dispute earnestly: *to contend against falsehood.*
–verb (used with object)
4. to assert or maintain earnestly: *He contended that taxes were too high.*

- I am compelled to share this letter with you during these uncertain economic times. (مجبور/ناگزیر بودن)

- Lier and Liar تلفظ هر دو لایر است
  Liar: *a person who tells lies*
  Lier: (noun) *to be prostrate[1] defeated[2] or disgraced[3]*

1.(مطیع کردن- از پادرآوردن) , 2.(شکست دادن- محروم کردن)
3.(رسوایی- خفت- ننگین- رسواکردن- ازنظرانداختن)

To be defeated → دی فی تد: شکست خوردن- مغلوب شدن
disgraceful → رسوائی آور- ننگین

- US, Secretary of state said Wed. that American's insatiable[1] demand for illegal drugs and its inability[2] to stop weapons from being smuggled into Mexico our fueling an increase in violence along the border.

1.(این سه ش بل: سیری ناپذیر- راضی نشو)
2.(این ابل تی: قادرنبودن)

insatiable: این سه ش بل:
Not satiable; incapable of being satisfied or appeased: *insatiable hunger for knowledge.*
<had an insatiable desire for wealth>
/in/sa/tia/bil/ity سیری ناپذیری- راضی نشدن

- *Heterosexual** men: of or relating to, or characterized by a tendency to direct sexual desire toward the opposite sex. *(حِ تِ رو سِک چوآل)
heterosexuality→ *noun*

A person whose sexual orientation is toward people of the opposite sex. Relating to or characteristic of **heterosexuality**. One whose interests and behavior are characteristic of **heterosexuality**. ... A person whose sexual orientation is toward people of the opposite sex.

- Police say faked death is apprehended.

معنی اول: (دریافتن- درک کردن) معنی دوم: (توقیف کردن)

<*A man who police say faked his death to avoid arrest last year was apprehended in Los Vegas .* توقیف شد >

- Have you lifted oppressive[1] sanctions[2]? 1.(اَپرِسیو:ستم آمیز- ظالمانه- دشوار)

2.در *(اقتصاد)* مجازات ، تصديق مجازات اقتصادي، تصويب كردن ، مجوز جريمه ، ضمانت اجرايي قانون)

sanction—***Count Noun***

A sanction is a severe course of action which is intended to make people obey the law.

<The ultimate sanction of the government is the withdrawal of funds.>

burdensome, unjustly harsh, or tyrannical:

<an oppressive king; oppressive laws.>

<oppressive legislation> ,<an oppressive climate>

- Pakistan plunges deeper into chaos.... هیولای روز اول- هرج و مرج و بی نظمی

- Have you ever given up mudslinging (مادِ اسلینگ اِینگ) and making accusations against the great Iranian nation and officials?

mudslinger تهمت زدن : *one that uses offensive[1] epithets[2] and invective[3] esp. against a political opponent.*

1.(برخورنده- اهانت آمیز- بد- تهاجمی یا متهاجم) -

2.(اِ پِ سِت س: صفت، لقب، عنوان، کنیه اصطلاح)

3.(سخن سخت- پرخاش- طعنه)

mudslinging: An attempt to discredit one's competitor, opponent, etc., by malicious or scandalous attacks.

epithets: اپ یت س: *Any word or phrase applied to a person or thing to describe an actual or attributed quality.*
<*"Richard the Lion-Hearted" is an epithet of Richard I.*>

- This very daunting[1] for us, but we are very resilient[2]

1.(ترسانیدن- بی جرات کردن), 2. (بحال اول برگشتن- بهبودپذیر)

(مطالب فوق را رئیس پلیس شهر اوکلنه در کالیفر نیا --- گفت شخصی 4 پلیس را کشت)

dauntless بی پروا- بی باک
dauntlessness بی باکی و بی پروایی

- Iran's powerful theocracy and how it will dictate the pace ad tone of any new steps by Obama… (تی آکـ راسی: حکومت خدا)

Theocracy → حکومتی که خدا پادشاه آن باشد

- benediction مرحله بعد از سخنرانی (اوباما) در موقع رئیس جمهور شدنش

- "The Iranian leaders are not about concessions at this stage. It's still about ideology from the Iranian side.

(امتیاز- واگذاری- تسلیم- تن دهی)

- Assistant sheriff wriggles in seat (ری گل : لولیدن- از اینسو به آنسو رفتن)

wriggles --Verb (used without object)
1. to twist to and fro; writhe; squirm.
2. to move along by twisting and turning the body, as a worm or snake.
3. to make one's way by shifts or expedients (often fol. by *out*): *to wriggle out of a difficulty.*
–verb (used with object) **4.** to cause to wriggle: *to wriggle one's hips.*
5. to bring, get, make, etc., by wriggling: *to wriggle one's way through a narrow opening.*
–noun **6.** act of wriggling; a wriggling movement.

- (Sue & suing)* → To institute a process in law against; bring a civil action against: <*to sue someone for damages.*>

* (تقاضا كردن، تعقيب قانوني كردن، دعوي كردن)

sewing : → (سُواینگـ: خیاطی)
sowing (سُواینگـ: کاشتن گیاه), <*sowing outdoors*> تلفظ هر دو یکجور است

- Who in 1967 sought to eradicate Israel?

(E ژ D کیت: از ریشه کندن- قلع و قمع کردن)

- There is just an extraordinary affinity[1] and kinship[2] that we have. We owe so much to England that…

1.(اَفِ نیتی : وابستگی- پیوستگی- قوم و خویشی بوسیلع وصلت-کشش)
2.(خویشاوندی- نزدیکی- بستگی- همانندی)

<Affinity between two language> ,<relationship by marriage>
<She was of kinship with the queen>
مطالب فوق را اوباما در سفر به انگلستان گفته است که چقدر وابستگی بین دو کشور زیاد است

- Would it be considered duping friends and family to have a real wedding?

(دُو پی اینگ: گول زدن)
(این مطلب درباره مرد (گِی gay) و زنِ straight بود که میخواستند ازدواج کنند)

- platonic soulmate. (پِ لِ تانیک: افلاتونی)

<ideological soulmate>
باشد مثل عقاید و خصیصه های شبیه به هم شخصی که بی اندازه از نظر روح و روانی شبیه شخص دیگری

- Trade commission sends a blunt warning to the fact-growing foreclosure fix -it industry.. (بی تعارف)

(مطلب فوق درمورد مردی است که چند سال زنش را رها کرده بود و یا با یک زن جوان دیگر رفته بود- حالا آمده و اظهار ندامت می کند و میخواهد زنش او را ببخشد.)

- I can see the benefit for you, but how will it benefit her? Better to find another avenue for redeeming. (بازخریدن- نجات دادن)

- List of purported* illegal immigrants mailed in Utah, terrifying[2] many in the state's Hispanic community. (وحشت زده کردن) 2 (بنظر امدن ، حاكي بودن از)*

- Chinese officials closely follow U.S. political rhetoric[1] and frequently decry[2] what they consider foreign interference in china's internal affairs.

1.(رِ تِ ریک:علم معانی و بیان)
2.(cry-d:رسوا کردن- تحقیرکردن- بی بها کردن)

rhetoric: *the art of speaking or writing effectively. As the study of principles and rules of composition formulated by critics of ancient times.*

- *unfetter*: *a*). to free from fetter→ (پایبند- قید- زنجیر)
  b). emancipate, liberate,
  <*unfetter the mind from prejudice*>, <*unfetter a prisoner*>,

  unfettered: *is adjective, free, unrestrained,* <*unfettered access*>
  Also yesterday, international aid organization called for the unfettered entry of humanitarian and building supplies into Gaza.

- Is a heinous act against the civil right of our unborn brothers and sisters? (هی نس:شنیع- زشت- تاثر آور)
  <*heinous crimes*>, heinously → بطورشنیع

  heinous ***–adjective***
  hateful; odious; abominable; totally reprehensible: *a heinous offense*
  Heinous means extremely evil; a formal word.

- *sibling:* سی بر لینگ هم نژاد، برادر یاخواه
  1. Sib also: *one of the two or more individuals having one common parent* **2.** *One of the two or more things related by a common tie or characteristic*

- I am victim of identity theft. (قربانی- دستخوش- شکار)

  victim ***–noun***
  1. a person who suffers from a destructive or injurious action or agency: *a victim of an automobile accident.*
  2. a person who is deceived or cheated, as by his or her own emotions or ignorance, by the dishonesty of others, or by some impersonal agency: *a victim of misplaced confidence; the victim of a swindler; a victim of an optical illusion.*
  3. a person or animal sacrificed or regarded as sacrificed: *war victims.*
  4. a living creature sacrificed in religious rites.

- She said "it sounds like there was at least one renegade juror from the get-go who didn't wants to convict". (رن گید : عیسوی مسلمان شده- مرتد)

  renegade ***–noun*** رن گید
  1. a person who deserts a party or cause for another. **2.** an apostate from a religious faith.
  –adjective **3.** of or like a renegade; traitorous.

- After an eight-day struggle to find the wreckage and pull it from the murky water. (مِر کی : تاریک- غلیظ)

–adjective, murk·i·er, murk·i·est.
1. dark, gloomy, and cheerless. **2.** obscure or thick with mist, haze, etc., as the air.
3. vague; unclear; confused: *a murky statement.* Also, **mirky.**
4. Murky places are dark and rather unpleasant. *We looked out into the murky streets.*
5. Murky water is so dark and dirty that you cannot see through it. *...murky ponds*

- He said he had already promised his family a plate of hot couscous for lunch. (کُوس کُوس: غذای آفریقائی ازگوشت و سبزیجات)

couscous ***–noun*** کُوس کُوس
A North African dish consisting of steamed semolina, served with vegetables and meat.

semolina consists of small hard grains of wheat that are used for making foods such as spaghetti and macaroni and for making sweet puddings with milk
Supplies of basics such as flour and semolina are available in the shops.... ...semolina pudding.

- Sclerosis Doctor says new pill might work against multiple sclerosis (اس کلِروسِس: سفت شدگی بافتها)
- nonetheless= *nevertheless* باوجود این- با این وصف- معهذا

- Lobbying for Oscar

معنی اول همان لابی هتل یا راهروی مجلس است- در اینجا یعنی رای دادن
یا با وسائل گوناگون طرف را به اسکار می رسانند
معنی دوم:لایحه ای که بوسیله دیدن نمایندگان و خواهش اصرار گذراندن لایحه ائی جمله زیر بکار برده می شود:

To lobby a bill through US.
Lobby, lobbies, lobbied
Lobbying: to conduct activities aimed at influencing police officials and esp. members of a legislative body on legislation.

- Peter Falk's wife (همسرِ کولمبو) and daughter clash[1], MR. Falk entrusted[2] his wife to manage his affairs and care before his health deteriorated[3], according to documents filed in LA court.

1.(درق صدا کردن- صدای بهم خوردگی چیزی با شکستگی- مخالف بودن- بصدا درآمدن)
2 .(سپردن- وگذار کردن)
3.(دی تی ریو ریت: بدتر کردن روبزوال گذاشتن-خراب کردن)

clashing: to conflict; disagree مخالف بودن

<Their stories of the accident clashed completely.>

deteriorate: *To make or become worse or inferior in character, quality, value, etc to disintegrate or wear away.*

- We will all be dead by their bravado. برواَدو: لاف دلیری

bravado ***–noun, plural*** -does, -dos.
a pretentious, swaggering display of courage.

- Her mother has a peculiar pattern. (پِ کیو لیر:ویژه-خاصیت مخصوص)

peculiar ***–adjective***
1. strange; queer; odd: *peculiar happenings.*
2. uncommon; unusual: *the peculiar hobby of stuffing and mounting bats.*
3. distinctive in nature or character from others.
4. belonging characteristically (usually fol. by *to*): *an expression peculiar to Canadians.*
5. belonging exclusively to some person, group, or thing: *the peculiar properties of a drug.*

- New Jersey man became alarmed by despondent California team.
(دسپاند نت: افسرده- دلسرد- محزون)

<*despondent about failing health.*

despondent ***–adjective*** دسپاند ت
feeling or showing profound hopelessness, dejection, discouragement, or gloom: *despondent about failing health.*

- Sheriff defended large number of deputies at hearing on concealed weapons permits but said she was appalled to see the misuse of the cameras. ترساندن

Appalling ترسناک ***–adjective***
causing dismay or horror: *an appalling accident; an appalling lack of manners.*

- Grand nephew of the old man hired a lawyer[1], who threatened[2] in a letter to the city to proceed[3] with our right…to have the property revert[4] back

1.(لایر **یا** لُ یر**:** وکیل دادگستري، مشاورحقوقي), **2.**(تِرتِن : تهدید کردن ترساندن)

3.(پُرسید : پیش رفتن، رهسپار شدن حرکت کردن ، ناشي شدن از عایدات، در جمع عایدات
(حقوق) اقدام کردن 4 (ریورت : برگشت کردن-برگرداندن)

lawyer **–noun** لایر
1. a person whose profession is to represent clients in a court of law or to advise or act for clients in other legal matters.
–verb (used without object) 2. to work as a lawyer; practice law.
–verb (used with object)
3. to submit (a case, document, or the like) to a lawyer for examination, advice, clarification, etc.

threaten **–verb (used with object)**
1. to utter a threat against; menace: *He threatened the boy with a beating.*
2. to be a menace or source of danger to: *Sickness threatened her peace of mind.*
3. to offer (a punishment, injury, etc.) by way of a threat: *They threatened swift retaliation.* **4.** to give an ominous indication of: *The clouds threaten rain.*
–verb (used without object) **5.** to utter or use threats.
6. to indicate impending evil or mischief.

(مطلب زیر در رابطه با فرمان بسته شدن زندان وآنتا منا که زندانیان را کجا و چگونه محاکمه کنیم؟)

- Jubilation[1] uncertainty[2] after Obama order to close….

1.(جُوبِ لِی شن: شادمانی)
2.(آن سِر تِن تی : نـا مـعـلـومـی- تردید- چیزنامعلوم یا امر غیرمسلم)

jubilation: *an act of rejoicing, the state of being jubilant.*
(خوشی کننده-هلهه کننده)

Another meaning of jubilation: *an expression of great joy.*

uncertainty **–noun, plural** -ties آن سِر تِن تی
1. the state of being uncertain; doubt; hesitancy:
His uncertainty gave impetus to his inquiry.
2. an instance of uncertainty, doubt, etc.
3. unpredictability; indeterminacy; indefiniteness.

- A Riverside mechanic is blamed for the conflagration that killed five federal firefighters in 2006. (کان فلگ ری شن: آتش یا حریق بزرگ)
conflagration: fire esp. a large disastrous fire

- In an online column the longtime leader appeared to be pondering[1] his mortality[2].

1.(سنجیدن-اندیشه کردن)
2.(فناپذیری- مرگ و میر- شمارمردگان)

<*to ponder on or/ over a mutter*[3]> در چیزی تفکر یا اندیشه کردن

3.(مادر : غرغر، من من کردن، غرغر کردن)

murmur ***–verb (used without object)***
1. to utter words indistinctly or in a low tone, often as if talking to oneself; murmur.
2. to complain murmuringly; grumble.
3. to make a low, rumbling sound.
–verb (used with object)
4. to utter indistinctly or in a low tone: *to mutter complaints.*
–noun
5. the act or utterance of a person who mutters.

- The smugglers did not want to give their real names for fear of retribution either Israelis or the Egyptian authorities.

(S ماگلر : قاچاقچي) (رتر b -u شن : کیفر- مکافات- تلافی)

retribution ***–noun*** رتر b -uشن : کیفر- مکافات- تلافی
1. requital according to merits or deserts, esp. for evil.
2. something given or inflicted in such requital.
3. *Theology* . the distribution of rewards and punishments in a future life.

- The purported property address is…پر پور تد: مفهوم بخشیدن- بنظر آمدن

<*The document purports that…*> آنچا از این سند مفهوم می شوداین است که

Purported: asserted[1] to be true or to exit or reputed[2] .

1.(اظهار/ادعا کردن/بنظر امدن / حاكي بودن از) ,**2**.(فرض کردن-دانستن-به حساب آوردن)

<*she is reputed to be the best engineer.*>

- The management of the IRS has purportedly told the auditors to "audit more rigorously and go collect some money".

(ری گرسلی : بسختی- بادقت زیاد)

rigorous ***–adjective*** ری گرسلی
1. characterized by rigor; rigidly severe or harsh, as people, rules, or discipline: *rigorous laws.*
2. severely exact or accurate; precise: *rigorous research.*
3. (of weather or climate) uncomfortably severe or harsh; extremely inclement.

- The will and any codicils are available for examination in the file kept by the court. (کادیسل: متمم وصیت نامه)

codicils **-noun** کادیسِل

1. a supplement to a will, containing an addition, explanation, modification, etc., of something in the will.

2. any supplement; appendix.

- Yelling "free free Palestine" and shouted retorts including, there is no Palestine from the pro-Israeli side.

رِتُورت : رد کردن- پس دادن- در اینجا یعنی جواب مطابق دادن- تلافی کردن

- For now, the stricter building requirements will only be applied to homes damaged or destroyed in the Nov. 2008 Friday

(S تِرِکت : سخت تر- اکیدتر- دقیق تر- بی کم و زیاد)

<under strict orders> or <a strict teacher>

strict ***-adjective,*** -er, -est. : S تِرِکت

1. characterized by or acting in close conformity to requirements or principles: *a strict observance of rituals.*

2. stringent or exacting in or in enforcing rules, requirements, obligations, etc.: *strict laws; a strict judge.*

3. closely or rigorously enforced or maintained: *strict silence.*

4. exact or precise: *a strict statement of facts.*

5. extremely defined or conservative; narrowly or carefully limited: *a strict construction of the Constitution.*

6. close, careful, or minute: *a strict search.*

- endure → اِین دُر : تحمل کردن- دوام آوردن

<I cannot endure to see that> طاقت یا تحمل دیدن آن را ندارم

***endure*—Verb with Object**

If you endure a painful or difficult situation, you bear it calmly and patiently. *It was more than I could endure.... There is no end to the humiliations you may have to endure.*

Verb, If something endures, it continues to exist....*a city which will endure for ever.... A world lay ahead where peace endured.* True **love endures** to the end

---

- They might have called a few former friends to apologize and mend fences for past squabbles . (S کُوآ بِل : داد و بیداد- دعوای جزئی- سروصدا راه انداختن)

squabble ***–verb (used without object)*** : S کُوآ بِل

1. to engage in a petty quarrel.

–verb (used with object)
2. *Printing* . to disarrange and mix (composed type).
–noun **3.** a petty quarrel.

- He says the event is tentative because he is not sure when the pilot will return home. (تن تی تیو : آزمایشی- امتحانی)

- Stopping the deflation cycle.

معنی این لغت یعنی تهی سازی باد- ولی در اینجا معنی زیر را دارد:

***deflation**: a contraction[1] in the volume of available money or credit that results in a general decline[2] in prices.*

1.(جمع شدگی- کلمه مخفف یا کوتاه شده) **2**.(سرازیر شدن- ردکردن، نپذیرفتن، رو بزوال گذاردن، تنزل کردن)

decline - ***–verb (used with object)***
1. to withhold or deny consent to do, enter into or upon, etc.; refuse: *He declined to say more about it.*
2. to express inability or reluctance to accept; refuse with courtesy: *to decline an invitation; to decline an offer.*
3. to cause to slope or incline downward.

- To make English the official language, this would unify our people and aid immigrant assimilation. اَسّی می لی شِن : یکسان- شبیه

Assimilate ***–noun*** اَسّی می لیت : یکسان کردن- برابر کرد

1. the act or process of assimilating; state or condition of being assimilated.
2. *Physiology* . the conversion of absorbed food into the substance of the body.

In an effort to curtail the abuse. کورتیل: موقوف کردن- کوتاه کردن

<*curtail the power of the executive branch*>
Noun --*Architecture*.
A horizontal, spiral termination to the lower end of stair railing.

- When a man has heart trouble, if he contemplate helplessness and dependency, even temporarily, may resurrect fear of being a Mama's baby. رِزِرَکت: زنده کردن- احیاء کردن- تجدید

resurrect ***--Verb (used with object)*** رِزِرَکت
1. to raise from the dead; bring to life again.
2. to bring back into use, practice, etc.: *to resurrect an ancient custom.*

–verb (used without object) **3.** to rise from the dead.

- Resumption of illegal traffic raises questions about success of Israel's war goals. (ازسرگیری- ادامه- اشغال دوباره)

اصل کلمه resume است یعنی از سرگیری- اشغال دوباره.

- Don't let shame get in the way of your Longevity.

Longevity means: *length of life* لان ج وِ تی: درازی عمر- عمر زیاد

The gender gap in longevity appears to be progressively declining.

Longevity **–noun** لان ج وِ تی: درازی عمر- عمر زیاد

1. a long individual life; great duration of individual life:
Our family is known for its longevity.
2. the length or duration of life: *research in human longevity.*
3. length of service, tenure, etc.; seniority: *promotions based on longevity.*

- Feeling low and despondent I entered my office and secretary, Janet said "good morning boss". دیس پان دِ نت :افسرده و دلتنگ

despondent **–adjective** دیس پان دِ نت

feeling or showing profound hopelessness, dejection, discouragement, or gloom:
<*despondent about failing health.*>

- Agents who are ambitious and are cleaning out his office. (جاه طلب)

<*Having or controlled by ambition*>, <*an ambitious young executive*>
<*Ambitious for power or Showing ambition*>, <*an ambitious film*>

ambitious: Having a desire to achieve a particular goal: aspiring
adjective: An ambitious person wants to be successful, rich, or powerful.
Mr Mellor is an ambitious and outspoken politician.
An ambitious idea or plan is on a large scale and needs a lot of work to be successful.
The government is taking its most ambitious and controversial step yet.

- Benediction[1] the invocation[2] of a blessing.

1.(بِ نِ دِک شِن: دعای خیر- دعای اختتام) **2.**(دعا- استدعا-استمداد- طلب یاری)

invocation: the act or process of petitioning for help or support

invocation ***–noun***
1. the act of invoking or calling upon a deity, spirit, etc., for aid, protection, inspiration, or the like; supplication.
2. any petitioning or supplication for help or aid.
3. a form of **prayer** invoking God's presence, esp. one said at the beginning of a religious service or public ceremony.

- White house counsel Grey Graig said Obama took the Oath from Robert Gate again out of an "abundance of caution"

آبا ندِنس:فراوانی- وفور

abundance ***–noun*** آبا ندِنس
1. an extremely plentiful or over sufficient quantity or supply: *an abundance of grain.*
2. overflowing fullness: *abundance of the heart.*
3. affluence; wealth: *the enjoyment of abundance.*

- City Council* an assembly or meeting for consultation advice or discussion.

*(شورا- انجمن- هیات)

Council of ministers	هیات وزیران
Town council	انجمن شهرداری
Council-board	جلسه هیات وزیران
White house counsel:	مشورت دادن- پند دادن

- The law had been embroiled in challenges to its constitutionality since it passed in 1998 and never took effect.

(ام بُرُیل : به نزاع انداختن- در هم بر هم کردن- پیچیده کردن)

<*embroiled with* آمیخته با یا آمیخته به>,
embroilment میانه بهم زدن- نزاع- درهمبرهمی

embroil ***–verb (used with object)***
1. to bring into discord or conflict; involve in contention or strife.
2. to throw into confusion; complicate.

- Congresswoman clenches fisrt around inauguration tickets.

(کلِن چِز :محکم بستن- از زیر پرچ کردن)

Clench: *to hold fast,* <*clenched the arms of the chair*>,
to set or close tightly, <*clench one's teeth*>, <*clench one's fists*>
Verb with Object---When you clench your teeth, you squeeze them together firmly.
She hissed through clenched teeth, `Get out of here.'

- Police identify mummified[1] woman. A woman whose mummified remains[2] were in parked car, the driver has not been arrested, but police are looking into possible health code violations for knowingly transporting a corpse[3].
  1.(مآ ما فای : موميايي كردن) 2.(بقايا ی عضو موميايي شده) 3.(کُرپس : نعش، لاشه، جسد)

  corpse–**noun** کُرپس : a dead body, usually of a human being.

- He challenged Americans to stop bickering and serve their nation.
  (بِ کِرینگ: پرخاش کردن- لرزیدن (شعله)

  ***bicker*–verb (used without object)**
  1. to engage in petulant or peevish argument; wrangle: *The two were always bickering.*
  2. to run rapidly; move quickly; rush; hurry: *a stream bickering down the valley.*
  3. to flicker; glitter: *The sun bickered through the trees.*
  4. ***–noun*** an angry, petty dispute or quarrel; contention.

- World leaders meeting in Egypt grapple with Gaza stability over the long term. گرَپل : کوشش فراوان در انجام کاری- دست به گریبان شدن- گلاویز شدن

  grapple –verb (used without object) : گرَپل

  1. to hold or make fast to something, as with a grapple.
  2. to use a grapple.
  3. to seize another, or each other, in a firm grip, as in wrestling; clinch.
  4. to engage in a struggle or close encounter (usually fol. by *with*):
  He was grappling with a boy twice his size. to grapple with a problem.
  7. to seize in a grip, take hold of: *The* ***thug**** *grappled him around the neck.*
  –noun *(ثاگ : ادم کش ، بي شرف ، قاتل ، گردن کلفت)
  8. a hook or an iron instrument by which one thing, as a ship, fastens onto another; grapnel. → قلاب، چنگک، چنگک يا قلاب كشتي

- Israel and Hamas ended up separately declaring cease-fire 12 hours apart after strenuous efforts by Egyptian mediators to get an agreement
  (S ترِن u- s : باحرارت- مصر- اصرارآمیز)

  strenuous ***–adjective*** S ترِن u- s
  1. characterized by vigorous exertion, as action, efforts, life, etc.:
  a strenuous afternoon of hunting.
  2. demanding or requiring vigorous exertion; laborious:
  To think deeply is a strenuous task.
  3. vigorous, energetic, or zealously active: *a strenuous person; a strenuous intellect.*

- Bush is leaving with no accountability[1] for eviscerating[2] poor constitution.

1 .(مسئوليت- جوابگويي) 2.(E وی ز ریتینگ : روده درآوردن از- شکم دریدن- در اینجا یعنی تهی کردن)

- "He has fun to be around very inclusive[1] always talked to everybody" said his friend. "He was just one of the guys. He was charismatic[2] and funny" said his friend. **1**.(دربردارنده- شامل- جامع), **2**.(کَرِزمَتیک)

charismatic: کرِزمتیک *Someone who is charismatic is able to attract, influence, and inspire people by their personal qualities.*

<..A *charismatic leader of people.... ...a charismatic figure and fiery orator*.*>
*، مستدعي، خطيب، ناطق‌پرداز، سخنران(سخن)

inclusive: Including the stated limit or extremes in consideration or account: *from 6 to 37 inclusive.* <*charismatic gifts*> *or* <*a charismatic leader*>

- King's words again filled the pews[1] and pulpits.[2] at black churches across the country.

1.(پی یو (در کلیسا) نیمکت، مقام ، درنیمکت قرار گرفتن، پیف (بوي بد) **2**.(پا ل پِتز : سکوی وعظ- منبر)

pew: *(in a church) one of a number of fixed, bench like seats with backs, accessible by aisles, for the use of the congregation.*

***pulpit*–noun** پا ل پِتز : سکوی وعظ- منبر

1. a platform or raised structure in a church, from which the sermon is delivered or the service is conducted.
2. the pulpit, **a.** the clerical profession; the ministry.
b. members of the clergy collectively: *In attendance were representatives of medicine, the pulpit, and the bar.*

- Crash inspectors report attests to quick thinking. گواهی دادن- تصدیق کردن

***attest*–verb (used with object)**
1. to bear witness to; certify; declare to be correct, true, or genuine; declare the truth of, in words or writing, esp. affirm in an official capacity: *to attest the truth of a statement.*
2. to give proof or evidence of; manifest: *His works attest his industry.*
3. to put on oath.
–verb (used without object)
4. to testify or bear witness (often fol. by *to*): *to attest to the reliability of an employee.*

- White House Speaker Nancy Pelosi veers (وِیرز-v) from Obama on tax cuts.
  Veer (وِیر-v) *To let out (as a rope)* تغییر جهت دادن- تغییر دادن-سست کردن

- Many black preachers[1] touted[2] the moment---the 23rd federal observance[3]of..

  1.(p ری چِر : واعظ) , 2.(تَ آت: مشتری جمع کردن) 3.(اَبزِر وِنس :تواضع- احترام- تعظیم)

  preacher–noun
  1. a person whose occupation or function it is to preach the gospel.
  2. a person who preaches.
  3. Friar Preacher.
  Tout: to spy on, watch

- A gradual deceleration (d سه لِ ری شِن: سرعت کم کردن)
  <*decelerate a car*>

- On the cockpit[1] voice recorder "the sound of thumps[2] and a rapid decrease in engine sounds" could be heard, said NTSB. They heard a thump, then eerie[3] silence.
  NTSB: ***N****ational* ***T****ransportation* ***S****afety* ***B****oard*

  1.(کاک پِت : اطاقک خلبان، اطاق فرمان در هواپیما- صحنه تئاتر، محل دعواومسابقه)
  2.(ثامپ : ضربت- مشت- توسری), 3.(اِ ری: وهم آور- ترساننده)

  thump–noun
  1. a blow with something thick and heavy, producing a dull sound; a heavy knock.
  2. the sound made by or as if by such a blow.
  –verb (used with object)
  3. to strike or beat with something thick and heavy, so as to produce a dull sound; pound.
  4. (of an object) to strike against (something) heavily and noisily.
  5. *Informal* . to thrash severely.
  –verb (used without object)
  6. to strike, beat, or fall heavily, with a dull sound.

- Court tosses slander[1] lawsuit against ex-superintendent[2] .

  1.(s لَندِر: بدگویی- تهمت- افترا زدن به) 2.(سوُ پِرین تِندِنت : مدیر، رئیس، سرپرست)
  slanderous تهمت زدن - بدگویی

  slander –noun s لَندِر
  1. defamation; calumny: *rumors full of slander.*
  2. a malicious, false, and defamatory statement or report:
  a slander against his good name.

3. *Law* . defamation by oral utterance rather than by writing, pictures, etc.
–verb (used with object) **4.** to utter slander against; defame.
–verb (used without object) **5.** to utter or circulate slander.

- a prisoner files claim against city, saying he got food poisoning while incarcerated. این کار سریت : زندانی کردن- نگاه د اشتن

incarcerated hernia → جمع شدگی کیسه فتق

incarcerate***–verb (used with object)*** این کار سریت
1. to imprison; confine.
2. to enclose; constrict closely.
–adjective
3. imprisoned.

- Dissident killings shook Northern Island. دیس سدنت: مخالف عقیده عموم

dissident: disagreeing esp. with an established religious or political system, organization, or belief

---

- Any expatriate[1] in financing difficulty knows the safest bet is to take the next outbound[2] flight

1.(اکس پی 3 -8:به کشور دیگری تبعید کردن)
2.(آت باند: عازم خروج از بندر)

expatriate: *banish exile,* (تبعید- دور کردن)
(صحبت درباره اوضاع بد اقتصادی دبی بوده در 2008 است که گفته شده)

- Expatriates from developing countries helped maintain Dubai's orgy of consumption during the boom years.

(اورجی: میگساری- هرزگی-عیاشی - ,جمع لغت Orgies است)

expatriate: to withdraw (oneself) from residence in or allegiance to one's nation country. (آلی جنس : بیعت- وفاداری)

- Recaptured[1] bobcat, scientists who fitted the predators[2] with tracking collars and spent three years studying their monuments say their existence is sometimes.

1.(ری کپ چر: مجدا دستگیر شدن)
2.(پریتورز: شکاری)

predator: an animal that lives by predation Rescue workers in surgical makes pulled 100 bodies from building pulverized (by bombs. .

(پالورایزد: سائیدن- نرم شدن- در اینجا قطعه قطعه کردن- گرد شدن)

- neutered (نُوتِر) male. (نُوتِر : بدون ed یعنی جانور اخته)
  spayed female (s پی د : اخته کردن- بی تخم کردن)

  neutralization: an act or process of neutralizing

- that is news to me برای من تازگی دارد
- Marriage of convenience ازدواج مصلحتی
- A haze hung in the air مه کم- غبار-در اینجا نامعلومی و گیجی
- *precarious.* پ رِ گریوس: ناپایدار- چندروزه- بی اساس- مشکوک)

- *corroborate* (کورابِ ریت): *to support with evidence or authority make more certain,*
  Synonym→ *confirm*
  Corroboration کورابِ ریشِن: تایید-تقویت-تاکید

- Government Opportunity Program (GOP) chief clarifies[1] stance[2] on abortion

1.(صاف روشن کردن- روشن شدن)
2.(طرز ایستادن ، ساختمان- حالت- وضع- ایستایش)

Stance= station, site, a way of standing or being placed.

- LA County rejects stimulus[1] money swaps[2]

1.(محرک- اثر- فشار) , 2.(عوض- مبادله کردن)
<*under the stimulus of hunger*> → از فشار گرسنگی- براثرگرسنگی

- Despite arrears[1] in payments, US is the mainstay[2] of the world body, he acknowledges

---

- Attorney general commemorate[1] civil rights march[2].

1.(یادگار- یادبود), **2**.(نظامی وار راه رفتن- مارش- رژه)

- Supporters and opponents of gay marriage. حمایت کنندگان و مخالفین ازدواج هم جنس بازان

- A convicted fugitive who mutilated[1] his own fingertips to avoid detection[2] and who was twice prosecuted[3] while assuming false identities was arrested.

1.(میو t لیت : نقص عضو کردن- اندام کسی را بریدن)
2.(ردیابي، کشف، بازیابي بازرسي، تفتیش، اکتشاف)

3.(پُرا سی کیوتِد : تعقیب قانوني کردن، دنبال کردن پیگرد کردن)

mutilate ***–verb (used with object),*** -lat·ed, -lat·ing.
1. to injure, disfigure, or make imperfect by removing or irreparably damaging parts: *Vandals mutilated the painting.*
2. to deprive (a person or animal) of a limb or other essential part

detection ***–noun***
1. the act of detecting. **2.** the fact of being detected.
3. discovery, as of error or crime: *chance detection of smuggling.*

prosecute–***verb (used with object)***
1. *Law* . **a.** to institute legal proceedings against (a person).
b. to seek to enforce or obtain by legal process.
c. to conduct criminal proceedings in court against.
2. to follow up or carry forward something undertaken or begun, usually to its completion: *to prosecute a war.* **3.** to carry on or practice.
–verb (used without object)
4. *Law* . **a.** to institute and carry on a legal prosecution. **b.** to act as prosecutor.

- US will dispatch two emissaries to Syria for "preliminary conversations" aimed at warning relations with an Arab. *emissary*← مفرد لغت
(إمیسری: مامور مخفی)

- Attention first time home buyer: *Time is of the essence* for new $ 10,000 tax credit.
(إیسِنس: هستي، وجود ماهیت، گوهر، ذات، اسانس)
Of the essence: *of the utmost importance, Time is of the essence.*

<she was the essence of punctuality>, *<the essence of the issue>*
<He was in essence an honest person>

- Citing[1] tenets[2] of Iran….
1.(ذکرکردن-اتخاذ سند کردن cite) 2.(تِ نِت: عقیده و اصول)

- Obama calling on the other nations to exert[1] their influence to compel[2] Iran to give up its suspected pursuit[3] of nuclear weapons.
1.(اگزِرت: اعمال کردن- بکاربردن), **2**.(کام پِل : مجبور- ناگزیر کردن) , **3**.(پِر سوت : تعقیب، پیگرد)
< زوربکار بردن *to exert force*> , < کوشش-تقلا-فشار *exertion*>

exert **-verb (used with object)** اِگزِرت
1. to put forth or into use, as power; exercise, as ability or influence; put into vigorous action: *to exert every effort.* **2.** to put (oneself) into strenuous, vigorous action or effort.

compel **-verb (used with object)** کام پِل
1. to force or drive, esp. to a course of action: *His disregard of the rules compels us to dismiss him.*
2. to secure or bring about by force. **3.** to force to submit; subdue. **4.** to overpower.

pursuit **-noun** پِر سوت
1. the act of pursuing: *in pursuit of the fox.*
2. an effort to secure or attain; quest: *the pursuit of happiness.*
3. any occupation, pastime, or the like, in which a person is engaged regularly or customarily: *literary pursuits.*

- He is responsible for this most heinous[1] and terrible crime will finally be held accountable[2] for his actions.

1.(هی نِس:زشت- شنیع), **2.**(مسئول- جواب ده)

<*accountability* بطور مسئول- چنانچه بتوان توضیح داد >
<*no scandal accountability* مسئولیت- مسئولیت محاسباتی >

- Police said, her clothing was strewn[1] form the path, down a steep hill toward the bottom of a ravine[2]

1.(اس ترون : افشاندن- پاره پاره شدن) , 2.(رَوِن: دره تنگ- دربند)

< *His path was strewn with flowers* مقدم اورا گلباران کردند>
<*As a destination, Strewn is unique.*>, <*Sawdust strewed the floor.*>

- Investigators spoke with him in 2001 and at one point gave him a polygraph test that was inconclusive.

(پالی گرَف ماشین کپي سازی، دروغ فاش کن) (این کان کلو سیو : ناتمام- بی نتیجه)

inconclusive **-adjective**
1. not conclusive; not resolving fully all doubts or questions: *inconclusive evidence.*
2. without final results or outcome: *inconclusive experiments.*

- What is your political affiliation ? پیوستگی- قبول
- Photographing underage girls for sexual gratification.... خوشی- لذت

Gratify → لذ ت دادن

Gratification: a source of satisfaction or pleasure.

- The charismatic (کَرِزمَتیک) 56-year-old mayors brought fresh visibility to an office with limited powers.

Charismatic: Of relating to or constituting charisma or charim.

<Charismatic gifts>

- regime → رژیم: یک نوع حکومت - با افزودن n در آخر می شود رژیم غذایی

regimen (رِجِ مِن): *a systematic plan (as a diet therapy or medication)*

He is sociable and energetic.

regimen **–noun**

1. *Medicine/Medical* . a regulated course, as of diet, exercise, or manner of living, intended to preserve or restore health or to attain some result.

- interpretation of the law evolves to reflect shifting social values.

(E وآلو: استنتاج کردن- بیرون کشیدن- باز کردن)

evolve ***–verb (used with object)***

1. to develop gradually: *to evolve a scheme.*

2. to give off or emit, as odors or vapors.

–verb (used without object)

3. to come forth gradually into being; develop; undergo evolution: *The whole idea evolved from a casual remark.*

4. *Biology* . to develop by a process of evolution to a different adaptive state or condition: *The human species evolved from an ancestor that was probably arboreal.*

- After bumpy tenure in Los Angels mayor gets new term.

(تِن یور: دوره تصدی)

tenure **–noun**

1. the holding or possessing of anything: *the tenure of an office.*

2. the holding of property, esp. real property, of a superior in return for services to be rendered. **3.** the period or term of holding something.

4. status granted to an employee, usually after a probationary period, indicating that the position or employment is permanent.

–verb (used with object)

5. to give tenure to: *After she served three years on probation, the committee tenured her.*

- Forty one bodies *have been* recovered; another 187 *have yet* to be found.

- He disdains دیس دین to talk with me. او عار دارد از اینکه با من صحبت کند.
- Palestinians had been hoping that Clinton would press Israelis to curtail Jewish settlement expansion in the west Bank.

(کِر تِ یل : موقوف- محروم- کوتاه کردن)

curtail **–verb (used with object)**
to cut short; cut off a part of; abridge; reduce; diminish.

- Why do women over react get emotionally **distraught**[1] and dump men they feel a strong spiritual connection of unequivocal[2] love for?

1.(دیس تِرات : آشفته وپریشان در اثر غم و غصهٔ فراوان وغیره)
2.(آن Eکوئی ویکال: روشن ، بدون ابهام)

distraught: (دیس تِرات) *agitated with doubt or mental conflict or pain.*
<distraught mourners>
The second meaning: *mentally deranged: crazed*
<As if thou wert distraught and mad with terror-shak>

distraughtly مشتقات آن
<A distraught father was arrested early Wednesday morning after firing several shots during a dispute.>

- Context[1]: The parts of a discourse[2] that surround a word or passage[3] and can throw on its meaning. (In this context: در این زمینه)

1.(کان تِکست : زمینه- محتوی- کلمات پس و پیش مطلب که مفهوم آنرا تسهیل میکند)
2.(دیس کُرس : سخنرانی- مقاله- خط به) **3**.(پَسیج :گذر- مرور)

discourse ***–noun***
1. communication of thought by words; talk; conversation:
<earnest and intelligent discourse>.
2. a formal discussion of a subject in speech or writing, as a dissertation, treatise, sermon,etc.
3. *Linguistics.* any unit of connected speech or writing longer than a sentence.
–verb (used without object) **4.** to communicate thoughts orally; talk; converse.
5. to treat of a subject formally in speech or writing.

- The latest signs of the government's growing confidence in quelling[1] unrest[2] on the streets. (*Unrest*: turmoil)

<*Quell a riot*> , <*quell fears*> 1. (کُوالینگ: فرو نشاندن-سرکوب کردن)
2.(آن رست: آشوب- اضطراب- بیقراری

- Man killed by Anaheime Police at *7-11 store* had altercation* with mom.

  *(A noisy heated angry dispute)→ ستیزه- جدال- مشاجره

  Synonym see *quarrel*

- Rival[1] warns of looming[2] Iraq's neighbor dictatorship….

  1.(رای وال: رقیب) 2.(از دور نمودار شدن- از زیر ابر بیرون آمدن)

- Hamas fighters in alleyways[1] and cellars[2]……

  1. آلی وی :پاساژ یا راه باریک **2.** سِ لِر : زیر زمین یا سرداب

- In Wednesday's debate, Mr. A. accused two former presidents of joining forces with Mr. M. to wage a campaign of "lies."

  معنی دیگر wage در اینجا بغیر از دستمز یا اجرت میشود ← سرو صدا بپا کردن- جنگ بر پا کردن

  Waging: To engage in or carry on <*wage war*>, <*wage a campaign*>, <*The riot waged for several hours.*>

- Although every project is different and has its peculiar[1] quirks[2]

  1.(پی کیو لی یر :ویژه- مخصوص)و 2.(کورک: ابهام- حیله- کلک)

quirk–noun

1. a peculiarity of action, behavior, or personality; mannerism:
<*He is full of strange quirks.*>
2. a shift, subterfuge, or evasion; quibble.
3. a sudden twist or turn: *He lost his money by a quirk of fate.*
4. a flourish or showy stroke, as in writing.

(مطلب زیر در رابطه با حیوانی بنام اسکانک است که درموقع خطر بوی بدی اسپری میکند)

- A rehabilitator[1] of maligned[2] animals shares ways to get rid of pesky[3] creatures. → کری چر: مخلوق، جانور

  1.(ری حبی لی تیت: توانبخشي کردن، داراي امتیازات اولیه کردن، تجدید اسکان کردن)
  2.(م لاین: زیان آور- شوم- نحس- خطرناک) 3 .(پس کی: آزار رسان- مزاحم)

Rehabilitate: *To restore to a condition of good health, ability to work, or the like.* Troublesome, <*pesky issues*>

creature **–noun** کِری چِر: مخلوق، جانور
1. an animal, esp. a nonhuman: *the creatures of the woods and fields; a creature from outer space.*
2. anything created, whether animate or inanimate.
3. person; human being: *She is a charming creature. The driver of a bus is sometimes an irritable creature.*

- The nocturnal animals are not only digging up lawns in search of bugs and spraying automobiles . (ناک تِر نو ل: شبانه)

Active at night (opposed to diurnal*): (جانوراني که درروزفعاليت دارند) *(روزانه، مربوط به روز
<*Nocturnal animals,* Nocturnal birds.>, <*Diurnal* دایورنُل *temperature*>

Nocturnal **–adjective** ناک تِر نو ل: شبانه

1. of or pertaining to the night (opposed to diurnal).
2. done, occurring, or coming at night: *nocturnal visit.*
3. active at night (opposed to diurnal): *nocturnal animals.*
4. opening by night and closing by day, as certain flowers (opposed to diurnal).

- So how can anyone be offended when you say " F " word?
(*حقوق*) مرتکب خلاف شدن- رنجانیدن- اذیت کردن-تجاوز کردن ، صدمه زدن، دلخور کردن

- In a rare and raucous election debate. (رآکِس : خشن نا هنجار-خیلی نا مرتب)
raucous –*adjective* رآکِس
1. harsh; strident; grating: *raucous voices; raucous laughter.*
2. rowdy; disorderly: *a raucous party.*

- "Your method (of Government) definitely leads to dictatorship," he told him, who fidgeted[1] in his chair often and gave scornful[2] smiles as Moos. spoke.
1.(فی جِت: بی آرامی- بی قراری- بخود پیچید ن) 2.(اِسکُورن فُول : تمسخر- تحقیر- خوار شمردن)

fidget–***verb (used without object)*** فی جِت
1. to move about restlessly, nervously, or impatiently.
–verb (used with object)

2. to cause to fidget; make uneasy.
–noun
3. Often, **fidgets.** the condition or an instance of being nervously restless, uneasy, or patient.   4. Also, **fidg·et·er.** a person who fidgets.

scornful ***–adjective*** اِسکُورن فُول
full of scorn; derisive; contemptuous: *He smiled in a scornful way.*

- It was my birthday, my wife even didn't say good morning, let alone "Happy Birthday and I thought may be the children will remember. They came in and didn't say a word, feeling low and despondent. دِ س پاَن دِنت افسرده و دلسرد

despondent ***–adjective*** دِ س پاَن دِنت افسرده و دلسرد
feeling or showing profound hopelessness, dejection, discouragement, or gloom:
<*despondent about failing health.*>
<*despondent about his health*>, <*despondent about yet another rejection*

- Agent perpetuates[1] service excellence[2]

1.(پِر پِ چوُ اِیت : همیشگي کردن، دائمي کردن، جاوداني ساختن)
2.(مزيت، برترى، خوبي، تفوق، رجحان، فضيلت)

***perpetuate–verb (used with object),*-at·ed, -at·ing.** پِر پِ چوُ اِیت
1. to make perpetual.
2. to preserve from extinction or oblivion: *to perpetuate one's <u>name</u>*
3. Perpetuating, Perpetuation, Perpetuator ← مشتقات آن
<*Perpetuate the species*> ← اس پی شیز: گونه- نوع
4. If someone or something perpetuates a situation or belief, they cause it to continue; a formal word. <*...an education system that perpetuates inequality.*>

Species--- ← اس پی شیز: گونه- نوع
A species is a class of plants or animals whose members have the same main characteristics and are able to breed with each other.
<*There are two hundred and fifty species of shark.*>

- She was dismayed to learn of their disloyalty.

Dismay→ ترسانيدن، بيجرات كردن، ترس، وحشت زدگي، بي ميلي
Oh, f…k it! ← در موقعیکه میترسید یعنی در حالdismay ناگهان میگوئید

dismay–verb (used with object)
1. to break down the courage of completely, as by sudden danger or trouble; dishearten thoroughly; daunt: <*The surprise attack dismayed the enemy.*>
2. to surprise in such a manner as to disillusion:

<*She was dismayed to learn of their disloyalty..*>
3. to alarm; perturb: <*The new law dismayed some of the more conservative politicians.*>

- Promise and peril in South Los Angels.

پ رول: خطر، مخاطره، بیم زیان، مسئولیت، درخطر انداختن، در خطر بودن

peril ***–noun*** پ رول
1. exposure to injury, loss, or destruction; grave risk; jeopardy; danger:
They faced the peril of falling rocks.
2. something that causes or may cause injury, loss, or destruction
<*Fire put the city in peril*>, <*They faced the peril of falling rocks.*>

Periled, periling, perilous, ← مشتقات
Perilous: Full of or involving peril, <*a perilous journey*>

- These trivial ترى وى يال issues are normal. جزئی- نا قابل ، ناچیز

trivial ***–adjective***
of very little importance or value; insignificant: *Don't bother me with trivial matters.*

- The savior of all, <*Jesus Christ is the savior.*> ناجی

savior ***–noun***
1. a person who saves, rescues, or delivers: *the savior of the country.*
2. (*initial capital letter*) a title of god, esp. of Christ.

- Former president Bush blunders[1], blessings[2]

1.(اشتباه بزرگ دراثر یک حماقت یا بی ملاحظه گی) 2.(برکت- دعای خیر)

blunder ***–noun***
1. a gross, stupid, or careless mistake: *That's your second blunder this morning.*
–verb (used without object)
2. to move or act blindly, stupidly, or without direction or steady guidance:
<*Without my glasses I blundered into the wrong room.* >
3. to make a gross or stupid mistake, esp. through carelessness or mental confusion:
<*Just pray that he doesn't blunder again and get the names wrong.*>

- There are not many words with the versatility of the "F" word.

(ورسه تی لیتی: تنو ع)

versatile ***–adjective*** ورسه تی لیتی)

1. capable of or adapted for turning easily from one to another of various tasks, fields of endeavor, etc.: *a versatile writer.*
2. having or capable of many uses: *a versatile tool.*
3. The quality or state of being versatile , < *a writer of great versatility*>

- He helped a family subdue[1] a burglary suspect who broke into their home looking for loot[2].

1.(سابدُو : مطیع کردن، مقهور ساختن، رام کردن)
2.(لوُت : غارت، چپاول، تاراج، استفاده نامشروع، غارت کردن)

مَعانی یا بکار گیری لغات فوق در جملات دیگر:

subdue : سابدُو To bring under one's control by force of arms
<*subdued the rebels and sent their leaders to the gallows*>
Synonyms : subjugate, vanquish. tame, break, discipline. suppress.
Antonyms : awaken, arouse و intensify.

loot **–noun** لوُت
1. spoils or plunder taken by pillaging, as in war.
2. anything taken by dishonesty, force, stealth, etc.: *a burglar's loot.*
3. a collection of valued objects: *The children shouted and laughed as they opened their Christmas loot.*

- Since last year City of Laguna Hills has been looking into spay[1] and neuter[2] programs and is now recommending that….. and license canvassing[3] program be created in the up coming biennial[4] budget to make it easer for pet owners....

1.(اِس پی: اخته کردن)   **2.**(نُوتِر: خنثی کردن یا خنثی سازی)
3.(براي جمع اوري اراء فعاليت كردن، الک یا غربال کردن)

4. (بای انی نیال: دو ساله – درخت دوساله)

مَعانی یا بکار گیری لغات فوق در جملات دیگر:

***spay* –object** *Veterinary Medicine.* وِت رِ نِری
to remove the ovaries of (an animal).

***neuter* –adjective** نُوتِر: خنثی کردن یا خنثی سازی

1. *Grammar*. **a.** noting or pertaining to a gender that refers to things classed as neither masculine nor feminine. **b.** (of a verb) intransitive.
2. *Biology*. having no organs of reproduction; without sex; asexual.
–verb (used with object) *Veterinary Science*. to spay or castrate (a dog, cat, etc.).

canvass ***–verb (used with object)***
1. to solicit votes, subscriptions, opinions, or the like from.
2. to examine carefully; investigate by inquiry; discuss; debate.
–verb (used without object) **3.** to solicit votes, opinions, or the like.
–noun **4.** a soliciting of votes, orders, or the like.
5. a campaign for election to government office.

Biennial: occurring every two years or lasting for two years. بای انی نیال

- Israeli troops thrust[1] deeper into Gaza City. As Egyptian mediators urged Hamas to accept a truce[2] proposal and Israel sent its head negotiator to Cairo.

1.(تراست : در علوم نظامي حمله کردن، حمله، ضربت فشار- رخنه کردن)
2. (تروس: متارکه جنگ – مهلت)

<u>مَعانی یا بکار گیری لغات فوق در جملات دیگر:</u>

thrust –verb (used with object) تِراست
1. to push forcibly; shove; put or drive with force: *He thrust his way through the crowd. <She thrust a dagger into his back.> <To push or drive with force>*
2. to put boldly forth or impose acceptance of: *to thrust oneself into a conversation between others; to thrust a dollar into the waiter's hand.*
3. to extend; present: *He thrust his fist in front of my face.*

Truce: a suspension of hostilities for a specified period of time by mutual agreement of the warring parties; cease-fire; armistice.:→ تروس متارکهء جنگ، صلح موقت

- 150 sexually suggestive[1] photographs of young girls on his home computer…
  1.(اشاره کننده- حاکی- دال)
- Sweating[2] the real budget… (2.(سوِات : زحمت کشیدن- جان کندن-عرق ریختن)

- Orange County woman ousted at Los Angeles Airport (LAX)..

  oust: to take away (as a right or authority) Bar, remove.

  oust :→ برکنار کردن، دورکردن، اخراج کردن-در *(حقوق)* خلع ید کردن از

- The woman’s baby was delivered stillborn at a hospital. *Stillborn:* dead at birth, failing from the start, abortive, unsuccessful.

abortive:→ رشد نکرده- بی ثمر-سقط

<*He is said to have been involved in an abortive coup in January*>

گو: *coup* برهم زدن، ضربت، کودتا

- An element of the peace effort that has proved elusive for years.

الی لو سیو: طفره آمیز - اغفال کننده

- They are Americans and Israelis who want to stoke[1] sectarian[2] conflict in the countr

1.(اس تُوک: آتش کردن- تابیدن)

2. فرقه گراي، کوته بین- *(حقوق)* فرقهاي، حزبي، عضو فرقه

Stoked, Stoking: To poke or stir up (as a fire): supply with fuel,
To feed abundantly بطور فراوان

- Mo’s wife arguments are paired with the revolutionary credentials[1] that bring grudging[2] respect from hard-liners.

1.گواهی نامه-اعتبارنامه 2. بی میل- لجدار

grudging :A grudging feeling or response is one that you feel or make very unwillingly. <*Others stood watching with grudging respect...*>
< *It does appear to mark a grudging realization by the authorities that some concessions* may be necessary.*> ‘

* اعطاء امتیاز، امتیازانحصاري

- Islamic militants[1] fired barrages[2] of rockets at cities in Southern Israel.

1. (میلی تنت: مبارز- جنگجو 2.(بِ راج: سدبندي، رگبارگلوله بطورمسلسل بیرون دادن)

barrage –noun بِ راج
1. *Military*. a heavy barrier of artillery fire to protect one's own advancing or retreating troops or to stop the advance of enemy troops.
2. an overwhelming quantity or explosion, as of words, blows, or criticisms:

<*a barrage of questions.*> , <*Barrage barrier fire*>, *a barrage of protests*>
3. *Civil Engineering*. an artificial obstruction in a watercourse to increase the depth of the water, facilitate irrigation, etc.

- My cat was sneezing and drooling, (اب از دهان تراوش شدن ← Drooling : دُورل)

Drooling, *Drool*: intransitive verb, to secrete saliva[1] in anticipation of food drivel[2.]

To let saliva dribble from the mouth→ 1.(سه لای وا: بزاق- آب دهان خیو)
2.(دیر یول : آب دهان جاري ساختن از دهن یا بیني- جاري شدن دري وري سخن گفتن)

saliva ----Fast and Simple Testing Process; Provides quantitative results in less. سه لای وا
than five minute **using** only a **saliva** sample. .

Saliva is the watery liquid that forms in your mouth.

<These chemicals are also secreted in our saliva.>

drivel –*noun* دیر یول آب دهان جاري ساختن از دهن یا بیني- جاري شدن دري وري سخن گفتن
1. saliva flowing from the mouth, or mucus from the nose; slaver.
2. childish, silly, or meaningless talk or thinking; nonsense; twaddle.

- ***Toll*** : A payment or fee exacted by the state, the local authorities, etc., for some right or privilege, as for passage along a road or over a bridge.

- *King* judge issued the maximum sentence after he heard poignant words from Luis, 54th victim's father.
  Before they recommending death for him on July 30 after they were shown a poignant 1993 videotape of *Jeanette* at age 15, letting her father how much she love him.

  پوی نِنت: تندوتیز- نیش دار- گوشه دار

  Tolling agency strikes a conciliatory note. صلح آمیز
  Conciliator → آشتی دهنده

- Provoking[1] US. with impunity[2] …., <*Provoking to anger* →خشمگین کردن>
  1.(تحریک کردن- بر انگیختن) 2. (بخشودگی- معافیت از مجازات- معافیت از زیان)

- I defy anyone to tell us what is Obama said during a March visit to Pittsburg.
  Defied, defying, defies (دیفای : بمبارزه طلبیدن- تحریک بجنگ کردن- شیر کردن)

- In a new overture[1] to Iran, the Obama administration has authorized US embassies to invite Iranian officials to Independence Day[2] parties.
  1.(أورچر: پیشنهاد- مطرح کردن- با پیش درآمد آغاز کردن) 2.(این دیپن دِنس دِی : روز استقلال)

- The complete guide to Home Wiring is a comprehensive[1] tour through the sometimes intimidating[2] subject of electricity .

1.(کام پری هن سیو : جامع) 2.(این تی میدیت : آگاهی دادن- خبر دادن) .

comprehensive ***–adjective*** **جامع** : کام پری هن سیو
1. of large scope; covering or involving much; inclusive:
<*a comprehensive study of world affairs.*
2. comprehending mentally; having an extensive mental range or grasp.
3. *Insurance.* covering or providing broad protection against loss.

intimidate ***–verb (used with object),*** **-dat·ed, -dat·ing.** آگاهی دادن- خبر دادن : این تی میدیت
1. to make timid; fill with fear.
2. to overawe or cow, as through the force of personality or by superior display of wealth, talent, etc.
3. to force into or deter from some action by inducing fear:
< *to intimidate a voter into staying away from the polls.* >
To force into or deter from some action by inducing fear:
<*to intimidate a voter into staying away from the polls.*>

- Three people are behind bars, accused of orchestrating[1] an elaborate[2] plan to kidnap a bank employee and rob her bank.

1.(اُر کِس ترِ ر یت : هم آهنگ کردن) 2. (انی لَبو ریت : استادانه درست کردن-بطور کامل تهیه کردن)

orchestrate ***–verb (used with object), verb (used without object),*** **-trat·ed, -trat·ing.**
1. to compose or arrange (music) for performance by an orchestra.
2. to arrange or manipulate, esp. by means of clever or thorough planning or maneuvering: <*to orchestrate a profitable trade agreement.* >

<*Orchestrated preparations for the banquet*>

elaborate ***–adjective*** استادانه درست کردن-بطور کامل تهیه کردن : انی لَبو ریت
1. worked out with great care and nicety of detail; executed with great minuteness:
< *elaborate preparations; elaborate care.*>
2. marked by intricate and often excessive detail; complicated.

- President Bush states his legacy on keeping America safe.

میراث- جمع آن legacies است

- Obama's nominee for attorney general says waterboarding crosses the line.

یک نوع شکنجه با آب

- Notorious[1] a big winner, the rapper's life story transcends[2] gangster flick[3] cliche`s[4]

1.(انگشت نما- مشهو ر به بدی- رسوائی) 2.(تِ رَن سِنت : ما فوق چیزی بودن-فائق بودن)

3.(فِلِک : تکان ناگهانی- ضربه آهسته) 4.(کیلی شه : کلیشه)

مَعانی یا بکار گیری لغات فوق در جملات دیگر:

Transcend ***–verb (used with object)*** تِ رَن سِنت : ما فوق چیزی بودن-فائق بودن

1. to rise above or go beyond; overpass; exceed:

<to transcend the limits of thought; kindness transcends courtesy.>

2. to outdo or exceed in excellence, elevation, extent, degree, etc.; surpass; excel.

–verb (used without object)

To be transcendent or superior; excel: *His competitiveness made him want to transcend.*

flick ***–noun*** فِلِک : تکان ناگهانی- ضربه آهسته

1. a sudden light blow or tap, as with a whip or the finger:

<She gave the horse a flick with her riding crop. >

2. the sound made by such a blow or tap.

3. a light and rapid movement: *a flick of the wrist.*

4. something thrown off with or as if with a jerk: *a flick of mud.*

–verb (used with object) **5.** to strike lightly with a whip, the finger, etc.

6. to remove with such a stroke: *to flick away a crumb.* خرده نان، خرده، هرچیزي شبیه خرده نان

clichéd ***–noun*** -----Cliché: a trite* phrase expression. *(پیش پا افتاده – کهنه- مبتذل)

a trite, stereotyped expression; a sentence or phrase, usually expressing a popular or common thought or idea, that has lost originality, ingenuity, and impact by long overuse, as *sadder but wiser,* or *strong as an ox.*

a. a stereotype or electrotype plate.

b. a reproduction made in a like manner.

–adjective **5.** trite; hackneyed; stereotyped; clichéd. کیلی شه : کلیشه

- Are you saying too many borrowers need a drastic[1] reduction in payments. In a lot of cases, you are just delaying inevitable[2]...

1.(دِرَستیک : جدی- موثر) 2.(این اِو تِبِل : چاره نا پذیر – غیر قابل اجتناب)

drastic ***–adjective*** درَستیک
1. acting with force or violence; violent.
2. extremely severe or extensive: *a drastic tax-reduction measure.*

inevitable :-----If something is inevitable, it cannot be prevented or avoided.
<If this policy continues, then violence is inevitable>

- I absolutely feel vindicated beyond… حمایت کردن از

  <San Francisco X-sheriff claims vindication> حمایت-دفاع-اثبات

- Baghdad's heavy fortified Green-Zone……

  برج و بارو دار- دارای استحکامات یا سنگر بندی کردن

  fortify ***–verb (used with object)***
  1. to protect or strengthen against attack; surround or provide with defensive military works.
  2. to furnish with a means of resisting force or standing strain or wear: *to fortify cotton with nylon.*
  3. to make strong; impart strength or vigor to: *to fortify oneself with a good breakfast.*
  4. to increase the effectiveness of, as by additional ingredients: *to fortify a diet with vitamins; to fortify a lotion with lanolin.*
  5. to strengthen mentally or morally: *to be fortified by religious faith.*

- Vanguard Co. mired in debt. مایر: گل-باطلاق- گرفتار شدن.

  A troublesome or intractable situation…

  <found themselves in a mire deb , *<hunt on the wing like a hawk>*

- We have to use up this glut of homes.

  سیر کردن – پر خوردن ولی در اینجا یعنی← زیادی-عرضه بیش از تقاضا

  <There is a glut in the market> کالا در مارکت بیش از حد نیاز است

- Mr. Paulson saying his department will not buy distressed loans and related assets. پریشان- مضطرب

- Am I doomed to a lifetime of being "the friend"?

<*felt he was doomed to a life of loneliness*> دُم:حکم- سر نوشت بد

doom–noun

1. fate or destiny, esp. adverse fate; unavoidable ill fortune: *In exile and poverty, he met is doom.*
2. ruin; death: *to fall to one's doom.*
3. a judgment, decision, or sentence, esp. an unfavorable one: *The judge pronounced the efendant's doom.*
4. the Last Judgment, at the end of the world.
5. *Obsolete.* a statute, enactment, or legal judgment.

- All it did was create an anomaly… أناملی : خلاف قاعده

anomaly **---Count Noun**

If something is an anomaly, it is different from what is normal or expected.

There was an anomaly making the theory unsatisfactory.... It is easy to criticize the elections as being undemocratic when such anomalies occur.

- Bob Hope's wife reached his husband 100th birth date, he was too frail to enjoy it…

David died on April at 87, was convinced[1] that 20th centaury life was a frail[2] shell of pretense[3] over strong, dark, violent impulses[4].

1. کانونس : متقاعد کردن، قانع کردن
2. فِ ریِل : زود گذر- فانی - سست- نحیف- شکننده- زود گذر

3. پری تِنس : این لغت با حرف c هم صحیح است یعنی وا نمود سازی
4. ایم پوُلس : انگیزه دادن به - انگیزه ناگهاني تکان دادن، بر انگیختن

<u>مَعانی یا بکار گیری لغات فوق در جملات دیگر:</u>

convince ***–verb (used with object),*****-vinced, -vinc·ing.**

1. to move by argument or evidence to belief, agreement, consent, or a course of action: <*to convince a jury of his guilt; A test drive will convince you that this car handles well.*>
2. to persuade; cajole: <*We finally convinced them to have dinner with us.*>

(It was quite a jog to convince her. مگر به این آسانیها حرف توي كله اش مي رفت)
<she took some convincing>

frail **----Adjective**
A frail person is not strong or healthy.
<Visitors who have met him in recent weeks say he has been looking frail....
...a frail old man.>
Something that is frail is easily broken or damaged. ...a frail structure.

impulse ***–noun*** : inspiration, motivation

1. the influence of a particular feeling, mental state, etc.: *<to act under a generous impulse; to strike out at someone from an angry impulse>.*
2. sudden, involuntary inclination prompting to action: *to be swayed by impulse.*
An impulse is a sudden desire to do something.
<I had a sudden impulse to turn around and walk out.>
If you do something on impulse, you do it suddenly without planning it... A waiting period does force some people to reconsider buying a gun on impulse.
Impulsive→ کسیکه از روی انگیزهائی و بدون فکر عمل میکند

- Former …?… president Mo said, he will see hard-line leader Ah. For slander over remarks he made during an election debate.

تهمت- افترا- تهمت زدن- بد نام کردن

slander ***–noun***
1. defamation; calumny: *rumors full of slander.*
2. a malicious, false, and defamatory statement or report:
<a slander against his good name.>
3. *Law.* defamation by oral utterance rather than by writing, pictures, etc.
Synonym: see malign, (a malign (م لاین) spirit → روح پلید)

- Change of venue sought for trail of man charged in accident in which he died

ون یو: در حقوق حوزه صلاحیت – محل دادرسی
(حقوق) محل وقوع جرم يا دعوي، محل دادرسي، محل تشكيل دادگاه

Venue : *< Requested a change of venue>*

The venue for an event or activity is the place where it will happen.

The talks were postponed until Monday after an argument over the venue.

- President Obama said the lesson from the Buchan Wald Concentration-Camp[1] is vigilance[2] against evil, against subjugation[3] of the weak and against the "cruelty" in ourselves

1. محل نگهداری زندانیهای سیاسی- اسیران جنگی- پناهندگان و فراریها
ولی کلمه Concentration به تنهائی یعنی تمرکز- غلیظ

2. وِج لِنس : مراقبت، مواظبت، شب زنده داري، کشیک، امادگي چالاکي، احتیاط، گوش بزنگ

3. ساب جِ گی شن: مطیع سازی- اطاعت

(Subjugator: مطیع سازنده) (Subjugate: مطیع کردن- منکوب کردن),

***vigilance* –noun** وِج لِنس : مراقبت، مواظبت، شب زنده داري .

1. state or quality of being vigilant; watchfulness:

<*Vigilance is required in the event of treachery.*>

2. *Pathology*. insomnia.

- Subject's family life had unraveled....

آن رَ وِل : از پیچ درآمدن-از شک بیرون آوردن-روشن کردن

***unravel* –verb (used with object)**

1. to separate or disentangle the threads of (a woven or knitted fabric, a rope, etc.).

2. to free from complication or difficulty; make plain or clear; solve:

< *to unravel a situation; to unravel a mystery.*>

3. *Informal*. to take apart; undo; destroy (a plan, agreement, or arrangement).

- Los Angeles Lakers team dispel Magic (one of the Player),

از هم پاچیدن- دور کردن

Dispelled, dispelling (synonym see scatter: پراکنده کردن-پخش کردن)

To drive away by or as if by scattering: dissipate

- Excerpts of Dr. Brown's speech in Cal poly University,

اقتباس کردن-انتخاب کردن

<*Book excerpts*>, <*Free book excerpts*>

- Other hypotheses[1]---even terrorism haven't been rubbed out, though officials say a jet fuel slick[2] on the ocean's surface suggests there was no explosion.

1. های پا تِیسِس: فرض

2. سطح صاف، سطح صیقلي لیز نرم ، یک دست، نرم وصاف

hypotheses a proposition assumed as a premise in an argument.

Slick: Having a smooth surface, slippery,
<*slick wet leaves*>, *slick advertising*>
<*an implement for producing a smooth or slick surface*>
Slang. wonderful; remarkable; first-rate.

- Explicit[1] communication refers to the things we say or write, often messages intended to influence the behavior of others. "Do this" and "Don't do that" count as examples of explicit communication. They leave as little room as possible for interpretation or ambiguity[2].

1. (صریح روشن- واضح- رک گو)
2.(اَم بی گیوُاتی : ابهام ، نامعلومي، سخن مشکوک، گنگي)

<u>مَعانی یا بکار گیری لغات فوق در جملات دیگر:</u>

explicit ***–adjective***
1. fully and clearly expressed or demonstrated; leaving nothing merely implied; unequivocal: *explicit instructions; an explicit act of violence; explicit language.*
2. clearly developed or formulated: *explicit knowledge; explicit belief.*
3. definite and unreserved in expression; outspoken:
<*He was quite explicit as to what he expected us to do for hi*
4. described or shown in realistic detail: *explicit sexual scenes.*
5. having sexual acts or nudity clearly depicted: *explicit movies; explicit books.*
<*Explicit books and films*>, < *an explicit plan*>,
<*Explicit instructions*>, < *An explicit notion of our objective*>

ambiguity ***–noun, plural*-ties.** گنگي ،ابهام ، نامعلومي، سخن مشکوک اَم بی گیوُاتی :
1. doubtfulness or uncertainty of meaning or intention: *to speak with ambiguity; an ambiguity of manner.*
2. an unclear, indefinite, or equivocal word, expression, meaning, etc.: *a contract free of ambiguities; the ambiguities of modern poetry.*
doubtfulness or uncertainty of meaning or intention:
<*to speak with ambiguity; an ambiguity of manner.* >

- Autopsies[1] suggest jet broke up aloft[2].

1.(جمع اَتا پسی یعنی کالبد شکافی) 2.(اَلافت: در بالا)

aloft: in the air, esp. : in flight (as in an airplane),

<*meals served aloft*>, <*measuring the winds aloft*>

- Chaos[1] reigns[2] in Iran during demonstration.

1.(کی یاس: هرج و مرج-بی نظمی)
2.(ری نز یا با این تلفظ*Rains*) : حکمفرما ئی – حکمران)
Silence reign→ حکفرما بودن

In the reign of → در عهد سلطنت
Reigning beauty→ ملکه وجاهت
Dominating power or influence: *the reign of law.*

- Sounds far-fetched. دور و دراز - بزور گرفته شده

< *a far-fetched simile* سه م لی: تشبیه دور>

- Vice president officers weren't trying to avenge of 9/11/2001 event in NY.

کينه جويي كردن (از)، تلافي كردن، انتقام كشيدن (از)، دادگیری کردن، خونخواهي كردن

***avenge–verb (used with object),*a·venged, a·veng·ing.**
1. to take vengeance or exact satisfaction for: *to avenge a grave insult.*
2. to take vengeance on behalf of: *He avenged his brother.*
<avenged their leader's death> (To avenge oneself, انتقام خود را کشیدن)

- Lender accused of bilking investors . بیل کینگ: گول زدن- کلاه برداری

- I find that the aggravating[1] circumstances do out weight "the mitigating[2] circumstances" he said .

Mitigate: →
1.(بد تر کردن- اضافه کردن- خشمگین کردن
2.(سبک کردن- تسکین دادن)

- Ralph Clark, died Saturday, there wouldn't have been a bus system in Orange County, if it hadn't been for Ralph Clark said Jim interim* chief executive of the OCTA. * موقتي، موقت، فيمابين، فاصله، خلال مدت

An intervening time; interval; meantime: in the interim.

- Crackdown[1] intensifies[2] in Iran. 1.(تا دیب - سختگیری)

2.(اصل لغت intensify است یعنی سختگیری کردن- شدید کردن- افزون کردن)

<my grief was intensified غصه من زیاد تر شد>

intense زیاد- سخت- شدید

intensely بطور جدی

intensifying سختگیری کردن- شدید کردن

intensification افزون سازی – تشدید

- "This is the best time to be embarking* on the project" he said

  <the troops embarked at noon> *(مبادرت بکاری کردن – دست بکاری زدن)

  To make a start, *<embarked on a new care*

- President A. has huge constituency,

  کانس تی چو ان سی: هیئت موکلان یا مئوسسان یک حوزه

Constituency: a body of constituents; the voters or residents in a district represented by an elective officer or,
The president in an electoral district; an electoral district
A group served by an organization or institution; a clientele: کلاین تل
<The magazine changed its format to appeal to a broader constituency.>

- This is also a chance, more likely, that to avoid such an outcome, the clerics[1] will jettison[2] or at least rein[3] in and weaken.

(*A cleric is a member of the Christian clergy; an old-fashioned use.*).1
2. (ج ت سن: از شر چیزی راحت شدن)
3 .(ر ی ن "مثل باران" : افسار کردن- ممانعت کردن- مانع شدن-کنترل)
< *Assume the reins of government,* → زمام امور را در دست گرفتن>

Cleric: a member of the clergy.

- Attract enough clerical[1] support to create high-level rifts[2]

  1.(دفتری، وابسته به روحانیون) 2. (ریفت: شکاف- چاك، دریدگي، چاك دادن)

- Many Iranian feel strong kingship[1] with the revolution, its heirs[2] and the system they created, and are reluctant to do anything that would trigger[3] bloody upheaval[4].

  1.(پادشاهی- سلطنت) 2.(ار: وارث – جمع آن میشود وراث)

  3.(شروع کردن حمله - برانگیزنده، رهاکردن، راه انداختن- ماشه تفنگ)

  4.(آپ هی ول : تغیر نا گهانی)

upheaval:

Extreme agitation or disorder: radical change, or
Strong or violent change or disturbance, as in a society: <*The upheaval of war.*>

- President A. Has broad support among the poor and pious[1], who also venerate[2] the country's supreme leader,

1.(پا یس : دین دار- مذهبی) 2.(وِنِ ریت : محترم داشتن- احترام کردن)

(*Pious foundation*→ اوقاف)

Synonyms: devout, godly, reverent.

pious –adjective پا یس : دین دار- مذهبی
1. having or showing a dutiful spirit of reverence for god or an earnest wish to fulfill religious obligations.
2. characterized by a hypocritical concern with virtue or religious devotion; sanctimonious.
3. practiced or used in the name of real or pretended religious motives, or for some stensibly good object; falsely earnest or sincere: *a pious deception.*
4. of or pertaining to religious devotion; sacred rather than secular: *pious literature.*
5. having or showing appropriate respect or regard for parents or others

---

- Many see as a blatant theft of the election.

(بِ لِی تِنت :پر صدا- خشن- در اینجا معنی کاملا بطور واضح)

Blatant: unpleasantly loud and noisy.

- Iran's power structure is opaque. (او پی ک : مات- غیر شفاف)

Not transparent or translucent; impenetrable to light; not allowing light to pass through.

- A rift[1] in high levels of the theocracy[2] could endanger even leader.

1.(شکاف- دریدگی) 2.(حکومت روحانیون- حکومت خدا)

- Mr. Raf. a fierce critic of both leader and Mr. Ah are wild cards.

(فی ارس: تند- خشم آلود)

Fierce: violently hostile or aggressive in temperament: give to fighting or killing:
Pugnacious (پاگ نی شی س) →Belligerent متحارب، متخاصم، جنگجو، داخل درجنگ

- The concession that have already come from the clerics

(Concessionaire→ صاحب امتیاز) امتیاز- امتیاز انحصاری- اعطا

Political concessions to reformists or watching the unrest grow to ever- more dangerous law levels.>

- *Quench*: To suppress; squelch:
  The disapproval of my colleagues quenched my enthusiasm for the plan.
  Quench: فرو نشاندن، دفع کردن، خاموش کردن، اطفا
  An unquenchable thirst for development.
  quenchable→ فرونشانی-خواباندنی

- We saw apathy among the new generation,
  بي حسي، بي عاطفگي، خون سردي، بي علاقگي

- He arrested in jewelry store heists, هایست
  Heist: *To commit armed robbery on: steal*

  To take unlawfully, esp. in a robbery or holdup; steal: to rob or hold up.
  <*To heist a million dollars' worth of jewels.*>
  های ست : بلند کردن، دزدي کردن، دزدي -سرقت مسلحانه
- It's heavy with the themes of hope and change.
  تیم: موضوع- مقاله- انشا ء
  A subject of discourse, discussion, meditation, or composition; topic:
  <*The need for world peace was the theme of the meeting*>

- Swine Flu officially now a pandemic,
  (پن دمیک : نا خوشی همه جا گیر)
  <Pandemic declared>, <Pandemic malaria>, <a pandemic disease>
  General; universal: *pandemic fear of atomic war.*

- Iran's raucous election complains goes quiet.
  روکس: زمخت ناهنجار، خیلي نامرتب
  <*Raucous* voices>, ...*raucous laughter. A raucous voice is loud and harsh.*
  Anti- Semitism آنتی سه م تی زم: ضدیت با سامي گرایي

- Hostility toward or discrimination against Jesus as religious, ethnic, or racial group.
  Anti-Semitic→ adj. آنتی سه م تیک :مخالف نژاد سامی از نسل سام ابن نوح
  Anti-Semite → noun آنتی سه مایت :

- Arab concessions to Israel urged. امتیاز یا واگذاری- تسلیم
  Al-Qaida member denounces his Orange County Jewish roots in video.
  خبردادن از- اشاره کردن بر- کسي یا چیزي را ننگین کردن تقبیح کردن

If you denounce someone or something, you criticize them severely and publicly.
<He has denounced the action as illegal....>
< Anti-apartheid groups denounced Mrs. Mandela last year.>

- US. rescinds July 4th invitation. ری سیند : فسخ یا لغو کردن

- Washington on Wednesday of seeking to "provoke[1] a second Korea War" as the regime prepared to hold maritime[2] military exercises off its eastern coast.
  1.(انگیختن- باعث شدن-تحریک کردن)
  2.(مِر تایم :دریائی- مربوط به بازرگانی از راه دریا

- Miss California ousted[1], she was dethroned[2] as Miss California USA by pageant[3] owner Donald Trump for "*Contract violation*" pageant official said.
  1.(اُست: بیرون کردن- محر و م)
  2.(Deet-رُن: خلع کردن- معزول کردن)
  3.(پَجِنت: صفحه نمایش، نمایش مجلل وتاریخي، مراسم مجلل، رژه)

<u>مَعانی یا بکار گیری لغات فوق در جملات دیگر:</u>

oust **:** To expel or remove from a place or position occupied: *<The bouncer ousted the drunk; to oust the Prime Minister in the next election.>*

dethrone **:** To remove from *any* position of power or authority. Or Ro remove from a throne[1] or place of power or prominence[2].

1.(ثْرُن: تخت سلطنت)
2.(برجسته، والا- *(علوم نظامي)* برجسته، حساس، مهم)

<He came to the throne by succession.> و *<dethrone a king>,*
<trying to dethrone the champion>

prominent: برجستگي، امتیاز، پیشامدگي برتري
dethronement: خلع، عزل از پادشاهي

- The pressure of electrical current is called voltage. This current carrying capacity of wires is called amperage

  Outlet=receptacle : رسِپ تی کال

  receptacle: A container, device, etc. that receives or holds something:
  In electricity. A contact device installed at an outlet for the connection of a portable lamp, appliance, or other electric device by means of a plug and

---

- When she is vacationing without him and uses a phrase like "stuck at home", which implies resentment, ری زنت منت : رنجش، خشم، غیض در *(روانشناسي)* تنفر

- Circuit Breaker Panel: ← در داخل جعبه برق منزل منیاتورهائی ردیف قرار دارند که میگویند

  Shroud: Burial garment, winding-sheet, something that cover. شِراد : کفن

- Singer gets off to a rousing start . بیدار کننده- محرک

  rouse → بیدار کردن- تحریک کرد
- Female impersonation

  Impersonation: اعطای شخصیت - یابازی کردن سهم کسی در نمایش
  جعل هويت، نقش ديگري رابازي كردن

Conform :To act or be in accord or agreement; comply:
<*A computer* that *conforms to the manufacturer's advertising claims.*>,
<*That does not conform to the original pattern.*>

کآن فُرم: همنوايي كردن، مطابقت كردن وفق دادن، پيروي كردن
(حقوق) تطبيق كردن *(كامپيوتر)* كار كردن مطابق با مجموعهاي قوانين

- Counsel objects to City of Fullerton redevelopment plan.

  مشورت-مشورت کردن- ولی در اینجا معنی آن وکیلی را میدهد
  که در جائی منسوب میشود تا مواد قانونی را متذ کر شود
  دراین صورت میتوان بان گفت ← Consultant

  Basic counseling techniques including active listening, body language tone, asking questions, paraphrasing, summarizing, note taking, <counsel with her husband>, <City Council meeting> <Council-board میز یا جلسهٔ انجمن>, <Counselor مشاور >

- 2008 Vice Presidential candidate will write memoir

  م موآر: یاد داشت .- درجمع وقایع

  Memoir: an official note or report / memorandum

memorandum :A short note designating something to be remembered, esp. something to be done or acted upon in the future; reminder.

- Obama challenges class of 2009 to continue making strides in life.

S تراید : شلنگ برداشتن- قدمهای بلند بر داشتن

astraddle→ با پاهای گشاد از هم

< Strode across the room>,

< To stand astride >

stride, strode, stridden, striding

- Two decades of stringent[1] regulation have help dramatically[2] cut pollution[3] level in Orange County, Los Angeles.

1.(Sترین جنت : سخت- دقیق)

2.(دُ رو- مَ تیک لی : نمایشي، مهیج - *(روانشناسي)* چشمگیر، نمایشي)

اصل کلمه Dramatic است ، یعنی وابسط به درام یا داستان- نمایش- ولی اینجا بصورت قید است.

- Wal-Mart Store to maintain staycation* strategy, (stay-at-home vacation)*

یک نوع مرخصی که از محلهای اطراف منزل مثل پارک وغیره استفاده میشود.

Example: Common activities of a staycation include use of the backyard pool, visits to local parks and museums, and attendance at local festivals.

The USA House speaker cites[1] a denial of waterboarding[2].

1.(ذکر کردن، اتخاذ سند کردن گفتن *(علوم نظامي)* اخطار کردن، به دادگاه خواندن

2.(یک نوع شکنجه با آب است

- North Korea says more by South Korea is tantamount[1] to declaration[2] of war.

1.(تَنتِ مأنت: برابر، معادل، هم کف همپایه، بمثابه- با to در حکم)

2.(بیان، اظهارنامه، اعلامیه اعلام ، اعلان*(حقوق)* بیانیه، بیان، اظهارنامه)

Equivalent, as in value, force, effect, or signification:

<His angry speech was tantamount to a declaration of war.>

Tantamount: equivalent in value, significance or effect.

< A relationship tantamount to marriage.>

- Obama Joked, working on his memoir[1], tentatively title, "How to shoot friends and Interrogate[2] people."

1.(مِ موآر: یاد داشت.، تاریخچه، سرگذشت شرح حال، خاطره)

2.(این ت رو گیت: استنطاق کردن، تحقیق کردن باز جویي کردن)

- Indian 's election ends indecisively[1].
  Not decisive: in conclusive[2] , <*an indecisive battle*>

1.(بطور غیر قطعي، بطورنامعلوم یامشکوک، ازروي دو دلي، بي عزمانه)
2 .(قطعي، قاطع، نهایي)

- I was appalled at the lack of due professional care in this transaction.

اَپال: ترساندن- ، وحشت زده شدن

appall: weaken, fail, shock or dismay* *بی جرأت شد گی

- My husband is adamant about ...... اَدِ منت. : سنگ خارا

To fill or overcome with horror, consternation, or fear; dismay:
<*He was appalled by the damage from the fire.*>, <*I am appalled at your mistakes.*>
<*We sere appalled by his behavior*> synonym see dismay

- When I received and reviewed these documents, I note that she had been charged for rent back which was preposterous[1], this resulted $1,500 being paid to, I presume[2] the buyer.

1.(پری پاس تِ رَس: نا معقول- مضحک- افتضاح
2.(پری زُم : فرض کردن- احتمال کلی دادن)

Completely contrary to nature, reason, or common sense; absurd; senseless; utterly foolish: <*A preposterous tale.*>پری پاس تِ رَس
To take for granted assume, or suppose: <*I presume you're tired after your drive.*>

- The ceiling has been completely opened up for your perusal.

پِرُزال: مطالعه- خواندن دقیق

Peruse: (پِرُز) To examine or consider with attention and in detail. a reading:
<*a perusal of the current books.* >

The act of perusing; survey; scrutiny: <*A more careful perusal yields this conclusion.*>

- No one believe that this incident[1] is spontaneous[2], arising from a momentary impulse

1.(این C دنت : شایع، روي داد، واقعه)
2 .(اِس پاَن تِ نی یِس : خود بخود، خود انگیز، بي اختیار، فوري)

spontaneous : coming or resulting from a natural impulse or tendency; without effort or premeditation; natural and unconstrained; unplanned:
<A spontaneous burst of applause.>

- Respective party مخصوص خود- مربوط بخود
respective :partial, particular, separate, *<their respective home>*

- Although I am sympathetic[1] to their plight[2] given the short time they were in the home prior to this unfortunate event.

1.(سیم پِ تتیک :همدرد، دلسوز، شفیق غمخوار، موافق)
2.(پلایت : مخمسه- گرفتاری

plight : A condition, state, or situation, esp. an unfavorable or unfortunate one:
<to find oneself in a sorry plight.> Synonyms→ See predicament.

- A seller's agent has the following affirmative[1] obligations[2] to the seller:

a. A fiduciary[3] duty of outmost care, integrity[4], honesty, and loyalty in dealing[5] with the seller.

b. To the buyer and the seller, diligent exercise of reasonable[6] skill and car performance of the agent's duties.

1.(مثبت، تصدیق امیز)
2.(التزام- وظیفه- تعهد- در *(حقوق)* تعهد، عهد، الزام)
3.(امانتي *-(بازرگاني)* معتمد، امین، امانتدار امانتي- سپرده *(حقوق)* معتبر، قابل اعتماد)
4.(درستي، امانت، راستي تمامیت، بي عیبي، کمال)
5.(خریدوفروش و معامله، طرزرفتار، رفتار- سر وکارداشتن)
6.(معقول- *(اقتصاد)* قابل قبول، منطقي -عقلائي)

A **fiduciary** duty is a legal or ethical relationship of confidence or trust between two or more parties, most commonly a *fiduciary* and a *principal*.

- Diligent exercise *or* diligent attention and observation. کوشنده- ساعی
<diligent worker>, careful, *Thorough→* از اول تا اخر، بطور کامل- کامل، تمام

- Consult a competent professional. لایق، ذی صلاحیت، شایسته، دارای سر رشته

- I acknowledge receipt of copy of this disclosure.
  Acknowledge: admit, agree, recognize
  تصدیق کردن قدرداني کردن، اعتراف کردن، تصدیق کردن، وصول نامهای را اشعار داشتن

- In the event home buyer assumes or takes title[1] subject[2] to existing loan, bond or assessment[3]....

1.(بخودی خود یعنی حق-لقب-یا عنوان-ولی در املاک یعنی سند یا حق نسبت به ملکی) **2** .(تابع- شامل)

3.(تشخیص، تعیین مالیات، وضع مالیات، ارزیابي، تقویم براورد، تخمین)

(Title to a property → داشتن حق نسبت به ملکی)
Title deed → قباله
(*Subject to the law* → تابع یا مطیع قانون)
(*Subject to your approval* → منوط به تصویب شما)
(*Subject to flood* → دستخوش سیل)
(*Under the title of* → تحت عنوان)

- Buyer is allowed 5 calendar days from receipt of the disclosure, to make future inquiries at buyer's lender...... پرسش- بازجوئی- تحقیق

<*To make inquiries into a matter* چیزی را رسیدگی کردن>
<*To make inquiries about a person*>
<*Court of enquiries*دادگاه رسیدگی > inquiry, inquiries

- From the year 1942 to 1950 inclusive .... شامل، مشمول - دربر دارنده

inclusive : An inclusive price includes payment for all the separate parts of something or for one particular part that is being specified.
<*All prices are inclusive of the return flights from London.*>

- Only the following paragraph "*A*" through "*M*" when initialed both home buyer and Home seller are incorporated in this agreement .
  یکي کردن، بهم پیوستن، متحدکردن، داخل کردن، جادادن داراي شخصیت حقوقي کردن ثبت کردن

(در دفتر ثبت شرکتها)، امیختن

- Subordination[1]: This agreement is contingent[2] upon both buyer and seller approving a subordination clause[3].

1.(سابِر دی نِی شِن : اطاعت، مرئوسي تبعيت، فرمان برداري)

2.(کان تین جِنت : محتمل الوقوع، تصادفي مشروط، موكول)

3.(کِلاز : ماده- شرط- عهد- تبعيت- جزئي از جمله)

<u>مَعانی یا بکار گیری لغات فوق در جملات دیگر:</u>

clause: A distinct article or provision in a contract, treaty, will, or other formal or legal written document. Such as , *Establishment Clause* or *Independent Clause*

Subordination agreement:
An expensive claims problem in recent years has been with respect to **Subordination Agreements**. The title insurance industry has experienced a significant number of claims on mortgagee's policies which involve these agreements.

What the heck is **subordination**? A double edged tool that if respected, understood and used properly, can be of great benefit to sellers, buyers, realtors and contractors alike! Faster Easier ... The request for the use of **subordination** isn't always restricted to the sale of vacant land or new home building,

---

- The prevailing party shall be entitled to reasonable attorney's fees and cost.

غالب، فائق- برتر

Predominant: *prevailing winds.*
Generally current: *the prevailing opinion.*
Having superior power or influence, , effectual.

- No extrinsic[1] evidence whatsoever may be introduced in any judicial or arbitration[2] proceeding[3].

1.(اکس تی- رین- زیک : بیرونی – خارجی)

2.(نتیجهء حکمیت، رای بطریق حکمیت، داوری)

3.(جریان عمل، اقدام ، پیشرفت طرز، روند- *(حقوق)* اقدام)

<facts that are extrinsic to the matter under discussion.>

- North Korea clarifies*intentions. But the network media coverage of North Korea's nuclear test was rather lackadaisical.

*شفاف کردن- روشن کردن
لَکه دِی- ذیکال ضعیف- سست- بیحال

< Someone who is lackadaisical does not show any interest or enthusiasm and acts as if they are daydreaming.> <*She was annoyingly lackadaisical and impractical.*>

–adjective
1. Without interest, vigor, or determination; listless; lethargic: *a lackadaisical attempt.* **2.** Lazy; indolent: *a lackadaisical fellow.*

- Some speculate that the brother-in-law may take over as a regent until the son, age 26, can fully emerge. ریجنت : نایب السلطنه

- Assertive → مثبت- قطعی

  Synonym see aggressive, <aggressive behavior>, <aggressive fighter> <an aggressive salesman>, <an assertive leader>

- According to the Syrian TV news, Protesters set fire to barricade[1] Saturday in Tehran in open defiance[2] of Iran's clerical government.

1.(بَرَ کید: سنگر بندی موقتی کردن-مسدود کردن)
2.(دی فایِنس: دعوت بجنگ کردن- مخالفت کردن)

Defiance: the act or an instance of defying challenge,

–noun
a. Any barrier that obstructs passage.
b. A defensive barrier hastily constructed, as in a street, to stop an enemy.

- Security forces that fought back with baton[1] charges, tear gas and water cannons[2] as the crisis over disputed elections lurched[3] into volatile[4] new ground.

1.(بَ تان: باتون یاچوب قانون، عصای افسران)

2.(توپ *(معمولا بصورت اسم جمع)*، استوانه، لوله، بتوپ بستن)
3.(لِرچ: کج شدن –تلوتلوخوردن- بیک سوی دیگر رفتن)
4.(وُلاتایِل:)، بخارشدني، سبك، لطيف- فرار)

Cannon : A mounted gun for firing heavy projectiles; a gun, howitzer, or mortar.

- Some bloggers and Twitter users said there had been numerous fatalities in Saturday's unrest; but reporters could not be immediately verified.

آن رِست: آشوب- اضطراب- ناارامي ، اشفتگي ، بيقراري، بيتابي

- Another blow[1] to authority or authorities who sought to intimidate protesters with harsh warnings and lines of black-clad[2] police three deep in places.

1.(ضربت- صدمه- در اینجا یعنی مصیبت) 2.(پوشاندن یا = Clad)

(To clothe oneself→ (لباس پوشیدن , *(Snow clothe mountains→* کوهای پوشیده از برف
(کِ لُتز : چنا نچهS در آخر clothe قرار گیرد معنی جامعه- لباس میدهد)

- Mountain bewildered[1] many followers by not directly replying to the ultimatum issued one day by Iran's most powerful figure, his stern[2] order to Mo. And others call off demonstrations or…..

To perplex or confuse esp. by a complexity, verity or multitude[3] of objects or considerations, *synonym see puzzle*
<The stern warning pushes the opposition movement into pivotal[4] moment>

1.(بی ول دِرد: گیج کردن، سردرگم کردن، گم کردن-کلمهٔ مترادف آن puzzle است
2.(اِستِرن : سخت- سخت گیر، عبوس)
3.(مُلتی چُود : گروه، گروه بسیار، جمعیت کثیر، بسیاری)
4.(پیِ وِ تال: با al در آخرش یعنی محوری-اساسی)
5.(محوری – پاشنهٔ → pivot)

stern: To strike an attitude. <To put on a stern look → قیافه گرفتن <
<Charity covers a multitude of sins > → صد قصه گناهان را پاك مي كند- صدقه رفع بلاست

- Police general said more than a week of unrest[1] and marches had become exhausting, bothersome[2] and intolerable[3].

1.(آن رِست: آشوب- اضطراب- ناارامي ، اشفتگي ، بيقراري، بيتابي)
2.(پر دردسر، پرزحمت، مزاحم- درد سر دار)
3.(این تا لِ ربِل : تحمل ناپذیر، سخت، غیر قابل تحمل، دشوار)

Unrest: a disturbed or uneasy state: Turmoil→ (غوغا – پریشانی- آشفتگی)
< A report on Press TV listed the fallout from the unrest, including 700 buildings, 300 banks damaged and 400 police hurt.

bothersome: *Causing bother: vexing, vexation,<a vexing problem>*

(وِک سینگ : ازردن، رنجاندن، رنجه دادن خشمگین کردن)

vexing : to irritate; annoy; provoke: <*His noisy neighbors often vexed him*>

- They've built a human-sized replica of the Statue of Liberty....

رِپ لِ کا : نسخه عین، عین، المثني- *(حقوق)* المثني

<*A replica of something such as a statue, machine, or building is an accurate copy of it.*>, <*His gun was later found to be a replica.*>

Noun; A copy or reproduction of a work of art produced by the maker of the original or under his or her supervision. Any close or exact copy or reproduction.

Synonyms : duplicate, facsimile; imitation.

- Some of the demonstrators grouped together to charge back at police, hurling stones. جِرلینگ- بدون ing حِ رْل : پرت کردن- انداختن

To utter with vehemence: <*to hurl insults at the umpire.*>

- Mr. Mo's silence was broken after the melee with another call to annul the election results. مِ لی :کشمکش- زدو خورد- جنگ تن بتن

- Opening the door for more militant factions[1] to breakaway[2].

Factions: a party or group (as within a government) that is often contentious or self seeking:

دسته، گروه، محفل- *(روانشناسي)* جرگه، گروهک ← Clique

1. (.دسته بندي، حزب، انجمن فرقه)

2. (فرار، استعفاء، جدايي، هجوم وحشيانه گله گوسفند و گاو رم . ..
(علوم نظامي) نفوذ کردن، شکستن خط محاصره- شکستن بند زندان فرار از زندان
(ورزشي) حمله یک یا چند بازیگر

- In Washington president ……urged Ir…. authorities to halt[1] "all violent and unjust[2] actions against its own people"

1.(ايست، مکث، درنگ، سکته ايست کردن، مکث کردن لنگيدن)
2.(غير عادلانه، غير منصفانه، بي عدالت، بي انصاف، ناروا ناصحيح)
(عدالت، انصاف، درستي دادگستری ← (Justice)

- An estimated 3000 marchers directly onto a blockade of security forces keeping them form approaching A…..Square,

بِ لاَ کید: راه بندان، محاصره، انسداد بستن، محاصره کردن، راه بندکردن، سد راه، سدراه کردن

- A week of epic events in Iran have brought countless images to the world.

اِ پیک : رزمي، حماسي، شعر رزمي حماسه، رزم نامه

An epic is a long book, poem, or film which usually tells a story of heroic deeds.
...Homer's epic poems `The Iliad' and `The Odyssey'.

- All witnesses[1] spoke on condition of anonymity[2] because they feared reprisal[3]

1 .(شهادت، شهادت دادن- گواه- شاهد- گواهی دادن)
2.(اَنْ نی م تی: گمنامي، بینامي)
3 .(رِپ رای زآل : جبران، تلافي، انتقام ، تلافي کردن)

reprisal :(in warfare*) retaliation against an enemy, for injuries received, by the infliction of equal or greater injuries.

* (جنگاوري، ستیز، جنگ، نزاع زدو خورد، محاربه)

- News reporter says state powers were abused to skew[1] the election results and re-elect some one else in a landslide[2].

1.(اِس کیو: منحرف کردن-کج کردن- چیزي به صورت نادرست)
2.(زمین لغزه، ریزش خاک کوه کنار جاده- ولی معنی لغت در اینجا در زیر است)

<u>مَعانی یا بکار گیری لغات فوق در جملات دیگر:</u>

landslide : a great majority of votes for one side or an over whelming victory, to win an election by a heavy majority, <US doubts claim of a landslide>

If an election is won by a landslide, it is won by a large number of votes.
<Taylor should win by a landslide...
< The National League for Democracy won a landslide victory in last year's multi-party elections.>
landslide : <*Win an election by a landslide*>
decisive victory, runaway victory, overwhelming majority.

- Among Ir…..'s security forces or the sacred[1] system that preserves the country's independence. We are confronting deviations[2] and lies.

1.(سِیک رِد : مقدس، روحاني، خاص موقوف، وقف شده)
2.(d -v- اِشن : انحراف، انحراف جنسي-(*علوم نظامي*) اختلاف سمت)
(منحرف شونده- رو گرداننده← Deviator)

- A week of rallies[1], conflict[2], violence[3] with protesters in Ir…. emboldened[4] government unleashes[5] a reckoning[6].

1.(صف ارایي کردن - اجتماع مجدد، دوباره جمع شدن، تجمع براي موضوعی)
2.(کان فِ لکت: ستیزه، کشاکش، کشمکش نبرد، برخورد، ناسازگاري تضاد)
3.(وآیو لنس: خشونت، تندي، سختي، شدت زور- بي حرمتي- (حقوق) عنف، بیحرمتي، سختي خشونت-
4 .(اِ م بُل دِن: جسور- شیر کردن)
5.(از بند باز کردن، رهاکردن)
6.(رِ کُ نینگ : حساب، تصفیه حسا ب- جمع بندی)

<u>مَعانی یا بکار گیری لغات فوق در جملات دیگر:</u>

embolden: To make bold or bolder; hearten; encourage.
unleash: To unleash a powerful or violent force means to release it; a literary
reckoning: The act or an instance of reckoning: as: Account, Bill, word. Computation, Calculation of a ship's position, a summing up.

- Others are the small but powerful vignettes[1] that will be tucked away as personal narratives[2]. 1.(وین یت : عکس، تصویر، شکل- آرایش سر صفحهٔ کتاب)
2.(قصه، شرح، داستان داستانسرایي، حکایت، روایت)

correspondents[3] and other witnesses,

3.(خبرنگار، مخبر، مکاتبه کننده طرف معامله، مطابق)

Recall the tumultuous[4] week after, <*a tumultuous celebration.*>
full of tumult[5] or riotousness; marked by disturbance and uproar:

4.(تِ مِل چو اِس: پر همهمه، پر اشوب، شلوغ بهم ریخته، بي نظم- آشوبگر)
5.(تِ مولت :غوغا شلوغ، جنجال، اشوب التهاب، اغتشاش کردن- جنجال راه انداختن)

A general outbreak, riot, uprising, or other disorder:
The tumult moved toward the embassy.

6. (.دسته بندی،گروه هوا خواهی- حزب، انجمن فرقه)

Ir…'s disputed election,
<*Tumultuous applause,*>< *tumultuous passions*> *The laws were violated by a tumultuous faction,*[6]

A general outbreak, riot, uprising, or other disorder: <*The tumult moved toward the embassy.*>

- Election day and the excitement in Ir…. is palpable[1] never mind the broiling head. As the day fades, however, sings of conflict loom[2].

1.(پَل پِ بِل: حس کردني، قابل لمس- اشکار، واضح)

2.(لوم: ازدور نمودارشدن)

palpable **:**Synonym see perceptible→ (محسوس- قابل درک - مشاهده کردنی)

<Deficits loomed large>

- The previous day's euphoria[1] is gone. Riot police in body armor swarm[2] Cpital's streets, blocking traffic and beating protesters with rubber truncheons[3].

1.(u - فو - re- یا : رضامندی، خوشي، خوشحالي- رضایت)

2.(سُ اِرم : گروه، دسته زیاد، گروه زنبوران، ازدحام ، ازدحام کردن، هجوم اوردن)

3.(تِ ران- شِن: چوب پلیس یا باتوم)

Euporia: none, a feeling of well-being or elation.→ (سرفرازی – شادی)

< A swarm of meteors >→ (مِی تی یِر: حادثهء هوائی – رعدو برق)

< swarm of sightseers>, <Swarm with flies or bees>

- A woman weeps[1] when the president appears. As night falls, some neighborhoods are alight[2] with bonfires[3] or trash cans set ablaze[4].

1.(ویپ :گریه کردن- اشک ریختن)

2.(روشن - شعله ور ، روشن کردن- اتش زدن ، راحت کردن تخفیف دادن)

3.(اتش بزرگ، اتش بازي-آتش سوزی بزرگ در فضای باز)

4.(اَب – لِی ز :سوزان، فروزان، درخشان مشتعل، برافروخته)

ablaze : burning; on fire: <*They set the logs ablaze.*>

- Country attempts to quash[1] news report, Mo's supporters demonstrate for a second day after the elections that favored[2] incumbent[3] president.

1.(نقض کردن، باطل کردن، الغاکردن، با ضربه زدن، له کردن، فرو نشاندن)

2.(التفات، توجه مرحمت، مساعدت، طرفداري مرحمت کردن، نیکي کردن به طرفداري کردن)

3.(متصدي، ناگزیر،واجب- لازم با (*on و upon*)

<u>مَعانی یا بکار گیری لغات فوق در جملات دیگر:</u>

Quash :to suppress[4] or extinguish summarily[5] and completely <quash a rebellion[6]

<Suppress a riot → فرو نشاندن، خواباندن ، مانع شدن- تحت فشار قرار دادن، منکوب کردن >

4.(موقوف کردن، توقیف کردن فرو نشاندن، خواباندن ، مانع شدن ، منکوب کردن)

5.(سام رلی : مختصراً)

6.(طغیان، سرکشي، شورش، تمرد)

< Authorities say incumbent won>, < suppress or subdue her anger>

< during his incumbency, در دوره‌ء تصدی او یا عهده داری او >

< it is incumbent on you to .... بر شما واجب است که >

<*To be dismissed summarily from one's job.*>

- Mr. Mo's refusal to bow to authorities could keep his passionate[1] youthful[2] supporters out in the streets.

1.(پَ شِ نیت : اتشي مزاج، سودايي احساساتي)

2.(یُوس فُول : داراي نیروي شباب یا جوانی)

- Skeptics[1] continued to assail[2] the government's declaration that Ah. had won with 62% of the vote, or more than 24 million ballots.

1.(اِس کِپ تیک : شک و تردید)

2.(اَ سِیل : حمله کردن، هجوم اوردن بر)

مَعانی یا بکار گیری لغات فوق در جملات دیگر:

skeptic: اِس کِپ تیک A person who questions the validity or authenticity of something purporting to be factual.

<Pertaining to skeptics or skepticism….>

assail : اَ سِیل To attack with arguments, criticism, ridicule, abuse, etc.:

< *To assail one's opponent with slander.*>

- Down a nearby side street, a group of four youths who supported Mo. sat glumly, "I think our society, our country is at a very critical time" said one young man who carried a rolled-up poster of a Ah.

گِلا ملی : بطور افسرده، کدر، رنجیده، ملول، اوقات تلخ

GLUM describes a depressed, spiritless condition or manner, usually temporary rather than habitual:

- If a situation is gloomy, it does not give you much hope of success or happiness.

گُ لومی : تاریک، تیره، افسرده - غم افزا

To give way to gloomy thoughts .→ فکرهاي بد بخود راه دادن

Something that is gloomy is dark and rather depressing.

<...the gloomy prison.... ...a gloomy day.>

<A glum shrug of the shoulders; a glum, hopeless look in his eye.>

- Sanctions[1] elicit[2] defiance[3] ,

1.(سَنک شِن : فرمان، تصویب، داراي مجوزقانوني دانستن، ضمانت اجرايي)

2.(ائی لِ سی ت: بیرون کشیدن، استخراج کردن استنباط کردن)

3.(دِ فا یِنس : مبارزه طلبي، دعوت به جنگ- بي اعتنايي، مخالفت، مقاومت اعتراض)

<u>مَعانی یا بکار گیری لغات فوق در جملات دیگر:</u>

sanction *Law*. سَنک شِن

a. A provision of a law enacting a penalty for disobedience or a reward for obedience.

b. the penalty or reward.

International Law. action by one or more states toward another state calculated to force it to comply with legal obligations

elicit **:** To draw or bring out or forth; educe; evoke: ائی لِ سی ت

<To elicit the truth; to elicit a response with a question.>, < her remarks elicited cheers>
< hypnotism elicited cheers>, synonym see *Educe* → (to bring out as something latent)

defiance open disregard; contempt (often fol. by *of*): the act or an instance of defying, challenge or disposition to resist: willingness to contend or fight.

defiance of danger; His refusal amounted to defiance.

< New UN sanctions with more defiance>,

defiance : دِ فا یِنس < in defiance of > =<contrary to, despite>,
<seemingly in defiance of the laws of physics>

- The country also vowed[1] never to give up its nuclear ambitions[2] as a way to protect it sovereignty[3].

1.(نذر، پيمان، عهد، قول، شرط عهد كردن)
2.(جاه طلبي، ارزو جاه طلب بودن ، بلند پروازي)
3.(ساورا نتی : حق حاكميت و سلطه، اقتدار و برتري ، حق حاكميت *(فقهي)* حاكميت)

<I am under a vow to …. ... عهد يا شرط كرده ام كه < و > < to make a vow>
Sovereignty: also sovranty= سلطه , supreme power

Sovereignty is the power that a country has to govern itself or to govern other countries.
<.a threat to national sovereignty...>.< ...the end of British sovereignty over Gibraltar.>

- South Korea has harbored deep-rooted suspicious[1] that the US. could invade to topple[2] its regime. <*Topple a dictator* **or** defeat[3]> to be defeated شكست خوردن

1.(حاكي ازبد گماني، مشكوك-سوء ظن-ترديد)
2 .(تاپل: واژگون كردن-بر انداختن-*overthrow*)
3.(شكست دادن، مغلوب ساختن- *(علوم نظامي)* شكست دادن، شكست - *(حقوق)* الغاء، نقض

- North Korea warned that any attemped[1] blockade by the US. and its allies[2] would be regarded as "an act of war and met with a decisive[3] military response".

1.(ملايم كردن، نرم كردن اميختن، معتدل كردن، جوركردن)
2.(أ لايز : *(علوم نظامي)* هم پيمانان، متفقين)
3.(دي ساى سيو : قطعي، قاطع- *(حقوق)* قطعي، قاطع *(فقهي)* محكم)

- Riots erupt[1] in Iran over disputed presidential vote; authorities say incumbent[2] won, but rival camp claims fraud and protests in street.
<War could erupt at any moment>, <The audience erupted in applause>

1.(ائى رايپت : جوانه زدن، درامدن، دراوردن منفجرشدن، فوران كردن جوش دراوردن، فشاندن)
2.(اين كام بنت : متصدى –تكيه كننده ناگزير، لازم با آن و آيان)

Incumbent: holding an indicated position, role, office, etc., currently:
<the incumbent officers of the club.>

- The hard-line Iraqi president was re-elected in a landslide[1]. The rival candidate said the vote was tainted[2] by widespread fraud, and his followers responded with most serious unrest[3] in the capital in a decade.

1.(زمین لغزه، ریزش خاک کوه کنار جاده- ولی معنی لغت در اینجا در زیر است)
2.(لکه دار کردن، رنگ کردن- الوده شدن، لکه، ملوث کردن)
3.(ناارامي، اشوب، اشفتگي اضطراب، بيقراري، بيتابي)

<u>مَعانی یا بکار گیری لغات فوق در جملات دیگر:</u>

landslide : a great majority of votes for one side or an over whelming victory, to win an election by a heavy majority, <US doubts claim of a landslide>

If an election is won by a landslide, it is won by a large number of votes.
<Taylor should win by a landslide...>
< The National League for Democracy won a landslide victory in last year's multi-party elections.

taint : A trace of something bad, offensive, or harmful.

Tainted ladies, Tainted love

unrest : If there is unrest, people are angry and dissatisfied, often to the extent of breaking the law or causing violence.

- Police chased bands of protesters roaming[1] the streets pumping their fists in the air. Officers beat protesters with swift[2] blows from their truncheons[3].

1.(رُمینگ : پرسه زدن، گشتن، سیرکردن، گردیدن، سرگرداني)
2.(سُوافت : سریع، چابک، تندرو، فرز باسرعت)
3.(تِرآن چِن : چوب پاسبان، چماق، باچماق یاباتون زدن، چوب باطوم)

Roam: to walk, go, or travel without a fixed purpose or direction; ramble; wander; rove:
<to roam about the world. > , To wander over or through: *<to roam the countryside.*
<A swift runner>, <a swift transition>.

- Mr. ?.... in a message on state TV, he urged the nation to unite behind Mr. A., calling the result a "divine assessment"→ (ارزیابی خدائی یا الهی- خدا داده)

- Plumes[1] of dark smoke streaked[2] over the city, as burning barricades[3] of tires and garbage bins glowed[4] orange in the streets. Protesters also torched[5] an empty bus, engulfing[6] it in flames on a Capitals' Streets.

1.(پِ لوم :آرایش دادن)
2.(اِس تی ریک : خط- رگه- بسرعت حرکت کردن، خط خط کردن)
3.(سنگربندي موقتي، مانع مسدود کردن- راه بندان)
4.(گ ِلُ : تابیدن، برافروختن، مشتعل بودن- سوختن)
5.(تُر چ :مشعل، چراغ قوه، مشعل دارکردن)
6.(این گالف اینگ : غرق کردن در- توي چیزي فروبردن، فراگرفتن خروشان کردن)

<u>مَعانی یا بکار گیری لغات فوق در جملات دیگر:</u>

to mark with a streak or streaks; form streaks on:
<*sunlight streaking the water with gold; frost streaking the windows.*>

A streak is a line, mark, smear, or band differentiated by color or texture from its surroundings. Like when you are wiping the mirror off with windex and there marks after you do it, those are streaks.

A glow is a dull, steady light. <*...the blue glow of a police station light.*>

Torch : something considered as a source of illumination, enlightenment, guidance, etc.
< *the torch of learning.*>

- Suggesting an information clampdown, تعقیب، آزار، سرکوبي، سختگیري

A clampdown is a sudden restriction on a particular activity by a government or other authority.<...*a clampdown on wasteful spending...*>
<. *The police are maintaining their tight security clampdown.*>

- Mr. ?.... in a message on state TV, he urged the nation to unite behind Mr. A., calling the result a "divine assessment"→ (ارزیابی خدائی یا الهی- خدا داده)

- Iran's raucous[1] election campaign goes quiet. *Synonym* see loud

1.(راکِس :خشن، زمخت ناهنجار، خیلي نامرتب)
A raucous voice is loud and harsh[2]. Or disagreeably harsh or strident[3]: hoarse
<...*raucous laughter.*>, <raucous voices>

Rough or harsh in sound, <*harsh* تند، درشت، خشن، ناگوار، زننده، ناملایم >.2

<A strident voice, 3.> دارای صدای مزاحم-صدای گوش خراش

< a *hoarse voice* > صدا ی کلفت : تلفظ آن درست مثل خُرس← اسب است

- The campaign reached a crescendo[1] in the past few days with dueling[2] rallies by supporters of Mr. A. and his main challenger[3].

1.(کِ رِ شین دو: قوي شدن صدا بطورتدريجي، اوج) 2.(دوئل کننده) 3 .(چَ لِن جِر : مبارزه طلب، حريف)

A steady increase in force or intensity: *<The rain fell in a crescendo on the rooftops.>*

- Regime may be willing to engage, but Western officials have meager expectations for change. (می گِر: بی حرکت نا چیز)

<leading a meager life>, <a meager diet>

- The regime officers, which is often involved in crackdowns[1] on dissidents[2] was key in helping Mr. A. win in 2005, said news agency.

1.(تا دیب - سختگیری)

2.(دِ سِ دِ نت: مخالف عقیده‌ء عموم بالاخص در مورد سیاست و مذهب)

A person who dissents., disagreeing or dissenting, as in opinion or attitude: *< a ban on dissident magazines.*

- Iranian woman atop* the Tochal Mountain area skiing .

*(اَتا پ یعنی On یا At the top)

- Mr. Mo. Has accused Mr. A. of attempting to whitewash the scope of Country's problems, which include double-digit inflation and....

(رو سفید قلمداد کردن- آب پنبه)

- The last time country was engulfed[1] in similar turmoil[2] was a decade ago.

1.(اين گالف : غوطه ورساختن، توي چيزي فروبردن، فراگرفتن خروشان كردن)

2.(تِر مو يل : غوغا، ناراحتي، پريشاني، بهم خوردگي، اشفتگي)

- We saw apathy[1] among the new generation, but we also saw the young people wanted new life, said Saeed a 35-year-old activist[2].

1.(آ پَ تی : بي حسي، بي عاطفگي، خون سردي، بي علاقگي)

2.(طرفدار عمل)

apathy : آ پَ تی

Lack of feeling or emotion: Impassiveness
Lack of interest or concern: Indifference

- For the first time in Iran, the forces of the web have been fully harnessed[1] in an election showdown[2]. It has catapulted[3]. → (کَ تَ پولت)

1.) افسار زدن - مهارکردن مطیع کردن، تحت کنترل دراوردن)

2.) مرحله نهايي مسابقات ازمايش- نيرو *(علوم نظامي)* نمايش

نمايش دادن- نمونه نشان دادن چيدن كليه تجهيزات براي بازديد نمايشي)

3.) سنگ انداز، هرجسمي كه داراي خاصيت فنري بوده وبراي پرتاب اجسام بكارميرود – تير كمان)

Catapult :An ancient military engine for hurling stones, arrows, etc.

- In the final hours of the fierce contest, Mo. Got a sharp warning from the country's powerful revolutionary guard that .... (فی اِرس : تندخو، خشم الود)
  <*A fierce argument*>, <*fierce pain*>

- But it's also another skirmish[1] in a running media battle with Iran's authorities. Iran's ruling clerics can easily muzzle[2] reformist publications but they have struggle to clampdown[3] on the web.

1.) اِس کِر میش: کشمکش، زد وخورد، جنگ جزئي، زد وخورد کردن)

2.) ماذِ ل : پوزه، پوزه بند، دهان بند)

3.) تعقيب، آزار، سرکوبي، سختگيري)

Any brisk conflict or encounter: *She had a skirmish with her landlord about the rent.*
To restrain from speech, the expression of opinion, etc.: *The censors muzzled the press.*

clampdown: The act or action of making regulations more stringent < *a clampdown on charge accounts, bank loans and other inflationary influences-time*>

An imposing of restrictions or controls: *"Advertisers and broadcasters would raise howls of protest against any strong clampdown" (Wall Street Journal)*. سختگيري - تعقيب، سرکوبي.

ولی اگر کلمهٔ *clamp down* سر هم نباشد معنی آن از این قرار است:

To impose restrictions: Crack down <*the police are clamping down on speeders*>.

- Hierarchy[1] of power Mr. k. : *wields[2] control over every major decision either directly or through a network[3] of ....*

1.)های رَآیر کی: سلسلهٔ سران روحانی و شیوخ)

2.(ویلد: گردانیدن، اداره کردن، خوب بکار بردن)
3.(شبکه، شبکه توري، شبکه ارتباطي، وابسته به شبکه)

Hierarchy --- **–noun, plural** -chies.
1. any system of persons or things ranked one above another.
2. government by ecclesiastical rulers.
3.the power or dominion of a hierarch.
4. an organized body of ecclesiastical officials in successive ranks or orders: *the Roman Catholic hierarchy.*
5. one of the three divisions of the angels, each made up of three orders, conceived as constituting a graded body.
6. Also called **celestial hierarchy.** the collective body of angels.
7. government by an elite group.
To exercise (power, authority, influence, etc.), as in ruling or dominating.

- "They feel lied to, and we are their voice outside of Country" she said , the mood[1] was a far cry from the optimism[2] expressed by expatriates[3] who filled the Irvine Hyatt Hotel less than a week earlier to vote in what was already shaping up as a heated contest.

1.(مُود : حالت، حوصله، حال سردماغ، خلق ، وضع رواني)
2.(آپ تی می زِم : فلسفه خوش بيني، نيک بيني)
3.(اِکس پی تِ رِت : از کشور خود راندن، تبعید کردن، ترک کردن میهن تبعیدی)

< I am in a good mood today.>, (Banish , exile → تبعید کردن- اخراج بلد کردن)
< I am in an exuberant mood today < امروز خيلي كيفم كوك است
< An exuberant welcome for the hero.>

- expediency* council: Mediates between the parliament and guardian council, but often favors the supreme leader's views. (*شتاب- عجله- اقدام مهم)

- US. Representative[1] of Irvine Said, Wednesday that he is co-sponsoring[2] a measure questioning the election results and denouncing[3] Ir…..n repression[4]

1.(نماينده، وكيل)
2.(ضمانت كردن، مسئوليت راقبول كردن، باني، باني چيزي شد ن- – در *(علوم نظامي)* حامي ، كفالت كردن)
3.(عليه كسي افهاري كردن كسي يا چيزي را ننگين كردن تقبيح كردن-در *(حقوق)* متهم كردن)
4.(رِپ رِشِن : سرکوبي- جلو گیری- فرو نشانی)

co-sponsoring: A joint sponsor, as of a legislative bill.

repression: سرکوبي- جلو گیری- فرو نشانی

The act of repressing; state of being repressed.
Psychoanalysis. The rejection from consciousness of painful or disagreeable ideas, memories, feelings, or impulses.

The act of repressing or the state of being repressed. *Psychology* The unconscious exclusion of painful impulses, desires, or fears from the conscious mind.

- Some people have expressed doubt about people's willingness to sustain[1] the momentum[2].

1.(ساس تِین: ادامه دادن، متحمل شدن، تحمل کردن، تقویت کردن، حمایت کردن از)
2.(مقدار حرکت، مقدار جنبش اني، نیروي حرکت اني)

- It is heavy with the themes of hope and change. موضوع، مطلب، مقاله، انشاء

- The movement eventually fizzled[1] leaving the system intact[2]. This time, though, the protester's base is wider. Swathed[3] in a long black *chador*, people wanted to let the government know that many people *from all walks*[4] of life are angry.

1.(فِ زِل: فش فش، زرزر، وزوز- *(صداي هیزم تر هنگام سوختن)*، کوشش مذبوحانه شکست، زه زدن)
2.(دست نخورده، بي عیب، سالم کامل، صدمه ندیده)
3. (سَ اَت : ردپا، ردیف باریک راه باریک- اثرماشین چمن زني)
4.(اهل حرفه ها و مشاغل مختلف)

To make a hissing or sputtering sound, esp.one that dies out weakly.

<The reform movement fizzled out because of poor leadership>

cut a swath, to make a pretentious display; attract notice:

< *The new doctor cut a swath in the small community.*>

- The government suppress* people easily, people feel alone.

*(ساپرس :سرکوب کردن– تحت فشار قرار دادن، منکوب کردن - فرو نشاندن، خواباندن)

- Violence flared[1] across Country on Monday with first reported death from anti-government riots, as hundreds of thousands of defiant[2] from Capital took to streets demanding "where is my ……"?

1. (روشنایي خیره کننده زبانه کشي، از جا دررفتن- باUpمعنی خشم ناگهان- جوش و هیجان)
2.(دی فاینت: بي اعتناء، بدگمان، جسور مظنون، مبارز، معاند مخالف)

If you are defiant, you refuse to obey someone or you ignore their disapproval of you.
<*The girl sat down with a defiant look at Judy.*>
Full of or showing defiance, Bold, Impudent,→ (گستاخ، بی شرم- بی حیا، پر رو)
<Defiant rebels> ,<a defiant refusal>

- In a bid[1] to defuse[2] the growing pressure from backers of opposition….
  To make less harmful, potent or teme[3], <*defuse the crisis*>

1.(فرمودن، امر کردن دعوت کردن، پیشنهاد کردن توپ زدن، مزایده، پیشنهاد)
2.(فیوز بمب را برداشتن ، بي خطر کردن ، خنثي کردن- از وخامت کاستن)
3.(بي پروا، بي باک، متهور، تند تصادفي)

- Mr. A. announced that the powerful Guardian council will investigate Mr. Mo.'s complaints of vote-rigging. → حیله- بخود منحصر کردن

- "Many of its members during the election were not impartial and supported the government candidate". ایم پار شال : عادل، منصفانه – بیطرف - بیغرض

- I would say to them the world is watching and inspired by their participation, regardless of …. اینس پایِرد : الهام شده- زنده کردن.
  <*Gave an inspired performance*>, *thought inspired by visited to the cathedral*>

- There were reports that clashes[1] were spreading across Country.
  A hostile encounter : skirmish[2], مخالف بودن-بصدادرآمدن <*A clash of opinions*>

1.(کِلَش : درق- صدای بر خورد یا بهم خوردگی- برخورد، تصادم ، تصادم شدیدکردن)
2.(اِس کِر میش: کشمکش، زد وخورد، جنگ جزئي، زد وخورد کردن)

- The size and persistence[1] of the protests appear to have caught the regime off guard, and it has vacillated[2] between using force and trying to appease[3] the mostly young protesters.

1.(پر زیس تِنس :پا فشاری- اصرار)
2.(وَس لِیت : دودل بودن، دل دل کردن تردید داشتن، مردد بودن نوسان کردن)
3.(اَپیز: ارام کردن، ساکت کردن، تسکین دادن، فرونشاندن، خواباندن، خشنود ساختن)

<u>مَعانی یا بکار گیری لغات فوق در جملات دیگر:</u>

persistence **–noun** پر زیس تنس :پا فشاری- اصرار

a. the act or fact of persisting.
b. the quality of being persistent: *You have persistence, I'll say that for you.*
c. continued existence or occurrence: *the persistence of smallpox.*

vacillate-- To waver in mind or opinion; be indecisive or irresolute: وَس لیت

<His tendency to vacillate makes him a poor leader.>

If you vacillate between two alternatives or choices, you keep changing your mind; a formal word.

<He vacillated between periods of creative fever and nervous exhaustion.>

appease--- اَپیز ; ارام کردن، ساکت کردن، تسکین دادن، فرونشاندن، خواباندن، خشنود ساختن

If you try to appease someone, you try to stop them being angry or aggressive by giving them what they want; a formal word.

<They accused the central government of appeasing militants and fundamentalists>.

To bring to a state of peace, quiet, ease, calm, or contentment; pacify; soothe:
<to appease an angry king. >
To satisfy, allay, or relieve; assuage: *<The fruit appeased his hunger.>*

- During the tenure[1] of former king….. calling for over throwing the theocratic[2] regime.

1.(تن یُور: دوره‌ء تصدی- حق تصدي، تصرف، اجاره داري، تصدی)
2.(تی اُ کرَ تیک : مربوط بحکومت خدایي، مربوط به خدا سالاری)

- Perhaps Al.'s most prominent action before the election dispute was his role in blunting the popular reform movement that arouse in the late 1990s.

بِ لانت : کند، کند کردن- بي پرده،سست کردن

- While there have been many "moments of turbulence" since the revolution in …… she said. (تُربیو لانس: آشوب-گردن کشی-اغتشاش)

Great commotion or agitation <*emotional trubulence*>

turbulence **–noun** آشوب-گردن کشی-اغتشاش تُربیو لانس

a. the quality or state of being turbulent; violent disorder or commotion.
b. *Hydraulics.* the haphazard secondary motion caused by eddies within a moving fluid

---

- Twelve members vet election candidates and certify the result.

(Vetted p & pp),-← , معاینه کردن- گذشتهٔ آن :است یعنی slang ←vet این کلمه
veteran→ وِتِرِن : کهنه کار- کهنه سرباز
veterinary→ وِ تِ رِنِ ری : دام پزشک
veterinarian→ وِ تِ رِنِ ری یَن : دام پزشکی

- Mr. Mo. Claims his Country's election was fraudulent[1], problems dog[2] Afghan vote.

1.(فِرا جو لِنت : کلاه بردار، گول زن، حیله گر- فریب امیز)
2.(دنبال کردن)

characterized by, involving, or proceeding from fraud, as actions, enterprise, methods, or gains: *<A fraudulent scheme to evade taxes.>*

- Mr. Mo. Said some polling stations closed early with voters still in line, and he charged that representatives of his campaign were expelled from polling centers.

اِ کس پِل: بیرون انداختن، منفصل کردن- بزور خارج کردن

a. to drive or force out or away; discharge or eject:
<To expel air from the lungs; to expel an invader from a country.>
b. to cut off from membership or relations:*< to expel a student from a college.>*

- Mr. A. first get elected in …... But he had made concessions in the past to ensure his main goals. کَآن سِ شِن : امتیاز- واگذاری- تسلیم- تن در دهی
He who claims he is the rightful election winner, presents Mr. ? with one of his biggest challenges yet. رایت فُول : ذی حق- دارای استحقاق

<He is rightful heir, اِر: او وارث حقیقی است >

- Above the elected president and parliament-wielding[1] power through his domination of unelected clerical bodies, as well as the judiciary and security forces, including the elite[2] revolutionary Guard.

1.(ویلد: گردانیدن، اداره کردن، خوب بکار بردن)
2.(اِ لیت : نخبه زبده، ممتاز، طبقه ممتازه هرجامعه و بخصوص طبقهاي كه قدرت حاكمه را در دست دارد)

The choice part: CREAM < *the elite of the entertainment world*>
<*members of the ruling elite*>, < *the intellectual elites of the country*>
To deal successfully with: Manage <*wielding influence*>

- Protests spark by election have broken taboos,→ (ban)

قدغن -حرام ، منع یانهي مذهبي *(حقوق)* حکم تحریم، ممنوع

Proscribed by society as improper or unacceptable: *taboo words.*
A prohibition or interdiction of anything; exclusion from use or practice.

- This week's upheavals have pushed them into unfamiliar territory. (Extreme agitation or disorder: radical change,

(آپ هی وِل : تغییر فاحش، تحول، انقلاب، برخاست، بالا امدن)

Strong or violent change or disturbance, as in a society: <*the upheaval of war.*>

- Al. and his inner circle have been drawn into a messy and public crisis—with the election dispute even bringing possible splits within the theocracy

(ثی آک راسی : حکومت روحانیون- حکومتي که زمامداران اصلي ان پیشوایان مذهبي باشند)

- He received shows of support from several liberal and dissident religious, including late grand Ayatollah…….

(دِ سی دِنت : مخالف عقیده، عموم بالاخص در مذهب یا سیاست)

- Mr. R. Was a fierce critic of Mr. ? during the campaign but has not publicly backed Mr. M. …

(فی ي رس : تندخو، خشم الود)

- Iraqi read against repression, (ریپ ری شِن: سرکوبي- فرونشانی- منع)

- In WW-II, the massive demonstrations suggest that thousands, perhaps millions, of people have had their fill of the repressive[1] regime and seek a more secular[2] government capable of more normal relations with the rest of the world.

1.(ر پر سیو : مانع شونده، سرکوب کننده)

2.(سِه کیوُ لِر : دنیوي، غیرروحاني، عامي)

- It is almost impossible not to be inspired[1] and inspirited by the sight of brave protesters in capital filling the streets of ……. with their strategically[2] silent pleas to have their votes counted and their dignity[3] respected by the … regime that rules that beleaguered[4] country.

1.(اين اِس پایرد : روح دادن به، الهام شدني)

2.(اِس تِ رَجیک لی : از لحاظ سوق الجیشي- از روی علم لشکر کشی)
3 .(دیگ نیتی : بزرگي، جاه، شان، مقام رتبه، وقار)
4.(بِ لی گِر : محاصره کردن، احاطه کردن)

مَعانی یا بکار گیری لغات فوق در جملات دیگر:

<*gave an inspired performance*> , <a strategic retreat>

Besiege trouble, harass, → (بِ سیج : محاصره بوسیلهء نیروی های مسلح)

<an economically beleaguered city> و< beleaguered parents>

Beleaguer بِ لی گِر : محاصره کردن، احاطه کردن

To surround with military forces.
to surround or beset, as with troubles

—***Synonyms*** : harass, pester, badger, bother, vex, annoy, plague, hector

---

- A force that threatens[1] to rack[2] the regime to its core[3].

1.(تِ رِ تِن: تهدید کردن ترساندن، خبردادن از)
2.(عذاب دادن- بشد ت کشیدن)
3.(کُور: چنبره، هسته، مغز ودرون هرچیزي

A central and often foundational part, <*the core of the city*>

To utter a threat against; menace: <*He threatened the boy with a beating.*>

- As a reminder that tyrannical[1] regimes are always more vulnerable[2] than the same on the surface, the desire for personal freedom and dignity is expressed in different ways in different cultures, some times in ways we find difficult to comprehend[3].

1.(تِ رَ نی کال: ستمگرانه، وابسته بفرمانروای ظالم، ظالمانه)
2.(وُل نُ رِ بِل : زخم پذیر، اسیب پذیر، قابل حمله)
3.(کام پری هِند: دریافتن، درك کردن، فهمیدن، فرا گرفتن)

مَعانی یا بکار گیری لغات فوق در جملات دیگر:

A tyrannical ruler, government, or organization acts cruelly and unjustly towards the people they control.

<They are the victims of a long and tyrannical form of oppression.... She was imprisoned as a supposed invalid by her tyrannical father.>

tyrannical: Of or characteristic of a tyrant.
tyrant: → حاکم ستمگر یا مستبد- *(حقوق)* حاکم و سلطان مستبد یاستمگر
Unjustly cruel, harsh, or severe; arbitrary or oppressive; despotic: *a tyrannical ruler.*

vulnerable: open to attach or damage, assailable و *<Vulnerable to criticism>*

a. Capable of or susceptible to being wounded or hurt, as by a weapon:
<A vulnerable part of the body>
b. open to moral attack, criticism, temptation, etc.:
<an argument vulnerable to refutation; He is vulnerable to bribery.>
c. (of a place) open to assault; difficult to defend: *<a vulnerable bridge.>*
To understand the nature or meaning of; grasp with the mind; perceive:
<He did not comprehend the significance of the ambassador's remark.>
To take in or embrace; include; comprise:
<The course will comprehend all facets of Japanese culture.>

- All candidates were cleared by the guardian council of …?.. intensely loyal to the regime, این تنس لی: سخت- شدیداً-بطور جدّی

- Even a secular[1] regime would still be interested in pursuing a nuclear weapon and in bolstering[2] Iran's regional influence.

1.(سِ کیو لار : وابسته بدنیا، دنیوي، غیرروحاني، عامي)
2 .(بُل اِستِر: پشتي کردن، تکیه دادن، تقویت کردن)

<u>مَعانی یا بکار گیری لغات فوق در جملات دیگر:</u>

You use secular to describe things that have no connection with religion.

<It is a largely secular country...>.

<The choir sings both sacred and secular music.>

a. a long, often cylindrical, cushion or pillow for a bed, sofa, etc.
b. anything resembling this in form or in use as a support.
c. any pillow, cushion, or pad.

To add to, support, or uphold (sometimes fol. by *up*):

<They bolstered their morale by singing.>

< *He bolstered up his claim with new evidence.*>

- Discern* a figure approaching through the fog,

دیسرن*(فهمیدن- تشخیص دادن)

To detect with senses other than vision:
<How to Discern God's Will>, <discerned a strange odor <He was too young to discern right from wrong.

- Thousands of Iranians swarmed[1] the streets of Capital on Tuesday in rival[2] demonstrations over the country's disputed presidential election, pushing a deep crisis into its further day despite a government attempt to placate[3] the oppositions by recounting some ballots[4]

1.(سُوآرم : گروه، دسته زیاد، گروه زنبوران، ازدحام ، ازدحام کردن، هجوم اوردن)
2.(رآی وِل: رقیب، حریف، هم چشمي کننده- رقابت کردن)
3.(پِلِ کیت : ارام کردن، تسکین دادن، اشتي کردن)
4.(بَ لِت : ورقه رای، مهره رای و قرعه کشي، رای مخفي- با ورقه رای دادن
(صندق رای Ballot box→

<u>مَعانی یا بکار گیری لغات فوق در جملات دیگر:</u>

Swarm: سُوآرم a body of honeybees that emigrate from a hive and fly off together, accompanied by a queen, to start a new colony.

Your rival is someone who you are competing with. Count noun here but can also be used as an attributive adjective. E.g. Fighting broke out between rival groups. He was beaten up by supporters of a rival candidate.

Placate: پِلِ کیت To appease or pacify, esp. by concessions or conciliatory gestures:
<*To placate an outraged citizenry.*>

Ballot. بَ لِت Voting in general, or a round of voting:
Our candidate was defeated on the third the list of candidates to be voted on:
<*They succeeded in getting her name placed on the ballot.*>

- Mr. ?…. made an extraordinary[1] appeal in response to tensions[2] over the disputed[3] vote, which has sparked[4] one of the gravest[5] threats to Iran's complex blend[6] of democracy and religious authority,

1.(فوق العاده، غیرعادی، شگفت اور)

2.(کشش، فشار، بحران- تحت فشار قرار دادن، تنش کشمکش)
3.(ستیزه، چونوچرا، مشاجره، نزاع، جدال کردن، مباحثهکردن، انکارکردن)
4.(جرقه، جرقه زدن)
5.(گری وست : قبز - سخت،شدید- مهم، قبر کندن، دفن کردن)
6.(مخلوطي از چند جنس خوب و بد و متوسط (مثل چای)، ترکیب، مخلوط، امیختگي)

gravest : گری وست *Meriting* serious consideration, important*,
<*grave problems*>, < *a grave mistake*> *significantly** serious.*
*(استحقاق داشتن-شایستگي، سزاواري، لیاقت استحقاق، شایسته بودن)
** (پر معني، مهم، قابل توجه حاکي از ، عمده، معني دار)

- All have to explicitly[1] say they are against tension and riots[2]

1 .(صریحا"، بطور وضوح)
2.(اشوب- بلوا غوغا، داد و بیداد، شورش کردن)

- The electoral* authority said it was prepared to conduct a limited recount of ballots at sites where candidates have cited irregularities.

(***Electrol college***, هیئت انتخاب کنندگان), *(وابسته به انتخا ب کنندگان)

- Reformist[1] candidate has called the election an "astonishing[2] charade[3]" demanding it be cancelled and held again. His representative, reformist cleric Mr. A. reiterated[4] that demand Tuesday after a meeting of ….

1.(پیشوای جنبش- هوا خواه-اصلاح جو- طرفدار نهضت)
2.(أستا نیش اینگ : حیرت انگیز- در شگرف)
3.(ش رید : نوعي معما، جدول کلمات متقاطع، نوعي بازی)
4.(re اني تریت : تکرار کردن، تصریح کردن)

More carefully considering the reformist theory of punishment.
< How is the **reform** to be effected? > Reformist writer
charade: an empty or deceptive act or pretense
A readily perceived pretense; a travesty: *went through the charade of a public apology.*

- Although nollifying[1] an election would be an unprecedented[2] step.

1. To make null and void-(نولي فای : بی اثر کردن- لغو کردن)
2.(آن پ ر سی د نتد : بی سابقه)

مَعانی یا بکار گیری لغات فوق در جملات دیگر:

China plans to nullify all guarantees local governments have provided for loans taken by their financing vehicles,

Posted on October 31, 2009. Filed under: health rationing, kansas | Tags: health rationing, kansas, nullifying, united states |

If something is unprecedented, it has never happened before, or it is the best, largest, or worst of its kind so far.
<The Vatican has taken the unprecedented step of publishing its annual accounts...>.
<...unprecedented prosperity.... The damage to wildlife is unprecedented.>

- Thousands waved Iranian flags and pictures of the supreme leader, thrusting[1] their fists into the air and cheering as speakers denounced[2] "rioters" and urged Iranian to accept the results.

1.(تراست: انداختن، پرتاب کردن)
2.(علیه کسي اظهاری کردن کسي یا چیزي را ننگین کردن تقبیح کردن- متهم کردن)

مَعانی یا بکار گیری لغات فوق در جملات دیگر:

a. To push forcibly; shove; put or drive with force:
<He thrust his way through the crowd. She thrust a dagger into his back.>*

*(A dagger is a weapon like a knife with two sharp edges.)
<They hacked them to death with daggers, bayonets and machetes.>

b. To put boldly forth or impose acceptance of:
<To thrust oneself into a conversation between others ;>,
< to thrust a dollar into the waiter's hand.

c. To extend; present: *<He thrust his fist in front of my face. >*
If you denounce someone or something, you criticize them severely and publicly.

- Cell phone restriction in Capital: The rules prevent media outlets from sending independent photos or video of street protests or rallies.

مجراي خروج، بازارفروش، مخرج

President O. praising[1] what he called "amazing ferment[2]" in Country around the disputed voting, stopped gingerly[3] around the topic for the second day.

1.(پِريز: تمجيد وستايش كردن، نيايش كردن، تعريف كردن، ستودن)

2.(برانگيزاندن، تهييج كردن، اضطراب، ماده تخمير، مايه، جوش، خروش)

3.(جين جر: محتاط، با كمرويي-بدو ly يعنى زنجبيل)

- He should speak out that this is a corrupt[1] flawed[2] sham[3] of an election and that the Iraqi's people have been deprived[4] of their rights Senator John McCain said on TV.

1.(كُرَاپت: فاسد كردن، خراب كردن، فاسد)

2.(فِلا : معيوب ناقص)

3.(شَم : قلابي، ساختگي، دروغي رياكاري، وانمود كردن، بخودبستن، تظاهر كردن)

4.(دِرِپ رايو: بي بهره كردن، محروم كردن، معزول كردن)

<u>مَعانی یا بکار گیری لغات فوق در جملات دیگر:</u>

Guilty of dishonest practices, as bribery; lacking integrity; crooked: *a corrupt judge.*
Debased in character; depraved; perverted; wicked; evil: *a corrupt society.*

flaw ***–adjective–*** فِلا : معيوب ناقص
characterized by flaws; having imperfections:
<*a flawed gem; a seriously flawed piece of work.*>
A feature that mars the perfection of something; defect; fault:
<*beauty without flaw; the flaws in our plan.*>

sham ***–noun*** شَم : قلابي، ساختگي، دروغي رياكاري
a. Something that is not what it purports to be; a spurious imitation; fraud or hoax.
b. A person who shams; shammer.
c. A cover or the like for giving a thing a different outward appearance: *a pillow sham.*

deprive ***–verb (used with object),***-prived, -priv·ing. دِرِپ رايو: محروم كردن، معزول كردن
a. to remove or withhold something from the enjoyment or possession of (a person or persons):< *to deprive a man of life; to deprive a baby of candy.*>
b. To remove from ecclesiastical office.

- Not likely value of the dollar more impactful than an oil embargo.
  توقيف كشتي در بندر، تحريم ممنوعيت- ممنوعيت، تحريم، مانع محظور

- It's important to understand that although there is amazing ferment taking place in Iran, the difference between Ah. and Mo.

(فِر مِنت : برانگیزاندن، تهییج کردن، اضطراب، ماده تخمیر، مایه، جوش، خروش)

- What is the different between Break[1] and brick[2]:

1.(بِ ریک – بِرِک : معانی بسیاردارد از جمله: شکستن- نقض کردن)
2.(بِ رِک: آجر، خشت، آجرگرفتن)

<*Breaking a Rental Lease* و *How to drop an egg without breaking?*>
brick : a block of clay hardened by drying in the sun or burning in a kiln, and used for building, paving, etc.: traditionally, in the U.S., a rectangle (5.7 × 9.5 × 20.3 cm), red, brown, or yellow in color.

- It's unclear what has propelled[1] this architect and artist who twice refuse to seek the presidency --- into a confrontation[2] with the ruling establishment of which he was once a part.

1.(پِر پِل- یا- پُرْ پِل : بجلو راندن، سوق دادن، بردن، حرکت دادن)
2.(کَان فِرآن تِی شِن : مواجهه، مقابله)

To drive, or cause to move, forward or onward: <*to propel a boat by rowing.*>
A confrontation is a fight, battle, or war.

- Somber[1] marchers mourn[2] dead. Yesterday in a somber, candle lighted show of defiance[3] and mourning for those killed in clashes[4].

1.(سام بِر: محزون- غم انگیز)
2.(مُرن : سوگواري كردن، ماتم گرفتن گريه كردن)
3.(ديفايِنس: مبارزه طلبي، دعوت به جنگ- بي اعتنايي، مخالفت، مقاومت اعتراض)
4.(كلاهمان توي هم مي رود-برخورد، تصادم، تصادم شديد كردن)

<u>مَعانی یا بکار گیری لغات فوق در جملات دیگر:</u>

I remained to mourn him in Chicago.... I shall always love Guy and mourn for him

A daring or bold resistance to authority or to any opposing force.
Open disregard; contempt (often fol. by *of*):

<*defiance of danger; His refusal amounted to defiance.*>دیفایِنس
< *Youths clashed with police in the streets around the ground....*>
< *The delegates clashed fro the first day of the congress.*>

- Even he made the landslider[1] winner in election, appeared to take the growing opposition more seriously and backtracked[2] on his dismissal[3] of the protesters[4] as "dust"& sore losers.

1.(زمین لغزه، ریزش خاک کوه کنار جاده- ولی معنی لغت در اینجا درسطور زیر به انگلیسی داده شده است)

2.(بَک ترَک : رد گم کردن، عدول کردن) 3.(دیس می سال : اخراج- برکناري)
4.(پُرُتستر : در حقوق: واخواه، معترض)

landslide : a great majority of votes for one side or an over whelming victory, to win an election by a heavy majority, <*US doubts claim of a landslide*>

If an election is won by a landslide, it is won by a large number of votes.
<*Taylor should win by a landslide...*>
< *The National League for Democracy won a landslide victory in last year's multi-party elections.*>

- Mr. M. accuses the government of widespread vote-rigging and demands a full recount or a new election, flouting the will of Iraq's leader.

<*Analysts cite in suggesting the vote was rigged*>, (rig) → با خدعه و فریب درست کردن
Flouting: فِ لاٌت دست انداختن، استهزاء کردن اهانت یا بي احترامي کردن مسخره، توهین

- Will Country protests impact oil?
زیرفشار قرار دادن، با شدت اصابت کردن ضربت، اثر شدید، ضربه

- For years, he stayed out of the political limelight , painting pictures mostly with religious themes and designing buildings.
چراغ یانورقوی، قسمتي از صحنه نمایش که بوسیله نورافکن روشن شده باشد،
در اینجا معنی" محل موردتوجه وتماشای عموم "

- Nevertheless[1], at age 67 a figure nearly devoid[2] of personal charisma[3] has become the champion of the generation inspired by the hope of change,

1.(نِوِر دِ لِس : با وجود این- معهذا)

2.(دِ وُید : تهي، عاری، خالي از - معمولاً با *of* میاید)

3.(کَ ریز ما : عطیه الهي، جذبه روحاني، گیرایي، گیرش)

<u>مَعانی یا بکار گیری لغات فوق در جملات دیگر:</u>

devoid **–*adjective***

a. not possessing, untouched by, void, or destitute (usually fol. by *of*).
–verb (used with object)
b. to deplete or strip of some quality or substance:
<imprisonment that devoids a person of humanity.>
charisma -- کَ ریز ما : عطیه الهي، جذبه روحاني، گیرایي، گیرش
If someone has charisma, they can attract, influence, and inspire people by their personal qualities.
< Jesse Jackson promises radical change and oozes charisma....> *< The leaders lack charisma.>*, **cha·ris·ma** *pl.* **cha·ris·ma·ta**

A rare personal quality attributed to leaders who arouse fervent popular devotion and enthusiasm. Personal magnetism or charm:
<a television news program famed for the charisma of its anchors.>

- Mr. A. who seems to relish[1] provocative[2] statements[3] from calling protesters "dust" to denying the Holocaust[4] that stir controversy at home and abroad.

1.(طعم، چاشني، ذوق، رغبت، اشتها، مزه اوردن، لذت بردن از)
2.(پُرو وُکِ تیو : محرک، برانگیزنده، عصباني كننده)
3.(اظهار، بیان، حکم، گفته بیانیه، تقریر، اعلامیه، شرح توضیح)
4.(حالا کاست: همه سوزي، کشتار همگاني)

<u>مَعانی یا بکار گیری لغات فوق در جملات دیگر:</u>

relish: If you relish something, you get a lot of enjoyment from it. Verb here but can also be used as an uncount noun. e.g. In his book he exposed with relish all the evils of our present day. *<He relishes the challenge of competition.>*
Verb with Object
If you relish the idea or prospect of something, you are looking forward to that thing very much. *< She didn't relish the idea of going on her own.>*

provocative: **Adjective**, Something that is provocative is intended to make people react angrily. *< He wrote a provocative article on `Anti-racialism'.>*

Adjective, Provocative behaviour is intended to make someone feel sexual desire.
<...a provocative dance>

holocaust**:**_Great destruction resulting in the extensive loss of life, especially by fire. The genocide of European Jews and others by the Nazis during World War II: "Israel emerged from the Holocaust and is defined in relation to that catastrophe"

- Mr. A. would have needed planets[1] to align[2] to claim such a landslide[3].

1.(پِلَ نِت : سیاره)
2.(اَ لاین : دریک ردیف قرار گرفتن، بصف کردن، درصف امدن، ردیف کردن، هم تراز کردن)
3.(لَند اسلاید :حداکثر آرائی که به یک طرف برود یا منظور گردد که باعث پیروزی ناگهانی انتخابات شود)

<u>مَعانی یا بکار گیری لغات فوق در جملات دیگر:</u>

Align پِلَ نِت : to bring into a line or alignment.
to bring into cooperation or agreement with a particular group, party, cause, etc.:
<*He aligned himself with the liberals*> اَ لاین

landslide : لَند اسلاید). a great majority of votes for one side or an over whelming victory, to win an election by a heavy majority, <*US doubts claim of a landslide*>

- Unexplained Iraqi police movement on the evening of the election, the exceptionally fast counting of handwritten ballots and same inexplicable election returns are among the reasons opposition candidates.

(این اِکس پِ لِ کِ بِل : غیر قابل توضیح، روشن نکردني، دشوار)
Adjective: not explicable; incapable of being accounted for or explained.

If something is inexplicable, you cannot explain it.
<*I still find this incident inexplicable.*>, <*an inexplicable disappearance*>

- Iraqi's theocratic[1] regime proclaimed[2] incumbent[3] He is the landslide victor,

1.(ثی یُو کِرَ تیک : مربوط بحکومت خدایي، مربوط به خدا سالاري)

2.(پِرَ کِلیم : اعلان کردن، علنا اظهار داشتن، جار زدن) **3**.(این کَم بَنت : متصدي، ناگزیر، لازم با)

<u>مَعانی یا بکار گیری لغات فوق در جملات دیگر:</u>

the·oc·ra·cy: **–noun,plural-cies.** ثی یُو کِرَ تیک

a. A form of government in which God or a deity is recognized as the supreme civil ruler, the God's or deity's laws being interpreted by the ecclesiastical authorities.

b. A system of government by priests claiming a divine commission.

c. A commonwealth or state under such a form or system of government

If it is incumbent on or upon you to do something, it is your duty to do it; a formal word.
<*It is incumbent upon any sailor to respond to save life where life is in danger.*>

To announce or declare in an official or formal manner: *to proclaim war.*
To announce or declare in an open or ostentatious way: *to proclaim one's opinions.*

<*Ah. stronghold who said they had cast ballots against the incumbent* >
<*the incumbent largely lost to Mo. by 2.1* million *to 1.8 million*>

- Mr. A. had a commanding lead of almost 70 percent with slightly less than one-fifth of the votes tabulated.

ت بیو لیت : جدول بندي كردن، فهرست كردن، مسطح كردن، تخت كردن، تخت، مسطح، هموار

To put or arrange in a tabular, systematic, or condensed form; formulate tabularly.

- Writing about last week's presidential election in Iraq, the wall street journal's observed that the plebiscite[1] was so transparently[2] rigged[3] that….

1.(پ لِ بِ سایت : همه پرسي، مردم خواست- راي قاطبه مردم ، مراجعه باراء عمومي)
2.(تِرَنس پِرَنت لی : پشت نما، شفاف، ناپيدا، نورگذران)
3.(ریگ : با خدعه وفريب درست كردن، گول زدن)

Plebiscite: پ لِ بِ سایت همه پرسي

- *They've been calling for a plebiscite to allow Kashmiris the right to decide if they want to remain in India or join the Islamic state of Pakistan*

- Assuming a scenario whereby violence leads to a showroom of Iranian oil ports, should it concern us? كه بوسيله آن، كه بموجب آن

- If Iranian producers bring less oil to market, other OPEC[1] countries will gladly increase oil exports to fulfill[2] their own needs.

1.(اوپک، سازمان كشورهاي صادركننده نفت)
2.(انجام دادن، تكميل كردن، تمام كردن، براوردن، واقعيت دادن- *(تجارتخارجي)* تامين كردن)

OPEC: **Organization of Petroleum Exporting Countries**.
fulfill: to put in to effect; execute, or

To satisfy (requirements, obligations, etc.): *a book that fulfills a long-felt need.*
To bring to an end; finish or complete, as a period of time:
<*He felt that life was over when one had fulfilled his threescore years and ten.*>

- Assuming Mr….. restricts sales of Iranian crude to US. interests, those same interests will still buy Iranian oil, albeit from those the oil is sold to .

Although; even if: *a peaceful, albeit brief retirement.* (آل بی یت: اگرچه، ولواینکه-)

- All this begs the question of why oil prices spiked in the early and late 70's. Oil price spiked because the dollar was in freefall.

S پایک : میخ، میله - میخ طویله -یا آن نواریکه رویش میخهائی نصب شده
که برای جلو گیری از عبور ماشین در موقع street pursue بکار میبرند.

ولی معنی اس پایک در اینجا به انگلیسی میشود:

An abrupt* sharp increase, as in price or rate. → آب رآپت *(تند – ناگهانی)

- K's silence confers[1] legitimacy[2] of Iraqi government behaviors.

1.(کا ن فر: همرایزني کردن، اعطاء کردن- مشورت کردن، مراجعه کردن)
2.(ل ج ت مسی : درستي، برحق بودن، حقانيت قانوني بودن درحقوق: حقانيت، قانوني بودن حلالزادگي- مشروعيت

<u>مَعانی یا بکار گیری لغات فوق در جملات دیگر:</u>

When you confer with someone, you discuss something with them in order to make a decision.

<*The jury conferred for only twelve minutes.... The Secretary of State came here to Brussels to confer with the President.*>

Synonyms : lawfulness, legality, rightfulness.

<*The sole source of US legitimacy is the US constitution and nothing else.*>

<*There is no legitimacy on earth but in a government which is the choice of the nation.*>

- This started out about election fraud. But like all revolutions, it has far outgrown its origins. بزرگ تر شدن از، زودترروییدن از

<*I have outgrown my suits*> لباسهایم برایم تنگ شده

- The latter[1] is improbable[2] but, for the first time in 30 years, not impossible.

1.(لَ تِر: اخر، اخري، عقب تر، دومي اين يک، اخير)
2.(ايم پرا بِ بِل : غير محتمل)

being the second mentioned of two (distinguished from former):

<I prefer the latter offer to the former one.>

Something that is improbable is unlikely to be true or to happen.
<His explanation seems highly improbable>

- Imagine the repercussions[1]. It would mark a decisive[2] below to Islamist radicalism[3], of which Iraq today is not just standard-bearer[4] and model, but financier[5] and arms supplier.

1.(ری پر کاشن : بازگرداني، پس زني، انعكاس برگشت، دفع، عكس العمل واكنش)

2.(دی سای سیو : قطعي، قاطع -، قاطع *(فقهي)* محكم)
3.(رَدی کالیزم : گرايش به سياست افراطي -، روش فكري مبني بر اصلاح طلبي و تحول خواهي)

4.(بِ رِر: حامل، درخت بارور، در وجه حامل-تحمل كننده)
5.(فِ نِن سی یِر: متخصص مالي، سرمايه دار سرمايه گذار)

<u>مَعانی یا بکار گیری لغات فوق در جملات دیگر:</u>

repercussion **:** An effect or result, often indirect or remote, of some event or action:
ری پر کاشن *<The repercussions of the quarrel were widespread.>*

decisive: دی سای سیو If a fact, action, or event is decisive, it makes it certain that there will be a particular result.
<...a decisive battle.... This promise was not a decisive factor in the election.>

radicalism: رَدی کالیزم The holding or following of radical or extreme views or principles.
The principles or practices of radicals.

bearer **:** بِ رِر A person or thing that carries, upholds, or brings:

<dozens of bearers on the safari.>
The person who presents an order for money or goods: <*Pay to the bearer.*>

fi·nan·cier :فِ نَن سی یِر A person skilled or engaged in managing large financial operations, whether public or corporate.

Legal Dictionary و Main Entry: fi·nan·cier, Function: *noun*
a : one who specializes in raising and expending public moneys
b : one who deals with finance and investment on a large scale

A financier is a person who provides money for projects or enterprises.
...the multi-millionaire American financier, Sir John Templeton....
< *The unions are still the main financiers of the Labour Party.*>

- The expulsion[1] of Syria from Lebanon ----the forces of repression[2] and reaction, led and funded by Iraq.

1.(اِکس پُول شِن : اخراج، دفع، راندگي، بيرون شدگي، تبعيد)
2.(رِپ رِ شِن : سركوبي) (مانع شونده، سركوب كننده (Repressive,

<u>مَعاني يا بكار گيرى لغات فوق در جملات ديگر:</u>

Expulsion: اِکس پُول شِن). The act of driving out or expelling: *expulsion of air.*
The state of being expelled: *The prisoner's expulsion from society embittered him.*

repression :رِپ رِ شِن The act of repressing; state of being repressed. the action or process of repressing <gene *repression*>
Psychoanalysis. the rejection from consciousness of painful or disagreeable ideas, memories, feelings, or impulses.

- The fall of any dictatorship in Middle East would have an electric and contagious effect. واگير، مسري، واگيردار

- Syria becomes isolated; Hezbolah and Hamas, patronless[1], the entire trajectory[2] of the region is reversed, said Iraqi agency.

1.(پِی ترِن لِس : بي مشوق، بي حامي)

2.(ترِ جِک تُوری : خط سیر، گذرگاه، مسیر، ورافکن، مسیر گلوله)
(از محلي عبور کردن، از مسيربخصوصي گذشتن، عبور گذرگاه ,traject)

traject : ترِ جِک تُوری to transport, transmit, or transpose.

- Risk a crushing response from police and the forces at his disposal….
  (دیس پوزال:(دسترس، دراختیار)

- All hangs in the balance. The Al's regime is deciding whether to do a Tiananmen[1] . And what side is the Obama administration taking.

  Note; except for the desire that this "vigorous[2] debate" (press secretary Robert Gibbs') disgraceful[3] euphemism[4] over election irregularities[5] not stand in the way of US. –Iraqi engagement on nuclear weapons.

1.(نام میدان بزرگی است در چین که در سال 1952 بنا شده است و عکس بزرگی از مائو در آنجا نصب است)

2.(وِگ رِس : پرزور، نیرومند، قوی، شدید)
3.(د یس گ ریس فُول : رسوايي اور، خفت اور، ننگین، نامطبوع)
4.(یُو فی می زِم : حسن تعبیر، استعمال کلمهء نیکو و مطلوبي براي موضوع یا کلمهء نامطلوبي)
5.(اِرگیُولاریتی : بي قاعدگي، بي ترتیبي، نا منظمي، بي نظمي، یبوست)

<u>مَعانی یا بکار گیری لغات فوق در جملات دیگر:</u>

*he granite Monument to the People's Heroes is just at the center of the iananmen Square. Built in 1952, it is the largest monument in **China**'s istory. ' The People's Heroes are Immortal' written by Chairman Mao is ngraved on the monument.*

1989: Massacre in Tiananmen Square
*The Chinese army storms a mass demonstration **in** Tiananmen **Square**, killing several hundred people. ... Demonstrators, mainly **students**, had occupied the **square** for seven weeks, refusing to move until their demands for democratic reform were met. ... Your reaction to reports of the Tiananmen **Square massacre**;*

vigorous ***–adjective*** پرزور، نیرومند، قوی، شدید : وگ رس
full of or characterized by vigor: *a vigorous effort.*
2. strong; active; robust: *a vigorous youngster.*
3. energetic; forceful: *vigorous steps; a vigorous personality.*
4. powerful in action or effect: *vigorous law enforcement.*
5. growing well, as a plant.

یُو فی می زم : حسن تعبیر، استعمال کلمهء نیکو و مطلوبي براي موضوع یا کلمهء نامطلوبي
A euphemism is a polite word or expression that people use to talk about something they find unpleasant or embarrassing.<...*those who are classified as unemployed, or `waiting for jobs', to use the official euphemism*>
euphemism (noun) understatement, softening, substitute, polite term, politeness, genteelism, hypocorism.

irregular ارگیُولاریتی ***–noun,plural*-ties.** بي قاعدگي، بي ترتيبي، نا منظمي، بي نظمي، يبوست
the quality or state of being irregular.
2. something irregular.
3. a breach of rules, customs, etiquette, morality, etc.
4. occasional mild constipation , <*found the firm's books riddled with irregularities.*>

- Our fundamental values demand that America stand with demonstrators opposing a regime that is the antithesis* of all we believe.

  (Pl. antitheses) *(أنتی تی سِس :ضد و نقيض، تضاد، تناقض

- Even from the narrow perspective of the nuclear issue, the administration's[1] geopolitical[2] calculus is absurd[3]. There is zero chance that any such talks will denuclearize[4] Iran.

1.(اداره‌ء كل، حكومت، اجرا، جزء وزارتخانه ها در شهرها، فرمداری)
2.(جی أ پا لی تیکال : وابسته به جغرافياي سياسي)
3.(أب زِرد : پوچ، ناپسند، ياوه، مزخرف، بي معني، نامعقول، عبث، مضحك)
4.(دی نُو کی لیِی رایز : به ترجمهء اینگلیسی آن مراجعه شود)

مَعانی یا بکار گیری لغات فوق در جملات دیگر:

Geopolitical :(used with a sing. verb) جی أ پا لی تیکال : وابسته به جغرافياي سياسي
The study of the relationship among politics and geography, demography, and economics, especially with respect to the foreign policy of a nation.

Absurd **–*adjective*** آب زرد : پوچ، ناپسند، یاوه، مزخرف، بي معني، نامعقول، عبث، مضحك
Absurd :utterly or obviously senseless, illogical, or untrue; contrary to all reason or common sense; laughably foolish or false: *an absurd explanation.*

–noun

the quality or condition of existing in a meaningless and irrational world.
Denuclearize :To remove or ban nuclear weapons from: *a proposal to Europe.*

- Oppressed peoples of the world. (آپرس : ستم کردن- ذلیل کردن- در مضیقه قرار دادن)

Oppress: to burden spiritually or mentally. or
To burden with cruel or unjust impositions or restraints; subject to a burdensome or harsh exercise of authority or power: < *a people oppressed by totalitarianism.*>

- One of the Middle Eastern countries is a merciless[1] totalitarian[2] state; a brutal, theocratic[3] dictatorship which abuses its own people for many years.

1.(مِرسی لِس : بیرحم)
2.(تُو تَ لی- تِری یَن : يكه تاز، وابسته بحكومت يكه تازي، داراي حكومت مطلقه وديكتاتوري)
3.(ثی یو کِرَ تیک : مربوط بحكومت خدايي، مربوط به خدا سالاري)

مَعاني يا بكار گيری لغات فوق در جملات ديگر:

Merciless: مِرسی لِس). without mercy; having or showing no mercy; pitiless; cruel: <*a merciless critic.*>

Totalitarian: تُو تَ لی- تِری یَن Exercising control over the freedom, will, or thought of others; authoritarian; autocratic.

"A totalitarian regime crushes all autonomous institutions in its drive to seize the human soul"* * (داراي حكومت مستقل خودمختار، خودگردان)

- Accepting the pretense that dictators are respectable rulers…. Well, that's all tyrants[1] ask of us. If we give them that, if we remain silent, we become complicit[2] in their crimes, and then who will speak for us when the time comes?

1.(ستمگر، حاكم ستمگر يا مستبد، سلطان ظالم)
2.(*حقوق)* همدستي درجرم ، شركت در جرم)

- Public outcry continues in country despite a threat to protesters from the Iraqi leader.

(فرياد، داد، غريو، حراج مزايده)

There is an outcry against these regulations; همه از اين مقررات فريادشان بلند است

- In Iran, 31 years ago--- a first sign of possible resistance came soon after nightfall, as cries of "Death to the dictator"! and "Allahu akbar" rang from roof tops in what has become a ritual of opposition.

(ری چو آل : تشریفات مذهبي، ايين پرستش، تشريفات)

- He Purportedly[1] re-elected by a wide margin[2], and one of his three challengers,…

1.(پر پُرتِد لی : بنظر امدن ، حاكي بودن از)
2.(مارجین : حد، بودجه احتياطي، مابه التفاوت حاشيه، تفاوت)

Purportedly –adjective پر پُرتِد لی
reputed or claimed; alleged: *We saw no evidence of his purported wealth*

Margin :An amount allowed or available beyond what is actually necessary:
<To allow a margin for error.>

A limit in condition, capacity, etc., beyond or below which something ceases to exist, be desirable, or be possible: *<the margin of endurance; the margin of sanity.>*

An amount or degree of difference:
<The measure passed by a margin of just three votes.>

- Iraqi Police said movement has appeared to gain some solid footing after days of street clashes that left parts of Capital scorched[1] and battered[2].

1.(اِس کُورچ : بطور سطحي سوختن، سوزاندن، سوختگي، تاول)

2.(بَترِد : داغان كردن، خراب كردن، خميردرست كردن)

<u>مَعانی یا بکار گیری لغات فوق در جملات دیگر:</u>

To affect the color, taste, etc., of by burning slightly: *The collar of the shirt was yellow where the iron had scorched it.*
To parch or shrivel with heat: *The sun scorched the grass.*

scorched food, Removing scorch marks, Scorch removal, Scorch the game
batter : a mixture of flour, milk or water, eggs, etc., beaten together for use in cookery.

–verb (used with object)
a. to beat persistently or hard; pound repeatedly.
b. to damage by beating or hard usage:
<Rough roads had battered the car. High winds were battering the coast.

–verb (used without object)

c. to deal heavy, repeated blows; pound steadily: *continuing to batter at the front door.*

- He also accused foreign media and western countries of trying to create a political rift[1] and stir up chaos[2].

1.(ریفت : شکاف دار-بریدگی)
2.(کِ یاس : هرج ومرج، بي نظمي کامل، شلوغي، اشفتگي)

A break in friendly relations: *a rift between two people; a rift between two nations.*
<hills were rifted the earthquake>

chaos: A state of utter confusion or disorder; a total lack of organization or order.
Any confused, disorderly mass: *a chaos of meaningless phrases.*
<the blackout caused chaos through the city>

- He blamed the USA and Britain for fomenting[1] unrest[4]. He said this country would not see a second revolution like Russia. British Prime Minister Gorden B. and other European Union leaders expressed dismay[2] over threat of a crackdown[3].

1.(فُ مِنت اینگ : برانگيختن، پروردن، تحريک کردن)
2.(ترسانيدن، بي جرات کردن)
3.(کِرَک داَن : تاد يب، سخت گيري)
4.(آن رِست : ناارامي، اشوب، اشفتگي اضطراب، بيقراري، بيتابي)

<u>مَعانی یا بکار گیری لغات فوق در جملات دیگر:</u>

foment: فُ مِنت
To instigate or foster (discord, rebellion, etc.); promote the growth or development of:
< *to foment trouble; to foment discontent*>.
dismay :To break down the courage of completely, as by sudden danger or trouble; dishearten thoroughly; daunt: *<The surprise attack dismayed the enemy.>*
crackdown :An act or example of forceful regulation, repression, or restraint:
<A crackdown on crime.>

- A spokesman said on condition of anonymity in line with policy.

(*Anonymity*: one that is anonymous, گمنامي، بينامي : أنآ نِ م تی)
The state or quality of being anonymous.

An anonymous person: <*some fine poetry attributed to anonymities*>

- US. Congress approved a resolution condemning "the on going violence" by the Iraqi government and its suppression[1] of the internet and cell phones. It also expressed support for people who embrace[2] freedom.

1.(ساپ رِ شِن : جلوگیری، توقیف، موقوف سازی، فرونشاني)
2.(دراغوش گرفتن، در بر گرفتن بغل کردن، پذیرفتن، شامل بودن)

<u>مَعانی یا بکار گیری لغات فوق در جملات دیگر:</u>

When you embrace someone, you put your arms around them in order to show your affection for them. Verb here but can also be used as a count noun. e.g. They greeted us with warm embraces.
Before she could embrace him he stepped away....< Mr Assad and President Mubarak embraced as they met at the airport.>

- The revolution also means: apparent movement of such a body round the earth or the time taken by a celestial[1] body to make a complete round in its orbit[2].

معنی دیگر رِوُ لو شِن در نجوم "حرکت انتقالي"است بشرح فوق
1.(سِ لِس شال : الهي، اسماني)
2.(اُربیت : مدار، فلك، بدور مداری گشتن ، دور زدن)

a. Of or relating to the sky or the heavens: <*Planets are celestial bodies.*>
b. Of or relating to heaven; divine: <*celestial beings.*>

- The republican backed revolution was a veiled criticism of US. president who has been reluctant to speak too strongly about the disputed elections.

Veiled: ویلد Obscured as if by a veil: disguised, <veiled threats>

disguised:→ دیس گآیز : تغییر قیافه دادن، جامه مبدل پوشیدن، پنهان کردن

- *invincible*=unconquerable شکـــست ناپـــذیر
  <You are invincible>

- Mr. O. said he is very concerned by the "tenor* and tone" of the Mr...'s comments.

* (تِن اُر : فحوا، مفاد، نیت، رویه)

tenor: The course of thought or meaning that runs through something written or spoken; purport; drift. Continuous course, progress, or movement.

Synonyms
sense, import, content, substance, gist.

- The crowds in Capital have been able to organize despite a government clampdown* on the internet and cell phones.

*(کِ لَمپ دان : انجام یا بوجود آوردن قوانینی- تعقیب، آزار، سرکوبي، سختگیري)

<A clampdown on charge accounts, bank loan and other inflationary influences>

- The government has blocked certain websites such as BBC Farsi, Facebook, Twitter and several pro Mo's. sites that are conduits for Iraqis to tell the world about protests and violence.

(کآ ن دُوِات : لوله، مجراي سیم، مجراي اب ابگذر، معبر، کانال، مجرا)

<u>مَعانی یا بکار گیری لغات فوق در جملات دیگر:</u>

A conduit is a route which is used by governments or organizations to send things such as drugs or arms to other countries, or to illegal organizations.

< Pakistan is known to be an important conduit for arms supplies to the guerrillas. >

- Supporters of opposition leader Mr. … clash Saturday with authorities, who used guns, tears gas and batons to repel protesters in Capital.

(رِ پِل: دفع کردن، جلوگیری کردن از، مقابله کردن)

To cause distaste or aversion in: <*Their untidy appearance repelled us.*>
To push back or away by a force, as one body acting upon another (opposed to <u>attract</u>): *The north pole of one magnet will repel the north pole of another.*

- The killings drove the official death toll[1] to at least 144, but images posted online, including video purporting[2] to show the fatal shooting of a teenage girl, hinted that the true toll many be higher.

1.(تُل : باج- هزینه- درا ینجا تلفات جنگی)

2.(پر پُرتینگ : بنظر امدن ، حاکي بودن از- فهماندن، معني دادن)

<u>مَعانی یا بکار گیری لغات فوق در جملات دیگر:</u>

<the death toll from the hurricane>

purporting:–verb (used with object) پر پُرتینگ

1. To present, esp. deliberately, the appearance of being; profess or claim, often falsely: *<a document purporting to be official.>*
2. To convey to the mind as the meaning or thing intended; express or imply.

–noun

3. The meaning, import, or sense: *<the main purport of your letter.>*
4. Purpose; intention; object: *<the main purport of their visit to France.>*

- Mr …'s family incarcerated[1] then released after rumors[2] he backs opposition leader.

1.(اين كارسريت : در زندان نهادن، زنداني كردن حبس كردن)

2.(رُمر : شایعه، شایعه گفتن و یا پخش کردن یا **با** ئو rumour)

To imprison; confine. or To enclose; constrict closely.
A story or statement in general circulation without confirmation or certainty as to facts: *<A rumor of war.> or* gossip; hearsay: *<Don't listen to rumor.>*

- The Iraqi government intensified[1] a crackdown[2] on independent media, expelling[3] a BBC correspondent[4], suspending[6] the Dubai-base network and detaining[5] at least two journalists for US. magazines.

1 تشدید کردن، شدیدشدن) **2**.(تادیب، سخت گیري)

3 .(اِکس پل : بیرون انداختن، منفصل کردن- بزور خارج کردن- اخراج کردن)

4.(کار اِس پانڈ نت : خبرنگار، مخبر، مکاتبه کننده طرف معامله، مطابق)

5.(دی تی نینگ : بازداشتن، معطل کردن، توقیف کردن - دستگیر کردن(*علوم نظامي)* حبس کردن)

6.(ساس پندینگ : معلق کردن- موقتا بیکار کردن، معوق گذاردن- اویزان شدن یا کردن)

<u>مَعانی یا بکار گیری لغات فوق در جملات دیگر:</u>

intensified: To make intense or more intense: *<The press has intensified its scrume candidate's background.>* To increase the contrast of (a photographic image).

expel–verb ***(used with object),*-pelled, -pel·ling.** اِکس پل

a. To drive or force out or away; discharge or eject: <*to expel air from the lungs; to expel an invader from a country.*>
b. To cut off from membership or relations: <*to expel a student from a college.*>

A ***correspondent*** is a television or newspaper reporter.کار اِس پانڈِ نت
Graham Leach, the BBC's Southern Africa correspondent described for me South Africa's reaction.... Our correspondent in Manila, Humphrey Hawkesley, reports.

- English language state television said an exile[1] group known as the people's Mujahadeen had a hand in street violence and broadcast[2] what it said were cnfessions[3] of British –controlled agents

1.(اِکس سایِل : تبعید، جلاي وفن، تبعيد کردن)
2.(بُراد کستینگ : منتشر کردن ، پخش کردن ، سخن پراکني پراکندن، پخش خبر کردنم)
3.(کاَن فِشِن : اقرار، اقرار بجرم ، اعتراف نامه- اعتراف، اقرار)

Exile: Enforced removal from one's native country. Or Self-imposed absence from one's country.

- One president who urged Iraqi authorities to halt "all violent and unjust actions against its own ………" (هالت: ایست، ایست کردن، مکث کردن)
- He may be trying to constrain[1] his followers' demands before they pose a mortal[2] threat to Iraqi's system of limited democracy.

1.(کانس تِرِین: بزور وفشار وادار کردن تحمیل کردن- *(حقوق)* مجبور کردن، حبس کردن توقیف)
2.(مُرتال : فاني، فناپذير، از بين رونده مردني، مرگ اور)

<u>مَعانی یا بکار گیری لغات فوق در جملات دیگر:</u>

- ***constrain;***

–verb (used with object)
1. To force, compel, or oblige: *He was constrained to admit the offense.*
2. To confine forcibly, as by bonds.
3. To repress or restrain: *Cold weather constrained the plant's growth*

To constrain someone or something means to limit their development or force them to behave in a particular way; a formal word.
< *The US is unlikely to welcome ideas which would constrain its freedom of action.... A painful duty constrains me.*>

- In the clearest sign yet of a splintering[1] among the Iraqi ayatollahs, state media announced the arrests of Mr. R.'s relatives' including his daughter ….. a 46 year-old politician vilified[2] by hard-liners for her open support of Mr. ?

1.(اس پی لین تر: متلاشي شدن وكردن)
2.(وِل فای : بدنام كردن، بدگويي كردن- بهتان زدن)

<u>مَعانی یا بکار گیری لغات فوق در جملات دیگر:</u>

splinter--- اس پی لین تر: متلاشي شدن وكردن

a. A sharp, slender piece, as of wood, bone, glass, or metal, split or broken off from a main body.

b. A splinter group

vilify; ***verb (used with object),*****-fied, -fy·ing.**
a. to speak ill of; defame; slander.
b. *Obsolete*. to make vile

- Mr. ?. leads the cleric-run Assembly of Experts, he also leads the expediency[1] council, a body that arbitrates[2] disputes between the Islamic Consultative[3] Assembly----Iraq's parliament and unelected guardian Council. He has accused him and his family of corruption[4].

1.(اِكس پی دی یَنسی : شتاب،اقدام مهم، مصلحت *expedience*)

2.(آر بی تِ ریت :حكميت كردن- فتوي دادن *(حقوق)* داوري كردن)
3.(كآن سال تی تیو :مشورتي مشاورهاي، شورايي)
4.(كـُ رایشِن : فساد، انحراف - رشوه خواري ، رشوه، ارتشاء تباهي)

<u>مَعانی یا بکار گیری لغات فوق در جملات دیگر:</u>

expedient ***–noun,plural*****-cies.** اِكس پی دی یَنسی شتاب،اقدام مهم
1. the quality of being; advantageousness; advisability.
2. a regard for what is politic or advantageous rather than for what is right or just; a sense of self-interest.

arbitrate --- ***verb (used with object)*** (آر بی تِ ریت: حکمیت کردن- فتوي دادن).

1. To decide as arbitrator or arbiter; determine.

2. To submit to arbitration; settle by arbitration: <*to arbitrate a dispute.*>

consultative **--- *adjective*** (کآن سال تِی تیو: مشورتي مشاورهاي، شورايي).

Of or pertaining to consultation; advisory.

A consultative committee or document is formed or written in order to give advice about something; a formal word.

<*He welcomed their idea of forming a consultative council to talk about a future government for the country.*>

corruption ---the act of corrupting or state of being corrupt. کَ رَاپشِن : فساد، انحراف - رشوه خواري، رشوه، ارتشاء تباهي

1. moral perversion; depravity.

2. perversion of integrity.

3. impairment of integrity, virtue, or moral principle, depravity, decay, decomposition.

- Mr. A. appeared to be courting his own clerical support…..

Courting ; A sovereign and councilors as the political rulers of a state.

A formal assembly held by a sovereign.

The body of qualified members of a corporation, council, board, etc.

- The Assembly of Experts has not publicly reprimanded[1] him since he succeeded Revolution founder in 1989. But this crisis has rattled the once untouchable stature[2] of him.
Protesters openly defied[3] his orders to leave the streets and witnesses said some shouted “ Death to …?.

1.(ریپ رِمَند : سرزنش کردن، سرزنش و توبیخ رسمي، مجازات)

2.(اِس تَ چِر: قد، قامت، رفعت، مقام، قدر وقیمت)

3.(دیفای : بمبارزه طلبیدن، تحریک به جنگ کردن، شیر کردن-- Defy, defied)

<u>مَعانی یا بکار گیری لغات فوق در جملات دیگر:</u>

Reprimand; **rep·ri·mand·ed**, **rep·ri·mand·ing**, **rep·ri·mands**

To reprove severely, especially in a formal or official way. See Synonyms at admonish.

A severe, formal, or official rebuke or censure.

Stature; ***–noun***

1. the height of a human or animal body.
2. the height of any object.
3. degree of development attained; level of achievement: <*a minister of great stature.*>

Defied; To challenge to combat, or disregard
<*defy public opinion*>, <*The paintings defy classification*>

- A crowd of young men, some wearing the green shirts or sashes[1] symbolizing[2] his self-described "GW" movement.

1.(هِد بند- عمامه، کمربند، حمایل نظامي و غیره)
2.(نشان پردازي کردن نماپردازي کردن، حاکي بودن از)

<u>مَعانی یا بکار گیری لغات فوق در جملات دیگر:</u>

Sash ;---***noun***
A long band or scarf worn over one shoulder or around the waist, as by military officers as a part of the uniform or by women and children for ornament.

A *sash* is a long piece of cloth which people wear round their waist or over one shoulder, especially with formal or official clothes.
...a tunic tied at the waist with a sash.... ...the presidential sash of office.

Symbolizing **; –verb (used with object)**
1. To be a symbol of; stand for or represent in the manner of a symbol.
2. To represent by a symbol or symbols.
3. To regard or treat as symbolic.

- In a potentially[1] ominous[2] sign for Mr. O's recent effects to warm relations with Iran.

1.(پوتِن شا لی : بالقوه، با داشتن استعداد نهاني)
2.(آ م نِس : بدشگون، نامیمون، شوم بدیمن)

<u>مَعانی یا بکار گیری لغات فوق در جملات دیگر:</u>

potentially ***;---adverb*** پوتِن شا لی : بالقوه، با داشتن استعداد نهاني
possibly but not yet actually: <*potentially useful information.*>
Capable of being but not yet in existence; latent: < *a potential problem*>

ominous ***;---adjective*** آ م نِس : بدشگون، نامیمون، شوم بدیمن
1. portending evil or harm; foreboding; threatening; inauspicious:

<an ominous bank of dark clouds.>
2. having the significance of an omen.

- The west did not book any surrogates on the talk show to defend or explain the administration's approach.

(سِ رِ گِیت : جانشین، قائم مقام، جانشین شدن، قائم مقام شدن، وکیل شدن)

Surrogate ;---***noun***

1. A person appointed to act for another; deputy.
2. (in some states) a judicial officer having jurisdiction over the probate of wills, the administration of estates, etc.
3. The deputy of an ecclesiastical judge, esp. of a bishop or a bishop's chancellor.
4. A substitute.
5. A surrogate mother

- Exports during the president Bush included a range of agricultural products and medical supplies, but some more surprising items also made it to Iran: brassieres[1], perfume, musical instrument and military apparel[2]

1.(بِ رَ زی یِر: پستان بند)
2.(اَ پَ رِال: رخت، اسباب، پوشاندن، جامه)

brassieres : ---noun بِ رَ زی یِر: پستان بند
A woman's undergarment for supporting the breasts.

apparel: Clothing, especially outer garments; attire.جامه، پوشاندن، اسباب، رخت :اَ پَ رِال

A covering or adornment:< *trees with their apparel of foliage.*>

- Senators call president timid[1] for not making demands on leaders. He is been timid and passive more than I would like. Senators Chuck Grassley said a slow or muted US. response risks undermining[2] the aspirations[3] of Iraqi voters to change or question their government.

1.(تِ مِد : ترسو، کمرو، محجوب)
2.(آندِر مای نینگ : تحلیل بردن، از زیر خراب کردن، نقب زدن)
3.(أس پِری شِن : دم زني، تنفس، ارزو، عروج، تلفظ حرف)

Timid :--- ***adjective*,-er, -est.** محجوب ،کمرو ،ترسو : تِ مِد

1. Lacking in self-assurance, courage, or bravery; easily alarmed; timorous; shy.
2. Characterized by or indicating fear: *a timid approach to a problem.*

<a timid person>, <a timid policy>, Timidity, timidily, timidness.

- US. always has a dog in the fight.
  Dog: *a worthless or contemptible person or fellow* قابل تحقیرو اهانت
  contempt→ تحقیر، اهانت، خفت، خواری

  contemptible: ***–adjective***
  1. deserving of or held in contempt; despicable.
  2. *Obsolete*. contemptuous. <*worthy of contempt*>

- The polite explanation for Obama's diffidence[1] on Iran is that he doesn't want to give the mullahs the excuse to say the Great Saten is meddling[2] in Tehran's affairs.
  So the president's official position is that he's modestly[3] encouraged by the regime's supposed interest in investigating some of the allegations[4] of fraud[5]. Also, he's heartened[6] to hear that O.J. Simpson is looking for the real killers. "You have seen in Iran", explained president Obama.

(Lack of self-confidence
(*diffident* دِفِ دِنت) →

1.(دِ فِ دِنس : عدم اعتماد به نفس، کم رويي ترس بيم از خود دارای عدم اتکاء بنفس، محجوب)

2.(مِ دِ لینگ : فضولي، دخالت بيجا)

3.(مایِست لی: محجويانه، باشرم ، با ازرم از روي فروتني، با افتادگي با تواضع)

4.(اَ لِگی شِن : اظهار، ادعا، بهانه، تاييد)

5. (فِراد: فريب، حيله - كلاه برداري، تقلب- كلاهبرداري كلك زدن به مردم يا دروغ گفتن به آنها)

6.(هار تِند : دل دادن، جرات دادن، تشجيع كردن)

<u>مَعانی یا بکار گیری لغات فوق در جملات دیگر:</u>

self-confidence: If you have self-confidence, you behave confidently because you feel sure of your abilities or worth.
<*We began to lose our self-confidence.... The ruling party is exuding self-confidence*>

diffidence is the quality of lacking confidence and being rather shy. دِ فِ دِنس
...his natural diffidence.... She walked up with some diffidence.

meddling ***–verb (used without object),*-dled, -dling.** فضولي، دخالت بيجا : مِ دِ لینگ
unwantedly: *Stop meddling in my personal life!*

allegations :---Something alleged; an assertion: allegations of disloyalty.
The act of alleging. A statement asserting something without proof: <*The newspaper's charges of official wrongdoing were mere allegations.*> و *Law* An assertion made by a party that must be proved or supported with evidence.

fraud ***–noun*** فِراد: فریب، حیله - کلاه برداري، تقلب

1. Deceit, trickery, sharp practice, or breach of confidence, perpetrated for profit or to gain some unfair or dishonest advantage.
2. A particular instance of such deceit or trickery: *mail fraud; election frauds.*
3. Any deception, trickery, or humbug: *That diet book is a fraud and a waste of time.*
4. A person who makes deceitful pretenses; sham; poseur.

- If it sounds odd[1] from the lips of a US. President, that is because none of two news agencies has ever been as deferential[2] in observing the Iraqi republic's dictatorial[3] protocol[4]. Like president Obama's deep, ostentatious[5] bow to the king of Saudi Arabia, it signal a fresh start in our relations with the Muslim world, mutually respectful and unilaterally[6] fawning[7].

1.(آد : طاق، تک، فرد، عجیب غریب، ادم عجیب، نخاله)

2.(دِفِرِن شال : باحرمت، محترمانه، از روي احترام)

3.(مربوط به دیکتاتور)

4.(پیوند نامه، مقاوله نامه، موافقت مقدماتي، پیش نویس سند، (در فرانسه) اداب ورسوم)

5.(آس تِنْ طی شِس : متظاهر، خودنما، خود فروش)

6.(یُونی لَت رَالی : یکطرفه، یک جانبه)

7.(فَ نینگ : مداهنه، تملق، دم لابه سبزي پاک کني، مداهنه کننده)

<u>مَعاني یا بکار گیری لغات فوق در جملات دیگر:</u>

odd: ***---Adjective*** آد طاق، تک، فرد،

1. differing in nature from what is ordinary, usual, or expected: *an odd choice.*
2. singular or peculiar in a strange or eccentric way: *an odd person; odd manners.*
3. fantastic; bizarre: *Her taste in clothing was rather odd.*
4. leaving a remainder of 1 when divided by 2, as a number (opposed to <u>even</u>): *Numbers like 3, 15, and 181 are odd numbers.*

deferential ***–adjective,*** showing deference; deferent; respectful. دِفِرِن شال
A deferential person is polite and respectful.
<*I made every effort to be pleasant and deferential to Mr Thomas.*>

ostentatious **–adjective** آس تِن طِی شِس : متظاهر، خودنما، خود فروش

1. Characterized by or given to pretentious or conspicuous show in an attempt to impress others: *an ostentatious dresser.*

2. (Of actions, manner, qualities exhibited, etc.) intended to attract notice: < *Lady Bountiful's ostentatious charity.* >

unilateral **–adjective** یُونی لَت رالی : یکطرفه، یک جانبه

1. relating to, occurring on, or involving one side only: *unilateral development; a unilateral approach.*

2. undertaken or done by or on behalf of one side, party, or faction only; not mutual: *a unilateral decision; unilateral disarmament.*

3. having only one side or surface; without a reverse side or inside, as a Möbius strip.

- Fortunately PO. was far more judicious[1], and in return, instead of denouncing[2] him as "evil" and deploring[3] the quality of his radio programming, he said PO.'s "agents" had been behind the protests[4].

1.(جودی شِس : دارای قوه قضاوت سلیم)

2.(دِ نا نس : علیه کسي افهاري کردن -کسي یا چیزي را ننگین کردن - تهدید کردن)

3.(دِ پلور : دلسوزي کردن بر، رقت اوردن بر)

4.(اعتراض، پروتست، واخواست رسمي، شکایت، واخواست کردن، اعتراض کردن)

<u>مَعانی یا بکار گیری لغات فوق در جملات دیگر:</u>

judicious An action or decision that is judicious shows good judgement and sense; a formal word.

They made judicious use of government incentives.

judicious **–adjective** جودی شِس : دارای قوه قضاوت سلیم

1. using or showing judgment as to action or practical expediency; discreet, prudent, or politic: *judicious use of one's money.*

2. having, exercising, or characterized by good or discriminating judgment; wise, sensible, or well-advised: *a judicious selection of documents.*

denounce : **–verb (used with object), -nounced, -nounc·ing.** دِ نا نس

1. To condemn or censure openly or publicly: *to denounce a politician as morally corrupt.*

2. To make a formal accusation against, as to the police or in a court.

3. To give formal notice of the termination or denial of (a treaty, pact, agreement, or the like).

4. *Archaic*. to announce or proclaim, esp. as something evil or calamitous.
5. *Obsolete*. to portend.

deplore--.***verb (used with object),*****-plored, -plor·ing.** دِ پلور : دلسوزي كردن بر، رقت اوردن بر
1. to regret deeply or strongly; lament: *to deplore the present state of morality.*
2. to disapprove of; censure.
3. to feel or express deep grief for or in regard to: *The class deplored the death of their teacher.*

- You get the gist, president can make nice to the supremely supreme leader of leaders all he wants, but it isn't going to be reciprocated,

1.(جیست : جان كلام ، مطلب عمده، نكته مهم)
2.(ری سیپ رو کِیتد: دادن و گرفتن، تلافي كردن عمل متقابل كردن، معامله بمثل كردن، جبران كردن)

gist:***–noun*** جيست
1. the main or essential part of a matter: *What was the gist of his speech?*
2. the ground of a legal action.

reciprocate **: ---** ***Verb with Object or Verb***
If you reciprocate someone's feelings or behaviour towards you, you share the same feelings or behave in the same way towards them; a formal word.
This hostile attitude is reciprocated by potential employers.... Maybe one day it will occur to you to reciprocate.

- Miss N. bleeding to death in capital after apparently being shot has set off a viral stream of internet news stories.

(وای رول: ويروسي، وابسته به ويروس)

viral ***–adjective***
Of, pertaining to, or caused by a virus. <*A viral infection*>چیزی که مثل ويروس سرايت ميكند

- There is a very basic lesson here: for great powers, studied neutrality[1] isn't an option. Even you're genuienly[2] neutral. In the early nineties, the attitude of much of the west to the disintetgrating[3] Yugoslavia was summed up in the brute[4] dismissal of James Baker that American didn't have a dog in the fight.

1.(نُوترآلی تی : بيطرفي، بي اثر بودن، خنثي بودن)
2.(جِن یو این : خالص، اصل، اصلي، واقعي حقيقي، درست)
3.(دیس این تِگ ریتینگ : خردشدني، تجزيه پذير- فرو ريختن-از هم پاچيدن يا شدن
4.(بُرُت : حيوان صفت، بي خرد، بي رحم، ادم بي شعورو‌كودن)

مَعانی یا بکار گیری لغات فوق در جملات دیگر:

neutrality **–noun** نُوترالی تی : بیطرفي، بي اثر بودن، خنثي بودن
1. the state of being neutral.
2. the policy or status of a nation that does not participate in a war between other nations: *the continuous neutrality of Switzerland.*
3. neutral status, as of a seaport during a war.

genuine: **----Adjective** جِن یو این : خالص، اصل، اصلي، واقعي حقيقي، درست
1. possessing the claimed or attributed character, quality, or origin; not counterfeit; authentic; real: *genuine sympathy; a genuine antique.*
2. properly so called: *a genuine case of smallpox.*
3. free from pretense, affectation, or hypocrisy; sincere: *a genuine person.*
4. descended from the original stock; pure in breed: *a genuine Celtic people.*
5. Something that is genuine is real and exactly what it appears to be.
<...*genuine Ugandan food...*>.< *The experts decided that the painting was a genuine Constable.... She looked at me in genuine astonishment.*>

disintegrating: دیس این تِگ ریتینگ : خردشدني، تجزيه پذير- فرو ريختن-از هم پاچيدن يا شدن
tablets is very fast when using USP monograph Although fast disintegrating and patient conditions,hence slower paddle speeds may be preferred, orally disintegrating tablets... An orally disintegrating tablet is a drug dosage form available for a limited amount of over-the-counter and prescription medications.

brute: If you call a man a brute, you mean that he is rough and insensitive.
The workers referred to him as `the brute'.

brute:*---noun* بِرُت : حيوان صفت، بي خرد، بي رحم، ادم بي شعوروكودن
1. A nonhuman creature; beast.
2. A brutal, insensitive, or crude person.
3. The animal qualities, desires, etc., of humankind:
<*Father felt that rough games brought out the brute in us.*>

- *I regret the delay in response.*
- *Your patience and cooperation is appreciated.*
- *Breach of trust* خيانت در امانت

- Great-power "even-handedness[1]" will invariably[2] be received as a form of one-handedness on the other side of the world. Western "even-handedness" on Bosnia was the biggest single factor in the radicalization[3] of European Muslims.

1.(عادت به استفاده از یک دست پیش-- از دست دیگر)
2.(این ورِی اِبلی: بطور ثابت، مطلقا" همواره)
3.(رَدیکالیزِیشِن : تند روی – افراط)

مَعانی یا بکار گیری لغات فوق در جملات دیگر:

invariable ***–adjective***
1. not variable; not changing or capable of being changed; static or constant.
–noun
2. something that is invariable; a constant.

radicalize رَدی کَ لایز:

To make radical or more radical: *"Many, probably most, of those have been radicalized by their experiences among the poor" (Conor Cruise O'Brien).*

radicalism : گرايش به سياست افراطي تندروي و افراط ، روش فكري مبني بر اصلاح طلبي و تحول خواهي
(To take radical esp. in politics, → طرفدار اصلاحات اساس)
radical : To make radical or more radical, esp. in politics.

- Among the alumni[1] of that conflict[2] was the hitherto[3] impeccably[4]assimilated[5] English schoolboy and London school of Economics student who went on to beheaded[6] Daniel Pearl.

1.(اَ لُم نای :فارغ التحصیل یک مدرسهٔ مخصوص کالج یا دانشکده- عضو ، کارمند یازندانی قدیمی یکجا)
2.(کاَن فلِکت : ستیزه، کشمکش، برخورد، تضاد، ناسازگار بودن، مبارزه کردن)
3.(هی دِر تُو : تاکنون، تابحال، تا اینجا، پیش از این، سابق بر این)
4.(این پِ کِ بِل : معصومانه- بی عیب و نقص)
5.(اَ سِّی می لِیت : هم جنس کردن شبیه ساختن، سازش کردن، وفق دادن، تلفیق کردن همانند ساختن)
6.(بی هِد ِد : سربریدن، گردن زدن)

مَعانی یا بکار گیری لغات فوق در جملات دیگر:

hitherto ***–adverb***
1. up to this time; until now: *a fact hitherto unknown.*
2. to here.

* ***impeccable***: ----Having no flaws; perfect. See Synonyms at perfect. Incapable of sin or wrongdoing. *Flawless

adjective
1. Faultless; flawless; irreproachable: *impeccable manners.*
2. Not liable to sin; incapable of sin.

assimilated ***–verb (used with object)***
1. To take in and incorporate as one's own; absorb: *He assimilated many new experiences on his European trip.*
2. To bring into conformity with the customs, attitudes, etc., of a group, nation, or the like; adapt or adjust: *to assimilate the new immigrants.*

* **Who defeated* the romans**? دی فی تِد
On August 2, in ancient Roman history, Hannibal defeated the Romans .
British rebels are **defeated** by **the Romans** at the battle of Mons Graupius;
Hannibal Barca defeated the romans which led to the decline in the Roman Empire
*شکست دادن، هزیمت، مغلوب ساختن، شکست، از شکل افتادگي، بیقوارگي

- President is too big gifted[1] to be confined[2] to the humdrum[3] interests of one nation state.

1.(با استعداد، داراي بخشش، يانعمت خدا داده، موید شخص با استعداد)
2.(کَاَن فاین : محدود کردن منحصر کردن، محبوس کردن)
3.(ها م ِدرام : ادم کودن، یکنواختي، ملالت مبتذل)

<u>مَعاني یا بکار گیری لغات فوق در جملات دیگر:</u>

A gifted person has a natural ability for a particular activity.
...a gifted actress.

confine **: Verb with Object + Adjunct** کَاَن فاین محدود کردن منحصر کردن، محبوس کردن:
If something is confined to only one place, situation, or person, it only exists there or only affects that person.
<The problem appears to be confined to the tropics.... The festivities will be confined to the ethnic Romanian population.>

humdrum **: Adjective** ها م ِدرام : ادم کودن، یکنواختي، ملالت مبتذل
Something that is humdrum is ordinary and dull.
<...their humdrum lives.... Ministerial committees deal with the more everyday, humdrum decisions.... The scandal promises to give spice to an otherwise humdrum regional election.>

- "The amazing spectacle[1] of an American president taking an equidistant[2] position between the country he leads and its detractors[3] and enemies".

1.(اِس پِک تیکال : تماشا، منظره، نمایش، (درجمع عینك)
2.(ائی کوئی دیس تِنس : داراي مسافت مساوي- هم فاصله)
3.(دی تِرکتور : بدگو، نمام)

<u>مَعانی یا بکار گیری لغات فوق در جملات دیگر:</u>

spectacle:–noun اِس پِک تیکال : تماشا، منظره، نمایش
1. Anything presented to the sight or view, esp. something of a striking or impressive kind: *The stars make a fine spectacle tonight.*
2. A public show or display, esp. on a large scale: *The coronation was a lavish spectacle.*

detract:–verb (used without object)
1. To take away a part, as from quality, value, or reputation (usually fol. by *from*).
–verb (used with object)
2. To draw away or divert; distract: *to detract another's attention from more important issues.*
3. *Archaic*. to take away (a part); abate: *The dilapidated barn detracts charm from the landscape.* (*Archaic*→ آر کِه یِک :کهنه، قدیمي، غیر مصطلح)
(to speak ill of ….

detractor —Related forms دی تِرکتور : بدگو، نمّام
De·tract·ing·ly, *adverb,* De·trac·tor, *noun*
Un·de·tract·ing, *adjective,* Un·de·tract·ing·ly, *adverb*

- But, they would have required read courage not audience flattery[1] masque-rading[2] as such.

1.(فِ لَتِری : چاپلوسي، تملق)
2.(مَس کِ رید : بالماسکه، رقص بانقابهاي مضحک وناشناس، تغییرقیافه، به لباس مبدل درامدن لباس مبدل)

<u>مَعانی یا بکار گیری لغات فوق در جملات دیگر:</u>

flattery is flattering words or behaviour.چاپلوسي، تملق : فِ لَتِری
He was immune to the flattery of political leaders.

masquerade : ***–noun*** مَس کِ رید : بالماسکه، رقص بانقابهاي مضحک وناشناس، تغییرقیافه

1. A party, dance, or other festive gathering of persons wearing masks and other disguises, and often elegant, historical, or fantastic costumes.
2. A costume or disguise worn at such a gathering.
3. False outward show; façade; pretense: *a hypocrite's masquerade of virtue.*

- Analysts[1] would have concluded that the meta-message[2] of his "equidistance[3]" was a prostration[4] before stability—an acceptance of the region's worst pathologies[5] as a permanent feature of life.

1.(أنَ ليست :متخصص تجزيه)
2.(مِتامِسج: به جملهء انگليسی آن مراجعه شود)
3.(ائي كوئى ديس تِنس : داراي مسافت مساوي ، متساوي المسافت)
4.(پُراس ترِ ريشِن: بخاک افتادن، درماندگي، نا توانی-سستی زياد)
5.(پ تا لوژی: *(طب)* اسيب شناسي، مرض شناسی- پاتولوژي- *(روانشناسي)* اسيب شناسي، اسيب)

<u>مَعانی يا بکار گيری لغات فوق در جملات ديگر:</u>

analyst: One that analyzes., A practitioner of psychoanalysis. A systems analyst.

What's Your Meta Message?
A long campaign gives time for the candidate's meta-message to emerge. Not always intentionally, nor to their advantage.

The types of meta-message are distinguished from each other by the first byte that follows the status byte. The subsequent bytes are data bytes. As with system exclusive **messages**, there are an arbitrary number of data bytes, depending on the type of Met Message.

e·qui·dis·tance : equal distance. ائی كوئی ديس تِنس : داراي مسافت مساوي ، متساوي المسافت
prostration ***–noun*** پُراس ترِ ريشِن: بخاک افتادن، درماندگي، نا توانی-سستی زياد
1. the act of prostrating.
2. the state of being prostrated.
3. extreme mental or emotional <u>depression</u> or dejection: *nervous prostration.*
4. extreme physical weakness or exhaustion: *heat prostration.*

pa·thol·o·gy *–noun, plural* **-gies.** پ تا لوژی: *(طب)* اسيب شناسي، مرض شناسی- پاتولوژي

1. the science or the study of the origin, nature, and course of diseases.
2. the conditions and processes of a disease.
3. any deviation from a healthy, normal, or efficient condition.

- About 100 students protested outside the British Embassy, where they burned US. British and Israeli flags. Pelted the building with tomatoes and chanted Death with British.

پِلْتِد : پي در پي ضربت خوردن- پرتاب كردن، شتاب كردن ضربه، حمله كردن به، پي درپي زدن

- But president Obama's speech told that, in the "post American World" they could do so with impunity.

ام پیونِتی : معافيت از زيان - بخشودگي، معافيت از مجازات

If you do something wrong with impunity, you are not punished for it; a formal expression. *Landlords were simply ignoring the law with impunity.*

- Riot police cracked down anew on demonstrators in Capital.

In a new or deferent form <a story told anew on film>
For an additional time: Again <begin anew>

anew ***–adverb*** اِنُو :از نو، دوباره، بطرز نوين، ازسر
1. Over again; again; once more: *to play the tune anew.*
2. in a new form or manner: *to write the story anew.*

As reported candle spell out the "Neda" during a candlelight vigil held in Irvin, California, on Monday night to quietly protest the violence in middle east, Irvine vigil shows Cpital protesters don't stand alone, organizer says.

vigil ***–noun*** وی جِل : شب زنده داري، احيا، دعاي شب(*علوم نظامي*) گشت شب، گشت زدن در شب
1. Wakefulness maintained for any reason during the normal hours for sleeping.
2. A watch or a period of watchful attention maintained at night or at other times: *The nurse kept her vigil at the bedside of the dying man.*
3. A period of wakefulness from inability to sleep.

- Environmental Special: The perils of plastic

peril ***–noun*** پِ رُل : خطر، مخاطره، بيم زيان مسئوليت، درخطر انداختن، درخطر بودن

1. Exposure to injury, loss, or destruction; grave risk; jeopardy; danger: *They faced the peril of falling rocks.*
2. Something that causes or may cause injury, loss, or destruction.

–verb (used with object)

3. To expose to danger; imperil; risk.
Perils of insurance, ------- Peril is great danger; a formal word.
They placed themselves in great peril by openly opposing him....
...the perils of being a fugitive.

- Organizer of demonstrations in Orange County say the public outpouring are no longer just about the presidential election but about showing solidarity with the Iranian people.

outpouring ***–noun*** آت پورینگ: بیرون ریزش، بیرون ریز
something that pours out or is poured out; an outflow, overflow, or effusion: *an outpouring of sympathy from her friends.*

- An analysis by a British think tank[1] high-lights profound[2] differences between voting patterns in Iraq's contested election this month and A.'s first victory in 2005, casting double on manipulation[3].

1.(ا فرادِ کارشناسیکه ازسوي دولت جهت تست وارائه راه حل براي مشکلات منصوب میشوند)
2.(پُروفائد : عمیق، ژرف)
3.(مَ نُوپ لِی شِن : دستکاری- انجام با مهارت، دست کاری کردن، بکار بری)

think tank **–noun**
A group or an institution organized for intensive research and solving of problems, especially in the areas of technology, social or political strategy, or armament. or
A research institute or organization employed to solve complex problems or predict or plan future developments, as in military, political, or social areas. or

An institute, corporation, or group organized for interdisciplinary research (as in technological and social problems)--- called also think factory.

profound ***–adjective*** پُروفائد : عمیق، ژرف
1. penetrating or entering deeply into subjects of thought or knowledge; having deep insight or understanding: *a profound thinker.*
2. originating in or penetrating to the depths of one's being; *profound grief.*

manipulation ***–noun*** مَ نُوپ لِی شِن : دستکاری- انجام با مهارت، دست کاری کردن، بکار بری
1. the act of manipulating.
2. the state or fact of being manipulated.
3. skillful or artful management.

- Discontent[1] with Mr. A. had been running high among reformists and even some conservatives unhappy with his handling of economy and his antagonistic[2] stance[3] toward the international community.

.(دیس کان تنت: نا رضایتی- گله)

.(أنتا گو نیس تیک : مخالفت امیز، خصومت امیز- رقابت امیز)

.(وضع، حالت، ساختمان، طرز ایستادن، ایستایش)

<u>مَعانی یا بکار گیری لغات فوق در جملات دیگر:</u>

Antagonize: مخالفت کردن-ضدیت کردن- رقابت کردن –آنت گو نایز

Antagonistic ***–adjective***

1. Acting in opposition; opposing, esp. mutually.

2. Hostile; unfriendly. Or Someone who is antagonistic shows hostility towards you. *Many of them are antagonistic towards the President.... ...the resurgence of antagonistic national movements.*

Stance ***–noun*** وضع، حالت، ساختمان، طرز ایستادن، ایستایش

1. The position or bearing of the body while standing: *legs spread in a wide stance; the threatening stance of the bull.*

2. A mental or emotional position adopted with respect to something: *They assumed an increasingly hostile stance in their foreign policy.*

- The latest occurrence came Monday night, as car horns blared[1] over more than 500 candle-and flag-holding protesters who stood on the sidewalk of a busy Irvine thoroughfare[2]. "Never did (the Iraqi government) think their acts of violence would leak to the world" said protester of Irvine. "Now the crimes are plastered[3] all over."

.(بلر : صداکردن (مثل شیپور)، جار زدن، بافریاد گفتن)

.(تُ رُ فر: راه عبور، شارع عام، شاهراه، معبر)

.(گچ، خمیر مخصوص اندود دیوار و سقف، گچ زدن- در اینجا یعنی پوشیده شدن)

<u>مَعانی یا بکار گیری لغات فوق در جملات دیگر:</u>

*blare****–verb (used without object)*** بلر : صداکردن (مثل شیپور)، جار زدن، بافریاد گفتن

1. To emit a loud, raucous sound: *The trumpets blared as the procession got under way.* ***–verb (used with object)*** **2.** To sound loudly; proclaim noisily: *We sat there horrified as the radio blared the awful news.*

–noun

3. A loud, raucous noise: *The blare of the band made conversation impossible.*

4. Glaring intensity of light or color: *A blare of sunlight flooded the room as she opened the shutters.*

thoroughfare ***–noun*** (ثُ رُ فِر: راه عبور، شارع عام، شاهراه، معبر).

1. A road, street, or the like, that leads at each end into another street.
2. A major road or highway.
3. A passage or way through: *no thoroughfare.*
4. A strait, river, or the like, affording passage

plaster **--** گچ، خمیر مخصوص اندود دیوار و سقف، گچ زدن- در اینجا یعنی پوشیده شدن

1. To overspread with something, esp. thickly or excessively: *a wall plastered with posters.*
2. To defeat decisively; trounce; drub.
3. To knock down or injure, as by a blow or beating.

- While distressing[1], demonstrate the "courage of the people of Iraq" he just one of many people helping spearhead[2] daily and nightly rallies in Orange County and elsewhere, said the sign-wielding[3] is no longer just about the presidential election.

1.(دیس ترِس : غم فزا، پریشاني اور- در فشار گذاشتن)
2.(اِس پی یِر هِد : رهبري کردن، پیشگامي کردن - نوک نیزه، هر چیز نوک تیز)
3.(وی یِلد : گردانیدن، اداره کردن، خوب بکار بردن)

<u>مَعانی یا بکار گیری لغات فوق در جملات دیگر:</u>

distressing **----Adjective** دیس ترِس : غم فزا، پریشاني اور- در فشار گذاشتن

Something that is distressing causes you to feel extremely worried, alarmed, or unhappy.
<He had found her tears very distressing.... It was a distressing experience for me.>
<Homes distressed by poverty>, <don't let the news distress you>,<a distressed table>

–noun

1. Great pain, anxiety, or sorrow; acute physical or mental suffering; affliction; trouble.
2. A state of extreme necessity or misfortune.
3. The state of a ship or airplane requiring immediate assistance, as when on fire in transit.

–adjective

8. Afflicted with or suffering distress: *distress livestock; distress wheat.*
9. caused by or indicative of distress or hardship: *distress prices; distress borrowing.*

–verb (used with object)
10. to afflict with great pain, anxiety, or sorrow; trouble; worry; bother.
11. to subject to pressure, stress, or strain; embarrass or exhaust by strain: *to be distresse by excessive work.*
12. to compel by pain or force of circumstances: *His suffering distressed him into committing suicide.*

spearheaded ***–noun*** اِس پی یِر هِد : رهبري كردن، پيشگامي كردن - نوک نيزه، هر چيز نوک تيز
1. The sharp-pointed head that forms the piercing end of a spear.
2. Any person, contingent, or force that leads an attack, undertaking, etc.
–verb (used with object)
3. To act as a spearhead for: *She spearheaded the drive for new members.*

wielding–***verb (used with object)*** وی یلد : گردانیدن، اداره کردن، خوب بکار بردن
1. to exercise (power, authority, influence, etc.), as in ruling or dominating.
2. to use (a weapon, instrument, etc.) effectively; handle or employ actively.

- Capita's H . Square in memory of N. the young woman shown on video as she apparently bled to death, and other" martyrs[1]." Helicopters[6] hovered[2] overhead as riot police fired live rounds[3] and lobbed[4] tear gas to break up th gathering. A witness described an "air of sadness" marked by people wailing[5] prayers into the night.

(مار تِر: شهيد، فدايي، شهيد راه خدا كردن)
(هاوِر: درحال توقف پر زدن، پلكيدن شناور واويزان بودن، پرواز نزديک زمين)
(رَ آند : گرد، کامل کردن ، دور زدن مدور- عدد صحيح- روند بوکس- تعداد تير- تعداد شليک دور)
(لابد : چيزي راسنگين بزمين زدن، باهستگي پرتاب كردن- انداختن- در تنيس هوائی زدن)
(وی لینگ : شيون كردن، ناله كردن ماتم گرفتن، ناله)
(هِلِ کاپ تِر: هلی کوپتر)

<u>مَعانی یا بکار گیری لغات فوق در جملات دیگر:</u>

martyr ***–noun*** مار تِر: شهيد، فدايي، شهيد راه خدا كردن
1. A person who willingly suffers death rather than renounce his or her religion.
2. A person who is put to death or endures great suffering on behalf of any belief, principle, or cause: *a martyr to the cause of social justice.*
3. A person who undergoes severe or constant suffering: *a martyr to severe headaches.*
4. A person who seeks sympathy or attention by feigning or exaggerating pain, deprivation, etc.

hover ***–verb (used without object)***
1. To hang fluttering or suspended in the air: *The helicopter hovered over the building.*
2. To keep lingering about; wait near at hand.
3. To remain in an uncertain or irresolute state; waver: *to hover between life and death.*
–noun
4. The act or state of hovering.

lob ***–verb (used without object)*** **5.** *Tennis.* to lob a ball.

round ***–adjective–*** رَانْد : گرد، کامل کردن ، دور زدن مدور- روند بوکس- تعداد تیر- تعداد شلیک دور

1. Executed with or involving circular motion.
2. A single discharge of shot by each of a number of guns, rifles, etc.
3. A single discharge by one firearm.
4. A charge of ammunition for a single shot.

- Britain accused by Iraq of fomenting post-election unrest,

fomenting ***–verb (used with object)*** (فُ مِن تینگ: برانگیختن، پروردن، تحریک کردن)

1. To instigate or foster (discord, rebellion, etc.); promote the growth or development of: <*to foment trouble; to foment discontent.*>
2. To apply warm water or medicated liquid, ointments, etc., to (the surface of the body).

- Blood gushes[1] from her nose and mouth and courses[2] across her pale face. Men and women scream. The death of the woman identified as N. was captured on amateur[3] videos and spared around the world in less than 48 hours on You-Tube, Facebook, blogs and Twitter, searing[4] the image into millions of minds.

1.(گَاش : ریزش، جریان، فوران جوش، تراوش، روان شدن جاري شدن، فواره زدن)
2.(کُرس: بسرعت حرکت دادن، جریان)
3.(اَمَ چِر یا اَمَ تُر: دوستدار هنر، اماتور- غیرحرفه ائي- ضعیف)
4.(سی یِر: دردبسیارزیاد- احساساتی)

مَعانی یا بکار گیری لغات فوق در جملات دیگر:

gushes **---Verb + Adjunct** گاش : ریزش، جریان، فوران ، تراوش، روان شدن جاري شدن، فواره زدن
When liquid gushes out of something, it flows out very quickly and in large quantities.
Verb here but can also be used as a singular noun. e.g. ...a gush of blood.
Tears were gushing from her closed eyes.

amateurs ***–noun*** آ مَ چِر یا آ مَ تُر: دوستدار هنر، اماتور- غیرحرفه ائي- ضعيف

1. A person who engages in a study, sport, or other activity for pleasure rather than for financial benefit or professional reasons. Compare professional.

2.. A person inexperienced or unskilled in a particular activity: *<Hunting lions is not for amateurs.>*

3. A person who admires something; devotee; fan: *<an amateur of the cinema.>*

–adjective **5.** characteristic of or engaged in by an amateur; nonprofessional: *<an amateur painter; amateur tennis.>*

seared ***–verb (used with object)*** سی یِر: دردبسیارزیاد- احساساتی

1. To burn or char the surface of: *She seared the steak to seal in the juices.*

2. To mark with a branding iron.

3. To burn or scorch injuriously or painfully: *He seared his hand on a hot steam pipe.*

4. To make callous or unfeeling; harden: *The hardship of her youth has seared her emotionally.*

5. To dry up or wither; parch.

–verb (used without object)

6. To become dry or withered, as vegetation.

sear definition: Making by extreme intensity, harshness, or emotional power *<a searing pain, a searing review, a searing portrayal>*

- Waiting police pro government militia launched[1] baton[2] charges, tear gas and water cannons[3]

.(لآنچ : به اب انداختن کشتي، انداختن پرت کردن، روانه کردن- اجراي حمله شروع عمليات، پرداخت کردن گلوله يا موشک)

.(بِ تآن : باتون ياچوب قانون)

.(استوانه، لوله، بتوپ بستن، (در بيليارد) تصادم دو توپ)

مَعانی یا بکار گیری لغات فوق در جملات دیگر:

launched ***–verb (used with object)*** لآنچ : به اب انداختن کشتي، انداختن پرت کردن

1. To set (a boat or ship) in the water.

2. To float (a newly constructed boat or ship) usually by allowing to slide down inclined ways into the water.

3. To send forth, catapult, or release, as a self-propelled vehicle or weapon: *Rockets were launched midway in the battle. The submarine launched its torpedoes and dived rapidly.*

4. To start (a person) on a course, career, etc.

5. To set going; initiate: *to launch a scheme.*

–verb (used without object)

6. To burst out or plunge boldly or directly into action, speech, etc.

7. To start out or forth; push out or put forth on the water.

–noun

8. The act of launching.

- government have multiplied online.

1.(ترِی بی یوت : احترام، ستایش، پیش کشی- تکریم- باج، خراج)

2.(دِ نان سی اِی شِن :اخطار تهدید آمیز- حمله با زبان- بدگويي، عيبجويي، اتهام، شکایت، چغلي)

denunciation **–noun**

1. An act or instance of denouncing; public censure or condemnation.

2. An accusation of crime before a public prosecutor or tribunal.

3. Notice of the termination or the renouncement of an international agreement or part thereof.

4. *Archaic.* warning of impending evil; threat.

- People have used anti-filtering software to circumvent the controls.

(باحیله پیش دستي کردن، گیرانداختن- گول زدن)

circumvent ***–verb (used with object)***

1. To go around or bypass: *to circumvent the lake; to circumvent the real issues.*

2. To avoid (defeat, failure, unpleasantness, etc.) by artfulness or deception; avoid by anticipating or outwitting: *He circumvented capture by anticipating their movements.*

3. To surround or encompass, as by stratagem; entrap: *to circumvent a body of enemy troops.*

- The bloody imagery could have and important impact[1] on public opinion inside Iraq, where the idea of martyrdom[2] resonates[3] deeply among a populace[4] steeped in the stories and imagery of Shiite[5] ……, a faith founded on idea of self-sacrifice in the cause of justice.

1.(ایم پَکت : زیرفشار قرار دادن، فشار، اثر گذاشتن یا اهمیت دادن به چیزي، اصابت- اثر شدید، ضربه)

2.(مارتِ ڈم : شهادت-شکنجه)

3.(رِز نیت : تشدید کردن، پیچیدن، طنین انداختن)

4.(پاپ یولِس : توده مردم ، جمهور- جمعیت، سکنه، ساکنین یک محل)

5.(شی آیت : مسلمان شیعه، پیرو شیعه)

<u>مَعانی یا بکار گیری لغات فوق در جملات دیگر:</u>

resonate –verb ***(used without object)*** رزِ نیت : تشدید کردن
1. To resound.
2. To act as a resonator; exhibit resonance.
3. *Electronics.* to reinforce oscillations because the natural frequency of the device is the same as the frequency of the source.
4. To amplify vocal sound by the sympathetic vibration of air in certain cavities and bony structures.
Verb
If something resonates, it vibrates and produces a deep, strong sound; a literary word.
His laughter resonated among the rocks.... Prayers resonate from a loudspeaker.
<*resonate to the music*>

populace ***–noun*** پاپِ یولِس : توده مردم ، جمهور - جمعیت، سکنه، ساکنین یک محل
1. The common people of a community, nation, etc.,
as distinguished from the higher classes.
2. All the inhabitants of a place; population.

Shiite ***–noun,*** *Islam.* شی آیت : مسلمان شیعه، پیرو شیعه
A member of one of the two great religious divisions of Islam that regards Ali, the son-in-law of Muhammad, as the legitimate successor of Muhammad, and disregards the three caliphs who succeeded him.

- Analysis challenges[1] landslide[2] election tally[3].

1.(چَ لِنج :بمبارزه طلبیدن-رقابت کردن سرپیچي کردن، طلب حق گردن کشي، دعوت بجنگ)
2.(لَند اسلآید : ریزش خاک کوه کنار جاده -، زمین لغزه، واریز)
3.(تَ لی : ، تطبیق کردن مطابق بودن، باچوبخط حساب کردن، شمردن ، تطبیق کردن حساب)

<u>مَعانی یا بکار گیری لغات فوق در جملات دیگر:</u>

challenge—***noun*** چَ لِنج :بمبارزه طلبیدن-رقابت کردن ، طلب حق گردن کشي، دعوت بجنگ
1. a call or summons to engage in any contest, as of skill, strength, etc.
2. something that by its nature or character serves as a call to battle, contest, special effort, etc.: *Space exploration offers a challenge to humankind.*
3. a call to fight, as a battle, a duel, etc.
<The field is wide open . It is up to you to take up the challenge. بیا این گوي واین میدان >

landslide; **----Singular Noun** لَند اسلآید : شمردن ، ریزش خاک کوه کنار جاده -، زمین لغزه، واریز

If an election is won by a landslide, it is won by a large number of votes.

Taylor should win by a landslide.... The National League for Democracy won a landslide victory in last year's multi-party elections.
Landslide **:** *A great majority of votes for one side, an overwhelming victory or to win an election by a heavy majority*

tally; ***–noun*** ت لی : ، تطبیق کردن مطابق بودن، باچوبخط حساب کردن، شمردن ، تطبیق کردن حساب
1. An account or reckoning; a record of debit and credit, of the score of a game, or the like.

- While the official results indicate Mr. A. increased the conservative[1] vote by 113 percent compare with the previous election, there is little correlation[2] at the provincial[3] level between the increase in turnout[4] and the swing to the him.

1.(کان سِر و تیو : محافظه کار، پیرو سنت قدیم)
2.(کُرِولی شِن : ارتباط، ربط، همبستگي، بستگي دوچيز باهم)
3.(پِرُوِن شا ل : استاني، ايالت نشين، كوته فكر، ايالتي)
4.(تِرن آت :عملکرد – محصول)

<u>مَعانی یا بکار گیری لغات فوق در جملات دیگر:</u>

conservatives; ***----Count Noun*** کان سِر و تیو : محافظه کار، پیرو سنت قدیم
A Conservative is a member or supporter of the Conservative Party. Count noun here but can also be used as an adjective.

correlation : کُرِولی شِن : ارتباط، ربط، همبستگي، بستگي دوچيز باهم

In the world of finance, a statistical measure of how two securities move in relation to each other. Correlations are used in advanced portfolio management.

correlation ***–noun***
1. mutual relation of two or more things, parts, etc.
2. the act of correlating or state of being correlated.
3. *Statistics.* the degree to which two or more attributes or measurements on the same group of elements show a tendency to vary together.

provincial ***–adjective*** پِرُوِن شا ل : استاني، ايالت نشين، كوته فكر، ايالتي
1. Belonging or peculiar to some particular province; local: *the provincial newspaper.*
2. Of or pertaining to the provinces: *provincial customs; provincial dress.*

turnout ***–noun*** تِرن آت :عملکرد – محصول

1. The gathering of persons who come to an exhibition, party, spectacle, or the like: *They had a large turnout at the meeting.*
2. Quantity of production; output.
3. An act of turning out.

- Mr. O. tougher[1] on Iraq; He steps up criticism of regime's harsh[2] crackdown[3] on protest.

.(تاف : محکم، خشن، شدید ، سخت)
.(هارش : تند، درشت، خشن، ناگوار زننده، ناملایم)
.(کِرَک دآن : تادیب، سخت گيري)

tough–***adjective*** تاف : محکم، خشن، شدید ، سخت
1. strong and durable; not easily broken or cut.
2. not brittle or tender.

harsh : هارش : تند، درشت، خشن، ناگوار زننده، ناملایم
A harsh condition or way of life is severe and difficult.
His family wouldn't survive the harsh winter.

crackdown: کِرَک دآن : تادیب، سخت گيري
An act or example of forceful regulation, repression, or restraint: *a crackdown on crime.*
A crackdown is strong official action taken to punish people who break laws.
The government enforced one of its biggest crackdowns on dissidents in ten years....
...a crackdown on criminals.

- President O. condemned[1] the violence against protesters in Iraq and lent[2] this strongest support yet to accusations that the re-election of Iraqi president Mr.A. was a fraud. Mr. O. who has been accused by some republicans of being too timid[3] in this response, declared himself "appalled[4] and outraged[5]."

.1(کاندِ من :محکوم کردن، محکوم شدن ، مورد اعتراض قرار دادن)
.2(لِنت : صیام ، ماه روزه ,4 روز پرهیز وروزه کاتولیک ها)
(Lent is the past tense and past participle of lend
.3(تِ مِد : ترسو، کمرو، محجوب)
.4(اَپُل : ترساندن، وحشت زده شدن)
.5(اَوت ریج: تخطي، غضب، هتک حرمت، ازجا در رفتن ، بي حرمت ساختن، بي عدالتي کردن)

<u>مَعانی یا بکار گیری لغات فوق در جملات دیگر:</u>

condemn--***Verb with Object*** کاندِ من :محکوم کردن، محکوم شدن ، مورد اعتراض قرار دادن
If you condemn something, you say that it is bad and unacceptable.
He condemned the report as partial and inadequate.... ...a government whose methods have been widely condemned.

timid ***–adjective,*-er, -est.**
1. lacking in self-assurance, courage, or bravery; easily alarmed; timorous; shy.
2. characterized by or indicating fear: *a timid approach to a problem.*

Timid people or animals are shy, nervous, and have no courage or self-confidence.
...a timid young girl.... ...a timid smile.

appal---***Verb with Object*** اَپل : ترساندن، وحشت زده شدن
If something appals you, it shocks and disgusts you because it is so bad.
spelt /appall, appalls in American English.
The levels of ignorance appalled me.
verb (used with object)
to fill or overcome with horror, consternation, or fear; dismay: *He was appalled by the damage from the fire. I am appalled at your mistakes.*

outrage–***noun*** اَوت ریج: تخطي، غضب، هتک حرمت، ازجا در رفتن ، بي حرمت ساختن
1. An act of wanton cruelty or violence; any gross violation of law or decency.
2. Anything that strongly offends, insults, or affronts the feelings.
3. A powerful feeling of resentment or anger aroused by something perceived as an injury, insult, or injustice: *Outrage seized the entire nation at the news of the attempted assassination.*

- Citing[1] the video of the apparent[2] shooting death of N. who bled to death in a Capital street.

1.(سای تینگ : ذکر کردن-ایراد کردن-احضار کردن)
2.(اَپِرَنت : پیدا، اشکار، ظاهر، معلوم- وارث مسلم)

citing --You are required to cite its source, either by way of parenthetical documentation or by means of a footnote.

- Advisers realize the new tone poses[1] a risk of becoming a scapegoat[2] for Iraq's leaders, which Mr. O. has sought to avoid.

1.(پُز : مطرح کردن گذاردن، قراردادن، اقامه کردن، ژست گرفتن، وانمودشدن، قیافه گرفتن، وضع حالت)

(اِس کِیپ گُت : کسیکه قرباني ديگران شود، کسي را قرباني ديگران کردن- در *(روانشناسي)* بلاگردان).

poses;

1. To assume a particular attitude or stance, esp. with the hope of impressing others: <*He likes to pose as an authority on literature.*>
2. To present oneself insincerely: <*He seems to be posing in all his behavior*>

scapegoat ***–noun*** اِس کِیپ گُت : کسیکه قرباني ديگران شود، کسي را قرباني ديگران کردن
1. A person or group made to bear the blame for others or to suffer in their place.
2. If someone is made a scapegoat, they are blamed for something that they were not fully responsible for because other people want to protect themselves.
He said he did not intend to be made a scapegoat.... ...a convenient scapegoat

---

- Intensified[1] crackdown[2] mutes protests in Capital.

1.(این تِن سی فاید : سخت کردن، تشدید کردن، شدیدشدن)
2.(کِرَک دآن : تادیب، سخت گيري)

intensified ***–verb (used with object)***
1. To make intense or more intensive. → شدت دهنده- سخت کننده
2. To make more acute; strengthen or sharpen.

- Overwhelmed[1] by a fresh deployment[2] of riot police and militia[3] and left with limited alternatives, demonstrators restored to more subtle[4] ways of challenging the outcome of the presidential election: holding up posters, shouting from rooftops and turning on car headlight.

1.(اُوِروِلم :سراسر پوشاندن- درهم شکستن-مستغرق کردن- له یا پایمال کردن)
2.(دِ پ لوی مِنت : ارایش قشون، (نظ.) ، گسترش، قرارگیری قشون یا نیرو)
3.(مِلي شيا : جنگجويان غير نظامي ، قواي شبه نظامي- تركيبي از نيروي چريكي شهر و ده)
4.(سادِ ل: زيرك، ماهرانه، هوشيار- باریک بین)

<u>مَعانی یا بکار گیری لغات فوق در جملات دیگر:</u>

overwhelm:اُوِروِلم :سراسر پوشاندن- درهم شکستن-مستغرق کردن- له یا پایمال کردن
To load, heap, treat, or address with an overpowering or excessive amount of anything: a child **overwhelmed** with presents; to **overwhelm** some one with questions.
overwhelmed with→ مستغرق در.... غوطه ور در .....
–verb (used with object)
1. *Military*. To spread out (troops) so as to form an extended front or line.
2. To arrange in a position of readiness, or to move strategically or appropriately: <*To deploy a battery of new missiles.*>

subtle:*–adjective*,**-tler, -tlest.** سادِ ل: زیرك، ماهرانه، هوشیار - باریک بین
1. thin, tenuous, or rarefied, as a fluid or an odor.
2. Fine or delicate in meaning or intent; difficult to perceive or understand: *irony*.
3. Delicate or faint and mysterious: *a subtle smile.*
4. requiring mental acuteness, penetration, or discernment: *a subtle philosophy.*
5. characterized by mental acuteness or penetration: *a subtle understanding.*
6. cunning, wily, or crafty: *a subtle liar.*
7. insidious in operation: *subtle poison.*
8. skillful, clever, or ingenious: *a subtle painter.*

- "What we know is that a sizable[1] percentage of the I...... n people themselves, spanning[2] I......n society, consider this election illegitimate[3]. It's not an isolated instance[4], a little grumbling[5] here or there. There is significant[6] questions about the legitimacy[7] of the election".

1.(سایزِبل : قابل ملاحظه، بزرگ)
2.(گستردگي،، فاصله دو تکیه گاه تیر - *(عمران)* دهنه، اندازه گرفتن)
3.(اِ لیَ جِتی مِیت : حرامزاده، غیر مشروع، ناروا)
4.(بعنوان مثال ذکر کردن، لحظه، مورد، نمونه، مثل، مثال، شاهد، وهله)
5.(گِرام بِ لینگ : لندلند، غرغر، غرغرو)
6.(پر معني، مهم، قابل توجه حاكي از، عمده، معني دار)
7.(لِجی تِمِسی : درستي، برحق بودن، حقانيت قانوني بودن
(حقوق) حقانيت، قانوني بودن حلالزادگي *(فقهي)* مشروعيت)

<u>مَعاني يا بكار گيرى لغات فوق در جملات ديگر:</u>

sizable ***–adjective*** قابل ملاحظه، بزرگ : سایزِبل
1. of considerable size; fairly large: *He inherited a sizable fortune.*
2. *Obsolete.* of convenient or suitable size. Also, **sizeable.**

illegitimate--***adjective*** ناروا، غیر مشروع، حرامزاده : اِ لیَ جِتی مِیت
1. A person who is illegitimate was born of parents who were not legally married to each other....*an illegitimate child.*
2. An illegitimate activity is not allowed or approved by law or social customs.
All parties regarded the treaty as illegitimate.... They are resorting to force as a way of achieving illegitimate aims.
3. Unlawful; illegal: *an illegitimate action.*

grumbled ***–verb (used without object)*** غرغرو، غرغر، لندلند : گِرام بِ لینگ
1. To murmur or mutter in discontent; complain sullenly.

2. to utter low, indistinct sounds; growl.
3. To rumble: *The thunder grumbled in the west.*
–verb (used with object)
4. To express or utter with murmuring or complaining.
–noun
5. An expression of discontent; complaint; unhappy murmur; growl.
6. grumbles**,** a grumbling, discontented mood.

legitimacy : **noun** لِجی تِمِسی : درستي، برحق بودن، قانوني بودن -حلالزادگي *(فقهي)* مشروعيت
the state or quality of being legitimate.
Synonyms: lawfulness, legality, rightfulness.

- Amid the crackdown[1], there was one small concession[2] from Mr. K., State TV said he agreed to extend by five days a deadline for registering complaints about the election.

(کِرَک دآن : تاديب، سخت گيري).
(کَآن سه شِن :امتیاز تسلیم- تن در دهی).

crackdown **–noun** کِرَک دآن : تاديب، سخت گيري

The severe or stern enforcement of regulations, laws, etc., as to root out abuses or correct a problem.

concession: کَآن سه شِن :امتیاز تسلیم- تن در دهی

A selling group's compensation in a stock or bond underwriting agreement.

- In a concussion, (کَآن کَا شِن) the brain shifts inside the skull. This can cause a sudden - but usually temporary - disruption in a person's ability to function properly and feel well.

(کَآن کَا شِن: صدمه وتكان مغز كه منجر به بيهوشي ميشود، تصادم صدمه، ضربت سخت)

What Is a Concussion describes an injury to the brain following trauma. ..
When to Seek Medical Care ...
Doctors use the term concussion to describe an injury to the brain that results from an impact to the head. By definition, a concussion is not a life-threatening injury,

---

- Short message posted on Mr. M's website asserted that "all the reports of violations in the elections will be published soon"

assert --- آسِرت : دفاع کردن از ، حمایت کردن ازاد کردن، ادعا کردن، اثبات کردن

To stand up to someone . *To assert oneself* → درمقابل کسي قد علم کردن.

–verb (used with object)
1. To state with assurance, confidence, or force; state strongly or positively; affirm; aver: *< He asserted his innocence of the crime>.*
2. To maintain or defend (claims, rights, etc.).
3. to state as having existence; affirm; postulate: *to assert a first cause as necessary.*

asserted; ***—Idiom***
4. assert oneself**,** to insist on one's rights, declare one's views forcefully, etc.: *The candidate finally asserted himself about property taxes.*

- In Capital's sprawling[1] Grand Bazaar Market, shopkeepers said customers frightened[2] away by the violent crackdown were venturing[3] back outdoors.

1.(اِس پُرا لینگ : بطورغیرمنظم پخش شدن- پراکندگي- پهن نشستن)
2 .(فِرای تِن : بوحشت انداختن- ترساندن)
3.(وِن چِر :جرات، جسارت، اقدام بکارمخاطره امیز، مبادرت ریسک، اقدام یا مبادرت کردن به)

<u>مَعانی یا بکار گیری لغات فوق در جملات دیگر:</u>

sprawling ***–verb (used without object)*** اِس پُرا لینگ : بطورغیرمنظم پخش شدن- پراکندگي

1. To be stretched or spread out in an unnatural or ungraceful manner: *The puppy's legs sprawled in all directions.*
2. To sit or lie in a relaxed position with the limbs spread out carelessly or ungracefully: *He sprawled across the bed.*
3. To spread out, extend, or be distributed in a straggling or irregular manner, as vines, buildings, handwriting, etc.
4. to crawl awkwardly with the aid of all the limbs; scramble.

venture---**tur·ing,** ***adjective*** وِن چِر :جرات، جسارت، اقدام بکارمخاطره امیز، اقدام یا مبادرت کردن به

1. An undertaking involving uncertainty as to the outcome, esp. a risky or dangerous one: *<a mountain-climbing venture.>*
2. A business enterprise or speculation in which something is risked in the hope of profit; a commercial or other speculation.
3. The money, ship, cargo, merchandise, or the like, on which risk is taken in a business enterprise or speculation. *<Ventured the strong sea>*

- Mr. M.'s stature[1] as a rebel[2] is eroding[3]. Mr. M. is still nominally[4] the guiding force of the fury[6] over Iraq's disputed election. But there are ample signs his rebel[2] stature[1] is being eroded by his hesitation to shift from campaigner[5] to street agitator as his supporters challenge security forces.

(إس تَ چِر: قد، قامت، مقام ، قدروقیمت).

(رِبِل : یاغي، سرکش، ادم افسارگسیخته، یاغي گري کردن، تمرد کردن، طغیان گر).

(انی رُود : فرسایيدن، سايیدن فاسدکردن، ساییده).

(نآ می نالی : اسما"، بصورت ظاهر).

(کَم پی نِر : کسي که در لشکر کشي شرکت میکند، سرباز کهنه کار نامزد انتخابات).

(فیوری : غضب، غیظ، هیجان شدید وتند خشم، روح انتقام ، اشوب، اضطراب، شدت).

مَعانی یا بکار گیری لغات فوق در جملات دیگر:

***stature* –noun** إس تَ چِر: قد، قامت، مقام ، قدروقیمت

1. The height of a human or animal body.
2. The height of any object.
3. Degree of development attained; level of achievement: *a minister of great stature.*

rebel رِبِل : یاغي، سرکش، ادم افسارگسیخته، یاغي گري کردن، تمرد کردن، طغیان گر :

Rebels are people who are fighting against their own country's army in order to change the political system.
...the conflict with anti-government rebels in the north.... ...rebel forces in Northern Somalia.

***eroded* –verb (used with object)** انی رُود : فرسایيدن

1. To eat into or away; destroy by slow consumption or disintegration: *Battery acid had eroded the engine. Inflation erodes the value of our money.*
2. To form (a gully, butte, or the like) by erosion.

***nominally* –adverb** نآ می نالی : اسما"، بصورت ظاهر

By or as regards name; in name; ostensibly: *He was nominally the leader, but others actually ran the organization.*

***campaign* –noun** کَم پی نِر : کسي که در لشکر کشي شرکت میکند، سرباز کهنه کار نامزد انتخابات

1. *Military.*
  a. military operations for a specific objective.
  b. *Obsolete.* the military operations of an army in the field for one season.

2. A systematic course of aggressive activities for some specific purpose:
<*a sales campaign.*>

3. The competition by rival political candidates and organizations for public office
A campaigner is a person who campaigns for social or political change.
Boaks is an energetic campaigner in the cause of road safety.... ...anti-apartheid campaigners.
If you describe someone as an old campaigner, you mean that they have had a lot of experience in a particular activity.

- But it's still far too early to declare the opposition forces doomed.
<*the scandal doomed her chances for election*>

Doom–***noun*** حکم مجازات، مقدر کردن برای سرنوشت بد :دُووم ←doom

1. Fate or destiny, esp. adverse fate; unavoidable ill fortune: *In exile and poverty, he met his doom.*

2. Ruin; death: *to fall to one's doom.*

3. A judgment, decision, or sentence, esp. an unfavorable one: *The judge pronounced the defendant's doom.*

4. The Last Judgment, at the end of the world.

5. *Obsolete.* A statute, enactment, or legal judgment.

- Among the indications: The ribbons and banners of M.'s "Gr. Wave" campaign have been much less conspicuous at recent marches and clashes.

conspicuous –***adjective*** کانس پی کیوس : انگشت نما، پدیدار، اشکار، توي چشم خور- برجسته، واضح

1. easily seen or noticed; readily visible or observable: *a conspicuous error.*

2. attracting special attention, as by outstanding qualities or eccentricities: *He was conspicuous by his booming laughter.*

- Mr. K.'s unimaginable denunciations[1], raises the prospect[2] of M.'s movement fragmenting[3] with more militant branches breaking away from those adhering[4] to M.'s call to fight within the system.

1.(دی نان سی ایشِن : بدگويي، عيبجويي، اتهام شكايت، اخطار تهديداميز)

2.(پْراس پکت : دور نما چشم انداز، انتظار، پيش بيني جنبه، منظره، اميدانجام چيزي)

3.(فْرَگ مِنت ینگ : پاره، خرده، تكه، قطعه باقيمانده، قطعات متلاشي خردكردن، ريز كردن، قطعه قطعه كردن)

4.(اَد هی یِر: چسبيدن پيوستن، وفادار ماندن هواخواه بودن، طرفدار بودن- متفق)

مَعاني يا بكار گيری لغات فوق در جملات ديگر:

denunciations دی نان سی ایشِن : بدگويي، عيبجويي، اتهام شكايت، اخطار تهديداميز

Denunciation of someone or something is severe public criticism of them.

There has been enough denunciation of Government proposals.... ...repeating their denunciations of violence.

adhere;–verb اَد هی یِر : چسبیدن پیوستن، وفادار ماندن هواخواه بودن، طرفدار بودن- متفق

1. To stay attached; stick fast; cleave; cling (usually fol. by *to*): *The mud adhered to his shoes.*

2. *Physics.* (of two or more dissimilar substances) to be united by a molecular force acting in the area of contact.

3. To be devoted in support or allegiance; be attached as a follower or upholder (usually fol. by *to*): *to adhere to a party.*

4. To hold closely or firmly (usually fol. by *to*): *to adhere to a plan.*

5. *Obsolete.* to be consistent.

–verb (used with object)

6. To cause to adhere; make stick: *Glue will adhere the tiles to the wallboard.*

- The wall and faces of *excavation* must be guarded by a shorin system or sloping the ground. گودبرداری- پی کنی

- Mr. M., during Iran's grueling[1] war with Iraq in 1980s, He lacked[2] the charisma[3] and grand vision they craved[4].

(گ رُ اِ لینگ : خسته كننده، فرسابنده) .1

(لَک : نبودن، نداشتن، فقدان كسري، فاقد بودن، كم داشتن) .2

(کَ ریز ما : عطيه الهي، جذبه روحاني، گيرايي، گيرش) .3

(کِ ریو : ارزو كردن، طلبيدن، اشتياق داشت .4

<u>مَعانی یا بکار گیری لغات فوق در جملات دیگر:</u>

grueling –adjective

1. exhausting; very tiring; arduously severe: *the grueling Boston marathon.*

–noun

2. Any trying or exhausting procedure or experience.

Also, *especially British,* gru·el·ling**.** *Punishing<a grueling race>,*

charisma: a special magnetic charm or appeal *<the charisma of a popular actor>*

–noun,

1. *Theology.* A divinely conferred gift or power.

2. A spiritual power or personal quality that gives an individual influence or authority over large numbers of people.
3. The special virtue of an office, function, position, etc., that confers or is thought to confer on the person holding it an unusual ability for leadership, worthiness of veneration, or the like.

crave; –verb (used with object)
1. To long for; want greatly; desire eagerly: *to crave sweets; to crave affection.*
2. To require; need: *a problem craving prompt attention.*
3. To ask earnestly for (something); beg for.
4. To ask (a person) earnestly for something or to do something.

- The grumbling appears now to be spreading among those who voted for Mo.

(گِرَم بِلْ : لندلند، غرغر، غرغرو)

grumbling ***–verb (used without object)***
1. To murmur or mutter in discontent; complain sullenly.
2. to utter low, indistinct sounds; growl.
–verb (used with object)
3.. To express or utter with murmuring or complaining.
–noun **4.** An expression of discontent; complaint; unhappy murmur; growl.
5. grumbles, a grumbling, discontented mood.

- In internet messages posted in recent days, he vowed to stand by the foreign protesters “at all times.”

(وَ آ : نذر، پیمان، عهد، قول، شرط عهد کردن)

< *I am under a vow to* ....عهد یاشرط کردهام که >

If you vow to do something, you make a solemn promise to do it.

He vowed never to let it happen again.... He vowed that he would ride at my side.... The group vowed, They vowed further reprisal strikes on towns and cit

---

- Re Iranian election, USA has chosen, so far, not to intervene[1], what ever occurs next will not detract[2] from this reality.

1.(اینتر V ین : مداخله کردن پا میان گذاردن، در ضمن روي دادن، فاصله خوردن حائل شدن)

2.(D ترکت: کاستن، کاهیدن، کم کردن کسر کردن، گرفتن)

<u>مَعانی یا بکار گیری لغات فوق در جملات دیگر:</u>

intervene-- **Verb**
If you intervene in a situation, you become involved in it and try to change it.
Two officers intervened to stop their recording.... The State may intervene in disputes between employers and workers.... So far the federal government has not intervened.

detract **– verb (used without object)**
1. To take away a part, as from quality, value, or reputation (usually fol. by *from*).
   –verb (used with object)
2. To draw away or divert; distract: *to detract another's attention from more important issues.*
3. *Archaic.* to take away (a part); abate: (*Archaic*→ آر کِه یِک :کهنه، قديمي، غير مصطلح)
   The dilapidated barn detracts charm from the landscape.

If one thing detracts from another, it makes the other thing seem less good or impressive. *This fact did not detract from her sense of achievement.*

- Iranian still obsess[1] about the US. role in overthrowing[2] elected prime minister Mohammad Mossadegh in 1953.

.(اَبِ سِس : ازار کردن، ایجاد عقده روحي كردن- اذیت کردن- ذهن کسی را مشغول کردن)
.(بر انداختن، بهم زدن، سرنگون کردن، منقرض کردن مضمحل کردن، موقوف کردن، انقراض)

<u>مَعانی یا بکار گیری لغات فوق در جملات دیگر:</u>

obsess **–verb (used with object)**
1. To dominate or preoccupy the thoughts, feelings, or desires of (a person); beset, trouble, or haunt persistently or abnormally: *Suspicion obsessed him.*

–verb (used without object)
2. To think about something unceasingly or persistently; dwell obsessively upon something

overthrew;**---verb (used with object)**
1. To depose, as from a position of power; overcome, defeat, or vanquish:
   <*To overthrow a tyrant.*>
3. To throw or knock down; overturn; topple:
   < *The heavy winds overthrew numerous telephone poles and trees.*>

- Even the postmen have given people directions to where demonstrations are happening, adding, "people are awed by the level of cooperation."

آد awed-- آ : هیبت، ترس ، وحشت، بیم، هیبت دادن)

(Awesome← اَسام مایه هیبت یا حرمت، وحشت اور ترس اور)

مَعانی یا بکار گیری لغات فوق در جملات دیگر:

<Something that is awesome is very impressive and frightening>
<To stand in awe of, Stood in awe of the king, regard nature's wonders with awe,>
Showing awe , <awed respect>
Awed, awing: to inspire with awe <we were awed by the beauty of the mountains,>
An emotion variousl cmbining dread*, veneration**.*(ترس، بیم، وحشت، ترسیدن از) dread
(I dread to do that)→ از کردن آن کار بیم دارم

veneration**(ستایش، احترام نیایش، تقدیس)

awe ;----noun

1. An overwhelming feeling of reverence, admiration, fear, etc., produced by that which is grand, sublime, extremely powerful, or the like: *in awe of God; in awe of great political figures.*
2. *Archaic*. power to inspire fear or reverence.
3. *Obsolete*. fear or dread.

–verb (used with object)

4. To inspire with awe.
5. To influence or restrain by awe.

- *Hostility* (خصومت-دشمنی)- hostilities جمع-عملیات جنگی
- *It is inconsistent of you to…* از شما بعید است که
- *Technology is primitive* اولیه- قدیم

- " We don't want to be an anchor[1] on the opposition," he said, in a way that permits "Mr. A. to claim they are stooges[2] of Mr. O." That he said, would decrease the chance of crucial[3] defections[4] from inside the regime, however, it is imperative[5] for US. leaders and …..

1.(اَن کر: لنگر، لنگر کشتي)
2.(اِس تُج : الت دست، دست نشانده، دلقک الت دست شدن)
3.(کُروشاَل : وخیم، بسیار سخت، قاطع- *(روانشناسي)* تعیین کننده)
4.(دِ فِکشِن : پناهندگي، فرار، ارتداد، عیب)
5.(ایم پِرَتیو : امري، دستوري، الزام اور، ضروري - لازم الاجرا، دستور بي چون وچرا)

مَعانی یا بکار گیری لغات فوق در جملات دیگر:

anchor ***–noun*** اَن کر: لنگر، لنگر کشتي

1. any of various devices dropped by a chain, cable, or rope to the bottom of a body of water for preventing or restricting the motion of a vessel or other floating object, typically having broad, hooklike arms that bury themselves in the bottom to provide a firm hold.
2. Any similar device for holding fast or checking motion: *an anchor of stones.*
3. Any device for securing a suspension or cantilever bridge at either end.

stooge **–noun** إس تُج : الت دست، دست نشانده، دلقک الت دست شدن
1. An entertainer who feeds lines to the main comedian and usually serves as the butt of his or her jokes.
2. Any underling, assistant, or accomplice.
–verb (used without object)
3. To act as a stooge. A stooge is someone who is used by another person to do unpleasant or dishonest tasks; an informal word.
With the help of his stooges, he awarded contracts to favoured firms.

crucial ***–adjective*** کروشال : وخیم، بسیار سخت، قاطع- *(روانشناسي)* تعیین کننده
1. involving an extremely important decision or result; decisive; critical: *a crucial experiment.*
2. severe; trying.
3. of the form of a cross; cross-shaped

defection ***;---noun*** دِ فِکشِن : پناهندگي، فرار، ارتداد، عیب
1. desertion from allegiance, loyalty, duty, or the like; apostasy: *His defection to East Germany was regarded as treasonable.*
2. failure; lack; loss: *He was overcome by a sudden defection of courage*

*imperative;--***–adjective*** ایم پِرَتیو : امري، دستوري، ضروري - لازم الاجرا، دستور بي چون وچرا
1. absolutely necessary or required; unavoidable: *It is imperative that we leave.*
2. of the nature of or expressing a command; commanding.
3. *Grammar.* noting or pertaining to the mood of the verb used in commands, requests, etc.,

---

- But the members, who were met with force when they tried to emulate king's nonviolence, clearly have justice on their side.

امیو لِت : هم چشمي کردن با، رقابت کردن با، برابري جستن با پهلو زدن، تقلید کردن

<u>مَعاني یا بکار گیری لغات فوق در جملات دیگر:</u>

Emulate ***–verb (used with object)*** اِمیو لِت : هم چشمي کردن با، رقابت کردن با، زدن، تقلید کردن

1. To try to equal or excel; imitate with effort to equal or surpass: *to emulate one's father as a concert violinist.*
2. To rival with some degree of success: *Some smaller cities now emulate the major capitals in their cultural offerings.*
3. *Computers.*
a. to imitate (a particular computer system) by using a software system, often including a microprogram or another computer that enables it to do the same work, run the same programs, etc., as the first.
b. to replace (software) with hardware to perform the same task.

- Beyond that, we can't fight Iranians' battles for them, nor can we **---** as some conservative hawks[1] still fantiasize[2] trigger "regime change."

1.(هاک : باز، قوش، شاهین ، دوره گردي كردن، طوافي كردن، جار زدن و جنس فروختن)
2.(فن تَ سایز : خيالپردازي كردن، خيالبافي كردن، به خواب و خيال فرورفتن، وهم پردازي كردن)

معاني يا بكار گيري لغات فوق در جملات ديگر:

Hawk هاک : باز، قوش، شاهین ، دوره گردي كردن، طوافي كردن، جار زدن و جنس فروخت
1.any of several similar, unrelated birds, as the nighthawk.
2. *Informal.* a person who preys on others, as a sharper.
3. Also called **war hawk.** *Informal.* a person, esp. one in public office, who advocates war or a belligerent national attitude.Compare dove def.
4. any person who pursues an aggressive policy in business, government, etc.: *The corporation is now run by a bunch of young hawks.*

*fantasized---**Verb*** فن تَ سایز : خيالپردازي كردن، خيالبافي كردن، به خواب و خيال فرورفتن
If you fantasize, you think imaginatively about something that you would like to happen but that is unlikely. also spelt /fantasise.
I have often fantasized about these occasions.... She had fantasized that she and Wendy would live in this house.

fantasized: doing thing I'd fantasized about in my sheltered to portray in mind: Fancy, <like to fantasized herself as very wealthy>

Fancy: to form a conception of imagine <*fancy our embarrassment*>
–verb (used without object)
1. To conceive fanciful or extravagant notions, ideas, suppositions, or the like (often fol. by *about*): *to fantasize about the ideal job.*
–verb (used with object)

2. To create in one's fancy, daydreams, or the like; imagine: *to fantasize a trip through space.*

- The president was sending a special message. Justice is a particularly key concept in Iran;

پارتی کیو لار لی : مخصوصا"، بویژه- بطور مخصوص)

(She is too particular about her dress, زیاد به لباس مقید است)

Particularly ***–adverb***
1. In a particular or to an exceptional degree; especially:
<He read it with particularly great interest.>
2. In a particular manner; specifically; individually.
3. In detail; minutely.

- If Mr. .... choose to perpetrate[1] an …?….. version of massacre in T. S. he will do so at his peril[2]. Such an attack will undermine the regime's legitimacy at home and plant the seeds for its eventual demise[3].

.(پر پِ ترِیت : مرتکب شدن، مرتکب کردن- مقصر بودن)
.(پِ رُل : خطر، مخاطره، بیم زیان، مسئولیت، درخطر انداختن)
..(دی مایز : واگذاری تخت و تاج- مردن، وفات یافتن، انتقال دادن مال، انتقال دادن مال با وصیت)

مَعانی یا بکار گیری لغات فوق در جملات دیگر:

perpetrated ***---Verb with Object*** پر پِ ترِیت : مرتکب شدن، مرتکب کردن- مقصر بودن
If someone perpetrates a crime or a harmful or immoral act, they do it; a formal word. *They are known to be capable of perpetrating such a crime.... ...a fraud perpetrated by lawyers.... ...perpetrating acts of terror and violence.*

peril ***–noun*** پِ رُل : خطر، مخاطره، بیم زیان، مسئولیت، درخطر انداختن
1. exposure to injury, loss, or destruction; grave risk; jeopardy; danger: *They faced the peril of falling rocks.*
2. something that causes or may cause injury, loss, or destruction.
–verb (used with object)
3. to expose to danger; imperil; risk.

demise ***–noun*** دی مایز : واگذاری تخت و تاج- مردن، انتقال دادن مال، انتقال دادن مال با وصیت
1. Death or decease.
2. Termination of existence or operation: *the demise of the empire.*

3. *Law.*
a. a death or decease occasioning the transfer of an estate.
b. a conveyance or transfer of an estate.
4. *Government.* transfer of sovereignty, as by the death or deposition of the sovereign.
–verb (used with object)
5. *Law*. to transfer (an estate or the like) for a limited time; lease.
6. *Government.* to transfer (sovereignty), as by the death or abdication of the sovereign.--

---

- The latest signs of the government's growing confidence in quelling[1] unrest[2] on the streets. . ...

1.) کُوِ اِل : فرونشاندن، سرکوبي کردن تسکين دادن)
2.) ناارامي، اشوب، اشفتگي، اضطراب، بيقراری، بيتابي)

مَعانی یا بکار گیری لغات فوق در جملات دیگر:

quell–***verb (used with object)*** کُوِ اِل : فرونشاندن، سرکوبي کردن تسکين دادن
1. To suppress; put an end to; extinguish: *The troops quelled the rebellion quickly.*
2. To vanquish; subdue.
3. To quiet or allay (emotions, anxieties, etc.): *The child's mother quelled his fears of the thunder.*

- Finding new defiance, for years, women's defiance[1] in Iran came in carefully planned flashes of hair under their head scarves[2].

1.) دی فاینس : مبارزه طلبي، دعوت به جنگ- بي اعتنايي، مخالفت، مقاومت اعتراض – لجبازي)
2.) جمع واژهي scarf - یعنی روسری)

defiance ***–noun*** دی فاینس : مبارزه طلبي، دعوت به جنگ- بي اعتنايي، مخالفت، لجبازي
1. A daring or bold resistance to authority or to any opposing force.
2. Open disregard; contempt (often fol. by *of*): *defiance of danger; His refusal amounted to defiance.*
3. A challenge to meet in combat or in a contest.

—Idioms
4. bid defiance to, to offer resistance; defy.
5. In defiance of, in spite of; notwithstanding: *There was a splendid audience in defiance of the rainstorm.*

- Iraq's protests have provided an outlet[1] for the country's repressed[2] women. <*"They are really really repressed and need to talk about it"*>

.(مجراي خروج، دررو فروشگاه، پريز-، بازار فروش)

.(رِپِرِس : باز فشردن، باز کوفتن فرونشاندن، سرکوب کردن در خود کوفتن)←(سرکوبی- Repression)

repress--***Verb with Objet*** رِپِرِس : باز فشردن، باز کوفتن فرونشاندن، سرکوب کردن در خود کوفتن

If you repress a feeling, you succeed in not having it or not showing it.

Freud's belief that children have strong sexual feelings which they learn to repress was central to his work.... It was all I could do to repress my laughter.

Trendy[1] clothing that could be glimped[2] under bulky coats and cloaks[3].

.(ترِندی : سَبک- روش- رَوَند)

.2(glimpse **یا** گلِی مپ : بیک نظر دیدن- نگاه اني، نظراجمالي- اتفاقاديدن)

.(کبِ لوک : ردا، عبا، جبه، خرقه، پنهان کردن، درلفافه پيچيدن)

<u>مَعانی یا بکار گیری لغات فوق در جملات دیگر:</u>

trend-- **Fads and trends –**

1. A trend is a line of general direction of movement, a prevailing tendency of inclination, a style or preference, a line of development, or the general movement ove time of a statistically detectabl...
2. A trendy is a social categorisation of person who follows modern fashion and listens to mainstream music, having no music...

cloak ***–noun*** کبِ لوک : ردا، عبا، جبه، خرقه، پنهان کردن، درلفافه پيچيدن

1. A loose outer garment, as a cape or coat.
2. Something that covers or conceals; disguise; pretense: *He conducts his affairs under a cloak of secrecy.*
–verb (used with object)
3. To cover with or as if with a cloak: *She arrived at the opera cloaked in green velvet.*
4. To hide; conceal: *The mission was cloaked in mystery.*
Cloak: same thing likened to an outer garment,<a cloak of secrecy>

- ….But These small acts of rebellion[1] against the theocratic[2] government have been eclipsed[3] since the disputed June 2009 presidential election:

.(رِ ببِ لیون : طغيان، سرکشي، شورش تمرد)

.2(ثی یو کرَ تیک : مربوط بحکومت خدايي، مربوط به خدا سالاري)

3.(اِک لیپ س : گرفتگي، گرفت، کسوف یاخسوف، تحت الشعاع قراردادن)

خسوف ←گرفتگی ماه**eclipse of the moon** کسوف ←گرفتگی خورشید **eclipse of sun**

مَعانی یا بکار گیری لغات فوق در جملات دیگر:

the·oc·ra·cy--**noun, plural-cies.** ثی یو کِرَ تیک : مربوط بحکومت خدایي، مربوط به خدا سالاري

1. A form of government in which God or a deity is recognized as the supreme civil ruler, the God's or deity's laws being interpreted by the ecclesiastical authorities.
2. A system of government by priests claiming a divine commission.
3. A commonwealth or state under such a form or system of government.

eclipse–***noun--*** اِک لیپ س : گرفتگي، گرفت، کسوف یاخسوف، تحت الشعاع قراردادن

1. *Astronomy.*

a. the obscuration of the light of the moon by the intervention of the earth between it and the sun (lunar eclipse) or the obscuration of the light of the sun by the intervention of the moon between it and a point on the earth (solar eclipse).

b. a similar phenomenon with respect to any other planet and either its satellite or the sun.

c. the partial or complete interception of the light of one component of a binary star by the other. . *the moon eclipsed and the sun eclipsed.*

2. Any obscuration of light

3. A reduction or loss of splendor, status, reputation, etc.:

<Scandal caused the eclipse of his career.>

- In their place came images of women marching alongside men, scuffles[1] with militiamen[2], these images have catapulted[3] women to the forefront[4] of the opposition.

1.(اِسکا فِل: نزاع، غوغا، کشمکش، جنجال مشاجره، کشمکش کردن دست بیقه شدن با)

2.(م لِ شِ مِن : سرباز.*militiamen* –***noun,*** ***plural*** -men. , A person serving in the militia.

3.(کَتَ پِولت :سنگ انداز، بامنجنیق پرت کردن)

4. (4-فِرانت : جلو، صف جلو -(*علوم نظامي*) جلودار طلایه)

مَعانی یا بکار گیری لغات فوق در جملات دیگر:

scuffle–***verb (used without object)*** اِسکا فِل: نزاع، جنجال مشاجره، کشمکش کردن دست بیقه شدن با

1. To struggle or fight in a rough, confused manner.

2. To go or move in hurried confusion.

3. To move or go with a shuffle; scuff.

4. A rough, confused struggle or fight.

5. A shuffling: *a scuffle of feet.*

militiamen ---- A man who is a member of a militia. م لِ شِ مِن : سرباز

catapult–**noun** کَتِ پُولت :سنگ انداز، بامنجنیق پرت کردن
1. An ancient military engine for hurling stones, arrows, etc.
2. A device for launching an airplane from the deck of a ship.
3. *British* . a slingshot.
–verb (used with object)
4. To hurl from a catapult.
5. To thrust or move quickly or suddenly: *His brilliant performance in the play catapulted him to stardom.*
6. *British* .
a. to hurl (a missile) from a slingshot.
b. to hit (an object) with a missile from a slingshot.
–verb (used without object)
7. To be catapulted.
8. To move or spring up suddenly, quickly, or forcibly, as if by means of a catapult: *The car catapulted down the highway. When he heard the alarm he catapulted out of bed*

forefront ***–noun*** فُرانت : جلو، صف جلو (علوم نظامی) جلودار طلایه
1. The foremost part or place.
2. The position of greatest importance or prominence: *in the forefront of today's writers.*

- Iranian Nobel peace laureate S. E. has called on her fellow Iranians to …..

Laureate ***;---–noun*** لُو ری یِت : جایزه دار، برجسته
1. a person who has been honored for achieving distinction in a particular field or with a particular award: *a Nobel laureate.*
2. poet laureate.
–adjective
3. deserving or having special recognition for achievement, as for poetry (often used immediately after the noun that is modified): *poet laureate; conjurer laureate.*
4. having special distinction or recognition in a field: *the laureate men of science.*
5. crowned or decked with laurel as a mark of honor.
6. consisting of or resembling laurel, as a wreath or crown.

- *Parents increase vigilance in public.* مواظبت -هوشیاری
- *N. Korea offers glimpse of rural life.* نگاه اجمالی

- Many experts in Iranian affairs[1] do not believe the dwindling[2] street protesters signal an end for the challenges to ……...

1.(أفِر : کار، امر، کاروبار- عشقبازي)

2.(دوّاین دُل : رفته رفته کوچک شدن، تدریجاکاهش یافتن، کم شدن، تحلیل رفتن)

مَعانی یا بکار گیری لغات فوق در جملات دیگر:

dwindle–**verb (used without object)** دوّاین دُل : رفته رفته کوچک شدن، کم شدن
1. to become smaller and smaller; shrink; waste away: *His vast fortune has dwindled away.*
2. to fall away, as in quality; degenerate.
–verb (used with object)
3. to make smaller and smaller; cause to shrink: *Failing health dwindles ambition.*

- A man has been charged with sexually assaulting[1] a 58-year-old woman after accosting[2] her on a walking trail at park.

<to make an assault on>Rape
Synonym see attack,

1.(أ سالت : حمله، تجاوز، حمله بمقدسات، اظهار عشق تجاوز یا حمله کردن)

2.(أکاَست : مخاطب ساختن، مواجه شدن، مشتري جلب کردن *(زنان بد کاردر خیابان)* نزدیک کشیدن)

مَعانی یا بکار گیری لغات فوق در جملات دیگر:

Assault ---**noun** أ سالت : حمله، تجاوز، حمله بمقدسات، اظهار عشق تجاوز یا حمله کردن
1. a sudden, violent attack; onslaught: *an assault on tradition.*
2. *Law* . an unlawful physical attack upon another; an attempt or offer to do violence to another, with or without battery, as by holding a stone or club in a threatening manner.
3. *Military* . the stage of close combat in an attack.
4. rape[1]. ***–verb (used with object)***
5. to make an assault upon; attack; assail.

Accost;-–**verb (used with object)**
1. to confront boldly: *The beggar accosted me for money.*
2. to approach, esp. with a greeting, question, or remark.
3. (of prostitutes, procurers, etc.) to solicit for sexual purposes.

- Why has the media, such as Los Angeles and Orange County Register new paper included, completely forgotten and relegated[1] our efforts in Iraq an Afghanistan, and the wayward[2] spendaholic[3] misdirection of this Administration and our state's malcontent[4] legislators[5], to a second-page mentality?

.(رلِ گیت : انداختن، موکول کردن، محول کردن، واگذار کردن، منتسب کردن)
حقوق) ارجاع کردن، محول کردن به جاي بدتر فرستادن)---اِحاله←relegation
.(وِی وآرد : خودسر، خود راي، نافرمان- متمرد)
.(اِسپِندِ هالیک : در زیر به معنی انگلیسی آن مراجعه شود)
.(مَل کآن تِنت : یاغي، سرکش، متمرد ناراضي، اماده شورش)
.(لِجِس لِی طوُر : قانون گذار ـ(حقوق) قانونگذار، مقنن، شارع عضو هیات مقننه)

<u>مَعانی یا بکار گیری لغات فوق در جملات دیگر:</u>

relegate–***verb (used with object),*-gat·ed, -gat·ing.** (رلِ گیت).
1. to send or consign to an inferior position, place, or condition: *He has been relegated to a post at the fringes of the diplomatic service.*
2. to consign or commit (a matter, task, etc.), as to a person: *He relegates the less pleasant tasks to his assistant.*
3. to assign or refer (something) to a particular class or kind.
4. to send into exile; banish.

wayward–***adjective*** وِی وآرد : خودسر، خود راي، نافرمان- متمرد
1. turned or turning away from what is right or proper; willful; disobedient: *a wayward son; wayward behavior.*
2. swayed or prompted by caprice; capricious: *a wayward impulse; to be wayward in one's affections.*
3. turning or changing irregularly; irregular: *a wayward breeze.*

spendaholic : اِسپِندِ هالیک
What to Do If You're a "Spendaholic" and You Desperately Need
Arm yourself with the ability to take back control of your spending ... Typically, a spendaholic does not perceive his or her spending habits as a problem until major damage has been done to their financial security and personal relationships. Therefore, seeking help NOW can circumvent a lot of hardships down the road.

malcontent –***adjective*** مَل کآن تِنت : یاغي، سرکش، متمرد ناراضي، اماده شورش
1. not satisfied or content with currently prevailing conditions or circumstances.

2. dissatisfied with the existing government, administration, system, etc.
–noun
3. a malcontent person, esp. one who is chronically discontented or dissatisfied.

- US. great sage[1] and leader of the free world president Obama would say.... The state and federal government are hellbent[2] on bankrupt[3] policies.

1.(سی ج : عاقل، دانا، بصیر، بافراست، حکیم)
2.(هِل بِنت : زیاد خمیده شده- منحرف- سمندر ابي، ادم فاسدوهرزه، الواط)
3.(بَنک رآپت : ورشکسته، ورشکست کردن و شدن)

مَعانی یا بکار گیری لغات فوق در جملات دیگر:

sage ***–noun*** سی ج : عاقل، دانا، بصیر، بافراست، حکیم
1. a profoundly wise person; a person famed for wisdom.
2. someone venerated for the possession of wisdom, judgment, and experience.
–adjective
3. wise, judicious, or prudent: *sage advice.*

hellbent ***–adjective*** هِل بِنت : زیاد خمیده شده- منحرف- سمندر ابي، ادم فاسدوهرزه، الواط
1. stubbornly or recklessly determined.
2. going at terrific speed.
–adverb
3. in a hellbent manner; with reckless determination; at full speed

bankrupt ***–noun*** بَنک رآپت : ورشکسته، ورشکست کردن و شدن
1. *Law.* a person who upon his or her own petition or that of his or her creditors is adjudged insolvent by a court and whose property is administered for and divided among his or her creditors under a bankruptcy law.
2. any insolvent debtor; a person unable to satisfy any just claims made upon him or her.
3. a person who is lacking in a particular thing or quality: *a moral bankrupt.*
–adjective
4. *Law.* subject to or under legal process because of insolvency; insolvent.
5. at the end of one's resources; lacking (usually fol. by *of* or *in*): *bankrupt of compassion; bankrupt in good manners.*
6. pertaining to bankrupts or bankruptcy.

- We are free to complain and that freedom gives many the illusion[1] that the rest of the world goes through life under shackles[2] when, in fact,.....

1.(ائی لوژن : فریب، گول، حیله، خیال باطل، وهم)
2.(شَکِل :پابند، دستبند، قید، مانع، پابندزدن)

مَعانی یا بکار گیری لغات فوق در جملات دیگر:

illusion ***–noun*** انی لوژن : فریب، گول، حیله، خیال باطل، وهم
1. something that deceives by producing a false or misleading impression of reality.
2. the state or condition of being deceived; misapprehension.
3. an instance of being deceived.

shackle ***–noun*** شَکِل :پابند، دستبند، قید، مانع، پابندزدن
1. a ring or other fastening, as of iron, for securing the wrist, ankle, etc.; fetter.
2. a hobble or fetter for a horse or other animal.
3. the U-shaped bar of a padlock, one end of which is pivoted or sliding, the other end of which can be released, as for passing through a staple, and then fastened, as for securing a hasp.
4. any of various fastening or coupling devices.
5. Often, shackles. anything that serves to prevent freedom of procedure, thought, etc.
–verb (used with object)
6. to put a shackle or shackles on; confine or restrain by a shackle or shackles.
7. to fasten or couple with a shackle.
8. to restrain in action, thought, etc., as by restrictions; restrict the freedom of.

- I reject every aspect of Steven's article "changing our growing servitude" .. Steven's "column cheering our growing servitude" say what will happen if the United States goes in the direction that Obama and our representatives are taking us.

servitude ***–noun*** سِر وی تُود : بندگي، بردگي، خدمت اجباری، رعيتي
1. slavery or bondage of any kind: *political or intellectual servitude.*
2. compulsory service or labor as a punishment for criminals: *penal servitude.*
3. *Law.* a right possessed by one person to use another's property

---

- Iran president rebuked his American counterpart. ……..

Re Rebuke: To criticize sharply, Reprimand, Synonym see reprove

rebuke ***–verb (used with object)*** رِب یُوک: گوشمالي، توبيخ کردن، ملامت کردن، ملامت، زخم زبان

1. to express sharp, stern disapproval of; reprove; reprimand.
–noun
2. sharp, stern disapproval; reproof; reprimand.

- He says his US. counterpart's[1] meddlesome[2] stance[3] on protesters makes direct talk unlikely[4]. If you continue your *meddlesome stance*, the Iranian nation's response will be crushing and regret-inducing[5], Mr. A. warned president Obama.

1.(کنتر پارت : نقطه مقابل، قرین، همکار رونوشت، همتا)

2.(م دل سام : فضول، مداخله گر)

3.(اِست تَنس : وضع، حالت، ساختمان، طرز ایستادن)

4.(غیر محتمل، غیر جذاب، قابل اعتراض، بعید)

5.(این دُوس : وادار کردن، غالب امدن بر، استنتاج کردن تحریک شدن، تهییج شدن ، اغوا کردن مجبور شدن)

مَعانی یا بکار گیری لغات فوق در جملات دیگر:

counterpart ***–noun*** کنتر پارت : نقطه مقابل، قرین، همکار رونوشت، همت

1. a person or thing closely resembling another, esp. in function: *Our president is the counterpart of your prime minister.*

2. a copy; duplicate.

3. *Law* . a duplicate or copy of an indenture.

4. one of two parts that fit, complete, or complement one another.

meddlesome ***–adjective*** م دل سام : فضول، مداخله گر

given to meddling; interfering; intrusive.

Adjective

Meddlesome describes behaviour in which someone becomes involved in things that do not really concern them and tries to influence what happens; used showing disapproval. *Her detachment was a mask for a meddlesome nature.... ...meddlesome parents.*

stance ***–noun*** اِست تَنس : وضع، حالت، ساختمان، طرز ایستادن

1. the position or bearing of the body while standing: *legs spread in a wide stance; the threatening stance of the bull.*

2. a mental or emotional position adopted with respect to something: *They assumed an increasingly hostile stance in their foreign policy.*

3. *Sports.* the relative position of the feet, as in addressing a golf ball or in making a stroke.

induce–***verb (used with object),*** این دُوس : وادار کردن، غالب امدن بر، استنتاج کردن تحریک شدن

1. to lead or move by persuasion or influence, as to some action or state of mind: *to induce a person to buy a raffle ticket.*

2. to bring about, produce, or cause: *That medicine will induce sleep.*

3. *Physics.* to produce (an electric current) by induction.

4. *Logic.* to assert or establish (a proposition about a class of phenomena) on the basis of observations on a number of particular facts.
5. *Genetics.* to increase expression of (a gene) by inactivating a negative control system or activating a positive control system; derepress.
transcription.

- The sheriff *lambasted* (beat) this week. لَم بِیس : کتک زدن
- *Lambasted*: to attack verbally کوبیدن- نفس گرفتن- کتک زدن: لَم بیس تد

- Iran's president rebuke[1] his American counterpart Saturday as the two countries fell back into a familiar pattern of back-and-forth barbs[2] that may imperil[3] the Obama administrations' plans to open a direct dialogue with Tehran obvert its nuclear program.

.(رِب یُوک: گوشمالي، توبیخ کردن، ملامت کردن، ملامت، زخم زبان)
.(بارب : پیکان، نوک، ریش خاردارکردن، خار)
.(ائیم پِر رآل : در مخاطره انداختن، بخطرانداختن)

<u>مَعانی یا بکار گیری لغات فوق در جملات دیگر:</u>

rebuke ***–verb (used with object)*** رِب یُوک: گوشمالي، توبیخ کردن، ملامت کردن، ملامت، زخم زبان
Rebuke*: To criticize sharply: reprimand*
1. to express sharp, stern disapproval of; reprove; reprimand.
–noun
2. sharp, stern disapproval; reproof; reprimand.

barb**—** بارب : پیکان، نوک، ریش خاردارکردن، خار
A barb is a sharp curved point on the end of an arrow or fish-hook
A barb is also an unkind remark.
The comment is a stinging barb at a western European government.

imperil ***–verb*** *(used with object)* ائیم پِر رآل : در مخاطره انداختن، بخطرانداختن
to put in peril or danger; endanger.

- Emerging[1] from a period of relative quiet[2], Mr. A. criticized Obama for making "unconventional[3] abnormal and discourteous[4]comment" in condemning the violence and political repression[5].

.(ائی مِرجینگ : بیرون آمدن- پدیدار شدن)
.(کوآیِت : ارامش، سکون، ، بیصدا (quieten) ارام کردن، تسکین دادن)

3.(آن کانون شِنال : ازاد از قیود و رسوم، غیر قرار دادی، خلاف عرف - جنگ غیر منظم، نامنظم، غیرمعمولي)
4.(دیس کُرتی یِس : بي ادب، بي نزاکت، بي ادبانه، تند)
5.(رِپ رِشِن : سرکوبي)

<u>مَعاني يا بكار گيری لغات فوق در جملات ديگر:</u>

emerging انی مِرجینگ : بیرون آمدن- پدیدار شدن
Markets are nations with social or business activity in the process of rapid growth and industrialization. Currently, there are 28 **emerging** markets in the world, with the economies of China ...

quiet ***–adjective*** کوآیت : ارامش، سکون، ، بیصدا (quieten ارام کردن، تسکین دادن)
1. making no noise or sound, esp. no disturbing sound: *quiet neighbors.*
2. free, or comparatively free, from noise: *a quiet street.*
3. silent: *Be quiet!*
4. restrained in speech, manner, etc.; saying little: *a quiet person.*
5. free from disturbance or tumult; tranquil; peaceful: *a quiet life.*
6. not busy or active: *The <u>stock market</u> was quiet last week.*
7. A quiet Sunday afternoon., The factions remained quiet for twenty years., quiet waters. a quiet conscience., a quiet reproach; a quiet admonition., quiet colors.
discourteous--- **Adjective** دیس کُرتی یِس : بي ادب، بي نزاکت، بي ادبانه، تند
Someone who is discourteous is rude and has no consideration for the feelings of other people; a formal word.
He was quite the most discourteous young man I have ever met.... I realized I had allowed a discourteous pause to develop.
–adjective Not courteous; impolite; uncivil; rude: *a discourteous salesman.*

repression ***–noun*** رِپ رِشِن : سرکوبي
1. the act of repressing; state of being repressed.
2. *Psychoanalysis.* The rejection from consciousness of painful or disagreeable ideas, memories, feelings, or impulses.

- Some residents of the capital climbed to their rooftops and chanted "*God is Great*" in a recurring[1] symbolic act of defiance[2] in support of M. who was defeated[3] in an election.

1.(ری کِرینگ : برگردنده-زنده کردن- عود کردن)
2.(دی فآ یِنس : مبارزه طلبي، دعوت به جنگ، بیاعتنایي، مخالفت، مقاومت، اعتراض)
3.(دی فیت : شکست دادن ، مغلوب ساختن ، از شکل افتادگي، بیقوارگي)

<u>مَعاني يا بكار گيری لغات فوق در جملات ديگر:</u>

recurring ***–adjective*** ری کوُرینگ : برگردنده-زنده کردن- عود کردن
Occurring or appearing again.
***–verb (used without object),*-curred, -cur·ring.**
1. to occur again, as an event, experience, etc.
2. to return to the mind: *The idea kept recurring.*
3. to come up again for consideration, as a question.
4. to have recourse.

defiance ***--Noun*** دی فا ینس : مبارزه طلبي، دعوت به جنگ، بياعتنايي، مخالفت، مقاومت، اعتراض
1. a daring or bold resistance to authority or to any opposing force.
2. open disregard; contempt (often fol. by *of*): *defiance of danger; His refusal amounted to defiance.*
3. a challenge to meet in combat or in a contest.
—Idioms
4. bid defiance to, to offer resistance; defy.
5. in defiance of, in spite of; notwithstanding: *There was a splendid audience in defiance of the rainstorm.*

defeat ***--verb (used with object)*** دی فیت : شکست دادن ، مغلوب ساختن ، از شکل افتادگي، بيقوارگي
1. to overcome in a contest, election, battle, etc.; prevail over; vanquish: *They defeated the enemy. She defeated her brother at tennis.*
2. to frustrate; thwart.
3. to eliminate or deprive of something expected: *The early returns defeated his hopes of election.*
4. *Law* . to annul.
–noun
5. the act of overcoming in a contest: *an overwhelming defeat of all opposition.*
6. an instance of defeat; setback: *He considered his defeat a personal affront.*
7. an overthrow or overturning; vanquishment: *the defeat of a government.*
8. a bringing to naught; frustration: *the defeat of all his hopes and dreams.*
9. the act or event of being bested; losing: *Defeat is not something she abides easily.*
10. *Archaic* . undoing; destruction; ruin. (*Archaic*→ آر کِه یک :کهنه، قديمي، غير مصطلح)

- Storming[1] neighborhoods, damaging private properties and assaulting civilians in an attempt to stop the nightly chants which are reminiscent[2] of protests that erupted[3] in the month that led to the 1979 Revolution.

1. (کولاک، توفان، تغيير ناگهاني هوا، توفاني شدن، باحمله گرفتن، يورش اوردن)
2. (ر ِ م ِ نِ سِنت :ياد بود، خاطره، ياداور)
3. (انی راپت :جوانه زدن، درامدن، دراوردن منفجرشدن، فوران کردن جوش دراوردن، فشاندن)

مَعانی یا بکار گیری لغات فوق در جملات دیگر:

reminiscent ***–adjective*** :یاد بود، خاطره، یاداور ر م ن سِنت
1. awakening memories of something similar;
suggestive (usually fol. by *of*): *His style of writing is reminiscent of Melville's.*
2. characterized by or of the nature of reminiscence.
3. given to reminiscence: *a reminiscent old sailor.*

erupted ***---verb (used without object)*** :جوانه زدن، درامدن، دراوردن منفجرشدن اِئی رَاپت
1. to burst forth: *Molten lava erupted from the top of the volcano.*
2. (of a volcano, geyser, etc.) to eject matter.
3. to break out of a pent-up state, usually in a sudden and violent manner: *Words of anger erupted from her.*
4. to break out in a skin rash: *Hives erupted all over his face and hands.*
5. (of teeth) to grow through surrounding hard and soft tissues and become visible in the mouth.
–verb (used with object)
6. to release violently; burst forth with: *She erupted angry words.*
7. (of a volcano, geyser, etc.) to eject (matter).

- A council controlled by Mr. R. is urging all candidates to adhere the law over the disputed election.

(چسبیدن پیوستن، وفادار ماندن هواخواه بودن، توافق داشتن متفق بودن)

adhere ***–verb (used without object)***
1. to stay attached; stick fast; cleave; cling (usually fol. by *to*): *The mud adhered to his shoes.*
2. *Physics*. (of two or more dissimilar substances) to be united by a molecular force acting in the area of contact.
3. to be devoted in support or allegiance; be attached as a follower or upholder (usually fol. by *to*): *to adhere to a party.*
4. to hold closely or firmly (usually fol. by *to*): *to adhere to a plan.*
5. *Obsolete*. to be consistent.
–verb (used with object)
6. to cause to adhere; make stick: *Glue will adhere the tiles to the wallboard.*

- Iraqi politicians to meet about impasse. They are close to breaking the eight-month political deadlock that has stalled the formation of a new government.

انیم پَس : حالتي كه از ان رهايي نباشد، وضع بغرنج و دشوار، گير، تنگنا، كوچه بن بست

An impasse is a difficult situation in which it is impossible to make any progress; a formal word. <*The talks had reached an impasse over the issue*>.

impasse **--noun** اَنپم پَس : حالتي كه از ان رهايي نباشد، وضع بغرنج و دشوار
1. a position or situation from which there is no escape; deadlock.
2. a road or way that has no outlet; cul-de-sac.

- **Analysts said both reports might be disinformation or an attempt to anger Mr. R. and coax[1] him back into the fold[2].**

.1 (کُکس یا کُ آکس : ریشخندکردن، نوازش کردن چرب زباني کردن)
.2 (اغل گوسفند، دسته یا گله گوسفند، حصار ، چندلا، بشکست خود اعتراف کردن- بکسب یا شغل پایان دادن)

coax **–verb (used with object)** کُکس یا کُ آکس : ریشخندکردن، نوازش کردن چرب زباني کردن
1. to attempt to influence by gentle persuasion, flattery, etc.; cajole: *He coaxed her to sing, but she refused.*
2. to obtain by coaxing: *We coaxed the secret from him.*
3. to manipulate to a desired end by adroit handling or persistent effort: *He coaxed the large chair through the door.*
4. *Obsolete.* **a.** to fondle. **b.** to fool; deceive.
–verb (used without object) **5.** to use gentle persuasion.
fold **–verb (used without object)**
اغل گوسفند، دسته یا گله گوسفند، حصار ، بشکست خود اعتراف کردن- بکسب یا شغل پایان داد
1. to be folded or be capable of folding: *The doors fold back.*
2. *Cards.* to place one's cards facedown so as to withdraw from the play.
3. *Informal.* to fail in business; be forced to close: *The newspaper folded after 76 years.*
4. *Informal.* to yield or give in: *Dad folded and said we could go after all.*

- The Obama administration hoped to brooch talks with Tehran this year (2010) to resolve a long-standing dispute over Iran's nuclear research program

brooch **-–noun** بـِ روچ : برای نخستین بار باز کردن یا مطرح کردن
a clasp or ornament having a pin at the back for passing through the clothing and a catch for securing the point of the pin.
Also**, broach.**

- Obama administration rescinded the invitations.

rescind ***–verb (used with object)*** رِسِیند: باطل ساختن، لغو کردن، فسخ کردن

Rescind: take back, cancel, remove, <*refused to rescind the order*>
1. to abrogate; annul; revoke; repeal.
2. to invalidate (an act, measure, etc.) by a later action or a higher authority.

- Some Middle East citizenries supporting the people's struggle in their fight to stop the theocratic[1] and suppressive[2] actions of the neighbor's regime.

1.(تی یُوکرَ تیک : مربوط بحکومت خدايي، مربوط به خدا سالاري)
2.(سابپ رِ سیو : جلوگيري كننده، فرونشاننده، خنثي كننده اتش سركوب كننده)

- "He also used to speak to the world from a position of arrogance[1] and egotism[2], but you saw how God brought him down to abjectness[3] and buried him in the dustbin of history" he said in comments broadcast on state radio.

1.(اَرِگنس : گردنفرازي، خودبيني، تكبر نخوت، گستاخي، شدت عمل)
2.(اِئی گو تیزِم : خودپرستي، منت، خودستاني خود بيني، خودپسندي)
3.(اَبجِکت نِس : پستي، خواري – سر افكنده)

<u>مَعانی يا بكار گيری لغات فوق در جملات ديگر:</u>

arrogance **–noun** اَرِگنس : گردنفرازي، خودبيني، تكبر نخوت، گستاخي، شدت عمل
offensive display of superiority or self-importance; overbearing pride

egotism **–noun** اِئی گو تیزِم : خودپرستي، منت، خودستاني خود بيني، خودپسندي
1. excessive and objectionable reference to oneself in conversation or writing; conceit; boastfulness.
2. selfishness; self-centeredness; egoism.

abject **–adjective** اَبجِکت نِس : پستي، خواري – سر افكنده
1. utterly hopeless, miserable, humiliating, or wretched: *abject poverty.*
2. contemptible; despicable; base-spirited: *an abject coward.*
3. shamelessly servile; slavish.

- Perhaps the anger will reignite on July 9, the 10th anniversary of a student rising that promoted[1] a campaign to crush reformist aspirations[2].

1.(پِرُموُت : ترفيع دادن، ترقي دادن، ترويج كردن- *(علوم نظامي)* بالا بردن)
2.(اَس پی ریشِن : دم زني، تنفس، استنشاق، اه ارزو، عروج، *(روانشناسي)* اشتياق)

promote ; ---- **Verb with Object** پِرُموُت : ترفيع دادن، ترقي دادن، ترويج كردن- بالا بردن

If people promote something, they help or encourage it to develop or succeed.
The government could do more to promote economic growth.... Did writers like Wilde and Britten promote homosexuality?... She founded Les Ballets Africans in 1952 to promote African dance and culture.

***aspiration*–noun** أس پی ریشِن : دم زني، تنفس، استنشاق، اه ارزو، عروج
1. strong desire, longing, or aim; ambition: *intellectual aspirations.*
2. a goal or objective desired: *The presidency is the traditional aspiration of young American boys.*
3. act of aspirating; breath.

- The elation[1] of a lively political season highlighted by a series of boisterous[2] debates was crushed by election results grossly out of whack[3] with Iraqi's understanding of their nation's demographics[4] and previous voting patterns.

.(اِلِی شِن : بالابري، رفعت، ترفيع سرفرازي شادي -(روانشناسي) سرخوشي)
.(بُویِس تِرِس : خشن وزبر، خشن وبي ادب قوي، سترک، شديد، مفرط بلند وناهنجار، توفاني)
.(وَک : صداي کتک زدن، صداي اصطکاک، صداي ضربت ضربت، سهم، زدن، محکم زدن، تسهيم کردن)
.(دِ ماگ رَفیک : وابسته به امارگيري نفوس)

مَعانی یا بکار گیری لغات فوق در جملات دیگر:

***elation* –noun** اِلِی شِن : بالابري، رفعت، ترفيع سرفرازي شادي
a feeling or state of great joy or pride; exultant gladness; high spirits
Uncount Noun
Elation is a feeling of great happiness and excitement.
This little incident filled me with elation.

***boisterous* –adjective** بُویِس تِرِس : خشن وزبر، خشن وبي ادب قوي مفرط بلند وناهنجار، توفاني
1. rough and noisy; noisily jolly or rowdy; clamorous; unrestrained:
the sound of boisterous laughter. <خنده‌ی قاه قاه و پر صدا ←a boisterous laughter>
2. (of waves, weather, wind, etc.) rough and stormy.

***whack* –verb (used with object)**
وَک : صداي کتک زدن، صداي اصطکاک، صداي ضربت ضربت، سهم، زدن، محکم زدن، تسهيم کردن
1. to strike with a smart, resounding blow or blows.
2. *Slang.* to divide into or take in shares (often fol. by *up*): *Whack the loot between us two.*

–verb (used without object) **3.** to strike a smart, resounding blow or blows.
–noun
4. a smart, resounding blow: *a whack with his hand.*
5. *Informal.* a trial or attempt: *to take a whack at a job.* **6.** *Slang.* a portion or share.
—Verb phrases **7. whack off,**
a. to cut off or separate with a blow: *The cook whacked off the fish's head.*
b. *Slang: Vulgar.* to masturbate.
8. whack out, *Slang.* to produce quickly or, sometimes, carelessly: *She whacks out a short story every week or so.*
—Idiom
9. out of whack, *Informal.* out of order or alignment; not in proper condition.
1. To strike (someone or something) with a sharp blow; slap.
2. *Slang* To kill deliberately; murder.

demographic **---Adjective** دِ ماگ رَفیک : وابسته به امارگیري نفوس
Demographic means relating to or concerning demography.
Several western countries are all suffering the same sort of demographic trends.
–noun
(*used with a plural verb*) the statistical data of a population, esp. those showing average age, income, education, etc.

- Country had anticipated a fair vote---within a system constrained[1] by rules set by the country's leaders. True, all candidates were vetted[2] by the Guardian Council for fealty[3] to Iran's system.

1.(کانس تْ رِین : اجباري- تحمیل کردن)
2.(وِت : دامپزشک، بیطاري کردن- کهنه سرباز)
3.(فی یِل تی : وفاداری، راستي، صداقت- بیعت-وظیفه شناسی)

<u>مَعانی یا بکار گیری لغات فوق در جملات دیگر:</u>

constrained ***–adjective*** کانس تْ رِین : اجباري- تحمیل کردن
1. forced, compelled, or obliged: *a constrained confession.*
2. stiff or unnatural; uneasy or embarrassed: *a constrained manner.*

–verb (used with object)
1. to force, compel, or oblige: *He was constrained to admit the offense.*
2. to confine forcibly, as by bonds.
3. to repress or restrain: *Cold weather constrained the plant's growth.*

vet ***–noun*** وِت : دامپزشک، بیطاري کردن- کهنه سرباز

1. مخفف → veterinarian., <Vet the candidates for a position ارزیابی شدن برای پذیرش و تائید
–verb (used with object)
2. to examine or treat in one's capacity as a veterinarian or as a doctor.
3. to appraise, verify, or check for accuracy, authenticity, validity, etc.: *An expert vetted the manuscript before publication.*
–verb (used without object)
4. to work as a veterinarian.

fidelity ***–noun, plural*-ties.** فی دِل تی : وفاداری، راستي، صداقت- بیعت-وظیفه شناسی
1. *History/Historical.*
a. fidelity to a lord.
b. the obligation or the engagement to be faithful to a lord, usually sworn to by a vassal.
2. fidelity; faithfulness.

- Iranians are willing to pay for quality, but don't want to spend for shoddy goods. The same is true in politics.

shoddy ***–adjective*** شادی :پارچه پست، پست، بدساخت جازده، جنس بنجل، كالاي تقلبي
1. of poor quality or inferior workmanship: *a shoddy bookcase.*
2. intentionally rude or inconsiderate; shabby: *shoddy behavior.*
–noun
3. a fibrous material obtained by shredding unfelted rags or waste.Compare mungo.
4. anything inferior, esp. a handmade item or manufactured product.
What is shoddy fabric, Shoddy lymph nodes, Shoddy thinking

- Someone broke precedent[1] by explicity[2] standing with one side of the political spectrum[3]. What's more many Iranians felt they were being patronized[4] that person depicted[5] any vote cast as one for the system,

1.(پری سی دِنت : سابقه داشتن، مقدم بر ، رویه قضایي، ماقبل).
2.(اکس پلی سیتی : صراحتا" یا ضمنا"- روشن –واضح)
3.(اس پک ترُم : بینايي، طیف، خیال)
4.(پیترونایز : رئیس وار رفتار کردن تشویق کردن، نگهداري كردن مشتري شدن)
5.(دِ پکت : نمایش دادن -(بوسیله نقشه ومانند ان)، نقش کردن، مجسم کردن، رسم کردن، شرح دادن)

<u>مَعانی یا بکار گیری لغات فوق در جملات دیگر:</u>

precedent ***–noun*** پری سی دِنت : سابقه داشتن، مقدم بر ، رویه قضایي، ماقبل

1. *Law*. a legal decision or form of proceeding serving as an authoritative rule or pattern in future similar or analogous cases.
2. any act, decision, or case that serves as a guide or justification for subsequent situations.
***–adjective*pre·ce·dent**
3. preceding; anterior.
<a moral depicting a famous battle> describe

explicit ***–adjective*** اِکس پلی سیتی : صراحتا" یا ضمنا"- روشن –واضح
1. fully and clearly expressed or demonstrated; leaving nothing merely implied; unequivocal: *explicit instructions; an explicit act of violence; explicit language.*
2. clearly developed or formulated: *explicit knowledge; explicit belief.*
3. definite and unreserved in expression; outspoken: *He was quite explicit as to what he expected us to do for him.*
4. described or shown in realistic detail: *explicit sexual scenes.*
5. having sexual acts or nudity clearly depicted: *explicit movies; explicit books.*
6. *Mathematics*. (of a function) having the dependent variable expressed directly in terms of the independent variables, as $y = 3x + 4$.Compare implicit def. 4.

spectrum-- اِس پِک تِرَم : بينايي، طيف، خيال
Physics The distribution of a characteristic of a physical system or phenomenon, especially:

a. The distribution of energy emitted by a radiant source, as by an incandescent body, arranged in order of wavelengths.
b. The distribution of atomic or subatomic particles in a system, as in a magnetically resolved molecular beam, arranged in order of masses.
c. A range of values of a quantity or set of related quantities.
d. A broad sequence or range of related qualities, ideas, or activities: *the whole*

patronizes ***–verb (used with object),*-ized, -iz·ing.**
پترونایز : رئيس وار رفتار كردن تشويق كردن، نگهداري كردن مشتري شدن
1. to give (a store, restaurant, hotel, etc.) one's regular patronage; trade with.
2. to behave in an offensively condescending manner toward: *a professor who patronizes his students.*
3. to act as a patron toward (an artist, institution, etc.); support.
Also, *especially British*, **pa·tron·ise**.

*depict***–*verb (used with object)***
دِ پیکت : نمايش دادن (بوسیله نقشه ومانند ان)، نقش كردن، مجسم كردن، رسم كردن، شرح دادن
1. to represent by or as if by painting; portray; delineate.
2. to represent or characterize in words; describe.
<a moral depicting a famous battle> describe

- In 1957 The day after his speech, as Capital burned, the slogans took a nast turn. "Rue[1] the day when we're armed!" protesters chanted as they hurlec rocks at the detested[3] ……. militiamen and rest or as a sign of defiance commerce has showed to a trickle[5],
In the capital Grand Bazaar, newly spruced[6] up with trees, pedestrian- only boulevards, business has collapsed in the month before Ramadon[7].

.(رُو : آرزو، افسوس خوردن، غصه، ندامت- در اینجا یعنی وای بروزیکه-وای اگر)
.(هِرُل : پرتاب، پرت، لگد، پرتاب کردن پرت کردن، انداختن)
.(دِ تِیست : نفرت کردن، تنفر داشتن از- بیزار بودن از)
.(دی فاینس : مبارزه طلبي، دعوت بهجنگ، بیاعتنايي، مخالفت، مقاومت، اعتراض)
.(تریکِل : چکیدن، چکانیدن، چکه-در اینجا یعنی کساد شدن)
.(اِس پرُس : اراسته، پاکیزه، قشنگ)
.(رَمَ دان : ماه رمضان)

<u>مَعانی یا بکار گیری لغات فوق در جملات دیگر:</u>

***rue* –verb (used with object)** رُو : آرزو، افسوس خوردن، در اینجا یعنی وای بروزیکه-وای اگر
1. to feel sorrow over; repent of; regret bitterly: *to rue the loss of opportunities.*
2. to wish that (something) had never been done, taken place, etc.: *I rue the day he was born.*
–verb (used without object)
3. to feel sorrow, repentance, or regret.
–noun
4. sorrow; repentance; regret.
5. pity or compassion.
With rue my heart is laden*→ (سنگین-پر- مملو)*

***hurled* ----Verb with Obje** هِرُل : پرتاب، پرت، لگد، پرتاب کردن پرت کردن، انداختن
1. If you hurl something, you throw it with a lot of force.
I took all his books and hurled them out of the window
Verb with Object
If you hurl abuse or insults at someone, you shout abuse or insults at them.
Abuse was hurled at the police

***detested* ---Verb with Object** دِ تِیست : نفرت کردن، تنفر داشتن از- بیزار بودن از
If you detest someone or something, you dislike them very much.
In his own lifetime he was detested by almost everybody.
–verb (used with object)

to feel abhorrence of; hate; dislike intensely.

defiance ***–noun*** دی فاینس : مبارزه طلبي، دعوت بهجنگ، بیاعتنایي، مخالفت، مقاومت، اعتراض
1. a daring or bold resistance to authority or to any opposing force.
2. open disregard; contempt (often fol. by *of*): *defiance of danger; His refusal amounted to defiance.*
3. a challenge to meet in combat or in a contest.
—Idioms
4. bid defiance to, to offer resistance; defy.
5. in defiance of, in spite of; notwithstanding: *There was a splendid audience in defiance of the rainstorm.*

trickle ***–verb (used without object)*** تریکل : چکیدن، چکانیدن، چکه-در اینجا یعنی کساد شدن
1. to flow or fall by drops, or in a small, gentle stream: *Tears trickled down her cheeks.*
2. to come, go, or pass bit by bit, slowly, or irregularly: *The guests trickled out of the room.*
–verb (used with object)
3. to cause to trickle.
–noun
4. a trickling flow or stream.
5. a small, slow, or irregular quantity of anything coming, going, or proceeding: *a trickle of visitors throughout the day.*

spruce ***–noun*** اِس پرُس : آراسته، پاکیزه، قشنگ
1. any evergreen, coniferous tree of the genus *Picea,* of the pine family, having short, angular, needle-shaped leaves attached singly around twigs and bearing hanging cones with persistent scales.
2. any of various allied trees, as the Douglas fir and the hemlock spruce.
3. the wood of any such tree.
–adjective
4. made from the wood of a spruce tree or trees.
5. containing or abounding in spruce trees.

- Mehdi, a 26-year-old fabric wholesaler, supported Mr. M., but declined to heed his strike calls. The economy is in terrible shape, he said.

heed ***–verb (used with object)*** هی د : اعتنا، توجه، اعتناکردن (به)، محل گذاشتن به
1. to give careful attention to: *He did not heed the warning.*
–verb (used without object)
2. to give attention; have regard.
–noun

3. careful attention; notice; observation (usually with *give* or *take*).

- Jewelers were among those who went on strike last year to protest a value-added tax, which the government rescinded. Those 3 days almost crippled the entire bazaar.

rescind--**Verb with Object** رسیند : باطل ساختن، لغو کردن، فسخ کردن

If a government or group of people in power rescind a law or agreement, they officially withdraw it and state that it is no longer valid; a formal word.
This law was later rescinded.... They had to summon a second conference and rescind the previous motion.
–verb (used with object)
1. to abrogate; annul; revoke; repeal.
2. to invalidate (an act, measure, etc.) by a later action or a higher authority.

- Reformist candidate Mr.? who according to official results placed last in the election, has spoken out forcefully and dared[1] to wade[2] into crowds to cheer on protesters.

1. (دِیر: جرات کردن مبادرت بکار دلیرانه کردن بمبارزه طلبیدن، شهامت یارایی)
2. (وید: به اب زدن، بسختي رفتن، دراب راه رفتن)

مَعانی یا بکار گیری لغات فوق در جملات دیگر:

I dare you to say it to his face.خيلي راست مي گويي (اگ؟ مردي) جلوي خودش بگ؟
I dare you to tell him yourself .اگر راست ميگ؟ خودت به اوبگ؟
Dont you dare tell anyone .مبادا بكسي بگويي

dare–***verb (used without object)*** دِیر : جرات کردن مبادرت بکار دلیرانه کردن بمبارزه طلبیدن، شهامت
1. to have the necessary courage or boldness for something; be bold enough: *You wouldn't dare!*
–verb (used with object)
2. to have the boldness to try; venture; hazard.
3. to meet defiantly; face courageously.
4. to challenge or provoke (a person) into a demonstration of courage; defy: *to dare a man to fight.*
–auxiliary verb
5. to have the necessary courage or boldness to (used chiefly in questions and negatives): *How dare you speak to me like that? He dare not mention the subject again.*
–noun
6. an act of daring or defiance; challenge.

—Idiom
7. dare say, daresay.

- Between beatings and interrogations[1] they mingled[2] and shared ideas. Political philosophies and tools of the trade--just as enemies of the Shah did inside those same prison walls 30+ years ago.

1.(اين ت رگِيشِن : باز جويي ، استنطاق بازپرسي *(حقوق)* بازپرسي)
2.(مين گِل : ممزوج شدن، اميختن، بخاطراوردن، ذكر كردن، مخلوط كردن)

<u>مَعانی یا بکار گیری لغات فوق در جملات دیگر:</u>

interrogation ***–noun*** اين ت رگِيشِن : باز جويي ، استنطاق بازپرسي *(حقوق)* بازپرسي
1. the act of interrogating; questioning.
2. an instance of being interrogated: *He seemed shaken after his interrogation.*
3. a question; inquiry.
4. a written list of questions.
5. an interrogation point; question mark.

mingles ***–verb (used without object)*** مين گِل : ممزوج شدن، بخاطراوردن، ذكر كردن، مخلوط كردن
1. to become mixed, blended, or united.
2. to associate or mix in company: *She refuses to mingle with bigots.*
3. to associate or take part with others; participate.
–verb (used with object) **4.** to mix or combine; put together in a mixture; blend.

- Abbas, a 48-year-old art teacher impulsively rushed to the polling station and cast a vote for Mo. even though he doesn't trust the former prime minister

Impulsive ***–adjective*** ايم پال سيولِي : با نيروي اني و بدون اراده از روي تحريک
1. actuated or swayed by emotional or involuntary impulses: *an impulsive child.*
2. having the power or effect of impelling; characterized by impulsion: *impulsive forces.*
3. inciting to action: *the impulsive effects of a revolutionary idea.*
4. *Mechanics.* (of forces) acting momentarily; not continuous.

- You are all aware that Russian! -----people have risen[1] against..?.. years of ….regime in …?. The electoral coup[2] was only one strike of matches on gunpowder[3] of anger and despise[4] for the regime oppressive[5] power.

1.(رِزِن : برخاسته، طلوع كرده,← *Risen* is the past participle of rise.)
(The water has *risen* over his head ← آب از سرش گذشته است)

(Coup d'état. کودتا ،برهم زدن، ضربت : کُو).
(گآن پاُدِر : باروت- مواد منفجر کننده)
(دیس پایز : خوار شمردن، حقیر شمردن تحقیر کردن، نفرت داشتن)
(آپِر سیو : خورد کننده ناراحت کننده، غم افزا).

مَعاني یا بکار گیری لغات فوق در جملات دیگر:

risen **–verb (used without object)** رِزِن : برخاسته، طلوع کرده
1. to get up from a lying, sitting, or kneeling posture; assume an upright position: *She rose and walked over to greet me. With great effort he rose to his knees.*
2. to get up from bed, esp. to begin the day after a night's sleep: *to rise early.*
3.to extend directly upward; project vertically: *The tower rises to a height of 60 feet. The building rises above the city's other skyscrapers.*
4.to advance to a higher level of action, thought, feeling, etc.: *to rise above the commonplace.*

coup **–noun,pluralcoups** Coup d'état.کودتا ،برهم زدن، ضربت : کُو
1. a highly successful, unexpected stroke, act, or move; a clever action or accomplishment.
2. (among the Plains Indians of North America) a brave or reckless deed performed in battle by a single warrior, as touching or striking an enemy warrior without sustaining injury oneself.
3. *Coup d'état*.
Count Noun, A coup is a military action intended to seize power in a country by gettin rid of its government or its president.
The Indian authorities say mercenaries and rebels were behind a coup attempt in the Maldives.

gunpowder **–noun** گآن پاُدِر : باروت- مواد منفجر کننده
1. an explosive mixture, as of potassium nitrate, sulfur, and charcoal, used in shells and cartridges, in fireworks, for blasting, etc.
2. Also called **tea**. a fine variety of green China tea, each leaf of which is rolled into a little ball.

despised **---de·spised, de·spis·ing, de·spis·es**
یس پایز : خوار شمردن، حقیر شمردن تحقیر کردن، نفرت داشتن
To regard with contempt or scorn: *despised all cowards and flatterers.*
To dislike intensely; loathe: *despised the frigid weather in January.*
To regard as unworthy of one's interest or concern:
despised any thought of their own safety.

Verb with Object
If you despise someone or something, you have a very low opinion of them.
They despise them for their ignorance.

oppressive **---Adjective** آپِرِ سیو : خورد کننده نار احت کننده، غم افزا
You can say that the weather is oppressive when it is hot and humid.
...the oppressive heat of the plains.

- The suppressive[1] machineries of government have become activated again. It is avenging[2] the fearless youths that has shown no fear of death. The extend of suppression[3] is unimaginable.

1.(سابِرِ سیو : *(suppressor)* جلوگیري کننده، فرونشاننده، موقوف سازنده- *(علوم نظامي)* خنثي کننده،)
2.(أون جینگ : کینه جویي کردن *(از)*، تلافي کردن، انتقام کشیدن *(از)* دادگیري کردن، خونخواهي کردن)
3.(سابِرِ شِن : جلوگیري، توقیف، موقوف سازي، فرونشاني - *(علوم نظامي)* سرکوب کردن، خنثي کردن)

<u>مَعانی یا بکار گیری لغات فوق در جملات دیگر:</u>

suppressive ***–verb (used with object)***
1. to put an end to the activities of (a person, body of persons, etc.): *to suppress the Communist party.*
2. to do away with by or as by authority; abolish; stop (a practice, custom, etc.).
3. to keep in or repress (a feeling, smile, groan, etc.).
4. to withhold from disclosure or publication (truth, evidence, a book, names, etc.).
5. to stop or arrest (a flow, hemorrhage, cough, etc.).
6. to vanquish or subdue (a revolt, rebellion, etc.); quell; crush.
7. *Electricity* . to reduce or eliminate (an irregular or undesired oscillation or frequency) in a circuit.

avenged ***–verb (used with object),*** a·venged, a·veng·ing. (Avenger انتقام جو)
1. to take vengeance or exact satisfaction for: *to avenge a grave insult.*
2. to take vengeance on behalf of: *He avenged his brother.*
<Swore to avenge his father>, <avenged their leader's death>

*suppression**–noun*** ستم- فشار
1. the act of suppressing. (Suppressor ستمگر)
2. the state of being suppressed.

- In Middle East, and USA it is not easy to break the resilience of millions of people standing for change.

ری لی ینس :(resiliency) جهندگي،حا لت ارتجائی- جهندگي (علوم مهندسي) برجهندگي، جهندگي)

resilience–noun
1. the power or ability to return to the original form, position, etc., after being bent, compressed, or stretched; elasticity.
2. ability to recover readily from illness, depression, adversity, or the like; buoyancy. (synonym for resilient is *elastic*)

- The Iraqi regime no longer has any other tools at its disposal[1] to deal with people. This government is set to destroy the movement by suppressing[2] the people tending[3] to it.

.(دیس پوزال : در دسترس، دراختیار، موجود، مصرف درمعرض گذاري
.(ساپ رِس : موقوف کردن ، خواباندن پایمال کردن، مانع شدن تحت فشار قرار دادن، منکوب کردن
.(نگهداري کردن از ، مواظب بودن، متمایل بودن به گرایش داشتن، گراییدن)

<u>مَعانی یا بکار گیری لغات فوق در جملات دیگر:</u>

disposal --- Words Stress: **dis•pos•al**
یس پوزال : در دسترس، دراختیار، موجود، مصرف درمعرض گذاري
1. If you have something at your disposal, you can use it at any time.
...a cottage put at her disposal by a friend.
Uncount Noun 2. Disposal is the act of getting rid of something....*the safe disposal of radioactive waste.*
3. at one's disposalو power, authority, control, direction, discretion, responsibility, management, government, determination, regulation.

suppress,---*Verb with Object*
ساپ رِس : موقوف کردن ، خواباندن پایمال کردن، مانع شدن تحت فشار قرار دادن، منکوب کردن
1. to put an end to the activities of (a person, body of persons, etc.): *to suppress the Communist party.*
2. to do away with by or as by authority; abolish; stop (a practice, custom, etc.).
3.If an army or government suppresses an activity, they prevent it from continuing.
The army soon suppressed the revolt.
If someone suppresses a piece of information, they prevent it from becoming known.
The committee's report has been suppressed.

tending **–verb (used without object)**

تند ینگ : نگهداري كردن از ، مواظب بودن، متمايل بودن به گرايش داشتن، گراييدن

1. to be disposed or inclined in action, operation, or effect to do something: *The particles tend to unite.*

2. to be disposed toward an idea, emotion, way of thinking, etc.: *He tends to be overly optimistic. Her religious philosophy tends toward pantheism.*

3. to lead or conduce, as to some result or resulting condition: *measures tending to improved working conditions; Governments are tending toward democracy.*

4. to be inclined to or have a tendency toward a particular quality, state, or degree: *This wine tends toward the sweet side.*

5. (of a journey, course, road, etc.) to lead or be directed in a particular direction (usually fol. by *to, toward,* etc.): *a path tending toward the beach.*

- "Our victory leans on our unity and fraternity[1]" said leader. He frightened by depth of the people militancy[2], warns over and over again that be ware not to fall in the trap of antiestablishments[3] slogans… we should turn to ......

1

.(فِر تِر نِ تی : برادري، اخوت، انجمن اخوت صنف، اتحاديه)

.2(می لی تَن سی : نزاع طلبي، جنگجويي)

.3(اَنتی- اِس تَب- لیش مِنت : مخا لف تأسيس يا استقرار- مخا لف تشكيل)

بكار گیری لغات فوق در جملات دیگر:

fraternity ***–noun,plural*-ties.** فِر تِر نِ تی : برادري، اخوت، انجمن اخوت صنف، اتحاديه

1. a local or national organization of male students, primarily for social purposes, usually with secret initiation and rites and a name composed of two or three Greek letters.

2. a group of persons associated by or as if by ties of brotherhood.

3. any group or class of persons having common purposes, interests, etc.: *the Medical fraternity.*

4. an organization of laymen for religious or charitable purposes; sodality.

5. the quality of being brotherly; brotherhood: *liberty, equality, and fraternity.*

6. the relation of a brother or between brothers.

militant ***–adjective*** می لی تَن سی : نزاع طلبي، جنگجويي

1. vigorously active and aggressive, esp. in support of a cause: *militant reformers.*

2. engaged in warfare; fighting.

–noun

3. a militant person.

4. a person engaged in warfare or combat.

Uncount Noun

Militancy is the behaviour and attitudes of people who are very active in trying to bring

about political change, often in ways that some people find unacceptable.
The unions themselves have lost much of their former militancy.... The new militancy wa also a reaction to the government's decision.

antiestablishment **–adjective** اَنتی- اِس تَب- لیش مِنت : مخا لف تأسیس یا استقرار - مخا لف تشکیل
opposed to or working against the existing power structure or mores, as of society or government: *Antiestablishment candidates promised to disband the army, Congress, and the cabinet if elected.*

- ......and he is exemplifying[1] the same constitution that is basic axion[2] is assumption[3] that people are like herds[4] of sheep and the Holly Power is the Sheppard; (Herder چوپان- گاو دار)
(Herdsman or herssmen means: breeder or tender of livestock: چوپان – رمه دار)

1. (اِگزَم پِ لی فآی : بامثال فهمانیدن، بانمونه نشان دادن)
2. (اَکسی یان : حقیقت آشکار - قضیهٔ حقیقی)
3. (اَسامپ شِن : فرض، خودبيني، غرور، اتخاذ قصد، گمان)
4. (هِرد : رمه، گله، گروه، جمعیت، گردامدن، جمع شدن، متحد کردن گروه)

<u>مَعانی یا بکار گیری لغات فوق در جملات دیگر:</u>

exemplify ***–verb (used with object),*-fied, -fy·ing.**
1. to show or illustrate by example.
2. to furnish or serve as an example of: *The plays of Wilde exemplify the comedy of manners.***3.** *Law.* to transcribe or copy; make an attested copy of (a document) under seal

axion ***–noun*** *Physics.* اَکسی یان : حقیقت آشکار - قضیهٔ حقیقی
a hypothetical particle having no charge, zero spin, and small mass: postulated in some forms of quantum chromo dynamics.
Find deals, pics, reviews, wholesale pricing, and more on **Axion Shoes**. ... Pictures, videos, and more of **Axion Shoes... Axion** looks like they are coming back. We will try to be the fan site for the new **Axion Shoes** and footwear this coming out. When more and more styles and pics come out we will be putting them up here.

assumption ***–noun*** اَسامپ شِن : فرض، خودبيني، غرور، اتخاذ قصد، گمان
1. something taken for granted; a supposition: *a correct assumption.*
2. the act of taking for granted or supposing.
3. the act of taking to or upon oneself.
4. the act of taking possession of something: *the assumption of power.*
5. arrogance; presumption.

6. the taking over of another's debts or obligations.
7. *Ecclesiastical.*
a. (*often initial capital letter*) the bodily taking up into heaven of the Virgin Mary.
b. (*initial capital letter*) a feast commemorating this, celebrated on August 15.

herd **–noun** هرد : رمه، گله، گروه، جمعیت، گردامدن، جمع شدن، متحد کردن گروه
1. a number of animals kept, feeding, or traveling together; drove; flock: *a herd of cattle; a herd of sheep; a herd of zebras.*
Sometimes Disparaging. a large group of people: *The star was mobbed by a herd of autograph seekers.*
any large quantity: *a herd of bicycles.*
4. the herd, the common people; masses; rabble: *He had no opinions of his own, but simply followed the herd.*
–verb (used without object)
5. to unite or go in a herd; assemble or associate as a herd.

- Demand the annulations[1] of law of enforced[2] covering and all inequalities[3] and punishments designed for women.

1.(آنیو لی شِن :تشکیل حلقه -(حقوق) فسخ، الغاء)
2.(این فورس : اجراکردن، (بازور) از پیش بردن، وادار کردن مجبورکردن، تاکیدکردن)
3.(این انی کُو آلی تیز : نا برابري، عدم تساوي اختلاف، فرق، ناهمواري)

annulation— آنیو لی شِن :تشکیل حلقه -(حقوق) فسخ، الغاء

The act or process of forming rings. A ringlike structure, segment, or part.

enforce – این فورس : اجراکردن، (بازور) از پیش بردن، وادار کردن مجبورکردن، تاکیدکردن–

verb (used with object),-forced, -forc·ing.

1. to put or keep in force; compel obedience to: *to enforce a rule; Traffic laws will be strictly enforced.*
2. to obtain (payment, obedience, etc.) by force or compulsion.
3. to impose (a course of action) upon a person: *The doctor enforced a strict dietary regimen.*
4. to support (a demand, claim, etc.) by force: *to enforce one's rights as a citizen.*
5. to impress or urge (an argument, contention, etc.) forcibly; lay stress upon: *He enforced his argument by adding details.*

inequality **–noun, plural** -ties. این انی کُو آلی تیز : نا برابري، عدم تساوي اختلاف، فرق، ناهمواري
1. the condition of being unequal; lack of equality; disparity: *inequality of size.*

2. social disparity: *inequality between the rich and the poor.*
3. disparity or relative inadequacy in natural endowments: *a startling inequality of intellect, talents, and physical stamina.*
4. injustice; partiality.
5. unevenness, as of surface.
6. an instance of unevenness.

- Mr. M. was also very instrumental[1] in establishing and consolidating[2] the regime. He was called the prime minister of massacres[3], since during his reign[4] political prisoners were executed amass[5],…
(Royal authority: sovereignty), <under the reign of the kings>, < amass a great fortune>.

.(اینسٹرو مِنتال : وسیله ساز، مفید قابل استفاده، الت)
.(کانسا لید یتینگ : محکم کردن، یکي کردن، یک رقم کردن)
.(مَ سِ کِر : قتل عام کردن، کشتار)
.(رِین : سلطنت، حکمراني، حکومت حکمفرمايي، سلطنت یاحکمراني کردن)
.(آ مَس : گرداوردن، توده کردن متراکم کردن)

<u>مَعانی یا بکار گیری لغات فوق در جملات دیگر:</u>

instrumental ***–adjective*** اینسٹرو مِنتال : وسیله ساز، مفید قابل استفاده، الت
1. serving or acting as an instrument or means; useful; helpful.
2. performed on or written for a musical instrument or instruments: *instrumental music.*
3. of or pertaining to an instrument or tool.

*consolidate***d** ***–verb (used with object)*** کانسا لید یتینگ : محکم کردن، یکي کردن، یک رقم کردن
1. to bring together (separate parts) into a single or unified whole; unite; combine: *They consolidated their three companies.*
2. to discard the unused or unwanted items of and organize the remaining: *She consolidated her home library.*
3. to make solid or firm; solidify; strengthen: *to consolidate gains.*
4. *Military* . to strengthen by rearranging the position of ground combat troops after a successful attack.

massacre ***–noun*** مَ سِ کِر : قتل عام کردن، کشتار
1. the unnecessary, indiscriminate killing of a large number of human beings or animals, as in barbarous warfare or persecution or for revenge or plunder. غارت، چپاول، غارت کردن
2. a general slaughter, as of persons or animals:
the massacre of millions during the war.
3. *Informal.* a crushing defeat, esp. in sports.
–verb (used with object)

4. to kill unnecessarily and indiscriminately, esp. a large number of persons.
5. *Informal.* to defeat decisively, esp. in sports.

reign ;-—***noun*** رین : سلطنت، حکمراني، حکومت حکمفرمايي، سلطنت ياحکمراني کردن
1. the period during which a sovereign occupies the throne.
2. royal rule or authority; sovereignty.
3. dominating power or influence: *the reign of law.*
–verb (used without object)
4. to possess or exercise sovereign power or authority.
5. to hold the position and **name** of sovereign without exercising the ruling power.
6. to have control, rule, or influence of any kind.
7. to predominate; be prevalent.

amass ***–verb (used with object)***). أمَس : گرداوردن، توده کردن متراکم کردن
1. to gather for oneself; collect as one's own: *to amass a huge amount of money.*
2. to collect into a mass or pile; gather: *He amassed his papers for his memoirs.*
–verb (used without object)
3. to come together; assemble: *crowds amassing for the parade.*
If you amass something such as money, or if it amasses, you gradually get a lot of it.
So far, 1.6 billion has been amassed.... The combined loot of the army amassed as it advanced through South East Asia.... You won't get anywhere if you don't amass a network of sympathetic, influential supporters.

- His disputes[1] with the coup[2] faction[3] of the system have nothing to do with the Iraqi interests. In the last few weeks, when radical youths was engaged in streets with the forces of suppression[4] the leaders of "G. Wave" were hiding in the safety of their homes or in the mosques.

1.(ديس پيوت : ستيزه، چون وچرا، مشاجره نزاع، جدال کردن مباحثه کردن، انکارکردن)
2.(کُو : پی خوانده نمیشود--- برهم زدن، ضربت، کودتا)
3.(دسته بندي، حزب، انجمن فرقه، نفاق -(*علوم نظامي*) مخالفت، دسته بندي، توطئه کردن)
(نفاق- فرقه بازی → factionalism)
4.(جلوگيري، توقيف، موقوف سازي، فرونشاني- سرکوب کردن - منع، بازداري)

<u>مَعانی یا بکار گیری لغات فوق در جملات دیگر:</u>

disputes ---- ديس پيوت : ستيزه، چون وچرا، مشاجره نزاع، جدال کردن مباحثه کردن، انکارکردن
A dispute is a disagreement or quarrel between people or groups.
...disputes between unions and employers.... There is some dispute about this.
–verb (used without object)

1. to engage in argument or debate.
2. to argue vehemently; wrangle or quarrel.
–verb (used with object)
3. to argue or debate about; discuss.
4. to argue against; call in question: *to dispute a proposal.*
5. to quarrel or fight about; contest.
6. to strive against; oppose: *to dispute an advance of troops.*
–noun
7. a debate, controversy, or difference of opinion.
8. a wrangling argument; quarrel.

coup ***–noun, plural*** coups گُو : پی خوانده نمیشود--- برهم زدن، ضربت، کودتا
1. a highly successful, unexpected stroke, act, or move; a clever action or accomplishment.
2. (among the Plains Indians of North America) a brave or reckless deed performed in battle by a single warrior, as touching or striking an enemy warrior without sustaining injury oneself.
3. coup d'état.
—Idiom
4. count coup, (among Plains Indians of North America)
a. to perform a coup.
b. to recount or relate the coups one has performed.
Count Noun
A coup is a military action intended to seize power in a country by getting rid of its government or its president.
The Indian authorities say mercenaries and rebels were behind a coup attempt in the Maldives

suppression ***–noun*** جلوگيري، توقيف، موقوف سازي، فرونشاني- سرکوب کردن - منع، بازداري
1. the act of suppressing.
2. the state of being suppressed.

- Some unkown and suspicious[1] characters became the spokespersons for the movement and tried very hard to monopolies[2] the solidarity[3] of the people in their gatherings.

(ساس پی شِس : بدگمان، ظنین، حاکي ازبدگماني، مشکوک)
(مِ نا پُولی : انحصار، امتیاز انحصاري کالاي انحصاري ، انحصار حق)
(سالی دِرِتی : اتحاد، انسجام ، بهم پیوستگي مسئولیت مشترک، همکاري همبستگي)

<u>مَعانی یا بکار گیری لغات فوق در جملات دیگر</u>

suspicious–***adjective*** بدگمان، ظنین، حاکي ازبدگماني، مشکوک : ساس پی شس **1.** tending to cause or excite suspicion; questionable: *suspicious behavior.*
2. inclined to suspect, esp. inclined to suspect evil; distrustful: *a suspicious tyrant.*
3. full of or feeling suspicion.
4. expressing or indicating suspicion: *a suspicious glance.*

Adjective

If you are suspicious of someone, you do not trust them.
The consignment of weapons was uncovered when a customs official became suspicious.... Nuclear disasters at Windscale and Three Mile Island have left people suspicious and disenchanted.... Labour, once so suspicious of the European Community, is now an eager champion of the EEC.... It's not only the Americans that are suspicious that this is truly a chemical weapon plant.

monopoly ***–noun, plural*-lies.** امتیاز انحصاري- کالاي انحصاري ، انحصار حق : م نا پُولی
1. exclusive control of a commodity or service in a particular market, or a control that makes possible the manipulation of prices. Compare duopoly, oligopoly.
2. an exclusive privilege to carry on a business, traffic, or service, granted by a government.
3. the exclusive possession or control of something.
4. something that is the subject of such control, as a commodity or service.
5. a company or group that has such control.

Also watch for this word: monopol<u>ise</u> and above word is monopol<u>**ies**</u> which is plural. You can write alos with <u>Z</u> monopoli**z**e.
Monopolizing; to get a monopoly of assume complete possession or control of <*monopolize a conversation*>, monopolization , noun,
(exclusive possession امتیاز انحصاری), (monopolize به خودانحصار دادن)

solidarity – ***Noun*** اتحاد، انسجام ، بهم پیوستگي مسئولیت مشترک، همکاري همبستگي : سالی برتی
If a group of people show solidarity, they show complete unity and support for eac other....*working-class solidarity*.

***noun, plural*-ties.**
1. union or fellowship arising from common responsibilities and interests, as between members of a group or between classes, peoples, etc.: *to promote solidarity among union members.*
2. community of feelings, purposes, etc. **3.** community of responsibilities and interests.

- A color used by one faction[1] against the other faction in the campaign trails[2].

1.(فک شِن : دسته بندي، حزب، انجمن فرقه، نفاق ـ(علوم نظامي) مخالفت، دسته بندي)
2.(تِ ریل : بدنبال کشیدن، بدنبال حرکت کردن ، دنباله دار بودن، دنباله داشتن، اثرپا باقي گذاردن)

مَعانی یا بکار گیری لغات فوق در جملات دیگر:

faction **–*noun*** فَک شِن : دسته بندي، حزب، انجمن فرقه، نفاق -(علوم نظامي) مخالفت، دسته بندي
1. a group or clique within a larger group, party, government, organization, or the like: *< a faction in favor of big business>.*
2. party strife and intrigue; dissension: *<an era of faction and treason>*

trail **--Count Noun** تِ ريل : بدنبال كشيدن، بدنبال حركت كردن ، دنباله دار بودن- اثرپا باقي گذاردن
You can refer to the places that are visited by someone who is seeking election to public office as their campaign trail.
Bush argued his case on the campaign trail in stops in Akron and Chicago.... Six months after multi-party elections in Hungary politicians are once again on the campaign trail.

- The demand for separation of state[1] and religion; annulations[2] of discriminatory[3] laws against the women and assembly[4] of the workers and other social strata's[5];……..

.(توضيح دادن، جزء به جزء شرح دادن ، دولت استان، ملت، جمهوري كشور، ايالت، كشوري، دولتي حالت)
سياستمدارانه Statesmanlike)
مرد سياسی يا سياستمدار Statesman)
زمامداري، سياستمداري Statesmanship)

.(أ نيو لِيت : تشكيل حلقه- (حقوق) فسخ، الغاء)
.(ديس كرى مِنِ تُورى : تميز، فرق گذاري، تبعيض -تبعيض اميز)
.(أ سِم بِلى : مجمع، اجتماع انجمن، مجلس، گروه، هيئت قانون گذاري)
.(اِس تِ ريتا :طبقه- قشر- لايه--- به كلمهء جمع آن در زير توجه كنيد)

مَعانی یا بکار گیری لغات فوق در جملات دیگر:

annulation–***adjective*** أ نيو لِيت : تشكيل حلقه- (حقوق) فسخ، الغاء
1. formed of ringlike segments, as an annelid worm.
2. having rings or ringlike bands. Also, **an·nu·lat·ed.**

discriminatory **–*adjective*** ديس كرى مِنِ تُورى : تميز، فرق گذاري، تبعيض -تبعيض اميز
1. characterized by or showing prejudicial treatment, esp. as an indication of racial, religious, or sexual bias: *discriminatory practices in housing; a discriminatory tax.*

assembly **–*noun, plural*-blies.** أ سِم بِلى : مجمع، اجتماع انجمن، مجلس، گروه، هيئت قانون گذاري

1. an assembling or coming together of a number of persons, usually for a particular purpose: *The principal will speak to all the students at Friday's assembly.*
2. a group of persons gathered together, usually for a particular purpose, whether religious, political, educational, or social.
3. (*often initial capital letter*) *Government.* a legislative body, esp. the lower house of the legislature in certain states of the U.S.: *a bill before the assembly;*
the new york State Assembly.
4. *Military.*
a. a signal, as by drum or bugle, for troops to fall into ranks or otherwise assemble.
b. the movement of forces, tanks, soldiers, etc., scattered by battle or battle drill, toward and into a small area.
5. the putting together of complex machinery, as airplanes, from interchangeable parts of standard dimensions.
6. *Machinery.* a group of machine parts, esp. one forming a self-contained, independently mounted unit.

Strata–***noun*** اِس تِ ریتا :طبقه- قشر- لایه--- به کلمهء جمع آن در زیر توجه کنی
1. a pl. of stratum. Or Strata is the plural of stratum.
2. (*usually considered nonstandard*) stratum.

- Many years ago Iraqi people in an anti imperialist[1] monarchic[2] revolution to radically change the face of Iraq and to help with the rest of the world, but the western power put the realm[3] of the revolution in hand of Mr. K. and prevented it from its victory.

1.(اِمپی ریا لیست : امپریالیست ، طرفدار حکومت امپریالیستي یاامپراطوری- استعمار طلبی)
2.(مِنار کیک : وابسته به حکومت سلطنتي وابسته به سلطنت- سلطنت خواه)
(ic در آخر کلمهٔ 2 یعنی وابسته به حکومت سلطنتی- بدون آ ن یعنی سلطان- پادشاه)
3.(رِلم : قلمرو سلطان، متصرفات مملکت، ناحیه- (حقوق) کشور، قلمرو، حدود، حوزه، سلطنت)

بکار گیری لغات فوق در جملات دیگر:

imperialist-- اِمپی ریا لیست : امپریالیست ، طرفدار حکومت امپریالیستي یاامپراطوری-
by 1882; originally "an adherent of an emperor," such as the emperor of Germany, France, China, etc. The shift in meaning came via the British Empire, which involved a worldwide colonial system. See imperialism. As a term of abuse in communist circles, attested by 1927.

imperialism-- ***Word Origin & History***
1826, originally in a Napoleonic context, also of Rome and of British foreign policy, from imperial + -ism. At times in British usage (and briefly in U.S.) with a neutral or positive sense relating to national interests or the spread of the benefits of Western civilization, but from the beginning usually more or less a term of reproach. General sense of "one country's rule over another," first recorded 1878. Picked up disparagingly in Communist jargon by 1918.

mon·arch ---n. مِنار کیک : وابسته به حکومت سلطنتي وابسته به سلطنت- سلطنت خواه
One who reigns over a state or territory, usually for life and by hereditary right, especially:

1. A sole and absolute ruler. **2.** A sovereign, such as a king or empress, often with constitutionally limite authority: *a constitutional monarch.* **3.** One that commands or rules: *"I am monarch of all I survey" (William Cowper).* **4.** One that surpasses others in power or preeminence: *"Mont Blanc is the monarch of the mountains" (Byron).* **5.** A monarch butterfly.

[Middle English monarke, from Old French monarque, from Late Latin monarcha, from Greek monarkhos : mono-, *mono-* + arkhein, *to rule*.]
mo·nar'chal (mə-när'kəl), **mo·nar'chic** (-kĭk), **mo·nar'chi·cal** (-kĭ-kəl) *adj.*, **mo·nar'chal·ly**, **mo·nar'chi·cal·ly** *adv.*
realm ***–noun*** لم : قلمرو سلطان، متصرفات مملکت، ناحیه- *(حقوق)* کشور، قلمرو، حدود، حوزه، سلطنت
1. a royal domain; kingdom: *the realm of England.*
2. the region, sphere, or domain within which anything occurs, prevails, or dominates: *the realm of dreams.*
3. the special province or field of something or someone: *the realm of physics; facts within the realm of political scientists.*
Count Noun--- A realm is also a country with a king or queen; a formal word.
...the established church of the realm.

- Be aware that this time they are trying to use your name and energy in this scheme.

scheme ---***Count Noun*** إس کیم : برنامه، طرح، نقشه ، نقشه طرح کردن، توطئه چید ن
A scheme is a plan produced by one person as a way of achieving something.
He had a crazy scheme to corner the champagne market.... ...some scheme for perfecting the world.
A scheme is also a large-scale plan produced by a government or by an organization.
...the State Pension scheme.... ...a 5.6 million pound scheme to build 63 houses and a motel.

- This is a disgrace[1] to Middle Eastern people fighting for their rights. This, by far, is a leap[2] forward in liberation of the Middle East and the world.

(Take leap in the dark دل بدریا زدن)

1.(دیس گریس : رسوایي، خفت، تنگ، فضاحت سیه رویي، خفت اوردن بر بي ابرویي- (فقهي) توهين)

2.(لیپ : جست، پرش، خیز، جستن دویدن، خیز زدن)

disgrace ***---Uncount Noun*** دیس گریس : رسوایي، خفت، تنگ خفت اوردن بر بي ابرويي

Disgrace is a state in which people disapprove of someone or no longer respect them.
My uncle brought disgrace on the family.... He himself had come back twice from political disgrace.
If you are in disgrace, you have done something which makes people disapprove of you or stop respecting you ... He was sent back to his village in disgrace.... Nixon was the first President ever to resign the office in disgrace.

leap ***–verb (used without object)*** لیپ : جست، پرش، خیز، جستن دویدن، خیز زدن

1. to spring through the air from one point or position to another; jump:
to leap over a ditch.
2. to move or act quickly or suddenly: *to leap aside; She leaped at the opportunity.*
3. to pass, come, rise, etc., as if with a jump:
to leap to a conclusion; an idea that immediately leaped to mind.

- A worlds without discrimination[1], exploitation[2] and injustice.

1.(دیس کری می نی شن : فرق گذاري، تبعيض)

2.(اکس پلوی تی شن : ، استثمار- بهره برداري، انتفاع استخراج)

مَعانی یا بکار گیری لغات فوق در جملات دیگر:

discrimination **---Uncount Noun**فرق گذاري، تبعيض : دیس کری می نی شن

Discrimination is the practice of treating one person or group of people less fairly or less well than other people or groups.
African students in China accuse the Chinese of chronic racial discrimination.... The police force has to stamp out sexual discrimination.
Discrimination is the ability to recognize and like things that are of good quality.
He showed a total lack of discrimination in the way he decorated his room.

exploitation ***–noun*** اکس پلوی تی شن : ، استثمار- بهره برداري، انتفاع استخراج

1. use or utilization, esp. for profit: *the exploitation of newly discovered oil fields.*
2. selfish utilization: *He got ahead through the exploitation of his friends.*
3. the combined, often varied, use of public-relations and advertising techniques to promote a person, movie, product, etc.

- *Hypoglycemia :* های پو گِلای 30 میا –**noun** *Pathology*
  Hypoglycemia (hy-po-gly-ce-mia) *means* low-blood sugar, (hypoglycemic).

  an abnormally low level of glucose in the blood.
  Alternate Name(s): Insulin shock; Low blood sugar ...... **Hypoglycemia** occurs when your blood sugar, called glucose, is abnormally low. The term insulin shock is used to describe severe **hypoglycemia** that results in unconsciousness .
- 2 hours after start of meal: Blood sugar should be 140-180 which 140 is optimal. → مربوط به کمال مطلوب

  I would **use** "**optimal**" **in a sentence** like, "It is impossible to come up with a recommendation that will be **optimal** for everyone" (i.e. because everyone's circumstanc is different). On the other hand, I think "**optimum**" conveys more of a sense of an ideal or best regardless of circumstances.

- If you are frantic[1] about your health and wellness…. We should be mindful[2] with our diet.

(فِرَن تیک : بي عقل عصباني، ازکوره در رفته- از خود بیخود چه از حیث خوشی یا نا خوشی) .

(مآیند فوُل: متوجه-با خبر- ملتفت- متفکر، اندیشناک، در فکر) .

<u>مَعانی یا بکار گیری لغات فوق در جملات دیگر:</u>

frantic **–adjective** فِرَن تیک : بي عقل عصباني، - از خود بیخود چه از حیث خوشی یا نا خوشی
1. desperate or wild with excitement, passion, fear, pain, etc.; frenzied.
2. *Archaic* . insane; mad. (آر کِه یک :کهنه، قدیمي، غیر مصطلح ← *Archaic*)

mindful **–adjective** مآیند فوُل: متوجه-با خبر- ملتفت- متفکر، اندیشناک، در فکر
attentive, aware, or careful (usually fol. by *of*): *mindful of one's responsibilities*

- Iran is working on ballistic[1] missiles[2], the missiles launched Sunday near the city of Qom were not the kind that can carry nuclear warheads[3].

(بالستیک : مربوط بعلم حرکت اجسامي که درهوا پرتاپ میشوند- *(علوم نظامي)* بالیستیک .
علوم نظامي) بالیستیک، منحني مسیر گلوله، وضع حرکت گلوله، علم حرکت گلوله

(میس زِل : اسلحه پرتاب کردني، گلوله موشک، پرتابه- *(علوم نظامي)* موشک) .
ballistic missile ←وقتی دو لغت با هم بیآیند معنی اسلحهء پرتاب کردنی

(وآر هِد : قسمتي از موشک که حاوي مواد منفجره میباشد، کلاهک *(علوم نظامي)* کلاهک جنگي .

کلاهک موشک سر جنگي، جمع آن با اِس معنی پرتاب شناسی میدهد)

مَعانی یا بکار گیری لغات فوق در جملات دیگر:

ballistics **–*adjective*** بالستیک : مربوط بعلم حرکت اجسامي که در هوا پرتاپ میشوند
1. of or pertaining to ballistics.
2. having its motion determined or describable by the laws of exterior.
—Idiom
3. go ballistic, *Informal.* to become overwrought or irrational: *went ballistic over the of a tax hike.*

missiles **–*noun*** میس زل : اسلحه پرتاب کردني، گلوله موشک، پرتابه
1. an object or weapon for throwing, hurling, or shooting, as a stone, bullet, or arrow.
2. guided missile.
3. ballistic missile.
–adjective
4. capable of being thrown, hurled, or shot, as from the hand or a gun.
5. used or designed for discharging missiles.

warhead --- وار هد : قسمتي از موشک که حاوي مواد منفجره میباشد کلاهک موشک سر جنگي
A warhead is the front end of a bomb or missile, where the explosives are carried.
Pakistan had fired a missile capable of carrying a nuclear warhead.

- In interviews broadcast Sunday, U.S. Secretary of State Hillary and Defense Secretary R. Gates signaled support for harsher[1] sanctions[2] on Iraq as a deterrent[3].

1.(هارشر: تند، درشت، خشن، ناگوار زننده، ناملايم)
2.(سنک شِن : ، تصدیق مجازات اقتصادي، تصویب کردن، مجازات کردن- ضمانت اجرایي قانون)
3.(دی تِ رنت : مانع شونده، منع کننده بازدارنده، ، میخکوب کننده)

مَعانی یا بکار گیری لغات فوق در جملات دیگر:

deterrent **---Count Noun** هارشر: تند، درشت، خشن، ناگوار زننده، ناملايم
A deterrent is something that makes people afraid to do something. Count noun here but can also be used as an attributive adjective. e.g. These sanctions will have a deterrent effect upon the actions of the government.
Severe punishment is the only true deterrent.

harsh **–*adjective*** سنک شِن : ، تصدیق مجازات اقتصادي، تصویب کردن، ضمانت اجرایي قانون
1. ungentle and unpleasant in action or effect: *harsh treatment; harsh manners.*
2. grim or unpleasantly severe; stern; cruel; austere: *a harsh life; a harsh master.*
3. physically uncomfortable; desolate; stark: *a harsh land.*

4. unpleasant to the ear; grating; strident: *a harsh voice; a harsh sound.*
5. unpleasantly rough, ragged, or coarse to the touch: *a harsh surface.*
6. jarring to the eye or to the esthetic sense; unrefined; crude; raw: *harsh colors.*
7. unpleasant to the taste or sense of smell; bitter; acrid: *a harsh flavor; a harsh odor.*

sanction–***noun*** دی تِر رِنت : مانع شونده، منع کننده بازدارنده، ، میخکوب کننده
1. authoritative permission or approval, as for an action.
2. something that serves to support an action, condition, etc.
3. something that gives binding force, as to an oath, rule of conduct, etc.
4. *Law.*
a. a provision of a law enacting a penalty for disobedience or a reward for obedience.
b. the penalty or reward.
5. *International Law.* action by one or more states toward another state calculated to forc it to comply with legal obligations.
–verb (used with object)
7. to ratify or confirm: *to sanction a law.*
8. to impose a sanction on; penalize, esp. by way of discipline.

- The "Iranians are in a very bad spot now because of this deception, in terms of all of the great power."

بیپ شِن : نیرنگ، فریب، گول، حیله فریب خوردگي، اغفال

No other argument against Obama can fundamentally change the way people feel about him deep down inside, EXCEPT, proof that precisely the way they feel about him deep down inside is because of Obama's own **deception** and **use** of hidden hypnosis.

- Israel has trumpeted[1] the latest discoveries as proof of its long-held assertion[2] that Iran is seeing nuclear weapons.

.(ترَامپِت : شیپور-جار زدن، شیپور زدن - *(علوم نظامي)* شیپور، شیپور زدن)
.2(أسِر شِن : تاکید، اثبات، تایید ادعا اظهارنامه، اعلامیه، بیانیه اگهي، اخبار، اعلان)

مَعاني یا بکار گیری لغات فوق در جملات دیگر:

trumpet ---***Verb with Object*** ترَامپِت : شیپور-جار زدن، شیپور زدن ، شیپور زدن
If you trumpet something that you are proud of or that you think is important, you announce it widely so that many people get to hear about it.
Newspapers have been trumpeting reports of Ali Shah's imminent resignation for weeks...The government was not inclined to trumpet the policies of the past four decades.

assertion ***–noun*** أسِر شِن : تاکید، اثبات، تایید ادعا افهارنامه، اعلامیه، بیانیه اگهي، اخبار، اعلان

1. a positive statement or declaration, often without support or reason: *a mere assertion; an unwarranted assertion.*
2. an act of asserting.

- Church aims to bolster tradition.

بُل اِستِر: بالش، متکا، پشتي کردن، تکیه دادن، تقویت کردن - تیري که بطورعمودي زیرپایه گذارده شود

Bolter: a long pillow or cushion, or a structural part designed to eliminate friction or provide support or bearing.

- Vatican to embrace[1] groups of Anglicans[2], and even their rituals[3].

1.(ایم برِس : دراغوش گرفتن، در بر گرفتن بغل کردن، پذیرفتن، شامل بودن)

2.(آن گیلی کَن : وابسته بکلیساي انگلیس)

3.(ریچوُ آل : شعائر دینی، مراسم عبادات، تشریفات)

<u>مَعانی یا بکار گیری لغات فوق در جملات دیگر:</u>

embrace ***–verb (used with object)*** ایم برِس : دراغوش گرفتن ، پذیرفتن، شامل بودن
1. to take or clasp in the arms; press to the bosom; hug.
2. to take or receive gladly or eagerly; accept willingly: *to embrace an idea.*
3. to avail oneself of: *to embrace an opportunity.*
4. to adopt (a profession, a religion, etc.): *to embrace Buddhism.*
5. to take in with the eye or the mind.
6. to encircle; surround; enclose.
7. to include or contain: *An encyclopedia embraces a great number of subjects.*
–verb (used without object) **8.** to join in an embrace.
–noun **9.** an act or instance of embracing.

Reciprocal Verb
When you embrace someone, you put your arms around them in order to show your affection for them. Verb here but can also be used as a count noun. e.g. They greeted us with warm embraces.
Before she could embrace him he stepped away.... Mr Assad and President Mubarak embraced as they met at the airport.

anglicans ***–adjective***: آن گیلی کَن وابسته بکلیساي انگلیس
1. of or pertaining to the Church of England.
2. related in origin to and in communion with the Church of England, as various Episcopal churches in other parts of the world.
3. <u>English</u> def. 1.
–noun
4. a member of the Church of England or of a church in communion with it.

5. a person who upholds the system or teachings of the Church of England.

ritual **–noun** ریچوُ آل : شعائر دینی، مراسم عبادات، تشریفات
1. an established or prescribed procedure for a religious or other rite.
2. a system or collection of religious or other rites.
3. observance of set forms in public worship.
4. a book of rites or ceremonies.
5. a book containing the offices to be used by priests in administering the sacraments an
for visitation of the sick, burial of the dead, etc.
6. a prescribed or established rite, ceremony, proceeding, or service: *theritual of the dea*

- She has temperamental[1] attitude[2].

(تم پرُ مِن تال : مزاجي، خلقي، خويي- *(روانشناسي)* خلق و خويي، تند مزاج).
(آ تِ تُود : حالت، طرزبرخورد، روش و رفتار ، حالت قرار گرفتن رفتار).

مَعاني يا بكار گيری لغات فوق در جملات ديگر:

temperamental **–adjective** پرُ مِن تال : مزاجي، خلقي، خويي- *(روانشناسي)* خلق و خويي، تند مزاج
1. having or exhibiting a strongly marked, individual temperament.
2. moody, irritable, or sensitive: *a temperamental artist.*
3. given to erratic behavior; unpredictable.
4. of or pertaining to temperament; constitutional: *temperamental differences.*

Unpredictable in behavior or performance,
< a temperamental child>,<a temperamental computer>
Marked by excessive sensitivity and impulsive mood changes,
<a temperamental child>

attitude **–noun** آ تِ تُود : حالت، طرزبرخورد، روش و رفتار ، حالت قرار گرفتن رفتار
1. manner, disposition, feeling, position, etc., with regard to a person or thing; tendency or orientation, esp. of the mind: *a negative attitude; group attitudes.*
2. position or posture of the body appropriate to or expressive of an action, emotion, etc. *a threatening attitude; a relaxed attitude.*
3. *Aeronautics.* the inclination of the three principal axes of an aircraft relative to the wind, to the ground, etc.
4. *Ballet.* a pose in which the dancer stands on one leg, the other bent behind.

- A thin icy coating that forms when rain or sleet freezes, as on trees or streets

اس لیت: برف وباران، بوران، تگرگ ریز باریدن - (برف و باران با هم میبارند → It sleets)

- A blizzard is a storm in which snow falls heavily and there are strong winds.

بِ لِ زِرد: بادشدید توام بابرف، کولاک

blizzard:

a. a storm with dry, driving snow, strong winds, and intense cold.
b. a heavy and prolonged snowstorm covering a wide area. an inordinately large amount all at one time; avalanche:

<*a blizzard of Christmas cards*>.

<*Scotland and the North of England have been hit by blizzards....*>,

< *A climber is feared to have been buried in an avalanche as blizzards swept cross the Scottish Highlands.*>

- Precipitation[1] in the form of ice pellets[2] created by the freezing of rain as it falls (distinguished from hail).

1. (پری سی پی تی شِن : شتاب زدگی- عجله، زیاد-بی ملاحظگی- ته نشینی- رسوب)

2.(پِ لِت: حب، گلوله، قرص، ساچمه یاخرج تفنگ، بشکل گلوله دراوردن)

precipitation-- پری سی پی تی شِن : شتاب زدگی- عجله، زیاد-بی ملاحظگی- ته نشینی- رسوب

1. A headlong fall or rush.
2. Abrupt or impulsive haste.
3. A hastening or acceleration, especially one that is sudden or unexpected:
< *He is responsible for the precipitation of his own demise.*>

pellet–noun پِ لِت: حب، گلوله، قرص، ساچمه یاخرج تفنگ، بشکل گلوله دراوردن

1. a small, rounded or spherical body, as of food or medicine.
2. a small wad or ball of wax, paper, etc., for throwing, shooting, or the like.

- Flurry[1] a light, brief shower of snow. sudden commotion[2], excitement, or confusion; nervous hurry:

1.(سراسيمگي، تپش، بادناگهاني سراسيمه كردن، اشفتن طوفان ناگهاني - باريدن ناگهاني)

2.(کُ موشِن : اشوب، اضطراب، جنبش اغتشاش، هیاهو)

<u>مَعانی یا بکار گیری لغات فوق در جملات دیگر:</u>

<*There was a flurry of activity before the guests arrived.*>

<*A flurry of activity or speech is a short, energetic amount of it.*>

<*There has been a flurry of diplomatic activity....*>

< *The decision raised a flurry of objections*>

commotion –noun کُ موشِن : اشوب، اضطراب، جنبش اغتشاش، هیاهو)

1. violent or tumultuous motion; agitation; noisy disturbance:

What's all the commotion in the hallway?

2. political or social disturbance or upheaval; sedition; insurrection.

- Hostile use استفاده به جبر و دشمنی
- Hostile use *entails* simply using the land without consent. مستلزم/متضمن بودن

- *significant* معنی- مقصود-اهمیت
- *Of no significance* بی معنی- بی مقصود

- Bar and grill نام یکنوع رستوران

- *The stranger became attentive.* (مواظب-توجه-اینجا یعنی گوشهایش تیز شد)

- *A stout man stood before the fire* (اِس تاوت:نیرومند)

- Predecessors/ ancestor (اَن سس تور) : پِرِدِس سورز : اجداد

- *During a mugging on X-max Eve.* کتک کاری کردن

- *Debutant* دبیوتانت دختری که برای اولین بار وارد کار می شود

- *Camaraderie* کام اِرا دِری همراهی-رفاقت-وفاداری
  Suing is for being humiliated by the so-called *camaraderie*–buildin exercise.

- < *How to create camaraderie in the workplace?*>
  <*Suing is for being humiliated by so-called camaraderie-building exercise*>

- *Published cartoons lampooning the president Bush.* هجوکردن

- *Disgraced*[1] *European scholars*[2] */pupil.*
  1.(رسوایی-خفت- بی آبروئی) 2.(اِس کالرز:شاگرد ممتاز)

- *Admonish* : <*The teacher admonished him about excessive noise.*>
  (ادمانیش)نصیحت کردن- اگاه کردن

- *Iran could intensify[1] the violence and defeat[2] the USA.*

1.سخت کردن- تشدید کردن   2.شکست دادن

- *The offender was brought before the magistrate*: مجستریت

(رئیس کلانتری-دادرس-رئیس دادگاه)

- *Counterintelligence* ضدجاسوسی

- *Interment* → بخاک سپاری

- *Sonship* پسری- فرزندی

<The Fatherhood of God and the Sonship of Man>

- *Entrench* تجاوز کردن *<So deeply entrenched>*

- *Rival's demotion* رقابت تنزل درجه

- Mitigate تخفیف دادن *<to make less severe: to mitigate a punishment>.*

- *Comedy-Club–Rant* کلوپ یاوه سرایی- بیهوده گویی
- *Rant*: to talk in a noisy, excited, or declamatory matter,
- *Declamatory: of relating to or marked by declamation[1]*, (سخنوری- نطق).1
- *< declamatory speeches>* , (یاوه گو ranter)
- *Prior preparation prevent poor performance* : ppppp

- *Tantrum* غیظ -اوقات تلخی , *<suffering from temper tantrum>*
- *Worried clients swarm Countrywide Mortgage Company.*

شلوغ کردن-ازدهام-هجوم دسته جمعی

- *The goal is an eclectic neighborhood done well.* گلچین کننده

- *Another county out for Arctic resources* شمالی- مربوط به قطب شمال

<Danish scientists are heading for an unprecedented expedition to the Arctic ice pack.>

- *Treaty* : is an international treaty which is a binding agreement under international law .* * معاهده ، پیمان

- He is egotist (انی گوتیست) کسی که خودپرستی را مایه اخلاق می داند
- He is arrogant (اروگِنت) متکبر - خودبین
  Arrogation (اَروگی شِن) ادعای بی خود- متکبرانه
- I am running like chicken with my head cut off! مثل مرغ سر کنده دویدن

- How to write a will: وصیت نامه

  I hereby devices[1] and bequeath[2] to my heirs and assign all my rea and personal property as follow: 1.-----------,2.----------,3. -------, etc

  Signature here..........jan.16, 2010 پس از نوشتن اقلام فوق انر امضاء میکنید
  صیت نامه دو نفره:
- *We hereby devise[1] and bequeath[2] to our heirs (our sons):*

  Twin-A & Twin-B, Also Known As (AKA): Steve & Paul.
  All our real and personal property are as follow:

  Whatever is listed under our name…..

. وصیت کردن – ارث گذاری 2. وقف کردن- از راه وصیت به کسی واگذار کردن

حوه امضا کردن بجای دیگری هنگام نوشتن وکالت:

Mr. Seller **by** Mrs. Seller *his attorney-in-fact*

ی وکالت زن از طرف شوهر: اسامی خانم و آقای فروشنده باید نوشته شود مثل

Charles Kim **by** *Elizabeth Kim as attorney-in-fact* or

Rahmat Moosavi **by** *Roubi Moosavi as attorney-in-fact*

- Notice of default[2], (NOD) 2.کوتاهی- قصور از عهده پرداخت
  Places you find foreclosure[3] properties:سلب حق فک رهن از خود 3.**1.**
- Trustee's office, **2.**Trustee's sales, **3.**County court
- My buyers are interested in resurrecting the deal. زنده کردن.

Right of reinstatement → حقِ تثبیت در مقام

لغاتی که بعلت تشابه اغلب با هم اشتباه می شوند:

مشورت دادن به- مشورت کردن (کَ آن سِل): *counsel*

- Broker has advised sellers to consult with legal and tax *counsel* prior to signing this listing. e.g. White house *counsel*

Council of Ministers هیات وزیران

- Statuary (اس تَ چو اِ ری): the art of making statues (اس تَ چو),
- sculptor مجسمه ساز- مجسمه سازی- مجسمه ای
- Statutory (اس تَ چ توری): enacted قانونی-مقرر

This report will satisfy the statutory obligations of the seller and his/her agent.

Statutes: a law enacted by the legislative branch of a government

Statute (اس تَ چی یُوت) قانون (مجلس)-فریضه

Statute of limitations قانون مورور زمان

- quite (کوایت) کاملا- بکلی-راستی-(زیاد-خیلی در اصطلاح آمریکائی

quite: wholly, completely <not quite finished>, to an extreme: positively <quite sure>

- **quiet** (کوآ یت) (e قبل از t), خاموش- ساکت-آرام

quiet : The quality or state of being quiet, tranquility. (On the quiet در نهان- در خفا)

- quit (کُو ات) فارغ-آزاد-رها

quit: released from obligation, charge or …

- (Feet (جمع کلمه فوت (پا) است), (Feat: act, deed شاهکار- کاربرجسته)
- devours (دی وَو رز) دریدن و خوردن

English idioms:

- ***Drop somebody a line:***

If you drop someone a line, you write a letter to them.
"I always ***drop her a line*** to wish her a Happy Birthday."

- ***Word of mouth:***

Information passed on through conversation is transmitted ***by word of mouth***,
"No announcement was necessary --- the news had already spread by word of mouth."

- ***Touch base:***

If you ***touch base*** with someone, you make contact or renew communication with them.
" I 'll try to touch base with you next week in California."

- ***Blow out of proportion:***

If you exaggerate the importance of something, you ***blow it out of proportion***.
"The importance of the event was blown out of proportion by the media."

- ***Keep someone posted:***

If a person asks you to ***keep them posted***, they want you to keep them informed about a situation. " Our agent promised to keep us posted on developments in the negotiations."

- ***Put someone in the picture:***

If you give somebody all the information necessary to enable them to fully understand a situation, you ***put them in the picture***.
" Let me put you in the picture about what happened during your absence."

- ***Spread like wildfire:***

If something such as news, rumors or gossip ***spreads like wildfire***, it becomes widely known very fast. "As soon as the nomination was announced, the news spread like wildfire."

- ***Speed networking :***

This refers to a relatively new urban trend which consists in making a potential business contact by briefly taking to a series of people at an organized event and exchanging contact details.

- ***Hit the airwaves:***

When someone ***hits the airwaves***, the go on radio and /or TV to be interviewed or to promote something. " The hospital was embarrassed when the patient hit the airways with his side of the story."

تعدادی اختصارات که بیشتر در آمریکا مورد استفاده قرار میگیرند

- AIDS : Acquired[1] Immune[2] Deficiency[3] Syndrome[4]
- AIG : American International Group inc. بانک معروف بین ا لمللی
- AARP : American Association Retired Persons
- ADHD : Attention Deficit Hyperactivity Disorder
- ADD : Attention Deficit Disorder
- AKA : Also Known As
- ARM : Adjustable Rate Mortgage
- BBB : Better Business Bureau
- BAR : Bureau of Automobile Repair
- CEDD: California Employment Development Dept.
- CENTO : Central Treaty Organization
- DSL : Digital Subscriber Lines
- ESP : Electronic Stability Program
- e.g. : exempli gratia برای مثال - مثلاً (x سیم p لی – گرَ ɛ یا):
- FDIC : Federal Deposit Insurance Corporation
- FEMA : Federal Emergency Management Agency
- GPS : Global Positioning System

- GFCI : Ground Fault Circuit Interrupter
- HMO *plan* : Health Maintenance Organization plan
- HIV : Human Immunodeficiency Virus
- IRA : Individual Retirement Arrangement
- IAEA : International Atomic Energy Administration
- NOD : Notice Of Default
- NATO: North Atlantic Treaty* Organization (معاهده ، پیمان)*
- NAFTA : North American Free Trade Agreement
- NPT or NNPT : Nuclear Non-proliferation Treaty* (معاهده ، پیمان)*
- OSHA : Occupational Safety & Health Act
- OPEC : Organization of Petroleum Exporting Countries
- P.P.P.P.P. : Prior Preparation Prevent Poor Performance
- PPO *plan* : Preferred Provider Organization plan
- PIN: Personal Identification Number
- REO : Real Estate Own
- RAM : Random Access Memory در کامپیوتر
- RADAR : Radio Detection and Ranging
- STD : Sexually Transmitted Disease
- SEP *plan* : Simplified Employee Pension plan
- USSR : Union Soviet Socialist Republic
- URL : Uniform or Universal Resource Locator در کامپیوتر
- USB : Universal Serial Bus در کامپیوتر
- HIV: Human Immunodeficiency Virus

List of English Irregular Verbs

Base Form	Past Simple	Past Participle	3rd Person Singular	Present Participle / Gerund
Abide	Abode/Abided	Abode/Abided/Abidden	Abides	Abiding
Alight	Alit/Alighted	Alit/Alighted	Alights	Alighting
Arise	Arose	Arisen	Arises	Arising
Awake	Awoke	Awoken	Awakes	Awaking
Be	Was/Were	Been	Is	Being
Bear	Bore	Born/Borne	Bears	Bearing
Beat	Beat	Beaten	Beats	Beating
Become	Became	Become	Becomes	Becoming
Begin	Began	Begun	Begins	Beginning
Behold	Beheld	Beheld	Beholds	Beholding
Bend	Bent	Bent	Bends	Bending
Bet	Bet	Bet	Bets	Betting
Bid	Bade	Bidden	Bids	Bidding
Bid	Bid	Bid	Bids	Bidding
Bind	Bound	Bound	Binds	Binding
Bite	Bit	Bitten	Bites	Biting
Bleed	Bled	Bled	Bleeds	Bleeding
Blow	Blew	Blown	Blows	Blowing
Break	Broke	Broken	Breaks	Breaking
Breed	Bred	Bred	Breeds	Breeding
Bring	Brought	Brought	Brings	Bringing
Broadcast	Broadcast/Broadcasted	Broadcast/Broadcasted	Broadcasts	Broadcasting
Build	Built	Built	Builds	Building
Burn	Burnt/Burned	Burnt/Burned	Burns	Burning
Burst	Burst	Burst	Bursts	Bursting
Bust	Bust	Bust	Busts	Busting

Buy	Bought	Bought	Buys	Buying
Cast	Cast	Cast	Casts	Casting
Catch	Caught	Caught	Catches	Catching
Choose	Chose	Chosen	Chooses	Choosing
5Clap	Clapped/Clapt	Clapped/Clapt	Claps	Clapping
Cling	Clung	Clung	Clings	Clinging
Clothe	Clad/Clothed	Clad/Clothed	Clothes	Clothing
Come	Came	Come	Comes	Coming
Cost	Cost	Cost	Costs	Costing
Creep	Crept	Crept	Creeps	Creeping
Cut	Cut	Cut	Cuts	Cutting
Dare	Dared/Durst	Dared	Dares	Daring
Deal	Dealt	Dealt	Deals	Dealing
Dig	Dug	Dug	Digs	Digging
Dive	Dived/Dove	Dived	Dives	Diving
Do	Did	Done	Does	Doing
Draw	Drew	Drawn	Draws	Drawing
Dream	Dreamt/Dreamed	Dreamt/Dreamed	Dreams	Dreaming
Drink	Drank	Drunk	Drinks	Drinking
Drive	Drove	Driven	Drives	Driving
Dwell	Dwelt	Dwelt	Dwells	Dwelling
Eat	Ate	Eaten	Eats	Eating
Fall	Fell	Fallen	Falls	Falling
Feed	Fed	Fed	Feeds	Feeding
Feel	Felt	Felt	Feels	Feeling
Fight	Fought	Fought	Fights	Fighting
Find	Found	Found	Finds	Finding
Fit	Fit/Fitted	Fit/Fitted	Fits	Fitting
Flee	Fled	Fled	Flees	Fleeing
Fling	Flung	Flung	Flings	Flinging
Fly	Flew	Flown	Flies	Flying
Forbid	Forbade/Forbad	Forbidden	Forbids	Forbidding
Forecast	Forecast/Forecasted	Forecast/Forecasted	Forecasts	Forecasting
Foresee	Foresaw	Foreseen	Foresees	Foreseeing
Foretell	Foretold	Foretold	Foretells	Foretelling

orget	Forgot	Forgotten	Forgets	Foregetting
orgive	Forgave	Forgiven	Forgives	Forgiving
orsake	Forsook	Forsaken	Forsakes	Forsaking
reeze	Froze	Frozen	Freezes	Freezing
rostbite	Frostbit	Frostbitten	Frostbites	Frostbiting
et	Got	Got/Gotten	Gets	Getting
ive	Gave	Given	Gives	Giving
o	Went	Gone/Been	Goes	Going
rind	Ground	Ground	Grinds	Grinding
row	Grew	Grown	Grows	Growing
andwrite	Handwrote	Handwritten	Handwrites	Handwriting
ang	Hung/Hanged	Hung/Hanged	Hangs	Hanging
ave	Had	Had	Has	Having
ear	Heard	Heard	Hears	Hearing
ide	Hid	Hidden	Hides	Hiding
it	Hit	Hit	Hits	Hitting
old	Held	Held	Holds	Holding
urt	Hurt	Hurt	Hurts	Hurting
nlay	Inlaid	Inlaid	Inlays	Inlaying
nput	Input/Inputted	Input/Inputted	Inputs	Inputting
nterlay	Interlaid	Interlaid	Interlays	Interlaying
eep	Kept	Kept	Keeps	Keeping
neel	Knelt/Kneeled	Knelt/Kneeled	Kneels	Kneeling
nit	Knit/Knitted	Knit/Knitted	Knits	Knitting
now	Knew	Known	Knows	Knowing
ay	Laid	Laid	Lays	laying
ead	Led	Led	Leads	Leading
ean	Leant/Leaned	Leant/Leaned	Leans	Leaning
eap	Leapt/Leaped	Leapt/Leaped	Leaps	Leaping
earn	Learnt/Learned	Learnt/Learned	Learns	Learning
eave	Left	Left	Leaves	Leaving
end	Lent	Lent	Lends	Lending
et	Let	Let	Lets	Letting
ie	Lay	Lain	Lies	Lying
ight	Lit	Lit	Lights	Lighting

Lose	Lost	Lost	Loses	Losing
Make	Made	Made	Makes	Making
Mean	Meant	Meant	Means	Meaning
Meet	Met	Met	Meets	Meeting
Melt	Melted	Molten/Melted	Melts	Melting
Mislead	Misled	Misled	Misleads	Misleading
Mistake	Mistook	Mistaken	Mistake	Mistaking
Misunderstand	Misunderstood	Misunderstood	Misunderstands	Misunderstan
Miswed	Miswed/Miswedded	Miswed/Miswedded	Misweds	Miswedding
Mow	Mowed	Mown	Mows	Mowing
Overdraw	Overdrew	Overdrawn	Overdraws	Overdrawing
Overhear	Overheard	Overheard	Overhears	Overhearing
Overtake	Overtook	Overtaken	Overtakes	Overtaking
Pay	Paid	Paid	Pays	Paying
Preset	Preset	Preset	Presets	Presetting
Prove	Proved	Proven/Proved	Proves	Proving
Put	Put	Put	Puts	Putting
Quit	Quit	Quit	Quits	Quitting
Re-prove	Re-proved	Re-proven/Re-proved	Re-proves	Re-proving
Read	Read	Read	Reads	Reading
Rid	Rid/Ridded	Rid/Ridded	Rids	Ridding
Ride	Rode	Ridden	Rides	Riding
Ring	Rang	Rung	Rings	Ringing
Rise	Rose	Risen	Rises	Rising
Rive	Rived	Riven/Rived	Rives	Riving
Run	Ran	Run	Runs	Running
Saw	Sawed	Sawn/Sawed	Saws	Sawing
Say	Said	Said	Says	Saying
See	Saw	Seen	Sees	Seeing
Seek	Sought	Sought	Seeks	Seeking
Sell	Sold	Sold	Sells	Selling
Send	Sent	Sent	Sends	Sending
Set	Set	Set	Sets	Setting
Sew	Sewed	Sewn/Sewed	Sews	Sewing
Shake	Shook	Shaken	Shakes	Shaking

have	Shaved	Shaven/Shaved	Shaves	Shaving
hear	Shore/Sheared	Shorn/Sheared	Shears	Shearing
hed	Shed	Shed	Sheds	Shedding
hine	Shone	Shone	Shines	Shining
hoe	Shod	Shod	Shoes	Shoeing
hoot	Shot	Shot	Shoots	Shooting
how	Showed	Shown	Shows	Showing
hrink	Shrank	Shrunk	Shrinks	Shrinking
hut	Shut	Shut	Shuts	Shutting
ing	Sang	Sung	Sings	Singing
ink	Sank	Sunk	Sinks	Sinking
it	Sat	Sat	Sits	Sitting
lay	Slew	Slain	Slays	Slaying
leep	Slept	Slept	Sleeps	Sleeping
lide	Slid	Slid/Slidden	Slides	Sliding
ling	Slung	Slung	Slings	Slinging
link	Slunk	Slunk	Slinks	Slinking
lit	Slit	Slit	Slits	Slitting
mell	Smelt/Smelled	Smelt/Smelled	Smells	Smelling
neak	Sneaked/Snuck	Sneaked/Snuck	Sneaks	Sneaking
oothsay	Soothsaid	Soothsaid	Soothsays	Soothsaying
ow	Sowed	Sown	Sows	Sowing
peak	Spoke	Spoken	Speaks	Speaking
peed	Sped/Speeded	Sped/Speeded	Speeds	Speeding
pell	Spelt/Spelled	Spelt/Spelled	Spells	Spelling
pend	Spent	Spent	Spends	Spending
pill	Spilt/Spilled	Spilt/Spilled	Spills	Spilling
pin	Span/Spun	Spun	Spins	Spinning
pit	Spat/Spit	Spat/Spit	Spits	Spitting
plit	Split	Split	Splits	Splitting
poil	Spoilt/Spoiled	Spoilt/Spoiled	Spoils	Spoiling
pread	Spread	Spread	Spreads	Spreading
pring	Sprang	Sprung	Springs	Springing
tand	Stood	Stood	Stands	Standing
teal	Stole	Stolen	Steals	Stealing

Stick	Stuck	Stuck	Sticks	Sticking
Sting	Stung	Stung	Stings	Stinging
Stink	Stank	Stunk	Stinks	Stinking
Stride	Strode/Strided	Stridden	Strides	Striding
Strike	Struck	Struck/Stricken	Strikes	Striking
String	Strung	Strung	Strings	Stringing
Strip	Stript/Stripped	Stript/Stripped	Strips	Stripping
Strive	Strove	Striven	Strives	Striving
Sublet	Sublet	Sublet	Sublets	Subletting
Sunburn	Sunburned/Sunburnt	Sunburned/Sunburnt	Sunburns	Sunburning
Swear	Swore	Sworn	Swears	Swearing
Sweat	Sweat/Sweated	Sweat/Sweated	Sweats	Sweating
Sweep	Swept/Sweeped	Swept/Sweeped	Sweeps	Sweeping
Swell	Swelled	Swollen	Swells	Swelling
Swim	Swam	Swum	Swims	Swimming
Swing	Swung	Swung	Swings	Swinging
Take	Took	Taken	Takes	Taking
Teach	Taught	Taught	Teaches	Teaching
Tear	Tore	Torn	Tears	Tearing
Tell	Told	Told	Tells	Telling
Think	Thought	Thought	Thinks	Thinking
Thrive	Throve/Thrived	Thriven/Thrived	Thrives	Thriving
Throw	Threw	Thrown	Throws	Throwing
Thrust	Thrust	Thrust	Thrusts	Thrusting
Tread	Trod	Trodden	Treads	Treading
Undergo	Underwent	Undergone	Undergoes	Undergoing
Understand	Understood	Understood	Understands	Understanding
Undertake	Undertook	Undertaken	Undertakes	Undertaking
Upset	Upset	Upset	Upsets	Upsetting
Vex	Vext/Vexed	Vext/Vexed	Vexes	Vexing
Wake	Woke	Woken	Wakes	Waking
Wear	Wore	Worn	Wears	Wearing
Weave	Wove	Woven	Weaves	Weaving
Wed	Wed/Wedded	Wed/Wedded	Weds	Wedding
Weep	Wept	Wept	Weeps	Weeping

Wend	Wended/Went	Wended/Went	Wends	Wending
Wet	Wet/Wetted	Wet/Wetted	Wets	Wetting
Win	Won	Won	Wins	Winning
Wind	Wound	Wound	Winds	Winding
Withdraw	Withdrew	Withdrawn	Withdraws	Withdrawing
Withhold	Withheld	Withheld	Withholds	Withholding
Withstand	Withstood	Withstood	Withstands	Withstanding
Wring	Wrung	Wrung	Wrings	Wringing
Write	Wrote	Written	Writes	Writing
Zinc	Zinced/Zincked	Zinced/Zincked	Zincs	Zincking

English Proverbs

ضرب المثلها ی فارسی و معادلهای انگلیسی آنها

- آدم بخیلی است آب از دستش نمی چکد

He is close-fisted. **Or** He won't give the droppings of his nos

- آب ازسرچشمه گل آلود است

Trouble starts with those at the bead of affair

- آب از سرش گذشته است

It is all up with him

- آب خوش از گلویش پائین نرفت

He was never happy. He led a dog's lif

- آب در کوزه و ما تشنه لبان میگردیم **یا** یار در خانه و ما گرد جهان میگردیم

We seek water in the se

- آبرا گل آلود میکند ماهی بگیرد

He makes mischief to gain his own end

- آبِ رفته بجوی بر نمی گردد

What is done cannot be undon

- آب زیر پوستش افتاده یا رفته است

He has put on flesh; also he has grown rich

- آبِ زیرِ کاه

Deep or shrewd (person

- آبشان از یک جوی نمی رود

They will never go in double harness; they will never agre

- آب که یک جا بماند می گند د

Caution against long periods of service in any one place.

- آب نمی بیند والاشنا گر قابلی است

Said of one who is deprived of chances to display his capabilities.

- آتش را با آتش خاموش نتوان کرد

Fire cannot be extinguished by fire.

- آدم بی اولاد پادشاه بی غم است

A man without children is a king without cares.

- آدم تا کوچکی نکند به بزر گی نمی رسد

Until a man has shown humility he cannot attain greatness. **Or** To learn to command one must learn to obey.

- آدم خوش حساب (**یا** خوش معامله) شریک مال مردم است

This is because he can borrow again and again.

- آدم دروغگو کم حافظه میشود

Liars should have good memories.

- آدم دست پاچه کار را دو بار میکند

Haste makes waste. **Or** More haste, less speed.

- آدم گرسنه دین و ایمان ندارد

A hungry man, an angry man. **Or** and empty belly bears nobody. **Or** A hungry belly has no ears.

- آدمی را عقل میباید نه زر

The wisdom of the old is far better than gold.

- آدمی را عقل میباید نه زور

Brains are better than brawn.

- آدمی فربه شود از راه گوش

From hearing comes wisdom; from speaking repentance.

- آدم دو روست **یا** پشت و رویش معلوم نیست
He is two faced or double face

- آرزو بگور بردن.To die frustrated in one's wished

- آشپز که دو تا شد آش یا شور است یا بی مزه.......همچنین ماما هم که دوتا......
To many cooks spoil the brot

- آفتابه خرج لحیم است
The game is not worth the candle **Or** (the play won't pay the candle

- آفتابه لگن هفت دست شام و ناهار هیچ
"Much bran, little meal" is not quite an equivalen

- آنانکه غنی ترند محتاج ترند
The more rich, the more in nee

- آنجا که عیان است چه حاجت به بیان است
- What is self evident needs no explanatio

- آنکه شیران را کند روبه مزاج احتیاج است احتیاج است احتیاج
Hunger will tame a lin

- آنچه عوض دارد گله ندارد
Fair exchange no robber

- آنرا که حساب پاک است از محاسبه چه باک است
A clear conscience fears no accusers. **Or** be true and fear no

- آن سبو بشکست و آن پیمانه ریخت **یا** آن ممه را لو لو برد
It is quite another story nov

- آه ندارد که با ناله سودا کند
He has not a penny to bless himself wit

- آهن سرد کوبیدن
To flog a dead horse. **Or** to bite a fil

- از آب رنگ گرفتن **یا** از ریگ روغن گرفتن
To draw blood out of a stone. **Or** to flay a flin

- از آن بید ها نیست که از این باد ها بلرزد

He has lived to near a wood to be frightened by owls.

- از آن نترس که های و هو داره ---- از آن بترس که سر بتو داره

Barking dogs don't bite.

- از این دُم بریده هر چه بگوئید بر میآید

This sly animal can do anything imaginable.

- از این ستون بآن ستون فرج است

Between one pillar and the other there is relief.

- در پی هر گریه آخر خنده ایست

After night comes the dawn. **Or** after sorrow comes joy.

- از تو حرکت از خدا برکت

1. God helps those who help themselves.
2. God helps the sailor, but he must row.
3. Begin your web, and God will send you the thread.

- از چاله در آمدن و توی چاه افتادن

To fall out of the frying-pan into the fire.

- از حلوا حلوا گفتن دهن شیرین نمیشود

Fair words butter no parsnips. **Or**
Wishes don't wash dishes.

- از خر میپرسند چهار شنبه کی است

What would you have an ass chop logic ?

- از دل برود هر آنکه از دیده برفت

Out of site, out of mind. **Or**
long absent, soon forgotten.

- از دماغ فیل افتاده

He is as proud as the peacock.

- از ضرر هر چه بر گردد نفع است

Whatever is recovered from a loss is a profit.

- از کف دست که موئی ندارد نمیتوان موئی کند
  You can't draw blood out of a stone
- از کوزه برون همان تراود که در اوست
  Every tree is known by its frui
- از کیسۀ خلیفه بخشیدن
  To be generous with other people's money.
- از هول حلیم توی دیگ حلیم افتادن
  To fall into the pot from greec
- اسب پیشکشی را بدندانش نگاه نمیکنند
  One does not look at the teeth of a gift horse.
- اصل بد نیکو نگردد زانکه بنیادش بد است --- تربیت نا اهل را گردگان بر گنبد است
  A lofty rank requires nobleness of soul. **Or** true blood will never stain.
- افسرده دل افسرده کند انجمنی را.
  A despondent person will depress the whole company.
- اگر بابا بیل زنی باغچهٔ خودت را بیل بزن
  - Physician, heal thysel
- العجلتهُ من الشیطان
  The more haste the less spee
- النظافته من الایمان.
  Cleanliness is next to Godlines
- المفلسُ فی امان الله
  The destitute are given immunity by Goo
- انسان جایز الخطا است
  To err is human. **Or** mankind is fallible.
- این شتری است که درِ خانهٔ همه کس خوابیده است
  We are all in the same boa

- این قافله تا بحشر لنگ است

It is an endless task.

- باد آورده را باد می برد

Light come, light go. **Or** easy come, easy go.

- با یک تیر دو نشان زدن

To kill two birds with one stone.

- بادنجان بد آفت ندارد

A cracking door hangs long on its hinges. **Or** A singed cat lives long.

- بار کج بمنزل نمی رسد

Cheating play never thrives. **Or** Honesty is the best policy.

- بجرم عیسی موسی را مگیر

Do not blame Moses for the sin of Jesus.

- بر گذشته حسرت خوردن خطاست

It is a mistake to grieve over the past.

- بریش کسی خندیدن

To snap one's finger at some one.

- بزرگی بعقل است نه بسال

Greatness is attained by wits, not by age.

- بزمین سفت یا سخت نشاشیده است

He has not experience hard times.

- بعد از مردن سهراب نوشدارو

After death the doctor.

- بقدر گلیمت پا دراز کن

Cut your coat according to your cloth. **Or** Set your sail according to your wind.

- بکچله گفتند چرا مو نمیگذاری یا نداری گفت دوست نمیدارم
Foxes, when they cannot reach the grapes, say they are not rip

- به لعنت خدا نمی ارزد
It is not worth a damn; it is not worth a curs

- لعنت بر شیطان !
Damn it ! Darn it ! Curse it

- بوزینه بچشم مادرش غزال است
The ape is a gazelle in its mother's ey

- بهر کجا رَوی آسمان همین رنگ است
Travelling to other places will not cause the effec

- پالانش کج است
She is a woman of easy virtue; she is loose in the hilt
she is a light-skirt

- پایش لب گور است
He has one foot in the grav

- پرده از روی کار برداشتن
To let the cat out of the ba

- پز عالی جیب خالی
Great boast little toast. **O**
He robs his belly to cover his bac

- پول حلاّ لِ مشکلات است
Money is a sword that can cut even the Gordian kno

- پول را از کاغذ نمی بُرند
Money doesn't grow on tree

- پولش از پارو بالا میرود
He is rolling in money. He is money-bag

- پیاده شو با هم راه برویم
Draw it mild.

- تا آب گل آلود نشود ماهی گیر نمی آید **یا** تا پریشان نشود کار بسامان نرسد
When things get to the worst they will mend.

- تا تنور گرم است نان باید پخت
Make hay while the sun shines. Or
Strike the iron while it is hot.

- تاس اگر نیک نشیند همه کس نرّاد است
He plays well who wins. Or
Throwing lucky dice makes every one a good players

- تا مار راست نشود بسوراخ نرود
Honesty is the policy. Or cheating play never thrives.

- تا مرد سخن نگفته باشد --- عیب و هنرش نهفته باشد
Until a man has spoken, his faults and vertues remain hidden.

- تخم مرغ دزد شتر دزد میشود
He that will steal an egg will steal an ox.

- توانا بود هر که دانا بود **یا** دانائی توانائی است
Knowledge is power.

- توبه گرگ مرگ است
You may end him, but you will not mend him.

- تو دعوا حلوا پخش نمیکنند
One can't make war with rose water.

- تو که لالائی میدانی چرا خوابت نمیرود؟
Physician, heal thyself.

- جای شما خالی بود
We missed you **Or** we thought of you.

- جنگ اول به از صلح آخر است

A word before is worth two after. O
Better an ounce of discretion than a pound of cur

- جواب ابلهان خاموشی است

The only answer to fools is silenc

- جوجه را در پائیز میشمرند

Don’t count your chickens before they are hatche

- جوینده یابنده است

Who seeks will fin

- جهان دیده بسیار گوید دروغ

Travelers tell fine tales. **Or** old men and travelers may lie by authorit

- چراغ از بهر تاریکی نگهدار

Put by something for a rainy da

- چراغی که بخانه رواست بمسجد حرام است

Charity begins at hom

- چیزی که عوض دارد گله ندارد

Exchange is no robber

- حرف را به آدم یک دفعه میزنند

A word to the wise is sufficien

- حسود هرگز نیاسود

The jealous never had tranquiallit

- حکم بچه از حکم شاه روان تر است

The baby is the king of the hous

- خایهٔ غول را شکستن

To perform a Herculean tas

- خایهٔ کسی را دستمال کردن

To crying before, **Or** fawn upon, some on

- خفته را خفته کی کند بیدار

He that is fallen cannot help him that is down. **Or** the blind cannot lead the blind.

- خودم کردم که لعنت بر خودم باد

As you make your bed, so you must lie on it.

- خون را با خون نمی شویند

One does not wash away blood with blood (but with water).

- خیاطان را احضار کرده بودند – پالان دوزها هم خود را قاطی کردند

Every ass thinks himself worthy to stand with the king's houses.

- درخت هرچه بارش بیشتر میشود سرش پائین تر میآید

The most fruitful branch is nearest the ground.

- دست بالای دست بسیار است

Every rogue is at length outrogued.

- دوری و دوستی

Absence makes the heart grow fond. **Or** friends agree but at a distance.

- دوست آنست که گیرد دست دوست--- در پریشان حالی و درماندگی

A friend in need is a friend indeed.

- ذرع نکرده پاره مکن

Look before you leap.

- روغن ریخته جمع نمیشود

No use crying over spilt milk.

- ریگ در کفش داشتن

To have something up one's sleeve. **Or** to have sly meaning.

- زیره به کرمان بردن

To carry coals to Newcastle.

- سالی که نکوست از بهارش پیداست--- بچهٔ مردنی از مدفوعش پیداست.
  A good beginning augurs well for a undertaking. O
  coming events cast their shadows befor

- سحر خیز باش تا کامرَوا باشی
  Early to bed and early to rise makes a man healthy, wealthy, and wise. o
  Early birds pick up the crumb

- سخن تا نپرسند لب بسته دار
  Speak when your are spoken t

- سرش بتنش سنگینی میکند
  The gallows groans for hin

- سکوت موجبِ رضا است
  Silence gives consen

- سگِ حق شناس به از آدمیِ نا سپاس
  A grateful dog is better than an ungrateful ma

- سگی که زیاد عوعو میکند گاز نمیگیرد
  Barking dogs don't bu

- شاهنامه آخرش خوش است
  Praise a fair day at night. O
  All is well that ends wel

- شتر در خواب بیند پنبه دانه --- گهی لُپ لپ خورد گه دانه دانه
  The cat dream of mice. O
  A lover dreams of his mistres

- صدقه رفع بلاست
  Alms are the golden key that opens the gate of heave

- عشق و مُشک پنهان نمی ماند
  Love and odor of musk cannot be hidden. O
  Love, a cough, and the itch cannot be hi

- عفو کردن بر ظالمان جور است بر مظلومان
He hurts the good who spares the bad.

- عقل قوت گیرد از عقل دیگر
Two heads are better than one.

- علاج واقعه را قبل از وقوع باید کرد
An once of prevention is worth a pound of cure.

- عنان مال خودت را بدست غیر مده --- که مال خود طلبیدن کم از گدائی نیست
Do not allow others to control your property;
for it is nothing less than beggary to ask for one's own.

- کسیکه گُل میخواهد باید منّت خار را بکشد
No pains, no gains.

- کسیکه منار میدزدد اول چاهش را میکند
You are a fool to steal , if you can't conceal.

- کور شود دکانداری که مشتری خود را نشناسد
A wool-seller knows a wool-buyer.

- کور کور را پیدا میکند آب گودال را
Birds of a feather flock together. **Or**
The goose goes with geese.

- کوزه گر از کوزه شکسته آب میخورد
The shoemakers's wife (or the cobbler's family) goes the worst shod.

- گاو پیشانی سفید
(A person) as well-known as the village-pump.

- گذشت آنکه عرب طعنه بر عجم میزد
Than is all past and done with. Or
It is quite another story now.

- گربه دستش بگوشت نمیرسید میگوید بو میدهد
Foxes, when they cannot reach the grapes say they are sou

- گوشت به دست گربه سپردن
To set the fox to watch the gees

- لالائی میدانی چرا خوابت نمیرود
He tells me my way but does not know his ow

- لایق هر خر نباشد زعفران
Do not cast pearls before swin

- مالَت را سفت نگهدار همسایه ات را دزد مکن
Better a lock than doub

- ماما که دو تا شد سرِ بچه کج در میآید
Too many cooks spoil the brot

- ماه همیشه زیر ابر نمی ماند
In the long run truth will ou

- مرگ یکدفعه شیون یکدفعه
Better face a danger once than be always in dange

- مشکلی نیست که آسان نشود
It is a long lane that has no turnin

- مصیبت بود پیری نیستی
Poverty on an old man's back is a heavy burde

- موی دماغ کسی شدن
To play gooseberr

- مهره گر نیک نشیند همه کس نرّاد است
He plays well that win

- مهمان تا سه روز عزیز است

Fish and guests stink after three days.

- نا برده رنج گنج میّسر نمی شود **یا** نوش خواهی نیش میباید چشید

No pains , no gains.

- نرو لاس با هم است

You must take the fat with lean.

- نفاق بینداز و فتح کن

Divide and rule.

- نمک بر زخم پاشیدن

To put one's finger in on other's one. **Or**
To make out to extinguish fire.

- نهال را تا ترَ است باید راست کرد

It is no use teaching an old dog new tricks.

- نه همین لباس زیباست نشان آدمیت

It is not the (gay) coat that makes the gentleman. **Or**
More goes to the making of a fine gentleman than fine clothes.

- هر آنکس که دندان دهد نان دهد

God never sends, a mouth, but he sends meat for it.

- هرچه پول میدهی آش میخوری

Pay the piper and call the tune.

- هرچه پیش آید خوش آید

All is for the best.

- هرچه (یا هرچیزکه) خوار آید روزی بکار آید

Lay things by, they may come to use.

- هر خوردنی پس دادنی دارد

One good turn deserves another

- هر کس درد ش در دلِ خودش است

No one knows the weight of another's burde

- هر که طا وس باید جور هندوستان کشد

No pains, No gain

- هر گردی گردو نیست

All is not gold that glitter

- هر نشیبی را فرازی در پی است

Every tide has its ebb. Or A flow will have an ebb. C
After sorrow comes jo

- همسایه را بپرس خانه را بخر

You must ask your neighbor if you shall live in peac

- همسایهٔ نیک در جهان فضل خداست

A good neighbor in this world is a blessing from God. C
A good neighbor, a good morrow

- همسایهٔ نزدیک به از برادر دور

Better a neighbor that is near you than a brother that is far from yo

- هیچ ارزانی بیعلت نیست --- هیچ گرانی بی حکمت نیست

Bad ware is never cheap. Or cheap is dear in the long ru

- یک ارزن از دستش نمی افتد

He won't give away the droppings of his nose. Or he is close-fiste

- Man who waits for roast duck to fly into mouth must wait very very long time. *Chinese Proverb*

- One man's poison is another man food.

END پا یا ن

Biography -- بیوگرافی

مؤلف درتهران متولد شده و یکی از دوازده خواهرو برادری است که تحصیلات متوسطهٔ خود را در دبیرستانهای امیر کبیر و ادیب تهران به پایان رسانده وپس از اخذ دیپلم ریاضی در سال 1343 مدتی در مؤسسهٔ روزنامهٔ کیهان زیر نظرمدیر عامل و مؤسس آن درقسمت حقوقی مشغول بکار بوده.

در اوایل تاسیس دانشگاه ملی بمدت یک ترم در دانشکدهٔ معماری مشغول تحصیل گردیده و پس از تغیر عقیده تصمیم گرفته که این رشته را در آمریکا ادامه دهد که این خود مستلزم انجام خدمت وظیفه بود-- تا اجازهٔ خروج از کشور صادر شود . پس از هجده ماه انجام وظیفه درسپاه بهداشت بعنوان دستیارِ پزشک موفق باخذِ پذیرش از یکی از دانشگاهای آمریکا گردید---و در نوامبر سال 1968 وارد نیویورک میشود

در آن زمان بندرت افرادی با وضع مالی نه چندان خوب به آمریکا سفر میکردند. تعداد دانشجویان ایرانی بسیار اندک و بعضی از دانشگاها اصلاً دانشجوی ایرانی نداشتند . نامبرده با کوشش فراوان بدون چشم داشت کمکهای مالی والدین با کوشش و کار و تحصیل موفق باخذ مدرک در رشتهٔ نقشه کشی طراحی و دکوراسیون داخلی ساختمان از لینی کالج اوکلند واقع در حوالی سا نفرنسیسکوگردید.

نا گفته نماند پروژهٔ نهائی ایشان پس از شرکت درAlamida County Fair in California بین دانشجویان در آن سال رتبهٔ اول را حائز شده که اخبار آن در روزنامهٔ سا نفرانسیسکو و ایران تایمزِ واشنگتن درج و همچنین مسئولین نمایشگاه مراتب را باطلاع کنسولگری ایران و از آنجا به وزارت امور خارجهٔ ایران در تهران رساندند. مدارکی مبنی بر قدردانی و تشویق وتبریک از داخل و خارج برای ایشان ارسال شده است که اصل آنها در آرشیو مؤلف میباشند.

سپس برای ادامهٔ تحصیل ترم اول را در دانشگاه برکلی- کالیفرنیا در رشتهٔ راه و ساختمان وپس از تغیر رشته به رشتهٔ آرشیتکت عازم دانشگاه ایالتی کالیفرنیا واقع در شهر سَن لوُئیسُ بِسپو تا پایان تحصیلات میشود. با انتشاراین کتاب این سومین اثری میباشد که ایشان در طی سی و پنج سال گذشته برشتهٔ تحریر در آورده که هر کدام آنها از نقطه نظرهائی حائز اهمیت و مثمر ثمر میباشد.

Resources: منابع و ماخذ

1. Los Angeles Times Daily paper
2. Orange County Register, California
3. New York Times
4. Weekly Time Magazine
5. EnglishDictionary.com
6. Dictionary Farsi.com
7. On line English Persian Dictioary.com
8. The Random House Dictionary
9. Webster's New World Dictionary
10. Pictorial English-Persian K.Barromand Dictionary
11. English-Persian Haim Dictionary
12. English-persian Aryan-poor Diction

خود آموز انگلیسی

This book designed for Farsi speaking students

این کتاب به علاقمندانی که عازم کشورهای: آمریکا- کانادا- انگلستان واسترالیا هستند توصیه میشود

A-Self-Teaching Guide

Improve and Expand
Your English Vocabulary
By
Learning Words in Context!

انگلیسی خود را تقویت کنید
با فرا گیری لغات و کاربرد درست آن
در جمله به
همراه تلفظِ متداولِ روز

نویسنده و گرد آورنده :

مهندس سید رحمت اله موسوی
ارشیتکت- فارغ التحصیل دانشگاه پلی تکنیک کالیفرنیا